The American Backwoods Frontier

THE AMERICAN

Creating the North American Landscape

Consulting Editors

Gregory Conniff
Bonnie Loyd
David Schuyler

BACKWOODS FRONTIER

An Ethnic and
Ecological
Interpretation

Terry G. Jordan and
Matti Kaups

The Johns Hopkins University Press
Baltimore and London

Softshell Books edition, 1992

The Johns Hopkins University Press
701 West 40th Street
Baltimore, Maryland 21211-2190
The Johns Hopkins Press Ltd., London

The paper used in this publication meets the
minimum requirements of the American
National Standard for Information Sciences —
Permanence of Paper for Printed Library
Materials, ANSI Z39.48-1984.

Library of Congress Catalog Card Number 88-9739

ISBN 0-8018-4375-8 (pbk.)

To Vera Belle Tiller Jordan, a loving and
indomitable mother, in whose American
backwoods genealogy stand, as comfortable
and natural companions, Scotch-Irish,
Welsh, Finn, and English hill folk.
Her prime virtue and legacy,
called in another tongue *sisu*,
is a spirit once resident on the frontier.

AND

In memory of a dear, loving mother,
Salme Tähe Kaups (1901–1987),
who encouraged me to realize other
worlds through different tongues.

CONTENTS

PREFACE

We are cultural geographers. As part of our disciplinary training, we learned to anticipate explanatory power in the greater human artifacts—the cultural landscape—produced during the occupancy of the earth's surface. For that reason, we both gravitated to the study of folk architecture—in particular, the wooden buildings of North America—with the expectation that we could read from their configuration much about the diffusionary events that shaped cultural regions. This book is, we hope, evidence of our success.

In explaining the origin of the backwoods colonization culture that swept so successfully across forested parts of North America, we present the thesis that colonial Finnish immigrants played a highly significant shaping role. A bit of background will help explain how we reached that seemingly far-fetched hypothesis. Jordan, who began his academic career as an unashamed Germanist and Teutophile, undertook in the middle 1970s to test the widely accepted but unproven notion that American notched log construction had German ethnic origin and was derived from Central Europe. He expected to find conclusive proof of this Germanic contribution to traditional American material culture, then use that evidence as a device to trace a pervasive Teutonic contribution in American folklife at large. Fluent in German and accompanied by his German-born wife, Jordan, during two lengthy field seasons, inspected every log construction region of Central Europe, even venturing into former German ethnic areas of Bohemia, Moravia, and Silesia. In brief, he went as a Germanist to German lands in search of Germanic prototypes of American log carpentry.

To his considerable surprise, he found very little evidence of such influence. The presumed antecedent forms did not exist. Puzzled and more than a bit perplexed, he turned to Scandinavia, to test the long-discarded notion that Swedish settlers of the short-lived colony of New Sweden on the Delaware River had introduced the prototype of American log construction. Still the Germanist, he expected to find little of relevance there. Jordan had not been in the field more than a week, however, when he discovered, in the back country of Sweden, a carpentry quite compatible with the American type. Closer inspection revealed that these techniques and forms appeared most often in a venerable Finnish ethnic area along the border of Sweden and Norway called the Finnskog, a district that had contributed abundantly to the New Sweden colony. The last glimmer of a Germanic connection faded; Finns, not Swedes, held the key.

At that point, the much-humbled Jordan invited Kaups into the project, recognizing that a specialist on Finnic culture had become essential. The scope of the research was enlarged, since both participants, following their cultural geographical instincts, wondered whether the Finnish contribution to carpentry had been paralleled by similar influence in other aspects of American backwoods pioneer culture. Adopting that line of inquiry and utilizing a cultural ecological methodology—also inherent in their geographical training—they produced the book now in hand.

We tell this story of Jordan's curious intellectual wanderings to demonstrate that the improbable conclusions presented in the book did not spring from special pleading. The principal author began as a proponent of an opposing viewpoint and was only gradually converted to the Finnish hypothesis by the weight of his own field and archival evidence. Kaups, a confessed Fennophile, did not steer this shift, but merely responded to the call of distress of a disillusioned Germanist who could not read Finnish and realized life was too short to learn that alien tongue, then master its scholarly literature. In the capacity of Finnic expert, Kaups proved not only essential but also creative and imaginative. The project began with Jordan. The initial enlightenment in the deep shade of the Finnskog was his, and the actual writing of the manuscript fell to him. But without Kaups's expertise and insight, the book could not have been completed. Kaups has fully earned and deserves the title of "coauthor." It has been a delightful collaboration between kindred spirits, and the hours spent discussing the day's fieldwork over a pitcher of strong Swedish beer in towns like Torsby were some of the most pleasant of our lives.

In carrying out the research, we became indebted to many persons in various ways. We are grateful to Richard M. Lieffort, a research assistant who accompanied us in Scandinavia and Finland; to Karl W. Butzer, Dickson Professor of Geography at the University of Texas at Austin, who freely shared his expertise in cultural ecology; to James M. Denny, chief of survey and registration at the Missouri Division of Parks and Historic Preservation, who provided abundant data and illustrations of folk architecture; to Lena Andersson Palmqvist of Nordiska museet in Stockholm, who greatly facilitated our work at that splendid museum; to Stig Appelgren, a librarian at the Nordiska; to Kirsti Melanko, and especially to Sirkku Dölle, of the National Museum of Finland in

Helsinki, who made our research in the archives there both enjoyable and productive; to Ivar Skre, director of Glomdalsmuseet in Elverum, Norway, who responded to our unannounced visit on a Sunday by coming down to the museum to assist us personally; to Hans Henrik Brummer, director of the Zornsamlingarna in Mora, Sweden, and his helpful assistant Bengt Mattsson; to Ove Koehler, curator of Sågudden museum at Arvika, who knows a Finn when he sees one; to Halvard Björkvik, director, and Lars Roede, architect, of the Norsk Folkemuseum in Oslo, who were both helpful and hospitable; to Rolf Kjellström and Janken Myrdal of Nordiska museet; to Erkki Jauhiainen, geographer at Joensuu University in Finland; to Nora Alajoki and Hanna Tynkkynen, volunteer guides and interpreters in the Laukaa district of Finland; to Paavo Tommonoksa of rural Laukaa; to Marlis A. Jordan, for her good company and assistance in archival work, editing, and proofreading; to Russell L. Gerlach and Robert Flanders of Southwest Missouri State University; to Harry and Doris Rink of Gibbstown, New Jersey, for their hospitality in showing the Nothnagle House; to Eugene Wilson, geographer at the University of South Alabama, who kindly gave us permission to use one of his photographs; to Madeline and William Stubbs, of Elkton, Maryland, who made the Boulden-Stubbs house available for inspection and offered useful information about that structure; and to Richard H. Hulan of Arlington, Virginia, who generously and enthusiastically shared his ideas on New Sweden, and whose name opens doors all through the Delaware Valley.

Our greatest debt is to Per Martin Tvengsberg of Hamar, Norway, a descendant of Finnskog settlers who shared with us his extensive knowledge of the local culture; who repeatedly provided us bed and board in Oslo, Hamar, and the forest; and who facilitated our work in Torsby and Helsinki. He is a kind, knowledgable gentleman and scholar who also agreed to read an early draft of Chapter 3, providing useful advice for improvement.

Cartographers Elaine Bargsley and John V. Cotter drew many of the maps in the book, and their patient attention to our often unreasonable demands for detail is appreciated.

Funding for the greater part of the research, including cartography, travel, photography, and field assistance, was provided from the endowment of the Walter Prescott Webb Chair, administered by Robert D. King, dean of the College of Liberal Arts at the University of Texas at Austin.

The American Backwoods Frontier

ONE

A BACKWOODS CULTURE

> *What manner of man are you,*
> *What kind of person, wretch?*
> Kalevala

The rise of distinctive regional cultures in the colonial eastern seaboard of the United States and their subsequent spread westward have long interested students of Americana. To what degree were various contemporary European cultures implanted, modified, simplified, or hybridized in the overseas colonial setting? How great were the cultural influences exerted by the American Indian and African slave? How potent a shaping force was the frontier experience? In what ways did the physical environment of the North American continent influence the colonial cultures?

In light of such questions, perhaps no traditional American way of life is more intriguing than that of the frontier backwoods pioneers, those highly successful forest colonizers who, forming the outer perimeter of European settlement in North America, swept in a scant generation from the Appalachians to the Mississippi, hesitated on the eastern margin of the great grasslands, and then leapt, in but one more generation, to the wooded mountain West, to halt reluctantly at the Pacific breakers. They constituted the vanguard of colonization in the temperate wooded areas of North America, opening the way for less adventurous but more enduring peoples to follow and complete the occupation of the continent's forests (Fig. 1.1).

A Distinctive Way of Life

These sylvan settlers knew they constituted a distinctive culture and very early sought a name for themselves. In the 1720s, pioneers on the Pennsylvania frontier preferred to be called "the Back Inhabitors" or "borderers," and other early contemporary accounts speak of "Back settlements," "Woodboys," "Woodsmen," "first settlers," "squatters," and "back settlers."[1] By at least the 1780s the favored appellation had become "back-woods men."[2]

Foreigners or other outsiders, confronted by such people but

Fig. 1.1. A latter-day backwoodsman. (Copied from "Surry County, North Carolina" 1862, p. 184.)

ignorant of the proper name for them, nonetheless felt obliged to set them apart from other Americans of their era. A German touring the westernmost settlements of Virginia about 1750 encountered "a kind of white people . . . who live like the savages," while seventy-five years later another traveler, near Niagara in Ontario, noticed people with "a half Indian appearance . . . living in the woods, surrounded by swamps."[3] New Englander Timothy Dwight also lacked the appropriate name, and upon observing backwoods pioneers, described them as "those who *begin* the cultivation of the wilderness, . . . cut down trees, build log-houses, lay open forested grounds to cultivation, and prepare the way for those who come after them."[4] Another traveler labeled them "a race which delight much to live on the frontiers." Backwoods pioneers, in their own view, lived "beyond the settlements" and clearly distinguished themselves from the inhabitants of the longer-populated districts.[5]

The bases of the cultural distinctiveness of the backwoods pioneers were numerous, and included

1. an essentially classless society;

2. a lack of appreciation or respect for centralized social institutions such as law, education, religion, and landownership;

3. high levels of personal freedom, individualism, and, paradoxically, mutual aid;

4. dominance by the nuclear family unit or, at most, small clans of blood kin;

5. considerable mixing with Indians, involving a lively cultural and genetic exchange, with more than occasional marriages to Indian women;

6. locational instability, amounting to an almost compulsive mobility, making it commonplace for persons to move three, four, or even five times during their lifespan;

7. frontier expansion not in the pattern of concentric rings or bark-growth, but instead in a "polynesian" manner, with backwoodsmen scattered islandlike through the forest, leaving unsettled land for miles around them;

8. considerable dependence upon nonagricultural pursuits, in particular hunting with traps and the muzzle-load long rifle, as well as upon fishing and the gathering of wild plants, all of which necessitated a sparse population density of two or fewer persons per square mile;

9. a lack of concern for conservation, leading to a wanton wasting of floral, faunal, and edaphic resources;

10. a subsistence slash-and-burn system of agriculture (including land rotation) based in small, impermanent fields created by ax and fire;

11. a settlement pattern consisting of dispersed farmsteads rather than clustered villages or hamlets;

12. the keeping of open-range livestock, particularly hogs and to a lesser extent cattle;

13. a crude form of notched, horizontal log construction;

14. a small number of simple, efficient, and interchangeable log house and barn plans;

15. a simple, high-protein diet containing unusually large amounts of meat — mainly pork and wild game — supplemented by breads and grits made from Indian corn, by garden vegetables, wild berries, and nuts from the forest, by peaches from a small orchard, and by distilled alcoholic beverages.[6]

It was, in sum, a culture ideally suited to the task at hand (Fig. 1.2).

Contemporary observers in various states cataloged these traits again and again as the culture passed west. In the 1780s, Benjamin Rush and Johann David Schoepf wrote two of the earliest lengthy descriptions of the pioneers, who were then in possession of western Pennsylvania.[7] "These hunters or 'backwoodsmen' live very much like the Indians and acquire similar ways of thinking," said Schoepf. Rush agreed, noting that the pioneer "soon acquires a strong tincture" of Indian manners. "An insignificant cabin of unhewn logs" with a floor "of earth" and a roof "of split logs" sufficed for them. In a small clearing, they planted corn, which "grows generally on new ground with but little care." Their open-range stock, "a few cows and pigs," fed upon "wild grass or the succulent twigs of the woods." The backwoodsman's "pleasures consist chiefly in fishing and hunting," but he also "loves spiritous liquors." He resists, wrote Rush, "the operation of laws" and "cannot bear to surrender up a single natural right for all the benefits of government." The German Schoepf agreed, noting that the pioneers "shun everything which appears to demand of them law and order, dread anything which breathes constraint." Even so, continued Schoepf, "they are not transgressors," but instead their object is merely "altogether natural freedom." Rush described their manner of living as "licentious" and noted, caustically, that "the flight of this class of people is always increased by the preaching of the gospel." In the words of an even earlier observer, William Byrd, the backwoodsman paid "no tribute, either to God or to Caesar."[8]

After a few years, continued Rush, "as population increases around him, he becomes uneasy and dissatisfied," both because the animals he hunts "fly from the face of man" and because the range of his "at large" livestock is restricted. "Therefore he abandons his little settlement, and seeks a retreat in the woods, where he again submits to all the toils which have been mentioned." Some backwoodsmen, Rush declared, "have broken ground on bare creation not less than four different times in this way, in different and more advanced parts of the State."[9]

A generation and a half later, in Illinois and Missouri, John Mason Peck provided another detailed description of the backwoods culture. He wrote of "the squatter race found on the extreme frontiers," living in "single log-cabins of the most inferior quality." To

Fig. 1.2. The backwoods farm. (Reproduced from Turner 1849, illus. facing p. 562.)

such a settler, it was "quite immaterial whether he ever [became] the owner of the soil." The backwoods pioneers "made a cornfield of a half-a-dozen acres, and a 'truck patch,' on which they raised cabbages, turnips, cucumbers, and melons," while swine and cattle foraged on the wooded "range." They depended considerably on "the proceeds of hunting." Among such people "there was no school, and a majority of the squatters wanted none." Worse, from missionary Peck's viewpoint, many woodland pioneers took a decided "stand against all organized efforts to publish the glad tidings to a sin-ruined world," with the result that they knew nothing "correctly of the progress of the kingdom of Christ on earth." Drifters all, they remained in a place only "till the range is somewhat subdued, and hunting a little precarious, or, which is more frequently the case, till neighbors crowd around . . . and he lacks elbow-room." Then they "cleared out for the frontier of Arkansas, or some other unsettled region."[10]

Such observers not only recognized the distinctiveness of the backwoods culture but also, on occasion, developed models or classifications of the settlement process, in which the pioneer occupied a separate, first phase. Long before the noted historian Frederick Jackson Turner proposed his famous model of frontier stages, one of which was the "pioneer farmer," similar schemes had been published.[11] In each of these early classifications, the backwoodsmen are displaced by more substantial settlers, who put down roots and complete the colonization process. Peck called them "the next class of emigrants" and "new-comers," while Rush described a *"second* species of settler."[12] In central

Texas, the secondary colonists were sarcastically called "the better sort" of people.[13]

New Englander Thaddeus Harris saw the two types—backwoods pioneers and their replacements—living side by side in the Ohio Valley about 1800, separated only by the river. "The industrious habits and neat improvements of the people on the west side of the river," he reported, "are strikingly constrasted with those on the east. *Here,* in Ohio, they are intelligent, industrious, and thriving; *there,* on the back skirts of Virginia, ignorant, lazy, and poor. *Here* the buildings are neat; *there* the habitations are miserable cabins. *Here* the grounds are laid out in a regular manner, and inclosed by strong posts and rails; *there* the fields are surrounded by a rough zigzag log fence." On the Ohio side "are thrifty young apple orchards; *there* the only fruit that is raised is the peach, *from which a good brandy is distilled."*[14]

A bit later the same juxtaposition shifted to central Ohio, where "the old pioneer log dwellings and the slovenly cultivation of the first settlers" stood alongside "lands well improved, with fields of moderate size, well fenced, with a good barn and neat dwelling-house."[15] Similarly, across Lake Erie in Ontario, backwoods homesteads provided a stark contrast to the "neat well-tilled farms of the . . . Pennsylvania Dutch."[16]

Clearly, the backwoods pioneers were not highly esteemed. Depicted as shiftless, lazy, dirty, drunken, ignorant, and sinful, as "land butchers" whose careless practices damaged the countryside, the backwoods people constituted, in the eyes of those who followed and observed them, an undesirable element.[17] Without question these accounts are biased, but the woodland pioneers left few written records to counterbalance their negative image. Few writers acknowledged the almost outrageous success of their colonization system. Few gave them credit for opening the land to settlement and for laying "the foundation of independent thought and feeling."[18]

Value judgments aside, we propose that the recognition of the backwoods pioneer as a distinctive type is essentially accurate. These are not simple classifications of convenience, nor are they merely arbitrary partitions of a colonization continuum. Instead, we feel, they describe an actual way of life, a genuine culture, or at least a subculture. True, Turner and his predecessors have been criticized for presenting an overly episodic view of the settlement process, and one must take care not to overstate the case.[19] To be sure, the woodland pioneers had much in common with their successors, and membership in their class was far from inviolable. People of the frontier could and frequently did choose to remain in a place and be absorbed into subsequent occupancy stages. For example, Peck in Missouri about 1820 noted that "mixed up with the ignorant, filthy, wretched squatters . . . were many decent, respectable, and religious families who were patiently waiting for the land to be brought into market, when the squatters would give place to an improved class."[20] Conversely, some people from longer-settled areas moved out onto the frontier and became acculturated into the backwoods way of life.[21] Even so, we maintain, initial European occupancy of the mesothermal woodlands of North America was accomplished by a distinct type of culture. It endured until there were no more forested settlement perimeters to inhabit, until the task of wilderness conquest ended on the shores of the Pacific. Even then, vestiges of the backwoods life lingered long in pockets unfavored by nature.

It is further our view, to be elaborated upon in succeeding chapters, that the American backwoods pioneer culture, while from a modern perspective flawed in diverse ways and perhaps partly responsible for certain ecological problems that plague us yet today, should be regarded as the basis of the most successful forest colonization process ever devised. We deal with a culture splendidly adapted to the forest and ideally suited for rapid westward expansion.

Some scholars have suggested analogous colonizations in other places and times. The millennium of Teutonic assault on the woodlands of central and western Europe, cruelly terminated by the Black Death around 1350, bore similarities to the American experience.[22] On close inspection these prove more superficial than real. The German colonists absorbed rather than displaced the native Slavic population, often annexing and enlarging their settlements. Through most of the period of Germanic clearance, the nobility and the church remained deeply involved, and compared to their counterparts in North America, the German axmen progressed at a snail's pace. They remained tied to tight villages and hindered by their compulsion to root out tree stumps as they cleared. Indeed, the German verb for clearing woods, *roden*, means literally "to root out," and from it came the host of Teutonic toponym suffixes—for example, *-rot, -rod, -reut*, and *-rud*—which today characterize villages in central Europe. Not surprisingly, given these restrictions, the Germanic folk took a thousand years to clear far less land than the American pioneers removed in a mere two centuries.

The Slavs—above all, the Russians—augmented the work begun by the Germans, shifting the major scene of forest removal to the expansive East European Plain. Their rate of progress also was rather slow, paling in comparison to that of the American pioneer. Truly, only in the United States and southern Canada "has there been so unified a frontier of settlement, nor another of comparable scale."[23] We deal with a quite remarkable, unique achievement.

Core, Domains, and Periphery

Spatially, the woodland pioneer culture in North America diffused from a hearth area, or core, through a primary domain, a secondary domain, and beyond into a peripheral zone of penetration, its traits weakening to the margins (Fig. 1.3).[24] The consensus has long held, and correctly, that the American backwoods pioneer culture emanated from the Middle Colonies, particularly Penn-

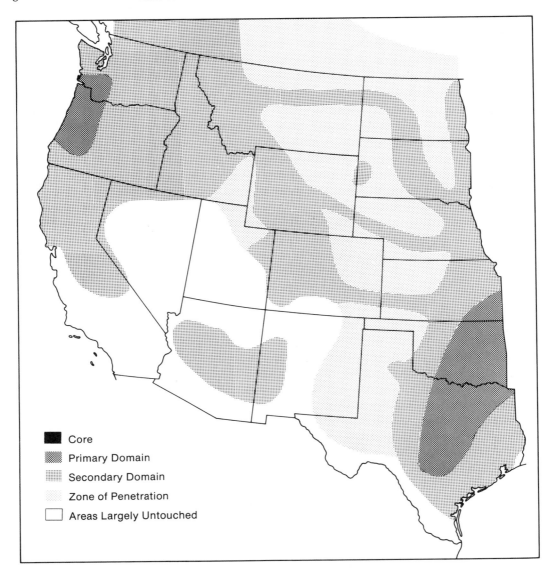

Fig. 1.3. Diffusion of the Midland American backwoods pioneer culture. **Core**: the nucleus where the Midland backwoods culture took shape in the period 1640–1680. **Primary domain**: most intense implantment of Midland backwoods culture, 1700–1850, by means of relocation diffusion; a zone where Midlanders made the dominant genetic input, and where secondary settlers (also dominantly Midland in origin) perpetuated a Midland-based culture that preserved many backwoods characteristics. **Secondary domain**: less intense implantment of Midland backwoods culture, accomplished through relocation and

sylvania.[25] A variety of possible core areas has been proposed over the years as the place of origin. Turner favored the Pennsylvanian section of the Great Valley of the Appalachians, while cultural geographer Milton Newton suggested a huge zone stretching from the vicinity of Lancaster, Pennsylvania, to Augusta, Georgia. Newton further proposed that the half-century from 1725 to 1775

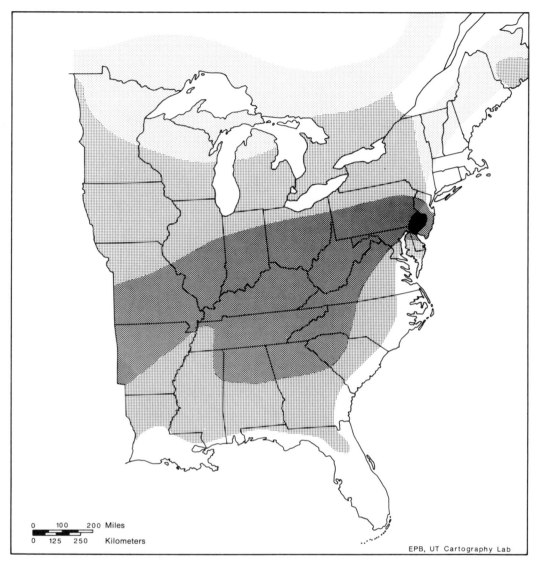

expansion diffusion, 1725–1875; a zone where the secondary cultures that supplanted the backwoods stage were essentially non-Midland, and where a few selected backwoods features survived; **Zone of penetration**: implantment of selected Midland backwoods traits, accomplished by means of contagious diffusion with little or no genetic input, and followed by the eradication of all backwoods traits. **Untouched areas**: no significant implantment of Midland backwoods culture. (Sources: in part, after Kniffen 1965; Meinig 1969; and Newton 1974.)

witnessed the blending necessary for evolution of the culture. Robert D. Mitchell, also a geographer, postulated several stages of core areas, including a primary hearth area in southeastern Pennsylvania and "secondary areas" of cultural fusion in the Shenandoah Valley and the northern Piedmont of North Carolina (Fig. 1.4).[26]

While we are aware that such matters necessarily remain some-

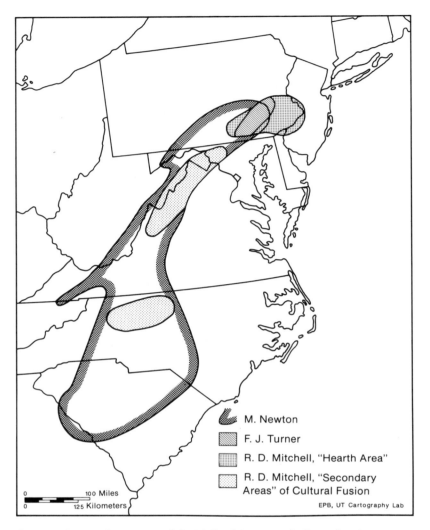

Fig. 1.4. Proposed core areas of the Midland American backwoods culture. (Sources: Turner 1962, p. 164; Mitchell 1978, p. 75; Newton 1974, pp. 148–49.)

what speculative, we point to a more confined, more easterly, earlier core. It is our contention that the backwoods culture arose in the very time and place where the Middle Colonies began—the lower Delaware Valley, below Philadelphia—in the period 1640–1680 (Fig. 1.3). From this core, backwoods pioneers spread between about 1700 and 1850 to create a *primary domain* (the zone of most intense implantment of their culture), a broad swath across the lower Midwest and the upland South (Fig. 1.3). Because of its location in the continental interior, this domain and its culture are well described by the adjective *midland*. In the primary domain, Pennsylvania-derived settlers made the dominant *genetic* as well as cultural imprint. That is, the spread of backwoods culture proceeded by means of *relocation* diffusion, in which the culture was transferred from place to place through the bodily migration of its bearers.[27] Moreover, the secondary settlers who displaced the woodland pioneers in the primary domain were also dominantly Midlanders by origin, perpetuating a Pennsylvania culture that preserved, in modified form at least, numerous features of backwoods culture.

To be sure, the Midland folk absorbed genetic and cultural minorities in the process of building the primary domain of their culture. Mitchell is likely correct in his designation of the specific areas where such absorption was greatest (Fig. 1.4). In particular, many Chesapeake English poor whites, displaced by enslaved black labor in the Tidewater plantation districts after about 1700, fled to the back country and became acculturated into the Pennsylvania pioneer culture through *expansion* diffusion.[28] In this process, elements of a desirable or useful culture spread through a population in a snowballing manner, by personal contact and example. By the same means, many basic elements of the Midland backwoods culture diffused to adjacent Indians, in particular the "Five Civilized Tribes" of the southeastern United States, producing generations of log cabin–dwelling, long rifle–hunting Indians such as the Cherokee and Creek (Fig. 1.5).[29]

The building of the primary domain began in earnest about 1725, and by the time of the first federal census in 1790, the pioneering prowess of the Pennsylvanians had permitted the old Delaware Valley colonies to place an imprint on a large, growing interior area. Our settlement frontier literally bulged in the middle, along the axis of the Cumberland Gap–Wilderness Road route, due to the expansion accomplished by the Midland backwoodsmen (Fig. 1.6). This bulge, in turn, served as the base for Midland military thrusts, followed by colonization. Kentuckians led by William Henry Harrison conquered the Old Northwest, while Tennesseans, following the likes of Andrew Jackson and Sam Houston, invaded and annexed the Gulf Coastal Plain.[30]

In the *secondary domain* of American backwoods culture—where forest pioneers were less prevalent—implantment was accomplished about equally by the relocation and expansion methods of diffusion (Fig. 1.3). There the people who displaced the backwoods folk in the second phase of settlement were bearers of non-Midland cultures, and as a result few features of the pioneer way of life persisted (Fig. 1.7). The backwoods Midland imprint faded rapidly as decades passed, and the present-day observer is hard-pressed to find much evidence of its former presence. In this manner, Midland artifacts and techniques diffused into areas such as upstate New York, Ontario, and the inner coastal plain of the Gulf of Mexico. The worth of the backwoods pioneers was as great in the secondary as in the primary domain, for they opened both to settlement, but their legacy was more fleeting in the secondary domain.

Still more peripheral is the *zone of penetration*, where selected Midland backwoods traits, unaccompanied by any significant genetic or relocation component, spread by means of expansion diffusion. Subsequently, and even more quickly and completely than

Fig. 1.5.   Chief McConico Battise of the Alabama-Coushatta tribe, Polk County, Texas. This Creek Indian holds a Kentucky long rifle and sits in front of a log cabin, revealing the acculturation of his tribe to the Midland backwoods way of life. (Photo by Dorothy Shill, Livingston, Texas; copy courtesy of The University of Texas Institute of Texan Cultures, San Antonio, and used with permission.)

in the secondary domain, Midland traits were eradicated here, leaving only the scantiest, most tantalizing traces. Beyond this zone were *untouched areas*, where for cultural or environmental reasons no noteworthy intrusion of Midland backwoods culture occurred.

Figure 1.3, a map portraying the spatial unfolding of the wood-

Fig. 1.6. The American frontier, 1740–1800. The bulge that centers on Kentucky demonstrates the more rapid westward penetration of the Midland pioneers. (After Gerlach 1976, p. 14; and Friis 1940.)

land pioneer way of life, falls short in the temporal dimension. At no single period did the backwoods pioneers reign over any substantial part of the several domains depicted. While they built their primary domain, they forfeited forever to successor cultures their Delaware Valley core. When they poured through Cumberland Gap to Kentucky, they surrendered the former major artery of their migration, the Great Valley of the Appalachians. In the early 1800s, a decade after statehood was achieved by Kentucky and Tennessee, F. A. Michaux, perhaps mistakenly, described them as already almost vanished from those two states.[31] A generation later Peck witnessed their flight from central Missouri.[32] Figure 1.3, then, suggests a durability, a staying power, that in reality never existed and would be antithetical to the essence of

Fig. 1.7. Diagram of the spatial evolution of the three principal Anglo-American subcultures. The Midland imprint was fleeting and confined to the backwoods stage on the northern and southern peripheries.

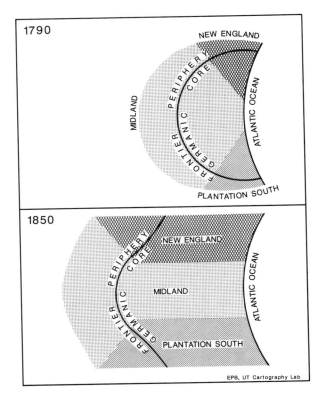

backwoods culture. The map represents at best a cumulative record of the presence of these restless people.

Competing Cultures

What of the practitioners of the other cultures who perched around the rim of colonial North America and might have seized all or part of the interior for themselves? What of the other two Anglo-American cultures—the Puritan New Englanders and the southern planters—as well as the Spaniards, Dutch, French, and Russians?

Neither of the other two Anglo-American groups made substantial progress toward the interior in colonial times. Both had failed to venture more than a day's journey from the Atlantic by the middle of the eighteenth century, even though the founding of Massachusetts and Virginia, their mother colonies, predated the arrival of Europeans in the Delaware Valley by twenty to thirty years.[33] In Puritan New England, Vermont, a scant ninety miles from the ocean breakers, remained unoccupied as late as 1750 and was settled largely after the Revolution, partly from the *west*. Indeed, the issue of whether Vermont would belong to New England or the Middle Atlantic states remained in doubt for many years. In addition, northwestern Massachusetts was not settled until after 1760.[34]

The Yankee New Englanders, then, progressed to the interior

of America with glacial slowness, even though, in 1650, they formed by far the largest European population in any of the colonial clusters. They chose instead to filter southward along the coast, settling Long Island and parts of New Jersey. Seeking a reason for the tardiness of New Englanders in penetrating the interior, various writers point to fierce Indian resistance, to the hostile French across the divide in the Saint Lawrence Valley, or to the low mountain barrier back from the coast.[35] The fact is, however, that the pious New Englanders failed for reasons based in their culture. They lacked expertise in forest colonization and often derived from towns rather than farms. Encumbered by a zealous theocracy and an overly centralized land-granting system, discouraged by winters colder than they had known in England, slowed by their reliance on sawmills and lumber, hindered by their insistence on rooting stumps from new fields in the ancient Germanic manner, retarded by their pursuit of communal perfection, and burdened by their English preference for mutton—which necessitated raising sheep alongside wolf-infested woods—these Anglo-Saxons scarcely crept inland.[36] Terrain cannot be blamed, for the New Englanders' access to the heart of the continent was easier than that faced by the Pennsylvanians.[37] No, they failed because they sprang from a deforested land and arrived on America's shores unprepared for the monumental task of woodland colonization. Look not to them for the spark of the westward movement.

Eventually, after about 1760, New Englanders finally stirred, seized their immediate hinterland, and soon, in another generation, poured through the Mohawk glacial gateway, the great natural route that had patiently waited for them, into the American heartland. This they achieved, however, only after adopting the essential Midland backwoods paraphernalia—the log cabin, axmanship, forest hunting skills—and by abandoning some of the traditional practices and institutions that had earlier hindered their progress. Moreover, they achieved this expansion largely as secondary settlers.

Plantation southerners, of English and French Huguenot ancestry in the main, similarly failed, awarding most of their backcountry, temporarily at least, to the Pennsylvanians. Tied to the coast by overseas markets and bound to the subtropics by the climatic demands of certain of their cash crops, the planters went only shallowly and late, as secondary settlers, to the interior. In South Carolina, settlements had been pushed hardly eighty miles from the coast by 1730, the close of the sixth decade of settlement. Not until the middle of the eighteenth century did Virginia planter families such as the Jeffersons leave the Tidewater districts and settle at the foot of the Blue Ridge, and only then as secondary settlers.[38] Had the planters chosen to go west early, their route would have been easy. Skirting the southern edge of the Appalachians, they would have found fertile plains leading to the Mississippi. Instead, they let Pennsylvania's children blaze this path for them, following at a cautious distance.

The planters, like their Calvinist cousins in New England, were culturally ill equipped to cope with forest colonization. Like the Puritans, they came from the long-settled, largely deforested, fertile core of Europe. In addition, the empty woods might have offered their slaves too tempting a goal for escape. The planters, then, also lacked the key to enter and seize the American heartland. Look not to them—cavaliers, criminals, and Calvert Catholics—for the roots of backwoods culture. They belong to the littoral.

However, South Carolina's plantation culture did spawn a subsidiary, a "poor white" subculture capable of westward expansion. It consisted of open-range cattle-hog herders based in "cowpens" scattered through the Charleston hinterland.[39] Dependent upon the grassy and caney undergrowth of the infertile belt of "pine barrens," paralleling the coast all the way to Texas, this herding subculture ultimately proved best adapted to the grasslands of North America. Reaching Texas and joining a Hispanic tradition, the Carolina herders exploded through the Great Plains in the late nineteenth century. But theirs was not a culture equipped to conquer the forests. They helped write the story of grassland colonization, but they did not challenge Pennsylvania in the woods.

The Spaniards, the earliest to arrive in North America, knew nothing of forests and shunned them, allowing first one, then another coastal foothold near the great woodlands to slip from their control—Louisiana, Florida, Texas, California. The Spanish governor of Louisiana, watching in 1794 as American backwoods pioneers bore down on the province he ruled, knew he had met his match. "Their roving spirit and the readiness with which they procure sustenance and shelter facilitate rapid settlement," wrote the governor. "With logs crossed upon one another he makes a house," and "when a family wearies of one place, it moves on to another and settles there with the same ease." The governor knew that "if such men [came] to occupy the banks of the Mississippi and Missouri," nothing could prevent them from entering Spanish territory (Fig. 1.8).[40] A scant few years later, after Spanish rule had been extinguished, prim New Englanders spoke of "the wild men on the Missouri" in vainly opposing the admission of Louisiana to the union.[41]

The Dutch, from an almost totally deforested land, clung tenuously to a river mouth and traded with Indians, ignoring the Hudson-Mohawk route, the easiest to the wooded continental interior. Look for their spoor along the banks of the Hudson, in old monied families and odd Dutch barns, not along the Ohio or the Mississippi.[42] Find it in their great city, New York, for they were town builders using masonry and bricks rather than woodland pioneers notching logs.

The Russians might have accomplished the task; certainly they knew how to colonize woodlands. But they reached North America too few in number and too late, after the issue of possession had been decided. They approached from the wrong direction, across interminable Siberia, and for the wrong reason—the

Fig. 1.8. Crockett at the Alamo. While fanciful, given Crockett's documented surrender in the siege, this drawing embodies many authentic traits of the backwoodsman. (Copied from *Crockett's Almanac*, 1848.)

plundering of wealth.[43] By the 1780s, when Russians first settled coastal Alaskan fur posts, Pennsylvanians had already poured through Cumberland Gap to claim the interior, and the infant United States, due in no small part to the work of its backwoods settlers, reigned as far as the Mississippi River. Moreover, by then Russia had bound its peasants to the soil in a neofeudal bondage that would persist until 1917, blocking any possibility of their emigration. Remarkable as the Russian reach for Alaska was, it came to naught.

And what of the French? Had they not, from bases on the lower Saint Lawrence and in the Mississippi Delta, explored and claimed the splendid network of internal waterways in North America? Had they not used those rivers, lakes, and short portages to tap the fur wealth of much of the continent? Yes they had, but the French did not achieve effective settlement of the interior, nor did they attempt to do so. Only their coastal entrepôts were truly colonized, and when New France was wrested from them in 1760, their western settlement frontier lay but a few miles upstream from Montreal, almost exactly where it had stood one hundred twenty years earlier, when the city was founded. The French-colonized area in that quarter formed only a narrow strip along the marine-inspired Saint Lawrence, and few *habitants* could not view the water from their front door.[44]

Beyond, in the continental interior, lay only a sprinkling of French fur posts and forts. Upstream from Montreal the French, as *couriers de bois*, adopted Indian culture; they did not seek effective control. Few French colonial females ever went beyond the Lachine Rapids, and the interior posts were peopled by half-breeds. Mostly, this happened by design. The French obsession with furs required that the interior be left wooded, wild, and in the possession of Indians. That was just as well, for the French were as ill equipped as the Dutch, Spanish, Puritans, and planters to colonize the North American forests. When approached and challenged by Midland backwoods culture, the French legacy in the North American interior evaporated like morning mist. It lacked substance.

Even in the Saint Lawrence Valley, little progress occurred. If New Englanders failed in colonial times to chop their way to the borders of Québec, so the French settlers of the Saint Lawrence never approached the British border. Small wonder, then, that Scotsman Patrick Campbell, passing from Montreal upstream to Kingston, Ontario, in 1791, found as he crossed the linguistic border that the swarming "loyalist" backwoods pioneers on the Ontario side, in possession of the land for only eight years, "do not fall much short of having as much land cleared as the French, who have been more than an hundred years in possession."[45]

By default, then, the task of forest pioneering fell to the Midlanders. How did the Middle Colonies succeed while all the others stood by? In what manner and from what human raw material was the colonizing culture formed? What explains the preeminence of the Pennsylvania pioneer?

The answers to these questions are of fundamental importance to an understanding of the American experience and of the territorial development of the United States into a continental, rather than a littoral, state. In offering them, we answer a call made to cultural geographers half a century ago by Carl O. Sauer, our founder-father, who challenged us to "characterize the culture complexes and successions" in the settlement of the United States.[46]

TWO

IN SEARCH OF A MAINSPRING

> *I blazed a trail . . .*
> *Broke branches,*
> *showed the way.*
> Kalevala

Scholars in several academic disciplines have studied the evolution of frontiers and overseas colonial European cultures. From a century or more of such inquiry and from work in other and related fields, we can distill at least five major categories of relevant concepts, models, and theses: cultural diffusion, environmentalism, economic determinism, societal models, and cultural ecology.[1] Advocates of some of these schools have claimed to offer the mainspring, the central causal mechanism explaining what happened to emigrating Europeans in one or more of the colonial settings. Each can profitably be brought to bear on the question of the Midland backwoods pioneer.

One of the goals of cultural geographers, as D. W. Meinig once said, is to gain "a better grasp of general process so as to understand an immensely complicated history." But an equally important goal is to find a causal mechanism that is applicable to a specific case—in this instance, the Pennsylvania pioneer.[2] While humanists glory in the variety of people, and social scientists level diversity in search of universal principles, we seek a joining of these approaches. While humanistic geographers delight in the uniqueness of place, and scientific geographers deal in spatial and ecological abstractions, we attempt to wed the two.

We realize at the outset that the American backwoods pioneer was an occupant of one particular type of frontier, an *external* or *insular* frontier, distant from and noncontiguous with the motherland. It was settled by individuals rather than groups, lay in mesothermal woodlands, and was an *agrarian* or *small-farm* frontier, to use the classification of James G. Leyburn, rather than one devoted to plantation exploitation or the rapid commercial extraction of mineral, faunal, or floral wealth.[3] We acknowledge, too, that the American frontier woodland involved both a habitat and a social process. It was not merely a spatially and temporally impermanent fringe area in which an expanding society adapted to a forested environment and to weakened ties to the European homeland; it was also a zone of contact with alien cultures and ethnic mixing.[4]

Diffusionist Studies

Perhaps the most obvious point of departure in our search for a mainspring is the time-honored methodology of cultural diffusion. In general, diffusionists believe that external, agrarian colonial cultures, in the main, were imported from the Old World. They suggest that people, particularly in the traditional or *folk* stage, were not very inventive. Even the more adventurous, who emigrated, remained sufficiently conservative as to transfer methods and artifacts, both singly and in cultural complexes, to the overseas settlement areas. Diffusionists, in the words of John C. Hudson, look "carefully behind what appear to be controls of the physical environment or imperatives of the economic system to learn more of who settled a region, or what their aims were, and, especially, from whence they came."[5] Or, as Carl Sauer once suggested, "No groups coming from different civilizations and animated by different social ideals have reacted to frontier life in identical fashion."[6]

Most diffusionists agree that a pronounced *simplification* of European culture occurred in the external colonial areas. Geographer R. C. Harris, echoing earlier statements by Albert G. Keller, George M. Foster, and Louis Hartz, wrote that "Europeans established overseas drastically simplified versions of European society." Europe, "a carpet of different human landscapes," mothered colonies far less diverse in character.[7] The causes of simplification are disputed but apparently multiple. Some considerable reduction occurs at the point of departure, since only areal and temporal fragments of European culture diffuse overseas, reflecting the sources and periods of emigration. Emigrants are never a typical cross section of the parent population. In addition, the diversity of their traits is further reduced in colonial settlements, under the action of strong selective frontier and environmental pressures. The German or "Dutch" dialect of Pennsylvania is an example of cultural simplification in diffusion. Immigrants in the colonial period introduced only two major dialects of German— Swiss and Pfälzer—out of the scores spoken in central Europe at that time, thereby reflecting the pattern of their origins. In Pennsylvania these two imported dialects collapsed into one, which drew upon both of its parent tongues.[8]

Another suggested phenomenon of diffusion is the principle of *first effective settlement*, proposed separately by cultural geographers Wilbur Zelinsky and Fred Kniffen.[9] In Zelinsky's words, "The first group able to establish a viable, self-perpetuating society in an empty land are of crucial significance for the later social and cultural geography of the area," regardless of how small the initial group may be.[10] The initial imprint tends to be durable, "surviving even where a new ethnic stock . . . succeed[s] the original settlers."[11] Following this principle, we can look to the very early settlement of the Middle Colonies for the prototype of the backwoods pioneer culture. Immigrants who arrived before 1700 presumably wielded greater formative influence than those who came in the eighteenth century. However, backwoods folk did not achieve a "self-perpetuating" settlement in any particular place, given the mobile nature of their culture. Secondary settlers, the "better sort," could and often did largely obliterate the pioneer way of life. Kniffen, cognizant of this problem, limited his version of the principle of first effective settlement to the postpioneer period.[12]

Perhaps the majority of diffusionists emphasize *fusion* of diverse Old World ethnic stocks as a key to understanding the simplified overseas European cultures. Much of the distinctiveness of colonial culture, in this view, derives from the juxtaposition and merging of groups that previously, in Europe, had little or no contact with one another. Midland culture, for example, reputedly took shape in the American Middle Colonies through "a fusion of more pluralistic complexes of primarily English, German, and Scotch-Irish origins."[13] From the English came common law and language; the Germans supposedly contributed the long rifle, Conestoga wagon, and "Dutch" barn; and the Scotch-Irish* are said to have brought whiskey, the Ulster cabin plan, and subsistence hill farming with an infield-outfield system.[14] These elements, in turn, were fused with numerous features of American Indian culture.[15] Indeed, Robin Wells lists direct contact by the expanding people with aboriginal cultures as one of four defining traits of all frontier sociocultural systems, and he, along with Irving Hallowell, assigns major importance to reciprocal cultural diffusion between Amerindians and backwoods pioneers.[16]

The working of cultural fusion is closely linked to simplification. Many ethnic cultures collapse into several, simplifying in the process.[17] The reduced cultural components crystallize into a new way of life. Some scholars, most notably Milton Newton, believe that the key to fusion and reduction is *syncretism*. That is, the traits most likely to survive are shared, in proximate form, by several or all of the constituent ethnic groups prior to emigration and fusion, in the several homelands.[18] Others attribute the survival of British traits in the American colonies to the dominance of the English host culture there.

A growing minority of diffusionists, in recent years, has downgraded fusion and syncretism, emphasizing instead Old World ethnic continuity in the American setting. Historians Forrest McDonald and Grady McWhiney, for example, propose that the colonial and antebellum American South, particularly the interior,

---

*Throughout the book, we have chosen to use the term *Scotch-Irish* instead of *Scots-Irish*. In so doing, we employ the vernacular American term, one that is also well established in the scholarly literature. We are aware that *Scots* technically refers to people and *scotch* to whiskey, but in the spirit of the frontier, we bow to the vernacular.

housed a largely unaltered Celtic ethnic group, reflecting an over-whelming majority of hill Britons in the regional population.[19] Further support for this view comes from geographer Russel Ger-lach, who writes of the "subconscious persistence" of Scotch-Irish ethnic identity in the Ozarks.[20] Similarly, after generations of scholars had discounted the possibility of significant African cultural influence in the Deep South, folklorist John Vlach and others countered with solid evidence of a substantial black cul-tural complex and ethnic identity derived from the old slave coast of Africa.[21] Such ethnic survival theses have lately come under sharp attack, but they do reflect growing attention to the transfer-ral and survival of substantial parts of ethnic cultural complexes, as opposed to isolated individual traits.[22] They serve as antidotes for the excesses of the fusionist school.

Perhaps the principal shortcoming of all diffusionist theses and models is their lack of explanatory power. They may accurately describe a procession, but they fail to explain process. Why were so few Old World items successfully transferred to the colonial areas? What mechanism governed success or failure? It is not enough to speak of syncretism, first effective settlement, simpli-fication, and selection. Moreover, culture in the diffusionist view often takes on a homogeneous and superorganic character, be-coming endowed with a leveling life force of its own that reduces individual people to the status of mindless worker bees concerned only to preserve the cultural hive.[23]

Clearly, to achieve explanatory power, the diffusion process must be linked to some causal mechanism, to some mainspring. Several of these have been proposed, and some of the most vener-able belong in the school of environmental determinism.

Environmental Determinist Theses

Certain scholars have proposed that the cultures evolving in Eu-rope's overseas colonial areas were shaped by their new and differ-ent natural settings. The famous frontier thesis of Frederick Jack-son Turner can best be placed in this environmental determinist category.[24] In the words of Ray Billington, an advocate of the Tur-nerian view, "The differences between American and European civilization [are] explained by the unique environment of the New World."[25] Turner saw the frontier as a place where Europeans met the physical environment, a place where, encountering a savage, remote, raw, untamed, wooded, and largely empty land, they fell into "the grip of overpowering forces."[26] In the western wilderness the tools of European civilization were out of place and of little value. Turnerians speak of "the corrosive influence of a forest en-vironment on imported cultures."[27] Ancestral institutions of law, religion, group discipline, agriculture, and finance suffered partial disintegration under physical environmental pressure.[28]

Because the frontier experience was prolonged by the huge size of the North American continent, being repeated for almost three centuries, its influence became magnified, in Turner's view.

American settlers were continually conditioned by the series of frontier environments they encountered, and their loss of European "cultural baggage on the road" increased with distance from the Atlantic.[29] This "steady movement away from the influence of Europe" produced a culture peculiarly American and largely indigenous.[30]

Turner is perhaps best remembered for his claim that the environmentally conditioned frontier way of life permanently stamped American civilization. In his view, democracy, individualism, anti-intellectualism, nationalism, optimism, innovative energetic ambition, and an idealistic view of progress and improvement all derived from the frontier.[31] "Forest philosophy," he wrote, "is the philosophy of American democracy."[32] Ultimately all rested upon free access to a demanding, forested wilderness.

Critics accuse Turner of underestimating European influence and placing too much importance on a transitory subculture. Powerful socioeconomic forces were afoot, such as the industrial revolution, the Age of Reason, and ascendant capitalism. Surely these rank at least alongside a demanding environment as factors to consider. Turner is also faulted for failing to explain the specific source, the cultural reservoir, from which flowed the new institutions needed to colonize the colonial forests. Why did the Pennsylvanians not simply perish as European misfits in the woods or cling, Puritan-like, to the coastland, where the umbilical tie to mother Europe had not yet been severed?

While Turner offered an environmental determinism based in the forest, his fellow historian Walter Prescott Webb presented a parallel thesis for the treeless, flat, semiarid western United States.[33] Pioneers hammered into Americans by two centuries of woodland colonization underwent a second traumatic pounding when they ventured west of the forests. Crossing an "institutional fault" line at the ninety-eighth meridian, Anglo-American civilization underwent a fundamental, forced modification on the Great Plains.[34] Presumably even more vestigial European characteristics died in the process, leaving behind an almost purely indigenous culture.

Turner and Webb, then, saw physical geography as the primary shaping force of frontier America. European cultures were irrelevant because they were ill equipped to cope with the environments of forest and grassland. Regionalism and sectionalism likewise had no standing in their systems. Western Texas was treeless, flat, and dry like North Dakota; Tennessee was the forested twin of New York. Technology, behavior, and ideology all were homogenized.[35]

The environmental determinist position was even more explicitly stated by early geographers such as Ellen Churchill Semple. Noting the central bulge in the American frontier at the time of the Revolution (Fig. 1.6), a "rude arc formed by the Tennessee and Ohio rivers," Semple postulated that "geographical conditions favored the expansion of the middle colonies." Through "many gateways" settlers were drawn to "the smiling lands of the Bluegrass" by "fertile soil, agreeable climate, and abundant salt springs," affording "all essentials for pioneer homes."[36]

The backwoods culture responsible for fashioning this "wedge driven into the great West" was itself, Semple claimed, created by the influence of the Appalachian mountains. The Great Valley of the Appalachians, stretching southwest from Pennsylvania, deflected Midland pioneers temporarily onto a more longitudinal course. A great mixing of stocks occurred as diverse streams of English, German, Dutch, Huguenot, and Scotch-Irish, passing from their coastal ethnic enclaves through gaps in the Blue Ridge, were caught up in the massive migration streaming through the valley. This mixing, facilitated by "the prevailing similarity of their physical environment," produced "the new type of the backwoods." Mountain-imposed isolation hindered markets and barred landed estates, thereby fostering classlessness.[37]

In Semple's view, formation of the backwoods culture continued and accelerated after the mountain wall had been breached and left behind. "In the cabin clearings of the western wilderness, beyond the barrier of the mountains," the last ties to Europe were severed and democratic backwoods pioneers sprang full grown onto the American stage.[38]

For all her explanatory efforts, all her references to the guiding and shaping influences of terrain, waterways, soil, and salt, Semple, and her imitators as well, did not address the central questions concerning the evolution of backwoods culture: Whence came the skills in woodcraft and pathfinding, the ability to survive and thrive in the woods? What first led settlers on the path west and taught them the ways of the wilderness? Why was such ability seen only in Midland America?

In any case, such determinism is an inappropriate motor to link to diffusion, since the two ideas are largely antithetical. Where diffusionists see transfer, determinists see the withering and death of imported traits. As Leyburn wrote, the "hostile environment" of the frontier required "development of folkways and mores different from the familiar ones 'back home.'"[39] Even Isaiah Bowman, not a determinist, argued that the pioneer breaks "the mold of the society that he leaves behind."[40]

Market Forces in the Wilderness

Casting aside consideration of physical environment, certain other scholars point to economic forces as central in human affairs. Economic deterministic models convey the image of humankind caught up in a giant economic web that allows little freedom of action. The most relevant examples of such work, from the perspective of backwoods pioneering, are spatial and deal with land use. Perhaps none is more valuable than the earliest such model—that of the *isolated state*—proposed in the 1820s by the German scholar-farmer J. H. von Thünen.[41] He suggested that the more intensive and commercialized forms of agriculture are located close to urban markets. Successive belts of progressively less intensive agriculture ring this core, at increasing distances. By implication, semisubsistence systems, such as that of the backwoods pioneer, survive only on the outer peripheries of the market-oriented system.

The explanation for von Thünen's concentric rings lies in the dictates of land rent. Land values are highest, and access to consumers easiest, near a market. Farmers can and must place nearly all their resources, in the form of capital and labor, into production, making only minimal outlays for the transportation of goods to market. Output per acre is thus high, and necessarily so, given the great value of the land. With increasing distance from a market, farmers have to spend progressively more on transportation and, as a result, invest less in production. Less intensive use of the land necessarily characterizes the hinterland. On the outer peripheries, where access to markets is poor or even impractical, subsistence systems can exist, since the land has little or no commercial value.

The von Thünen model, developed on a small, local scale, has been applied to the Western world as a whole.[42] If we envision, about the year 1800, that western Europe, particularly Britain, constituted the market, or "world city" as it has been called, then the American backwoods pioneers of that time occupied a portion of the remote periphery of the market system, where land values were low and land use was extensive (Fig. 2.1). If we add a temporal dimension to the model, setting it in motion, we begin to see expansion occur. As the world city grew, markets also grew. Improved transportation links reached ever farther from the world city, and the various agrarian belts migrated away from the expanding, industrialized core as massive numbers of Europeans migrated toward the peripheries. As transportation routes extended into new areas, the land became more accessible to the market and its value rose, causing an influx of cash farmers and an intensification of land use. One cannot but be reminded of the backwoods pioneers' flight to more remote areas when their land was "brought into market."[43] As the industrial revolution fueled the continued growth of the world city, allowing it, at least by 1850, to reach the American eastern seaboard, the continual displacement and eventual extinction of backwoods culture was assured. Caught in an immense and powerful economic machine, the pioneers and their highly extensive land-use system could not endure.

Implicit in von Thünen's model is the concept of *core versus periphery*, which has been the basis for a burgeoning academic literature in recent decades.[44] In the core, exemplified by Europe and von Thünen's world city, an elite operates the industrial, wealth-accumulating system, while residents of peripheral areas, enjoying little of the core's power, produce staple goods. The two, periphery and core, engage in an unequal exchange of surplus, causing the core elites, by capitalist accumulation, to grow richer and more powerful while the peripheral population is progressively impoverished. So-called *isolated areas* may exist beyond

Fig. 2.1. An adapted von Thünen model, ca. 1800. Key: **1** = the European "world city" or market; **2** = belt of highly intensive farming, such as market gardening; **3** = belt of stock-fattening, feed grains, and plantations; **4** = belt of food grains, especially wheat; **5** = peripheral backwoods pioneer belt, with hunting, open-range herding, and subsistence cropping; **6** = acculturated Amerindian zone. Arrows indicate expansion thrusts.

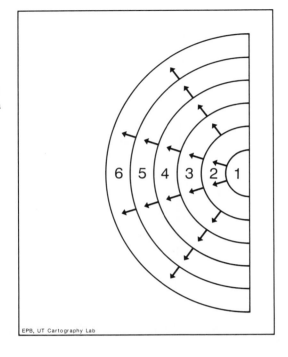

EPB, UT Cartography Lab

the periphery, and only there can an unstratified or classless society exist. In core/periphery terms, backwoods pioneers occupied such isolated areas.

Walter Prescott Webb, a generation after his youthful excursion into environmentalism, ventured as a mature scholar into core/ periphery economic determinism. Though unaware of von Thünen's work, in 1951 he proposed a quite compatible thesis for frontier development.[45] Europe, in Webb's view, was the "metropolis," or center, from which a four-hundred-year economic boom, lasting from about 1500 to 1900, emanated. At the beginning of that era, Europe retained much of its medieval character, with a rigidly stratified class society, a subsistence economy, little money, not much food, minimal personal freedom or individualism, and considerable rural communalism. Then, as a result of the Age of Discovery, Europeans quickly found vast, essentially unclaimed resources in the rest of the world. Seizing and exploiting them, they precipitated the unprecedented economic boom. In the process, Europe and Western civilization underwent fundamental changes, for the boom, in Webb's view, produced capitalism, free enterprise, democracy, and individualism. So vast were the new-found resources, including land, that almost every European could take a share, causing wealth to be widely distributed, the class system to weaken, and communalism to vanish.

To share in the bonanza and acquire a piece of the wealth, many Europeans emigrated in the greatest mass movement of people in history, providing the human raw material for overseas colonies. According to Webb's thesis, then, the backwoods folk were a completely new type of European, living on the outer margins of a massive annexation of resources. Because of their access to these resources, the pioneers could cast off all that was oppressive and confining about Europe in 1500, as indeed could the inhabitants of Europe itself. The backwoodsman, personified in Webb's book as the fictitious "Jim Brown," lived on the leading edge of a spatially expanding, exploitative system.[46] America formed only one arena of the expansion, for this was ultimately a global phenomenon.

Webb's thesis, like von Thünen's model, promised eventual doom, not just for the pioneer, but for the entire Neo-European culture complex built on resource annexation. The backwoods people, who specialized in the initial processing of land resources, became obsolete around 1900, when all the good land had been taken. The boom ended when all the resources had been seized. Pioneers vanished, wealth once again began to be assembled in the hands of the few, and Western civilization began an irreversible descent into neofeudalism.

Archaeologist Kenneth E. Lewis, seeking a model to explain the entire transition from initial settlement to full integration, also resorted to economic determinism.[47] "Frontier expansion is a decision of economic cost" and can be explained by a least-cost model, he wrote. Settlement of the American frontier, like that of other colonial areas, "was linked to the nature and organization of the economic system in which it took place." Expansion of the settled areas was, in Lewis's view, a "response to increasing demand for staple export production," and while these settlements varied "in response to their roles in the changing economic system of the frontier period," all were firmly enmeshed in a von Thünenian mechanism.[48] Backwoods individualism and freedom were but illusions.

Geographer Robert D. Mitchell applied such concepts of European economic mainsprings to a key segment of the old Midland frontier, the Shenandoah Valley of Virginia, part of the Appalachian Great Valley.[49] Though he acknowledged no inspiration from either von Thünen or Webb, the conclusions he reached were closely akin to theirs. Commercialism, he argued, was the mainspring, the shaper of colonial American cultures. Europeans arrived on the eastern seaboard with their newfound belief in private property, competition, a money-based economy, and freedom of trade. With Webbian quickness their medieval communalism vanished. Even the backwoods pioneer was meshed into the commercial system, and thus, Mitchell suggested, the classification proposing distinct occupancy stages of subsistence, semisubsistence, and market orientation was misleading. "Commercial tendencies were present from the beginnings" of settlement, and the traditional view of a pioneer economy as "equated with subsistence, the production of goods primarily for local, on-site consumption rather than for sale" was inaccurate. Subsistence conditions "were, at most, a temporary feature of the first year or two" of occupancy, and right from the start "most settlers were committed to commercialized perceptions of their new environment."[50] According to Mitchell, ethnicity and ethnic contributions to pioneer culture have been exaggerated.[51] Private property and the market ruled.

Provocative and illuminating as such economic models and theses are, they leave the same basic questions unanswered. Why was the backwoods pioneer outer ring dominated by midlanders, while southern planters and New Englanders lagged behind as the more intensive, "better sort" of farmers? Why did some Pennsylvanians likewise remain in the rear while others sought the frontier? What economic mechanism could have produced the skills and techniques needed for woodland pioneering? Why did those skills arise, consummately, in only one segment of the colonial American frontier? While economic models possess great explanatory power, they do not suffice for the task at hand. Economic determinsm is as hostile and incompatible with cultural diffusion as is environmentalism.

Societal Theory

Other writers, seeking to smooth the raw edges of economic determinism, have injected complementary societal forces, joining economy to ideology. While they have yet to produce a comprehensive explanatory model, these scholars have clearly revealed that the development of overseas colonial cultures is far more complex than simplistic, deterministic theory suggests. In common with other aspects of culture, "colonization reflects the organizational complexity of the society from which it has originated."[52]

The work of geographer R. C. Harris is representative.[53] He listed four elements that provided the underpinnings for simplified colonial European societies: (1) the availability of abundant cheap land; (2) societal dominance by the nuclear family unit; (3) the preexisting desire for private control of land and other resources; and (4) the absence of good markets. The essential ideological inheritance from Europe was family-level commercial-mindedness, and Harris suggested that the collapse of feudalism had already produced this ideology prior to American colonization. Communalism had perished with serfdom, as Webb earlier claimed. The colonial areas, through their offer of land and their denial of easy market access, provided the ideal setting for the new, family-based, egalitarian system to blossom. The common ideology helped integrate the frontier and simplify imported European culture.

The colonial phenomenon of dispersed farmsteads in unit-block landholdings provides an illustrative example. Suited to the new ideology, this settlement pattern was difficult to establish in the Old World. In Europe, the breakup of clustered farm villages and the restructuring of fragmented rural properties into independent family farms, a process known as *enclosure* in Great Britain, required enormous effort. To reshape an existing cultural landscape is both troublesome and time-consuming. The process of land consolidation and farmstead dispersal still drags on in much of Europe, four centuries after it began. The desire for unit-block farms and scattered dwellings had developed in western Europe by 1500 or 1600, but only slowly could it be brought to reality. By contrast, the new ideal could be realized at once in an overseas pioneer setting. Colonial European culture, then, came about when a postfeudal, capitalistic, family-based ideology was transported to empty overseas lands.

James Lemon, also a geographer, presented a similar view in his study of early southeastern Pennsylvania.[54] Settlers arriving in the Middle Colonies, he argued, were already imbued with a classic European liberalism, in which individual freedom and material well-being were placed above public interest. The ideology of these settlers rested on a desire for individual material success. As the frontier conditions that permitted this ideology to flourish waned in the Midland hearth, a backguard conservatism designed to preserve family wealth and freedom from institutional restraints arose among those who stayed in Pennsylvania. The pioneer, by contrast, fled to newer frontiers, preserving classical liberalism by becoming mobile. Our crude backwoods pioneer has become a fugitive ideologue.

Such societal and ideological injections do, indeed, make an economic mainspring more acceptable to the humanist, but the apparatus they produce comes no closer to answering the questions we are asking. Such theory is not sufficiently place-specific and personalized to become a suitable marriage partner for diffusion. Our search for a mainspring must continue.

Normative Cultural Ecology

A thriving subfield of both geography and anthropology, cultural ecology is based upon the premise that culture is the uniquely human method of meeting physical environmental challenges, that culture is an adaptive system.[55] People are studied by the methods of animal and plant biogeography, with the assumption that floral and faunal adaptations are relevant to the study of human beings. In this perspective the frontier becomes an ecosystem, a habitat undergoing transformation, and pioneering is the process by which a cultural system's niche is expanded.[56]

Now, many cultural ecologists engage in the same social scientific, normative leveling of human diversity practiced by the economic determinists. They seek universal principles and relationships among key variables or processes, at the expense of understanding regional variations in culture. In the process, they regularly draw upon the biosciences, as is the case with the ecological principle of *competition*. One competing organism may supplant another, occupy interstitial areas, or attain some form of symbiotic adjustment with other species. *Competitive exclusion* refers to the inability of two organisms using the same resource base to coexist over any considerable length of time.[57] Cultural analogies are clearly possible. If we regard the distinctive lifestyle of the backwoods pioneer as one competing species and the woodland Indian culture as another, we can see that both required extensive land resources. Biologists tell us that the weaker competitor in such contests must change either habitat or resource base. To a degree, the backwoods pioneers filled an ecological niche left vacant when large numbers of Indians died in epidemics. The remaining Indians were killed, absorbed, or driven west. The Anglo-American pattern of largely obliterating the native population, rather than forming a mestizo race, is perhaps partly explained by the success of the pioneer in competitive exclusion.

The backwoods folk proved less able to defend the rear, however, where secondary settlers competed for the same resource—land. The extensive land-use practices of the pioneers could not tolerate any substantial increase in population density, and in order to retain their lifestyle, they were obliged, repeatedly, to change habitat through migration. The trek westward, in this view, became an ongoing competition for resources, for ecological niche, a contest ultimately fatal to the pioneers when no more suitable new habitats could be found.

In this biological and ecological sense, the backwoods pioneers behaved as a "fugitive" or "tramp" species, possessing a wide range of ecological skills and for that reason "more likely to become established during early stages of colonization." Such plants and animals take advantage of transitory and unstable situations and exhibit preference for scattered habitats. They possess excellent dispersal mechanisms.[58] Later, however, such species are more likely to become extinct, since they are "less able to cope with competitors." Zoologists even speak of "supertramp" species, in which selection for dispersal and reproductive potential has occurred "at the expense of competitive ability," leaving them vulnerable to species that can "harvest resources more thoroughly and tolerate lower resource levels."[59] The analogy to backwoods pioneers becomes almost compelling when one reads biological descriptions of such species. "They are forever on the move, always becoming extinct in one locality as they succumb to competition and always surviving by reestablishing themselves in some other locality as a new niche opens."[60]

The winner in such competition, according to the *law of cultural dominance*, will be the group that more effectively exploits the energy resources of a given environment. It will successfully spread in that setting at the expense of less effective systems. In other words, a particular culture will be found "precisely in those environments in which it yields a higher energy return per unit of human labor" than any competitor culture.[61] This concept, which emphasizes the adaptive advantage of acquiring the needed output of life's necessities—food, housing, and clothing—from the minimal expenditure of labor, seems particularly appropriate for the frontier setting, where labor was in short supply. We will return repeatedly to the virtue of labor minimization in later chapters.

Some ecologists have also resorted to physics in their search for general principles. Nonequilibrium thermodynamics has been applied to the study of evolution, producing the thesis that all life consists of *dissipative structures*, temporary systems dependent upon a continuous supply of energy from an outside source—the sun—and thus temporarily able to escape the law of entropy. By analogy, frontiers can be thought of as temporary "boundary or edge phenomena," systems that interact with, and draw energy from, their neighbors.[62]

Our unlettered, anti-intellectual backwoods pioneers might profit from this lesson in physics. Frontiers, in the thermodynamic view, "are transitory structures that exist at the edge of . . . more stable physical systems" and depend upon "energy, materials, and information links to those systems."[63] The temporary character of backwoods pioneering, in other words, finds a logical basis in the physical sciences. As a culture, it was doomed not just by economics but by physics as well. Even if this argument were, true, however, thermodynamics brings no enlightenment at the specific level of Pennsylvania prowess, nor is the issue of a place-specific culture addressed through such physics.

Clearly, the central and most relevant concept of cultural ecology is *adaptation*.[64] Culture serves to facilitate long-term, successful, nongenetic human adaptation to nature and to environmental change. Adaptive strategy is based in culturally transmitted, or learned, behavior that permits a population to become viable and to reproduce in its natural environment.[65] Maladaptive strategies lead to extinction, since "man's cultural and reproductive histories tend to coincide."[66]

The concept of cultural adaptation has frequently been utilized in such a manner as to level the differences among cultures. For example, Stanton Green, studying the agricultural colonization of temperate woodlands, hypothesized that pioneer farmers there, in order to minimize effort and risk, gravitated to a long-fallow slash-and-burn cropping system and dispersed-settlement pattern. Temperate forests respond to clearance and burning with a short-term boom in crop yields, based in the sudden conversion of a large biomass into nutrient form. To avoid the long-term decline in land productivity, the laborious clearing and burning of new tracts must be perpetuated, bringing about highly extensive land use and a natural selection for young, rapidly increasing populations. In this manner, the "process of frontier settlement generates a series of social, economic, and demographic pressures that tend to self-perpetuate the colonization process."[67] If we accept this sort of model, then we must assume, in common with the environmental determinists, that all temperate woodlands will produce parallel adaptations by agrarian colonizers. Such an assumption permits us no substantial progress toward understanding the unique success of the Pennsylvania pioneer.

Particularistic Cultural Ecology

If, instead, we recognize that more than one path of adaptation exists in any given environment and that the choice among them is a function of culture, then the methods of cultural ecology can be more effectively applied to our research problem. In this perspective, separate adaptive pathways result from the interplay between the unique history of a culture and its physical environment. Culture channels the adaptive strategy by helping to determine what resources are meaningful in a particular setting, but the individual person gains considerable decision-making and innovative power. Further particularism is injected by the fact that traits exist within cultural complexes, and selection acts on these complexes. The value of one trait depends in part on the other traits present. In attempting to understand the ecology of forest pioneering, in other words, we must analyze cultural units. Peoples "varied greatly in dispersal ability," and the key to that variability lies in cultural complexes.[68]

Viewed in this way, the particular farming-hunting-gathering complex of Midland America becomes *an* adaptive strategy in the temperate woodlands, and our task is to explain, in cultural ecological terms, why it was so successful. Essential to that explanation, we believe, is the ecological concept of cultural *preadaptation*.[69] Migration to a new environmental setting forces a change in adaptive strategy. In such situations, preadaptation involves a complex of traits "possessed by a particular human society or part of that society" in advance of migration, giving the group "competitive advantage in occupying a new environment."[70]

For example, British immigrants arriving in the American Middle Colonies encountered a much more thickly forested land with colder winters than they had experienced in their former island home. Newly disembarked in Pennsylvania in 1683, Englishman Thomas Paschall at once complained that "the winter is sharp," and his contemporary, the English governor of New York, lamented that "our winters are extream cold and long."[71] The English were, in respect to climate and natural vegetation, poorly preadapted to the area. Indeed, "Englishmen were at first unsuited to survive in the New World."[72]

Successful cultural preadaptation tends to be a matter of chance, particularly when prior knowledge of the new land is sketchy or when migrants have little control over their destination. Typically, the relocation favors certain adaptive strategies that were deviant, obsolete, condemned, or even latent in the former homeland.[73] Of minimal value or possibly even maladaptive in the Old World, these minority practices became favored in the colonial area, serving to return individuals and entire groups to a state of adaptedness.

Among what kind of people are such deviant adaptive strategies most likely to be found? What factors favor adaptive versatility, or *diversifying selection*, to use the jargon of cultural ecologists, and which ones foster conformity, or *stabilizing selection?* These questions are of fundamental importance, because the success of pioneers in a new and stressful environment depends upon their toleration of rather considerable behavioral variability. The adaptive repertoire needs to be large, and the individual person should be receptive to new ideas. A nonspecialized culture is more efficient in dealing with the extensive, open frontier.[74] Dogmatism in such situations is maladaptive.

Abundant evidence suggests that stable, fruitful environments diminish behavioral or adaptive variability, engendering conservatism and intolerance. Stablilizing selection is the result. Jared Diamond refers to "stable, saturated environments" and to "a sluggish system in a very constant environment."[75] By contrast, stressful marginal environments, where considerable areal and temporal contrasts in climate, soil, vegetation, or terrain exist, encourage and reward diversifying selection.[76] In fringe stress zones, where nature is volatile, two or more adaptive norms may develop and coexist even within a single cultural population. New strategies are normally welcomed, and old, seemingly obsolete ones are held in reserve for an uncertain future.[77] When environmental change comes, the key to resiliency is diversification and open-mindedness.[78] A cultural system "with a rapid response time can adapt quickly to a new maintained set of environmental conditions," and diversity facilitates rapid response.[79] Fringe peoples are pragmatic. In such marginal settings, the deviant behavior necessary for diversifying selection is also more easily tolerated because population density is low. The culturally based decision-making process in adaptation here rests heavily upon the individual person, providing a promising prototype for individualism.

If we view seventeenth-century Europe from the perspective of diversifying versus stabilizing selection, a core/periphery contrast becomes apparent (Fig. 2.2). In the heart of Europe lay a stable, fertile Germanic core, home of the medieval three-field system of husbandry and of a large, relatively prosperous agrarian population. From this core came most of the English, French, German, and Dutch who settled colonial North America. Following the doctrines of cultural ecology, we would find these people poorly preadapted for forest pioneering. They were better suited to be secondary settlers, in which capacity they reestablished something like the stable, conservative agrarian system of the Germanic European core. They could model their colonial culture to fit the Neo-European ideology, but it would remain Germanic and stable at heart.

Fringing the core on all sides in Europe was a hardscrabble zone consisting of British hill areas, the subarctic north, a mountain-hill belt centered on the Alps, and the cold, marginally fertile East European Plain. There, in the periphery, diversifying selection prevailed, and a great variety of adaptive strategies coexisted. Agricultural systems ranged from slash-and-burn to infield-outfield types. Population was sparse and ecological stress high. British geographer Estyn Evans nicely captured the essence of the Euro-

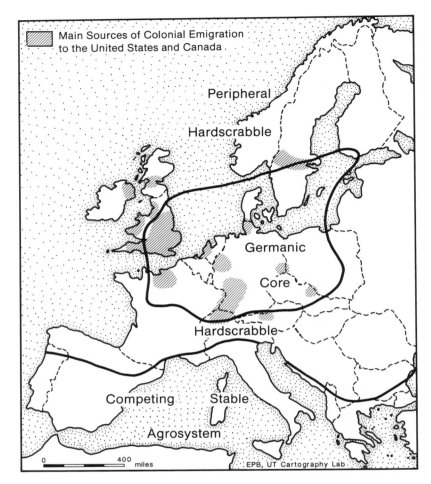

Fig. 2.2. The ecological core and periphery in Europe, 1650. In lands north of the Mediterranean peninsulas, a fertile, temperate, Germanic core was surrounded by a hardscrabble periphery of mountains, hills, glaciated lake plains, and cold continental climate.

pean core/periphery cultural configuration when he contrasted the disciplined, law-abiding village folk of the central plains, who expended enormous labor on their tiny strip fields, with the individualistic, lawless dwellers of the Atlantic fringe, who lived scattered about the countryside behind a maze of walls and hedges.[80]

From the European hardscrabble periphery came the Scotch-Irish, Welsh, Alpine Swiss, Salzburger, and Finnish settlers of colonial America. Among them we are more likely to find the nonconformist human raw material of the backwoods pioneers. The greater variability of their adaptive repertoire prepared them well for pioneer life. Migration to a new environment only heightened their versatility and receptiveness to new ideas. Preconditioned to meet, mix, and pool strategies, these peripheral folk seem attitudinally well prepared for the task.

Cultural ecology also helps explain the simplification process that took place in Europe's overseas colonies. Some anthropologists view cultural simplification as an adaptation to a new physical environment, involving the sacrifice of traits that possessed adaptive value in the old homeland but became liabilities in the new. In this manner, American pioneer culture became simplified to an Iron Age level, except in its use of firearms.[81] In particular, by stripping away unsuitable *specialized* traits, the pioneering process uncovered a more ancient, almost forgotten versatility, leading to diversifying selection.

Cultural ecology, then, suggests that the backwoods pioneer lifestyle was an adaptive strategy pursued by an unspecialized, fugitive culture with possible roots in the hardscrabble zones of the European periphery. By seeking its progenitors among people who possessed preadapted skills and techniques suited to the North American woodland, we find at last a place-specific methodology firmly linked to the nuances of niche and locale.

Methodology and Theses

From the concepts, models, and theses discussed above, we achieve a breadth of potential understanding and explanatory ability concerning the American backwoods pioneer. Viewed in conjunction, the several approaches promise insight. Two, in particular, are joined and emphasized in the present study. We feel that the mechanism of cultural diffusion, linked to the explanatory ability of particularistic cultural ecology, best yields the elusive, place-specific mainspring. Our work is thus subtitled "An Ethnic and Ecological Interpretation."

We do not ignore the other approaches. However, the crucial role of environmental influence is better and more objectively treated through the approach of particularistic cultural ecology than through determinism. We do not deny the roles of economy, society, physics, or ideology, but we view those forces as providing merely the *prerequisites, conditions*, and *limitations* for the backwoods drama. Yes, access to empty temperate forest land was necessary, as was the prolonged boom of the world city/metropolis. Yes, the decline of medieval communalism and the resultant rise of the nuclear family, private enterprise, commercialism, individualism, and perhaps even Protestantism also were essential prerequisites. Yes, economic land rent, resource limitations, and possibly even the laws of thermodynamics dictated that backwoods culture could not endure. No, the Midland pioneers did not pursue a strictly subsistent economy, for they were at least partly caught up in the European-based market system. They were periphery, Europe core. But in attempting to learn why a particular, highly successful forest colonization culture arose in a specific place and time, we find that only the joining of diffusion to particularistic ecology becomes explanatory.

Our main thesis, to be defended in ecological, diffusionary terms in succeeding chapters, is that *American backwoods culture had significant northern European roots*. To be sure, the pioneers possessed a fused, syncretic culture, but the preadapted prototypes for some of its essential features are to be found in the backcountry of seventeenth-century Finland and Sweden. As principal agents of diffusion, *we propose the ethnic Finns* who formed a substantial part of the population in the colony of New Sweden, founded on the lower Delaware River in 1638. More specifically, the *eastern*, interior Finns of Karelian and Savoan background, bearers of a well-developed, beautifully preadapted forest colonization cultural complex, were the most significant shapers of the American backwoods way of life. Their contributions to pioneer land settlement techniques exceeded in importance those of the highland Britishers, in particular the Scotch-Irish, and other settlers from the European peripheral hardscrabble zone (Fig. 2.3). The eastern Finns, more than anyone else, in the spirit of their great epic poem, the *Kalevala*, blazed the trail, broke branches, and showed the way, thereby launching the backwoods folk on their epic transcontinental surge.

Over three centuries ago, not long after their arrival in the Delaware Valley, the Finns were judged by an astute and perceptive Dutch colonial official to be "particularly fitted" to colonize the area.[82] Modern Finns, described by their prime minister, Kalevi Sorsa, as a people able to adapt to difficult situations, as headstrong and endowed with *sisu*—a mixture of pluck, gumption, and obstinacy—seem still to embody many of the traits of the ideal frontiersman. Indeed, forest colonization has never really ceased in Finland, and today pioneer farms push far into Lappland.[83]

Our main thesis is not unprecedented. Northern European origin for American pioneer log construction has traditionally been favored and was recently defended against undocumented counterclaims by Germanists.[84] As early as 1930, geographer Carl Sauer proposed that the Midland American forest pioneer culture had "its roots in the log cabin building and clearing activities of the Delaware Swede-Finn colony," and certain other scholars have made similar proposals in more recent years.[85] However, the prevailing academic consensus in a variety of disciplines holds that the Finns and Swedes of the New Sweden Colony made no lasting or meaningful imprint on colonial American culture. Among those who deny significant northern European influence are historian Thomas J. Wertenbaker, folklorist Henry Glassie, and geographer Fred Kniffen.[86] Even Wilbur Zelinsky, proposer of the doctrine of first effective settlement, declared in an ancillary statement that the principle did not apply to New Sweden.[87] In the main, then, our thesis is revisionist.

We also propose, as a secondary thesis, that after the Finns, *the next most significant contributors to the backwoods pioneer adaptive system were the eastern woodland Indians of colonial America*, in particular the Delaware tribe. In short, we suggest that early European settlers along the Delaware River borrowed significantly from the preexisting, highly successful aboriginal adaptive system, and that this accounts for much of the subse-

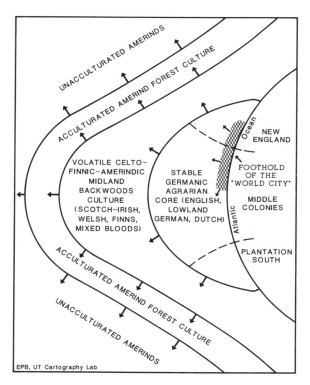

Fig. 2.3. A spatial/ethnic model of North American woodland colonization.

quent prowess of the Midland colonization culture. Accompanying and following this borrowing, we propose, frontier racial mixing occurred on a scale previously unrecognized, with the result that a substantial proportion of the "white" pioneer population acquired some measure of Indian blood.

While the resultant backwoods adaptive strategy can best be described as "Fenno-Indic," the greatest genetic input to the pioneer population was highland British, especially Scotch-Irish. These hill folk, we suggest, contributed many aspects of the pioneer culture that had little or no adaptive significance—folk music, speech, tales, and the like—but their part in shaping the colonization system was minimal. In our view, the role of the Celts in frontier America has traditionally been greatly overstated, the Indian influence consistently underestimated, and the Finnish contribution almost wholly ignored or, without adequate scholarly evidence, dismissed.[88] We seek here to correct the record, while at the same time explaining how a small band of colonists could have shaped an entire frontier adaptive system. An appropriate topic with which to begin our investigation is the traditional eastern Finnish forest culture and the migrations of its bearers, first to Sweden and later to colonial America.

THREE

EASTERN FINNISH CULTURE AND ITS
SPREAD TO COLONIAL AMERICA

Whence comes the stranger
from beyond the water?
Kalevala

Finland, in common with most countries, displays a vivid internal regionalism in culture and habitat. The most fundamental division is between coast and interior, between west and east.[1] A littoral arc in the west and southwest, largely coextensive with the traditional provinces of Uusimaa (Nyland), Varsinais Suomi (Egentliga Finland), Satakunta, and Pohjanmaa (Österbotten), offers the best agricultural land—moderately fertile, mild by the standards of Finnish climate, and capable of supporting permanent-field farming under traditional methods (Fig. 3.1). Indeed, the coastal arc proved sufficiently inviting to attract Germanic farming folk of the European core, represented by Swedes, as colonists. Early taxes and tribute from these districts came in the form of butter and grain—the yield of a fat land.

To the east, in the Finnish interior, lies a very different environment and culture. In provinces such as Savo (Savolax) and Karelia (in Finnish, *Karjala*), snow covers the ground one hundred fifty or more days each year. The stony, forested country north of the great moraine walls called the Salpausselkä is a huge lake plateau laced with waterways and marshes (Fig. 3.1). Except for some lakeshore clays, its soils are morainic drift, sterile sands, and ash-colored podsols covered with conifers, mainly pine and spruce.[2] Environmental hardship increases with distance from the coast. Traditionally, the scattered inhabitants of the Finnish interior, clinging to the microthermal edge of the agricultural world, cleared and cultivated small, impermanent fields but relied heavily upon hunting, fishing, and gathering for their livelihood. The taxes and tribute wrung from them came most often in the form of furs. Finland, then, straddles the European core/periphery boundary (Fig. 2.2). Our concern is with the boreal folk of the inhospitable Finnish east, with a fringe people noted for diversifying selection and its inherent individualism.

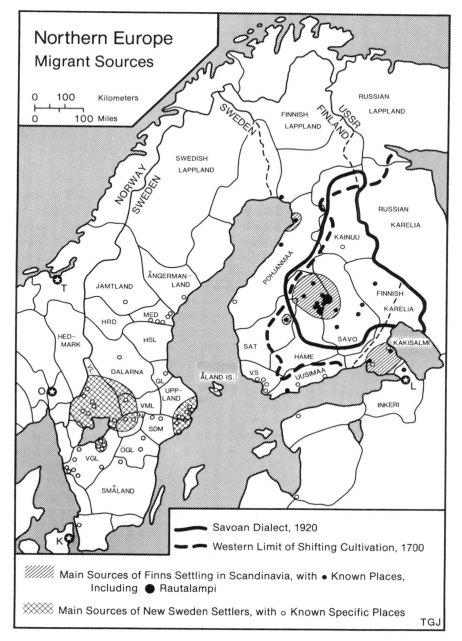

Northern Europe
Migrant Sources

0   100   Kilometers
0   100   Miles

RUSSIAN
LAPPLAND

FINNISH
LAPPLAND

SWEDEN

FINLAND

USSR

SWEDISH
LAPPLAND

NORWAY

SWEDEN

RUSSIAN
KARELIA

KAINUU

POHJANMAA

ÅNGERMAN-
LAND

JÄMTLAND

FINNISH
KARELIA

HRD

MED

T

HED-
MARK

HSL

SAT

SAVO

KÄKISALMI

HÄME

DALARNA

ÅLAND IS.

VS

UUSIMAA

L

VL

GL

UPP-
LAND

VML

INKERI

N

SDM

ÖGL

VGL

SMÅLAND

—— Savoan Dialect, 1920

- - - Western Limit of Shifting Cultivation, 1700

///// Main Sources of Finns Settling in Scandinavia, with ● Known Places,
Including ● Rautalampi

XXXXX Main Sources of New Sweden Settlers, with ○ Known Specific Places

K

TGJ

Fig. 3.1. Key to abbreviations: **GL** = Gästrikland; **HRD** = Härjedalen; **HSL** =
Hälsingland; **K** = København; **L** = Leningrad; **MED** = Medelpad; **N** = Närke; **O** =
Oslo; **OGL** = Östergötland; **SAT** = Satakunta; **SDM** = Södermanland; **T** =
Trondheim; **VGL** = Västergötland; **VL** = Värmland; **VML** = Västmanland; **VS** =
Varsinais Suomi. (Sources of data: Armstrong 1860, pp. 78–79; Fernow 1877, pp. 145,
156, 186; Gothe 1942, p. 31; Gothe 1945, pp. 67, 102, 125; Gothe 1950, pp. 493–95;
Gottlund 1931, pp. 79, 145; Hämäläinen 1945, pp. 9–10; Johnson 1911, vol. 1, pp. 243,
267; vol. 2, pp. 678, 693, 697, 699, 706–26; Kalm 1929, p. 219; Keen 1878b, p. 225; Keen
1879c, pp. 462–64; Kerkkonen 1969–70, p. 30; Kuopion museo exhibit, Kuopio,
Finland; Leiby 1964, p. 95; Linderholm 1974, p. 58; Linderholm 1976, p. 47;
Lindeström 1925, pp. 125–26; Lönborg 1902, pp. 68, 70; Louhi 1925, pp. 37–47;
Nordmann 1888, p. 146; Rising 1912a, p. 133; Springer and Springer 1954–55, pp. 143–
44; Suomen maantieteellinen seura 1960, map 14-10.)

Traditional Karelian Culture

The distinctiveness of the traditional eastern Finnish, originally Karelian, culture can be described in diverse ways. Linguistically it is represented principally by the Savoan (Savolais) dialect and, to the east, the Kaakois or Karelian dialect (Fig. 3.1). Eastern Finns were also distinguished by their systems of *burnbeating*, or shifting cultivation, in particular the types known as *huuhta* and *kaski* (Fig. 3.1). Settlers, dispersed through the subarctic, microthermal forest on isolated farmsteads, cut down or deadened trees in small clearings that were later burned, enclosed with a split-rail fence, and sown with grain (Fig. 3.2). *Huuhta*, an innovation that seems to have reached Ladogan Karelia in the eleventh or twelfth century, was especially well adapted to agricultural colonization in the virgin spruce forests of the Finnish interior, rendering the soil highly productive for one or, rarely, two crop years. Farmers practicing *huuhta* felled or girdled trees in the clearing in the early spring of the first year, allowed the wood to dry until midsummer of the third year, then burned the land. A specially adapted rye was sown in the ashes, without benefit of plowing or hoeing. It came to harvest in the fourth summer, whereupon the field was abandoned and usually no attempt was made to gain a second crop. Not only were previously uncultivatable needle-leaf evergreen forests opened to Karelian pioneer agriculture by *huuhta*, but in addition the one-year rye yields were extraordinarily high, commonly reaching 20- to 50-fold or even 100-fold in some instances. The delayed burning of the clearing permitted a more complete rendering of the vegetative material into crop nutrients; the burning process sharply reduced soil acidity while at the same time modestly increasing microorganic activity; and this, in turn, improved the ability of the growing rye to exploit soil nitrogen reserves.[3] The principal disadvantage of *huuhta* was that a new clearing had to be prepared each year, absorbing a considerable amount of hard labor and requiring a large expanse of land—at least 2,500 acres—for each family.[4]

A second Finnish method of burnbeating, *kaski*, was employed in areas covered with deciduous trees, perhaps most often second-growth forests that appeared after twenty to fifty years in the *huuhta* oldfields. Farmers practicing *kaski* felled their trees in late summer at maximum leaf and burned them early the following summer. This method created the spectacular sight of soot-blackened, infernal-looking men and women rolling flaming tree trunks over the surface of the cleared area to ignite all the leaf mold. The crop was usually either rye or barley, the latter a crop not possible in the *huuhta* system, and turnips, oats, and flax also were planted. *Kaski* lands were commonly cultivated for two or three consecutive years.[5]

In the Karelian agricultural system, crops were supplemented by livestock raising. The forests, oldfields, and marshes provided forage for open-range stock, particularly cattle, and wild hay was cut either from the abandoned fields or in marshes, often at con-

Fig. 3.2. Savo-Karelian Finns burning a clearing for cultivation, Eno Parish, northern Finnish Karelia, 1893. (Photo courtesy of National Museum of Finland, Helsinki, Archives, no. 4878:15.)

siderable distance from the farmstead. A lengthy section of the Finnish national epic, *The Kalevala*, consisting of folklore collected mainly in the Savoan and Karelian districts, deals with cattle charms. "Take care of them when they are without a caretaker" and "Keep them out of harm's way," implore some representative charms.[6]

Eastern Finns also relied greatly upon hunting, fishing, and gathering. In years when the harsh subarctic climate caused a crop failure, the diversified Karelians fell back upon game, fish, livestock, and the yield of wild plants to carry them through the lean period. Lengthy hunting and fishing expeditions during the winter half of the year took the men far to the north, up to 125 miles (200 kilometers) from their waterside homes, even into Lappish territory. The intricate network of lakes and streams in this region provided routes for the hunters, who used dugout canoes, boats, skis, and sleighs for transportation.[7] Private enterprise prevailed, and farmers owned specific tracts in the distant hunting and fishing grounds. Marked by blazed trees, these were regarded as outlying parts of their farms, and a hunter's shanty—a small log shelter with a single-pitch roof and completely open on the front side, facing the campfire—was built at the site of each tract (Fig. 3.3).[8] To a degree, these hunting activities eventually became commercialized. At least from the rise of medieval Novgorod, Karelian hunters provided furs for that city's market. Some men belonged

Fig. 3.3. An open-faced log hunter's shanty (*asento*) in the Savo-Karelian settlement area of Kainuu Province, Finland. (Photo by Samuli Paulaharju, 1910, courtesy of National Museum of Finland, Helsinki, Archives, no. 3490:977, used with permission.)

to organizations of backwoods trappers and traders engaged largely in the commercial exploitation of furs.[9]

Women, children, and the elderly did not accompany the hunters. They spent the long winters at the farmstead by the frozen lake, caring for the livestock and performing such tasks as spinning and weaving (Fig. 3.4). Sitting beside an open hearth in the winter darkness, they crafted various wooden objects, including many made of birchbark.

Above all, the hallmark of traditional eastern Finnish culture was forest pioneering. The Karelians were responsible for the rapid agricultural colonization of the greater part of interior Finland and Russian Karelia after about 1350 (Fig. 3.5). Three elements of their way of life in particular preadapted them for success as woodland pioneers: their hunting skills, the mobility and pathfinding ability linked to the hunt, and *huuhta*-style cultivation.[10] Gradually they converted their privately owned hunting and fishing grounds into new farms. A hunter's shanty was initially erected at each site, to be inhabited as needed during the hunting and fishing seasons. As the colonization process contin-

Fig. 3.4. Savo-Karelian carding and spinning wheels, at the Pielaveden kotiseutumuseo in northern Savo. (Photo by T.G.J., 1985.)

ued, the open-faced shanty was replaced by a one-room, ceiling-less log cabin, an ancient east Baltic type called a *pirtti*, which functioned as a combination dwelling, sauna, and grain-drying shed (Fig. 3.6). It had a chimneyless corner fireplace of unmortared stones, a door in one gable end, and often several small windows consisting of sliding boards. Smoke escaped through these apertures and a special hole high in the gable or roof.[11] At the same time, a *huuhta* clearing was made near the cabin, still well in advance of actual settlement, since its productive season lay three years in the future. The pioneering process was completed when the family, or a newly married son, moved permanently to the outlying cabin and clearing, perhaps in the year of cultivation.[12] In this manner, hunting grounds were converted into farms. New sites for hunting and fishing were then claimed even deeper in the watery wilderness.

The mobility and private enterprise of the Karelians imply yet another characteristic of their traditional culture—freedom from feudal duties. Eastern Finns remained freemen, even in medieval times, and they often exhibited contempt for central authority. Many escaped the detection of tax collectors in the Finnish backwoods. Their status as a free peasantry was an anomaly in the late Middle Ages, demonstrating once again the core/periphery contrast within Europe and Finland.

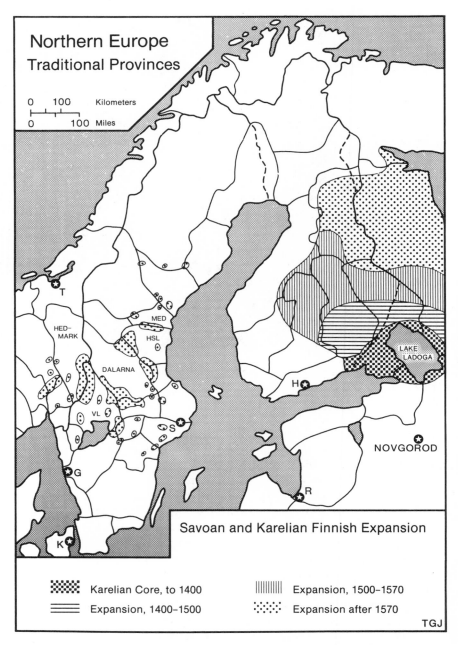

Northern Europe
Traditional Provinces

0   100   Kilometers
0   100   Miles

T

HED–
MARK

MED

HSL

DALARNA

VL

S

H

NOVGOROD

LAKE
LADOGA

G

R

K

Savoan and Karelian Finnish Expansion

Karelian Core, to 1400   Expansion, 1500–1570

Expansion, 1400–1500   Expansion after 1570

TGJ

Fig. 3.5.   Key to abbreviations: **G** = Göteborg; **H** = Helsinki; **HSL** = Hälsingland;
K = København; **MED** = Medelpad; **R** = Riga; **S** = Stockholm; **T** = Trondheim;
VL = Värmland. (Sources of data: Broberg 1967, pp. 76, 94; Campbell et al. 1957, p. 49;
Hämäläinen 1930, p. 14; Jutikkala and Pirinen 1974, pp. 13, 62–63; Lönborg 1902, p.
83; Østberg 1931, p. 443; Segerstedt MS, vol. 1, pt. 1, map following p. 740; Soininen
1959, pp. 150–51; Soininen 1961, pp. 125–36, 428; Värmlands museum, archiv, item
no. 27577.)

Fig. 3.6. A Finnish one-room log cabin, or *pirtti*, with typical gable entrance and small windows, in interior Finland. (Source: Retzius 1885; p. 63.)

Initial Expansion

The Karelian pioneering system based in *huuhta* rye farming, herding, hunting, fishing, free peasantry, mobility, pathfinding skills, and remote hunting grounds coalesced in about 1200 on the shores of Lake Ladoga. *Huuhta* seems to have been the last and most essential element to fall into place. The trigger, the initial stimulus that set the Karelian colonization system into motion and resulted in the settlement of the Finnish interior, cannot be known with certainty. The start of any type of colonization cycle is sometimes "sudden and mysterious," though usually keyed to unique historical events, to changes in climate, habitat, technology, competition, or food supply.[13] Apparently *huuhta* offered the technological change, while a problem with fur supply presented a modification of habitat. The Karelian link to the fur market at Novgorod became endangered by overtrapping of the lands near Ladoga. Novgorod, faced with declining fur yields in its immediate hinterland and engaged in a military contest with Sweden for control of the Karelian Isthmus, west of the lake, sought in the 1300s to consolidate its hold on the hinter shores of Ladoga, and the Karelian colonization system was perhaps initially employed in the service of Novgorod in the Vuoksi River area around Käkisalmi (Kexholm), presently Soviet Priozersk, on the isthmus. Agricultural pioneering of the coniferous forests there extended the range of Karelian trappers by allowing them to establish more remote bases while at the same time strengthening Novgorod's control. In 1323 Sweden and Novgorod partitioned the isthmus.[14]

However, the greater importance of the isthmus was as a zone of cultural contact and mixing, where the Russian Orthodox, eastern Karelians passed their skills as pioneers to their Swedish-influenced, Catholic (and later Lutheran), western Karelian kinfolk. North of the isthmus the two Karelian groups would go their separate ways on either side of a political border that has shifted slightly but persists to the present day. The easterners spread northward to the shores of the White Sea, bearing the Orthodox faith, Cyrillic alphabet, and Karelian tongue with them (Fig. 3.5).[15] They played no role in the American backwoods drama, but their western Karelian cousins achieved a truly spectacular expansion that was destined to cross the Atlantic.

The first goal of Karelian agricultural pioneers was to reach the lake plateau of interior southeastern Finland, beyond the Salpausselkä moraine walls.[16] It is possible that increased hunting pressure caused the northward retreat of fur-bearing game, drawing Finns to the interior; but other causal forces also were at work. In fact, a *decline* of commercial hunting may have spurred agricultural colonization. The fur trade dwindled in the 1400s, culminating on the Russian side of the border in closure of the Novgorod market in 1494. *Huuhta* cultivation, with its huge yields, had meanwhile made grain farming much more attractive. Moreover, continued warfare on the isthmus between Swedes and Russians drove some to the interior for refuge, while others fled rising taxes.[17] But the most important force pushing pioneers into the interior was the colonization system itself. From the first it had encouraged selection for an increased reproductive rate in the Karelian population, both because it produced abundant food and due to the demand for labor during the annual forest clearance. Fragmentary surviving records suggest an annual rate of population increase of ten or eleven per thousand. Such rapid growth demanded, in turn, continual habitat expansion.[18] Colonization, once set in motion, became a perpetual process powered by the extravagant consumption of forest resources, moving northwestward from the Karelian Isthmus. On Ladoga's far shore, a pioneer culture that would touch America sprang into motion.

Savo-Karelian Culture

Beyond the Salpausselkä moraine wall, Karelian pioneers from the isthmus colonized the lake-studded former hunting ground in southern Savo Province. There they encountered and mixed with a small population of indigenous Finns, producing the hybrid Savo-Karelian culture. Identified by its Savoan dialect, this culture retained the Ladogan, eastern methods of pioneering.

In the tales and lore of *The Kalevala*, the Savo-Karelian lifestyle is vividly portrayed.[19] Kalevalans are a free-spirited, boisterous, alcohol-guzzling, party-loving backwoods folk, capable of prodigious feats, bravery, foolhardiness, violence, and sundry foul deeds. Witches, wizards, and charms abound in a setting only dimly Christianized. Central authority and law rarely enter the epic.

These lusty Savo-Karelians inhabited isolated farmsteads consisting of numerous small, notched-log buildings strewn about in no apparent order. Included were house, stalls, storage shed, grain-drying shed, freestanding summer kitchen, bathhouse, and perhaps a haybarn.[20] Building functions were to a remarkable degree interchangeable, and the original *pirtti* might later be demoted to the status of sauna, kitchen, or grain-drying shed. In the early pioneer years, a dwelling often served most of these functions.[21] If the rye harvests were abundant and the hunts yielded many furs, the settlers displayed their prosperity in a larger house. The abundant children typical of Savo-Karelian pioneer families also encouraged enlargement of the *pirtti*. In contrast to the eastern, Orthodox Karelians, who erected huge, Russian-influenced, multistory house-barns with impressive gable façades, the Savo-Karelians, under western Finnish and Swedish influence, normally enlarged their dwellings by adding a second room across an often open breezeway from the first, forming an elongated, side-gable log double house (Fig. 3.7).[22]

The carpentry on these structures was crude in the early years, and one should not be misled by the finer log craftsmanship that prevails today in interior Finland. The Savo-Karelian pioneer buildings consisted of round logs crudely fitted together, the cracks or chinks stopped up with clay or moss.[23] Some such rough carpentry can occasionally be observed in northern Finland today (Fig. 3.8). Given the mobility of the Savo-Karelian pioneer culture, craftsmanship and durability were probably not highly esteemed. This was particularly true among a minority within the Savo-Karelian pioneer population known as the *kirvesmiehet*, or "ax-wielders," who did not bother to establish landownership, choosing instead to move every few years to another clearing, exercising squatters' rights.[24] The *kirvesmiehet* represented Savo-Karelian pioneer culture in its purest form, and their extreme mobility was perhaps the result of a desire to perpetuate the highly productive *huuhta*, rather than resort to the lesser yields of *kaski*, and to seek undiminished hunting grounds. We have not heard the last of them.

The huge amounts of labor expended in *huuhta* land clearance normally could not be supplied even by the large families typical on the Savo-Karelian settlement frontier. A considerable amount of cooperation developed within kin groups and the scattered neighborhoods, particularly in the seasons when clearing and burning were done. Sometimes these became formalized as working associations, but in any form they represented egalitarian mutual aid.[25] The Savo-Karelian love of feasts and parties complemented nicely this spirit of cooperation. Individualism, which permeates *The Kalevala*, was apparently little dampened by the reliance upon mutual assistance.

Fig. 3.7. A Savo-Karelian log double house from Taipalsaari in the lake district of southern Savo, now at the Karjalainen kotitalo-ulkomuseo, Imatra, Finland. The once-open central passage was later filled in, as can be seen where the wall changes texture. (Photo by T.G.J., 1985.)

Savo-Karelian Expansion

The hybrid Savo-Karelian culture, formed in southern Savo Province in the fourteenth and fifteenth centuries, continued the expansion earlier begun around Lake Ladoga. New hunting grounds were established to the north and west as southern Savo was settled, and in turn those grounds were colonized.[26] In the late 1400s, agricultural settlement began along the waterways of northern Savo, followed in less than a century by occupation of northern Häme (Tavastland) and bordering parts of the lake plateau in Satakunta and Pohjanmaa. By 1550, Savo-Karelian pioneers had even penetrated beyond the rocky, forbidding Suomenselkä ridge to the shores of Lake Oulu in southwestern Kainuu (Fig. 3.5).

The sixteenth century was the era of most explosive Savo-Karelian expansion in interior Finland.[27] Never before, anywhere in the world, had an agricultural frontier advanced so rapidly, some two hundred linear miles in about three quarters of a century. A characteristic pattern had developed in which the more adventurous pioneers, in particular the *kirvesmiehet*, moved well beyond existing farms, leaving unsettled lands in their rear, to be occupied by later arrivals.

By the time the Savo-Karelians had settled northern Savo Province, the Swedish government had become involved in the process. Wanting the remaining interior wilderness to be occupied,

Fig. 3.8. Crude round-log carpentry of the pioneer Savo-Karelian type, with chinking, in northern Finland. The structure is a storage building and stands in Peräpohjola Province, on Highway 78 north of Ranua. (Photo by T.G.J., 1985.)

the Swedish crown encouraged colonization.[28] Coastal western Finns and Swedes responded poorly, for they were not skilled pioneers and practiced no *huuhta*-type shifting cultivation. Swedish authorities thus turned to Savo-Karelian *kirvesmiehet*, who scarcely needed government encouragement to seize the remaining hinterlands of the western Finns.[29] Another link had been forged in the chain of events leading Savo-Karelians to colonial America, for the Swedish authorities now knew to whom to turn when they needed able, willing, mobile, ax-wielding pioneers capable of rapidly expanding agricultural settlement in the forests of the north.

Finland and all of northern Europe would soon prove too small to contain the Savo-Karelians. In the 1600s they occupied northern Finnish Karelia and, beyond, the remainder of Kainuu (Fig. 3.5).[30] Simultaneously, Savo-Karelians leaped the Gulf of Bothnia to colonize interior Scandinavia.

Savo-Karelian Settlements in Scandinavia

Eastern Finnish settlement of crown forest lands in Sweden began about 1570, around the time the Savo-Karelians completed their explosive occupancy of interior Finland.[31] Several causes have been proposed for this migration across the gulf, but we need not

look beyond the incessant demand for new lands inherent in the
Savo-Karelian colonization system and the desire of Swedish authorities to convert their interior Scandinavian forests into productive, taxpaying districts.[32] The immigration of eastern Finns
continued for three quarters of a century, ending about 1650. Vast
areas of coniferous woodland were settled, particularly between
1600 and 1630.[33]

The eastern Finnish colonists came to Sweden principally from
the northern part of the traditional province of Häme and bordering parts of northern Savo and eastern Satakunta (Fig. 3.1). The
extended church district of Rautalampi lay at the core of the emigration area. Some colonists came directly from the Karelian
Isthmus, including the Käkisalmi and Viipuri (Viborg) districts, as
well as Inkeri (Ingermanland).[34] Studies of Finnish folklore, dialect, colonization methods, and folk architecture in Scandinavia
all reveal Savo-Karelian cultural dominance.[35] A physical anthropologist claimed Karelian racial features to be the most common
among the Finns in one part of Sweden, followed by Savoan and
Hämean physical traits.[36] Even to the present day, some Swedish
residents in the interior of the country insist they are able to distinguish persons of Finnish ancestry on the basis of facial features
alone.[37]

The eastern Finns scattered widely through central Sweden,
founding settlements in the forests of sixteen traditional provinces (Fig. 3.5).[38] One hundred fifty place names containing the
component "Finn" occur in modern Sweden, scattered in twenty-
one different provinces.[39] Värmland received the largest number
of immigrants and was home to perhaps 6,000–9,000 Finns by the
end of the seventeenth century.[40] Other major concentrations developed in the Finnmarks of Dalarna, Västmanland, Gästrikland,
Medelpad, Hälsingland, and Ångermanland.[41]

As early as the 1620s, Savo-Karelian pioneers spilled over the
poorly defined international boundary into southeastern Norway,
where they quickly spread as far as the Oslo area (Fig. 3.5).[42] The
forest known as the Finnskog, or "Finns' Forest," straddling the
Swedish-Norwegian border in western Värmland and eastern Hedmark provinces, became the greatest Savo-Karelian stronghold in
Scandinavia. Only there did the Savolais dialect survive as late as
1900, and the region retains an ethnic flavor to the present day.[43]

The Finns occupied a particular ecological niche in central
Scandinavia. As late as 1600, Swedes and Norwegians had settled
the core of the peninsula only along stream corridors and lakes,
colonizing narrow alluvial valley strips, where they established
typically Germanic fixed-field farming.[44] At most they used the
rugged interfluves for seasonal pasture, haymaking, and hunting.
Most of the hilly, stony morainal and drumlin lands between the
settled valleys remained empty, covered by dense coniferous forests. The eastern Finns settled these interfluves, using the Savo-
Karelian colonization system, and they did so with almost outrageous success.[45] Leaping from one glacial hill district to the

next, the Finns required only one century to fill the niche open to
them, ignoring an international boundary in the process. The
Germanic valley folk awoke to find Finns perched in the heights
above them, and the new ethnic map of south-central Scandinavia
had topographic contour lines as borders.

Remarkably, the Savo-Karelian dispersal through Scandinavia
progressed rapidly in spite of the absence of a waterway network
like that of the Finnish Lake Plateau. While the settlers did not
abandon the use of boats in transportation and migration, they
had to rely much more in Scandinavia upon horses, overland
trekking, pathfinding, and sleighs—skills inherent in their traditional hunting activities. As in Finland, they moved forward in
leaps, leaving unsettled districts at their rear.[46] The ability of the
Finns to move through and between rugged interfluvial lands and
to transport the abundant rye surpluses from their burned fields
down to valley markets, in the absence of roads, was remarkable.
On occasion during our field research, we hiked on paths far back
into isolated, abandoned Finnish farmsteads located on the high
ground between Sweden and Norway, in the process gaining considerable respect for the ability of the Finns to move through such
rough, roadless country.

In Scandinavia the Finns could no longer situate their farmsteads on streams and lakes, since those lowland sites belonged
to their Germanic predecessors. A south-facing slope with a view
of a distant highland lake became a new ideal, but the Finns did
not forget their love of watersides. The interfluvial niche they
found in Scandinavia did, however, provide much that was familiar to them. The stony, acidic soils responded well to *huuhta*, and
the familiar coniferous forests teemed with the game they were
accustomed to hunting.[47]

The resultant Finnish lifestyle in Scandinavia was thus not
substantially altered from its Savo-Karelian prototype.[48] Settlers
lived in the same one-room cabins or log double houses, and mul-
tistructure, isolated farmsteads strewn through the forests remained the dominant pattern (Fig. 3.9).[49] Each pioneer family required a considerable expanse of land to make a living in the
inhospitable hills. For their rye fields, they burned clearings on
the rocky hillsides, high on the slopes where the soil was dry.
Every year they burned and fenced new clearings, and few settlers
attempted initially to create true, permanent fields cleared of
rocks. Their cattle herds grew, but they raised no fodder crops. In
summer the stock ran loose and untended, browsing in the woods.
Winter fodder was cut from natural meadows and bogs, as well as
from oldfields. Such wild hay was harvested even far from the
farmstead, as in Finland.

Hunting remained an essential livelihood, and the Finns
roamed for many miles in the wilderness to kill moose, bear, bea-
ver, deer, fowl, and other game, living in their traditional open-
faced shanties. To the horror of Swedish authorities, they at times
killed animals for the hides only, leaving the carcasses to rot.[50]

Fig. 3.9. A recently abandoned Finnish farmstead called Ritaberg (Ritamäki), near Lekvattnet in the high ground along the Swedish-Norwegian border, Värmland Province, and accessible only by footpath and jeep trail. (Photo by T.G.J., 1985.)

They fished in small mountain lakes and streams. As in earlier times east of Bothnia, hunting and fishing expeditions often provided the information base for subsequent migrations.

The witches, wizards, superstitions, and charms of *The Kalevala* came with the Savo-Karelians to Scandinavia, as did their joy in the sauna, beer, distilled spirits—particularly vodka made from rye—and boisterous social gatherings.[51] "Like all coarse barbarians," wrote one Swede concerning seventeenth-century Värmland, "Finns were very fond of vodka."[52] In addition, the Finns displayed a disdain for both church and state in Sweden, acquiring the reputation of lawless heathen.[53] Tradition says they were "perpetually in conflict with the law" due to such activities as smuggling, tax evasion, poaching, squatting, trespass, and public drunkenness.[54] The border location of Värmland's Finnskog district contributed to the lack of law and order. Nor was a violent criminal element lacking. For example, a Finn named Big Jacob, a large, strong fellow, terrorized the Finnskog in the 1640s. In a drunken rage, Jacob killed a fellow Finn, after which he fled across the Norwegian border, only to return several years later and, with ax and rifle, murder his half-brother (also named Jacob). The following year he again emerged from the woods, and when a sizable group of armed men came to seize him, he wounded one in hand-to-hand combat before being overpowered.[55]

While the Finns in Scandinavia preserved most aspects of their traditional Savo-Karelian culture, aided by the relative isolation of their highland domains, they also interacted very early with the neighboring Swedes and Norwegians. The marketing of grain surpluses in the lowland towns encouraged contacts, as did the highly fragmented distribution of Finnish settlement areas (Fig. 3.5). A modest level of acculturation apparently occurred rather early, and Finns accepted certain aspects of Germanic culture. Bilingualism developed, even in the 1600s, especially among the men. In the principal Savo-Karelian enclave, the Finnskog along the border of Värmland and Hedmark, both Swedish and Norwegian influences were felt.[56]

The Savo-Karelians' success in Scandinavia did not come, however, without generating opposition from indigenous Germanic farmers and the Swedish crown. With their hunting, fishing, haymaking, forest burning, and lawlessness, the Finns came into conflict with the Swedish villagers and royal authorities, especially the *kirvesmiehet.*[57] Too much woodland and game were destroyed by the newcomers, too much summer pasture and wild meadow was lost by the valley folk, and too much rye from the prolific burned clearings flooded the markets. The resulting conflict, as well as news of another frontier, where their shifting cultivation could be freely practiced, brought some of the Finns to colonial America.

Savo-Karelians in Colonial America

In 1638 the Swedish Empire, then at the height of its power, established a trading colony named Nya Sverige, or "New Sweden," on the lower Delaware River in parts of present-day Pennsylvania, New Jersey, and Delaware.[58] For seventeen years the colony remained under Swedish rule, but in 1655 it fell to the Dutch, who in turn lost it to the English in 1664. While administering the colony, the Swedes created a string of settlements along the west bank of the river, reaching from a point near present-day New Castle in northern Delaware upstream to the site of Philadelphia (Fig. 3.10). Forts, blockhouses, trading posts, mills, and scattered farm communities lined the west bank. The population of New Sweden remained small, numbering about two hundred by 1647 and twice that at the time the colony was surrendered to the Dutch.[59]

Immigration from the Swedish Empire continued for at least a decade after 1655.[60] By the time large-scale English colonization of the lower Delaware Valley had begun with the arrival of William Penn in 1681, the Swedes had not only occupied the west bank but had also spread up many tributary creeks and crossed the river to settle parts of the New Jersey side. Penn encountered a population of roughly one thousand derived from the Swedish Empire, and he noted that their families were remarkably large.[61] He and others credited the Swedes with making the first "considerable Improvement" in the valley.[62]

New Sweden's population was diverse in origin. At that time,

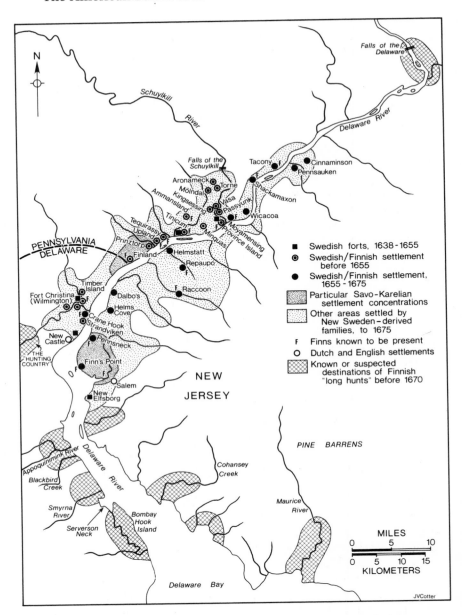

Fig. 3.10. New Sweden: Settlement of the Midland hearth, 1638–1675. (Sources: Johnson 1911, maps following pp. 496 and 514 in vol. 2; the sources listed in nn. 96, 98, 99, 100, 111, and 112 of this chapter; Fernow 1877, p. 130; Brodhead 1853–58, vol. 2, p. 88; Holm 1702, maps following pp. 26 and 36; Acrelius 1874, map following p. 66.)

Sweden ruled a multiethnic Baltic empire that included all of Finland and sizable parts of present-day Poland, the Soviet Union, and Germany. All corners of the empire were represented on the Delaware, and Sweden drew mercenary soldiers from an even wider Hanseatic area (Fig. 3.1). Ethnic Swedes, Finns, Germans, Danes, Frisians, English, and Dutch all lived in the colony.[63] Most

of the Swedes came from Uppland, Västergötland, and Södermanland. Our thesis demands that we demonstrate that a substantial
part of the population also was Finnish, or more exactly, Savo-
Karelian.[64]

Finns were present in New Sweden very early, though they are
often difficult and sometimes impossible to distinguish in the records. They were normally required to take Swedish names, and
only occasionally was Finnish identity suggested in names such
as Andries Matysen or Mathys Echelson.[65] Often or even typically,
observers referred to the entire population of the colony as
"Swedes," and as decades passed, the Finns were more than willing to accept this appellation, further confusing the issue.

Data on specific origin are the exception rather than the rule
for New Sweden, but the first Finns to arrive were thought to be
four families who came in 1640.[66] The number initially was very
small, but from 1641 on, references to persons such as "Måns
Jurrensson the Finn" or "Karin the Finnish woman" appeared regularly and, as the years passed, with increasing frequency in the
colonial records.[67] After the Dutch annexed the colony, official
references to Finns living in and migrating to the Delaware Valley
continued to appear, including mention of quarrels between Finns
and Swedes.[68] English authorities and observers after 1664 also
noted the Finnish presence and mentioned them at least as late as
1698.[69]

The available evidence, though fragmentary, strongly suggests
that the proportion of Finns in the population of New Sweden
increased steadily after the mid 1640s. At first the Finnish migration was forced, involving deportations for crimes committed in
Sweden, but the early exiles sent back glowing reports to their
kinfolk.[70] By the late 1640s, hundreds of Finns had petitioned for
the right to emigrate to New Sweden.[71] They began flocking
to the Delaware Valley in the early 1650s, and "America fever"
raged in the Finnmarks of Scandinavia.[72] The colony's governor
grumped in 1654 that "a good part" of the immigrants were "lazy
Finns."[73] By the end of Swedish rule the following year, at least
one third of the Delaware Valley population was Finnish.[74]

Under Dutch rule, the number and proportion of Finns continued to grow rapidly, for several reasons.[75] Many of the ethnic
Swedes, who had been army officers and administrators, left the
colony and returned to Europe.[76] More important, Finnish immigrants continued to arrive in the Delaware Valley. One shipload,
which had departed Sweden ignorant of the Dutch takeover,
reached the colony in 1656, bearing 33 Finnish men, 27 Finnish
women, and 32 Finnish children under the age of thirteen. Dutch
authorities were unable to prevent the disembarkation of these
people.[77] In 1663 local officials reported that 32 more Finns were
expected, having been "notified by their countrymen in the afore-
said colony of the good opportunity there." By that time, the
Dutch were welcoming "Swedes and Fins," noting that "many
families or households are from time to time expected." The
Swedish ambassador in Amsterdam lodged a protest, complaining

that the Dutch were "even drawing and conveying from Finland and Old Sweden additional inhabitants to be employed in their service in New Sweden."[78] In the following year, 1664, some 140 Finns, including many children, arrived in Amsterdam bearing a Swedish pass and, lured by the "glories of the country," requested transportation to the Delaware Valley colony. One of them displayed a letter from New Sweden dated 1657. After some delay, this group reached the Delaware Valley, in spite of the British takeover of the colony.[79]

Moreover, Finnish immigration did not stop with the advent of English rule. As late as 1678, for example, a Finnish farmer in the hills of southern Hälsingland Province, Sweden, sold his land to obtain money for the journey to the American colony.[80] In view of the growing Finnish presence and probable majority on the Delaware, it is not surprising that an English traveler in 1675 described one settlement where the inhabitants were mostly "Dutch and Finns," but did not mention Swedes.[81]

To be sure, not all of the colonial Delaware Finns were of Savo-Karelian origin. The records mention some settlers from the coastal margins of Finland, including the provinces of Uusimaa, Pohjanmaa, Varsinais Suomi, and Ahvenanmaa (Åland Islands), as well as Estonia (Fig. 3.1).[82] Many or most of these may, in fact, have been ethnic Swedes. One of the families reputedly from Pohjanmaa, the Mårtenssons of Vaasa, would generations later produce a signer of the American Declaration of Independence, John Morton.[83]

However, the great majority of the Finns on the Delaware were of Savo-Karelian background, derived mainly from the diaspora in Sweden. A remote ancestral link to the Rautalampi church district in northern Häme, the single greatest source of the Finns who settled Sweden, is well documented for the American colonists, and a monument to the Delaware settlers presently stands in the churchyard at Rautalampi.[84] It is equally clear that New Sweden's Finns came preponderantly from Värmland Province, the largest Savo-Karelian cluster in Sweden. The first four Finnish families known to have arrived in the American colony, in 1640, came from Sunne parish in Värmland, and a 1649 petition on behalf of 200 Finns who wished to emigrate to New Sweden also emanated from that province.[85] In the 1650s, the same pattern prevailed as Värmland Finns departed for America from the Finnskog bordering Norway, including Lekvattnet, one of the principal Finnish parishes; from the districts of Brunskog, Fryksdal, and Sunneskog; from along the Letstigen, a road in the southeastern part of the province; and from Bergslagen settlements in the east.[86] Experts on Värmland culture mention in particular that a fragment of the migratory Finnish population in the province was sent to New Sweden.[87]

Numerous other Delaware Valley settlers came from the scattered Savo-Karelian enclaves in Västmanland, Närke, Dalarna, Hälsingland, Medelpad, and possibly also Ångermanland.[88] The previously mentioned 1664 emigrants who reached Amsterdam, displaying astounding mobility by journeying overland in sleighs through Dalarna to Oslo, came from homes along the border of Medelpad and Hälsingland.[89] Clearly, an efficient communications network linked the many Savo-Karelian settlement areas in Sweden, and these Finns possessed remarkable geographical knowledge of the Scandinavian peninsula. Embarking at Oslo, the 1664 group sailed to Amsterdam, knowing that New Sweden had come under Dutch rule. The image of these free-spirited forest Finns loping about the streets of Calvinistic Amsterdam, dressed in what the Dutch considered summer clothing, is compelling and perhaps without parallel since the Goths visited Rome. The European core, however briefly, encountered the periphery face to face.

Still other settlers reached the Delaware Valley directly from the Karelian and Savoan heartland in Finland. Included were a few colonists from the Viipuri and Käkisalmi districts on the Karelian Isthmus and from Kajaani on Lake Oulu in Kainuu.[90]

The Savo-Karelians' dominance among the colonial Delaware settlers had several causes. Their prowess as forest pioneers and eagerness to migrate to new areas were perhaps the key factors, as both Swedish and Dutch administrators had recognized. But these very skills and tendencies had also gotten the Finns in trouble in Sweden. The honeymoon between royal officials and Savo-Karelian pioneers was over. The eastern Finns had destroyed far too much woodland with *huuhta* cultivation and had greatly diminished wild game through wasteful hunting practices. Their colonization of Sweden unfortunately coincided with the rise of the copper and iron industries in Bergslagen District, on the Dalarna-Värmland-Västmanland border, an activity that demanded large amounts of wood for the smelters. The forest Finns quickly fell from royal favor, and in the seventeenth century, laws were passed in an attempt to curtail their use of Sweden's woodlands.[91] The vitriolic Forest Law of 1647, for example, condemned those "who come into the forests with a ravenous appetite, without explicit prior permission," and instructed authorities "to capture and, as with other noxious animals, strive to get rid of them."[92] Earlier orders denounced people who "destroy the forests by setting tracts of woods on fire, in order to sow in the ashes, and who mischievously fell trees" and those who poach game. Expulsion of these criminals from the crown forests was demanded, and New Sweden proved to be a logical place of exile for captured "forest-destroying Finns."[93]

Particularly despised by the Swedes were the landless vagabond *kirvesmiehet* among the Savo-Karelians, who refused to establish permanent farmsteads and remain in the lands originally allotted to them, but instead roamed through the crown forests, relocating every few years to perpetuate *huuhta* and good hunting. In short, royal law was directed particularly against the most mobile, volatile, disrespectful, and boisterous among the Savo-Karelians in Sweden, and this resulted in a kind of cultural selection.[94] Some of these seminomadic squatters were rounded up as early as 1640 and transported to America, where a vast continental forest of unimaginable dimensions awaited them.[95] Such banishment of backwoods Finns was a bit like tossing Br'er Rabbit into the brier patch. As the decade progressed, news of the fine American forests filtered back to Sweden from the exiled Finns, prompting many other Savo-Karelians voluntarily to flee the harassment inflicted upon them by the Swedish government. In all, the Savo-Karelian migration to colonial America lasted for at least a quarter of a century.

Finns dispersed widely through New Sweden, and almost every settlement acquired some, but several districts became known as Finnish concentrations (Fig. 3.10). These areas gain a special importance, since, if our thesis is valid, they became focal points in the development of American backwoods pioneer culture out of the Savo-Karelian prototype. The oldest and largest dominantly Finnish settlement, dating from 1641 and appropriately called "Finland" (near present-day Marcus Hook, Pennsylvania), was a district on the west bank of the Delaware River (Fig. 3.10). This principal Savo-Karelian nucleus gradually expanded upstream to reach modern Chester, called Upland in the time of New Sweden, and downstream to present-day Claymont in the state of Delaware. At a later time Finns were said to be dominant still farther down the river, around Crane Hook and present-day Wilmington, and many also lived upstream at places such as Tacony and Shackamaxon, both now part of Philadelphia (Fig. 3.10).[96]

The west bank of the Delaware presented a rather different environmental setting for the Finns. Instead of the familiar microthermal coniferous and birch forest, they found a mesothermal broadleaf deciduous woods of oak, walnut, chestnut, maple, hickory, and tulip (yellow poplar) trees. In place of the sterile podsols and sands of subarctic northern Europe, they encountered fertile clays overlaid by a rich black mold, the gift of a temperate land.[97] Great oaks yielded readily to their axes and rolled ablaze across the *huuhta* clearings. Watersides and marshes were abundant, stirring memories of distant Värmland or Finland, and a good number of the area's wild animals and fish were remarkably similar to those the Finns had hunted and caught in their homeland.

Initially they hunted and traded with Indians on the opposite, eastern shore of the Delaware. By the late 1650s, following those paths, Finns began migrating to the east bank, in New Jersey, and in that setting they established a second major Savo-Karelian waterside settlement around Finns Point, centered at old Penn's Neck, the present-day Churchtown (Fig. 3.10).[98] On a 1685 map this district on the inner coastal plain was labeled "Finn's Land," and a local river was called the "Finnish." Three years later the ethnic character of the settlement was further revealed in the statement of an unwed, pregnant girl there, who said she had lain with "a young Youdas," meaning "a divill in ffinns language."[99] In the 1660s other Finns settled among Swedes at several other east-bank places, most notably Raccoon (present-day Swedesboro) and Repaupo.[100]

The east-bank environment was quite different from that on the opposite side of the Delaware River, and surely more familiar to the Finns. In the higher portion, near Swedesboro, a poor, sandy soil prevailed, covered only by a thin black stratum, and while oaks and hickories remained dominant, groves of coniferous trees—outliers of the expansive Jersey Pine Barrens to the east—occurred. Around Finns Point, a large lower-lying district, marshes and swamps were common, interspersed with wooded tracts. The Finns there lived along the rivulets that flowed into the Delaware and on necks of land that jutted into the river.[101] Later-arriving groups did not desire the sandy and marshy lands, and this permitted a much longer survival of northern European culture on the east bank than on the west. Indeed, much of the area east of the Delaware River remains quite rural today.

In the Delaware Valley as a whole, the population of Finns and Swedes never attained great size, but a first effective colonization was definitely achieved. Numbering perhaps 400 or 500 at the close of Swedish rule, the inhabitants by 1663 had established "110 good bouweries," and by 1697 their Swedish-speaking descendants totaled 1,200.[102]

The Implantment of Savo-Karelian Culture

In these two nuclei, one on each bank of the lower Delaware River, Savo-Karelian Finnish culture took root in colonial America, as evidenced by a variety of contemporary Delaware Valley records and reports. We read, for example, of "certain fields sown in rye and barley upon a burnt clearing," the likes of which, after a few years of declining yields, "its possessor therefore leaves . . . fallow, and proceeds to another part of his ground, which he treats in the same manner." We listen as Indians complain to the Dutch that the typical settler of New Sweden "builds and plants, indeed, on our lands, without buying them or asking us."[103] We learn that the colonists "on their arrival here, made such enclosures as are usual in Sweden," which is to say they built split-rail fences.[104]

Early observers also tell us that the early settlers of New Sweden built *pirtti*-style cabins consisting of "one little room" with a fireplace "in a corner," windows that were mere "holes before which a moveable board was fastened," and walls with chinks between the logs stopped "without and within with clay."[105] Later the Finnish log double house, with its open central passage, appeared near the banks of the Delaware.[106] The Finns' New World farmsteads also included the beloved sauna, usually referred to in the records by its Swedish name, *badstoe* or *badstua*.[107] One such bathhouse was owned by a certain Lace Colman (Kolehmainen) at Upland, in the oldest Finnish settlement nucleus.[108] Following old Savo-Karelian custom, these farmsteads were strewn along the waterfront "at considerable distance one from the other" or, inland, were "scattered in the country."[109]

The Finns on the Delaware continued to hunt in their traditional manner, ranging far in ancestral boats and dugout canoes made of oak, juniper, chestnut, and tulip trees up and down the river and along the shores of Delaware Bay.[110] One favored hunting ground lay along the lower Maurice River in southern New Jersey.[111] Evidence suggests that they also hunted along the Appoquinimink River on the Delaware coast in southern New Castle County and near the falls of the Delaware at present-day Trenton, for they later requested British permission to colonize those sites (Fig. 3.10).[112]

Kalevalan sorcerers lurked along the Delaware, too. The Finns Lasse and Karin were imprisoned for wizardry and witchcraft by the governor of New Sweden, and another Finnish woman, Margaret Mattson, was accused but acquitted of the charge.[113] Beer and vodka also reached the American colony, causing an observer on the Delaware in 1671 to remark that "the Distilling of Strong Liquors out of Corn" was "the Cause of a great Consumption of the Grain, as also the Debauchery and Idleness of the Inhabitants."[114] A few years later a British clergyman in the Delaware Valley complained of "Finns . . . addicted to Drunkenness."[115] Typical was the behavior of a certain Moens Staecket, who "in drinke" lured Andries Boen into a sauna and assaulted him.[116] Lawlessness of a more serious nature also occurred frequently among the Delaware Valley frontier Finns, plaguing three different colonial administrations. These crimes, sometimes provoked, included smuggling and insurrection, and violence was not uncommon.[117]

The old Savo-Karelian woodworking skills also were transplanted to New Sweden. A century after the colonization, a traveler visiting Swedesboro in New Jersey was told that, in former times, "the Finlanders, who are settled here, made dishes, bowls," and other objects from knoblike protuberances growing on the local ash trees.[118]

Savo-Karelian culture was celebrated with full exuberance in the colonial Delaware Valley. A rowdy fringe folk reached an ultimate forested periphery and took root with skill and gusto, surviving even a six-year span during which no supply ships arrived from mother Sweden. Soon masses of other Europeans of very different cultural origin followed the Finns and Swedes to this remote place, creating an odd, unique ethnic juxtaposition and providing the opportunity for an altogether new hybrid culture to form.

Babel along the Delaware

The ethnic composition of the early colonial Delaware Valley population was very complicated. William Penn, shortly after arriving, noted that "the People are a Collection of divers Nations in Europe," including "French, Dutch, Germans, Sweeds, Danes, Finns, Scotch, Irish and English."[119] The Dutch had actually preceded the Finns and Swedes to the lower Delaware, establishing a foothold at Lewes on the bay in the 1630s. A generation later, before seizing political control of the valley, they strengthened their position by founding New Castle; and during the decade of Dutch rule, between 1655 and 1664, their ethnic element grew, though it remained concentrated downstream from the two Finnish settlement areas.[120]

English colonists entered the valley long before William Penn or even the advent of British rule in 1664. As early as 1641, an English settlement developed near the later site of Salem, New Jersey, close to the Swedish Fort Elfsborg (Fig. 3.10).[121] By the 1670s, English settlers had again occupied the Salem site, adjacent to the Jersey Finnish concentration, while others lived among the Finns at Chester (Upland), Pennsylvania. Upstream, English Quakers settled at both Trenton and Burlington on the Jersey side of the river in the 1670s.[122] After the establishment of Penn's colony, the English influx became a flood, accounting for half the west-bank population by 1685.[123] The majority of the English immigrants to the Midland hearth came from the Anglican Plain, or lowland Britain, and should be regarded as Germanic core Europeans accustomed to stabilizing selection and ill suited for frontier life. Others, however, had been born in highland fringe counties of England, such as Yorkshire, Dorset, Westmorland, and Cornwall. In spite of being ethnically English, they were fringe folk very like the Celts, attuned to diversifying selection. It should not be surprising, therefore, to learn that English highlanders settled on the American frontier—for example, the Yorkshireman living on the Susquehanna in 1705.[124]

Continental Calvinists also sought homes in America's Delaware Valley. French Huguenots, far less numerous than either the English or the Dutch, lived in the Delaware colony at least as early as 1656, and the young city of Philadelphia later lured many more.[125]

Welsh surnames began appearing on local tax lists in the valley in 1670, and just over a decade later Welsh immigrants began flocking to the Quaker refuge, the "Great Welsh Tract" west of the Schuylkill River above Philadelphia. Suggestive toponyms such as Bryn Mawr and Radnor survive to the present there.[126] Fellow Celts, the Scots also were represented in the valley, including at least one who settled among the Finns at Chester.[127]

The Scotch-Irish, who were ultimately to form perhaps the majority of the Midland backwoods population, began arriving in 1680, and "many" Irish settled in Pennsylvania, eastern Maryland, and Delaware before 1700. New Castle and Upland (Chester), on the Delaware River, became two major early points of disembarkation, and from there Ulster pioneers moved before 1710 into the tristate border area where Pennsylvania, Maryland, and Delaware join (see Fig. 4.1).[128] In these ports and their hinterland, the Scotch-Irish had abundant exposure to established settlers of Finnish and Swedish origin. The largest Scotch-Irish immigration, the swarming of perhaps a quarter of a million people, began in 1717 and lasted until the American Revolution. Philadelphia became the major receiving port, once again placing the Scotch-Irish in close contact with the descendants of Finns and Swedes as the newcomers trekked to the back country.[129]

Some Danes, Frisians, Holsteiners, and other Jutlanders entered the Delaware Valley in the service of the Dutch and Swedish governments as early as the 1640s.[130] Among them was a scattering of north Germans, the vanguard of a Teutonic host. Long before the founding of the Germantown colony near Philadelphia in 1683, small numbers of Pomeranians, East Prussians, Silesians, Brandenburgers, and German-Swiss arrived in the valley.[131] The Rhenish German colony at Germantown added relatively little to the Teutonic population, but other Germans continued to arrive through the remainder of the century. By 1714, Germans lived among the Finns and Swedes at Finns Point and Swedesboro on the Jersey side of the river.[132] Large-scale Teutonic immigration to the Delaware Valley began about 1717, coinciding with the Scotch-Irish influx. Lasting for over half a century, this major colonization placed a permanent German stamp on much of southeastern Pennsylvania. Switzerland and southwestern Germany were the leading contributing areas.

This "extremely diverse population," derived from Europe, encountered the local Indians, who were village-dwelling farmers, hunters, and gatherers.[133] Known in the white vernacular as "Delawares," these Indians largely died out or were displaced, and relatively little violence developed on the frontier of the valley. Abundant interactions between Europeans and Indians occurred locally in the 1600s.

Conclusion

We have established that a highly successful Savo-Karelian woodland pioneering culture arose on the shores of Lake Ladoga in the late Middle Ages and was set in motion by the conjunction of economic, political, and ecological forces. We described how its bearers spread northwestward to claim the watery interior of Finland and crossed the Gulf of Bothnia to colonize much of central Sweden. Subsequently, we have shown, Savo-Karelian pioneers from Sweden migrated to colonial America, where they formed a substantial part of the colonial population of the Delaware Valley. We further noted the development of two major predominantly Savo-Karelian settlement nuclei along the Delaware River by 1670, in which the traditional eastern Finnish pioneering methods prevailed.

Further, we have seen the Finns and Swedes joined by a bewildering array of other European groups in the Delaware Valley, well before 1700. The subsequent arrival of masses of Germans, Swiss, and Scotch-Irish further complicated the ethnic picture, as did the lingering presence of a potentially important Indian population.

From this diverse human raw material, European and Indian alike, American backwoods pioneer culture was formed, yielding the most successful woodland colonization in history. Elaborate claims were long ago put forward for the contributions of the Scotch-Irish—the "first true backwoodsman"—to this culture, and German influence has likewise been proposed.[134] Even the American Indian has not wholly lacked champions.[135] In subsequent chapters we carefully evaluate these claims, and to them join our assessment of the possible Savo-Karelian role.

Our core/periphery model of Europe (Fig. 2.2), coupled with the ecological concept of diversifying selection, suggests that the Finns, highland British, and Alpine Swiss, along with the American Indian, deserve the closest scrutiny. We expect less from the Germanic core of Europe, including the English, Dutch, Danes, Swedes, and Germans.

In Chapters 4–8, we describe in some detail the American backwoods culture and seek prototypes in the various potential parent peoples. Throughout, we focus attention on the Savo-Karelian Finns, since they form the basis of the principal revisionist thesis we are testing, but we also consider the contributions of the other groups. Let us begin, then, with an analysis of backwoods society on the Midland American frontier.

FOUR

BACKWOODS SOCIETY IN MIDLAND AMERICA

Move your cottage to somewhere else,
Your dwelling place farther off.

Kalevala

A distinctive "sociocultural type" characterized the Midland American frontier.[1] Centralized social institutions such as law, religion, and education were weakly developed, as were central places and social classes. Pioneers were said to "manifest a great degree of apathy towards benevolent institutions."[2] Personal freedom, individualism, and even licentiousness filled this institutional void, and many forms of deviant behavior were stigmatized weakly, if at all. "Sloth and independence are prominent traits in their character," wrote a New Englander of the Midland backwoods pioneers, adding that "to indulge in the former is their principal enjoyment, and to protect the latter their chief ambition."[3] They were labeled "uncouth," the bearers of a "promiscuous society." Another early traveler, anticipating Turner's frontier thesis, suggested that, for all their excesses, the backwoods pioneers had laid the basis of a democratic society.[4] At the same time, self-reliance and independence from social institutions were partially canceled by the need for mutual aid and community effort in some endeavors, particularly defense.

Attachment to place was perhaps even weaker in pioneer society than in contemporary America, and migration, at least locally, was frequent. No sooner was the land brought into a market than "the squatter class would sell their pre-emptions to industrious immigrants and clear out."[5] Mobility tore at the fabric of society, helping to elevate the nuclear family at the expense of blood clan. Extended family networks survived, though in a weakened state. Partly as a result, ethnicity played no particular role in backwoods society, and intermarriage with persons of different origin or even race was common.

Demographic Traits

In part, the unusual character of American backwoods society derived from its basic demography. As noted earlier, the cultural ecology of forested agricultural frontiers favored selection of a young, rapidly growing population.[6] The large amount of physical labor required for clearing woodlands demanded healthy, strong people in their youth and prime. Each family needed an abundance of children to help in the task, and early marriage was the rule. John Mason Peck, traveling in 1820 in Missouri, reported "children and youth in almost countless numbers," a typical frontier situation.[7]

Demographically, as in many other aspects of society and culture, the early colonial Delaware Valley set a pattern consistent with the subsequent Midland frontier. A rapid rate of natural increase characterized the population in the formative years there. Contemporary accounts suggest that exceptionally high birth rates and large nuclear families were typical of the northern European pioneers of New Sweden, following the earlier Savo-Karelian frontier model. In part, perhaps, their fertility derived from the royal instruction to authorities in Sweden to deport to America only those forest-destroying Finns who were "strong and able-bodied."[8] Two generations later, William Penn, discussing the resident "Sweeds and Finns" of his colony in the early 1680s, marveled at their proliferation and noted that "they have fine Children, and almost every house full," adding that it was "rare to find one of them without three or four Boys, and as many Girls," and even some with "six, seven and eight Sons."[9] Censuses in the 1690s revealed an average household size of between five and six for the Delaware Valley Swedes and Finns, and on the Jersey side of the river, church records indicate that ten to twelve children "was more likely the rule than the exception."[10] The 1693 census of 188 "Swedish" families in the Valley revealed 7 containing ten or more persons and an additional 47 families consisting of seven to nine individuals.[11] By contrast, British families living in nearby Delaware, along Cedar, Saint Jones, and Duck creeks in 1680, reported to the census taker an average household size of only 2.75 persons.[12] It seems that the later-arriving Germanic groups had difficulty matching the Swedish/Finnish birth rate.

Had Penn been a cultural ecologist, he might have drawn some conclusions from the fecundity of New Sweden's early settlers. Population growth is perhaps the best measure of successful adaptation, providing convincing circumstantial evidence for the ecological fitness of a group.[13] Penn's observation strongly suggests that a successful woodland pioneering culture, a first effective settlement, had been developed in the Delaware Valley by northern Europeans before the arrival of English, Scotch-Irish, Welsh, and German immigrants. Significantly, those persons of Swedish and Finnish ancestry who remained in the valley rather than follow the receding frontier, experienced a marked decline in fertility in the eighteenth century.[14]

The American backwoods population from earliest times was so dominated by youth and birth that it produced an incomplete society, one in which the elderly were far underrepresented. Often, to age meant to be left behind when younger elements of the family migrated with the moving frontier. Lacking the elderly, whose role in moderating the excesses of the young and helping to civilize them is rather considerable in demographically normal societies, frontier folk remained boisterous and unruly, in many ways an assemblage of undisciplined juveniles. "Children were left to act out their vicious propensities, without the least effort on the part of the parents to assuage and restrain their ungovernable passions," wrote one early traveler, with the result that when grown to adulthood they were "unfit for social life."[15]

Like children, frontier folk were little concerned with personal hygiene. Fastidious New Englander Peck, ever the core European, faulted Missouri backwoods people for their "habitual neglect" of cleanliness, and was repulsed by "their tangled and matted locks, dingy faces, and squalid dress."[16] Similarly, the backwoods pioneers of early Ontario were flawed by "dirty habits."[17]

In effect, society in the demographic sense of the word had ceased to exist, yielding to dominance by the youthful, undisciplined nuclear family.[18] An atomization and weakening of society had occurred which, in turn, facilitated syncretism, re-networking, and the demise of ethnicity.

In contrast to the abnormality of age distribution on the frontier, sex ratios within the agricultural pioneer population remained near normal. Male-dominated frontiers tended to be confined to commercial resource exploitation, especially mining. By contrast, the Midland backwoods pioneer, pursuing hunting, gathering, and farming, required a family-based society. Males outnumbered females only slightly. For example, in the pioneer farming districts of the Willamette Valley of Oregon, one of the last American backwoods frontiers, the population in 1850 was 58 percent male.[19] Such sexual balance acted to preserve the stability partly undermined by the skewed age distribution.

For what it is worth, the sex ratio of the immigrant Finnish population along the Delaware River also was close to normal. The male domination of early exploitive colonies such as Virginia and New Netherland did not characterize the Finnish element in New Sweden. For example, in the group arriving in 1656, 55 percent of the adult Finns were male.[20] Clearly, family immigration was the norm among the Delaware Valley Finns, a demographic trait that greatly assisted their efforts to establish a viable forest pioneer culture in America and to provide a model for later-arriving groups.

In spatial terms, the outstanding demographic trait of the backwoods frontier was a low density of population. While it is arbitrary to assign any particular number, the often-cited figure of two or fewer European persons per square mile to define frontier conditions in the humid forested east is perhaps useful. Such a density necessarily retarded central-place formation and caused many or most of the functions typical of market and service towns to be dispersed or, more commonly, nonexistent. The only group in the Delaware Valley that had known in Europe so low a population density and so weak a central-place network were the Savo-Karelians. That, in turn, reflected the fact that the Finns alone, among the many ethnic groups implanted in colonial America, had previous experience as forest colonizers.

Individualism

One of the primary contributions of proponents of the cultural ecological paradigm is their recognition of the importance of the individual in decision-making processes. For decades, the prevailing view in disciplines such as anthropology and geography was of culture as superorganic.[21] Sweeping its human members docilely along, culture enjoyed a life force of its own. Individuals possessed little ability to depart from the cultural norm and minimal power to instigate change. Cultural ecologists, in contrast, regard the individual and deviant behavior as crucial to adaptation, to taking advantage of new opportunities or responding to environmental stress, thereby creating new ecological structures. Individual variation is important as the basis for selection.[22] One might well argue that the superorganic interpretation of culture was best suited to the Germanic core of Europe, where stablizing selection ruled, while the cultural ecological emphasis on individualism worked better in the European hardscrabble peripheries, the realm of diversifying selection (Fig. 2.2).

In any case, the frontier setting required that the decision-making process in adaptation rest heavily upon the individual person. In cultural ecological terms, individualism is essential on settlement frontiers. We should not be surprised, then, that the stereotyped image of the Midland American backwoods pioneer as individualistic is valid. Not only did adaptation demand as much, but the low population density, the atomization of society into basic family-unit nuclei, the banishment of the elderly, and the decline of discipline all fostered the rise of the individual. It has been said that the Midland pioneers of early Texas, who clumsily wrested that state from Mexican rule, were excellent fighters but poor soldiers.[23] Perhaps no better capsule description of American frontier individualism could be presented.

One might assume that the pioneer's individualism triggered innovation, that the American frontier was a zone where necessity mothered invention. Such was not the case, however. Instead, as noted earlier, simplification and cultural fusion occurred. The genius and energy of individualism were directed not to innovation but to a careful winnowing of imported European and indigenous Amerindian traits, in order to select those preadapted for frontier life. Implicit was an open-mindedness, a willingness to try something new from a different culture, an individualistic ability to experiment—in short, diversifying selection. Turner, viewing the American frontier, saw invention; we see selected continuity and blending, a penchant both to borrow and to discard.[24]

The winnowing of traits and a concordant syncretism, then, thrived in an essentially classless, individualistic, weakly disciplined, and tolerant society that was free of ethnic biases and other restrictive affiliations beyond the nuclear family level. To a degree, all European immigrant groups were preconditioned to membership in such a society. Transatlantic migrants were younger than the norm, as is true of most voluntary relocations, and as suggested in Chapter 2, the demise of feudalism and rise of capitalism had already thrust the nuclear family to the forefront in Europe. The normal demographic texture of society was torn by the migration process itself, opening the way for some of the related societal changes.

Even so, we suggest that the Delaware Valley and its hinterland enjoyed certain advantages in the creation of an individualistic pioneer way of life that were not shared by other Atlantic seaboard colonies. By drawing more heavily upon the northern and northwestern peripheries of Europe for its population than did New England, New Netherland, New France, or the Tidewater South, the Delaware Valley acquired people who had long been accustomed to diversifying selection, to classlessness, deviant behavior, and individualism. As a result, long before they left their Old World homelands, these peripheral folk were labeled "savage" or "uncivilized" by Germanic core Europeans, who later applied the same disparaging adjectives to backwoods pioneers and American Indians.[25]

The Scotch-Irish, in particular, had the reputation among the English of being quick-tempered, impetuous, reckless individualists.[26] The mobile, Savo-Karelian Finns, who were untouched by feudalism or even landlordism and had lived for generations in northern Europe as classless individuals, remained repulsive savages to their Swedish neighbors, a Germanic prejudice that has not entirely vanished even today. In Ireland, feudalism touched only the south and east, excluding rural Ulster, where freeholders composed almost one fourth of the population.[27] Thus both the Finns and the Scotch-Irish constituted a free peasantry prior to their migration to the Middle Colonies.

In short, individualism was a virtue and advantage on the American frontier, and the Delaware Valley settlements imported it in abundance. Ancestral diversifying selection showed the path to successful Midland pioneering, and the Delaware colonies inherited a legacy unknown elsewhere on the seaboard. Neither the narrow-minded Calvinist conformists of New England nor the neofeudal planters of the Tidewater South possessed these essential attributes.

Disregard for Government and Law

The harvest of individualism all too often is license; its price, lawlessness. For a variety of reasons, a partial disintegration of the

Germanic institutions of law and central government occurred on
the Midland frontier. A traveler near Pittsburgh in 1772, in a region that would soon spawn the Whiskey Rebellion, found that
"the inhabitants . . . seem to feel themselves beyond the arm of
government."[28] They and their western descendants lived "without the pale of civil law," lacking "the restraints upon manners
and actions imposed by refined society," and as a result formed "a
law unto themselves."[29]

One common expression of the backwoods pioneer's disregard
for government was a disdain for formal landownership. Squatter's right, a concept alien to Germanic law, assured a small pay-
ment upon departure, and the Midland pioneer desired nothing
more. Even as late as 1900 in Appalachia, squatter's right rather
than legal title remained the norm.[30] Nor did the backwoods pioneers in the wooded east generally look to government for defense. Instead, they raised volunteer militias and erected private
forts or blockhouses, as at one place on the colonial Pennsylvania
frontier, where during troubled times in 1755 "the people of the
path valley . . . Gethered Unto a Small fort."[31] Additional protection was in places provided by roving bands of hired gunmen,
often called "rangers," described around 1820 in Missouri as
"men who furnished their own horses, equipments, forage, and
provisions, and received one dollar per day for guarding the frontier settlements."[32]

While backwoods pioneers had little use for codified law, it
would be incorrect to assume that crime was rampant on the frontier. A contemporary observer declared, with some exaggeration,
that "nowhere are doors barred for the safety of those sleeping
within," while one Texas settler claimed that locks became necessary only after the secondary, postpioneer wave of people arrived.[33] It is probably fair to say that typical backwoods pioneers
did not commit criminal acts and were concerned to prevent and
punish crime. In so doing, they usually by-passed the Germanic
legal heritage and resorted to lynch law. "Regulators" administered spontaneous justice in many districts, taking prompt and
decisive measures against wrongdoers, in disregard of due process
and courts.[34]

While perhaps the majority of the pioneers were honest folks,
the frontier, from earliest times, did attract a rowdy, lawless element. "Drinking, debauchery, and all kinds of vice reign in this
frontier of depravity," wrote a visitor to the Pittsburgh area in
1775, and similar observations were made in many other frontier
areas.[35] Violence was not uncommon. Apparently a rather vivid
geography of crime developed in which certain Midland frontier
districts became outlaw havens and bases. Examples of such
crime pockets included the early Kentucky Barrens, between the
Cumberland and Green rivers; the South Carolina back country
centered on Camden; the area where Alabama, Mississippi, and
Tennessee join; and the southeastern corner of Texas.[36] In Illinois,
the Macoupin settlement consisted of "real frontier rowdies" be-

longing to a dozen families. Remarkably, some of these districts remain centers of rural crime today.[37]

Now, in some measure lawlessness and disrespect for government institutions might be expected on the frontier, since people were moving farther from the centers of administration into regions poorly served by transportation facilities and central-place services. In Midland backwoods culture, however, we find more than mere institutional deprivation; we find an active contempt for government and law among almost every element of society. Indeed, attempts to impose central authority were occasionally resisted violently, as in the Whiskey Rebellion. By contrast, in New England, township administration advanced with the agricultural frontier and outlaw havens did not develop. The Midland situation seems to have been unique.

What provided the model for the Midland frontier's mixture of lynch law, crime, and contempt for central authority? Elaborate and no doubt valid claims have been advanced for the influence of the Scotch-Irish, a people twice selected for frontier life by the time they arrived in the New World. The American frontier population, some say, reverted to medieval Scottish methods of suppressing violence and depredation.[38] The right of squatters to claim land by mere possession was reputedly derived from traditional Ulster tenant rights.[39] There is also evidence that habitual criminality was part of imported Ulster culture. According to contemporary observers, migration from Scotland to Ireland "was looked upon as a miserable mark of a deplorable person." The participants were often "breaking and fleeing from justice" and had previously led "scandalous lives." In a word used at the time, they were the "scum" of Scotland. Arriving in Ulster, not all of these wrongdoers reformed. A "deplorable laxity of morals" existed "among the early settlers of the Ulster plantation" and "iniquity abounded, with contention, murder, adultery," and the like. The massive genetic contribution of the Ulster immigrants to the American backwoods population convincingly supports a claim of detrimental societal influence.[40]

Others point to the transported habitual criminals of English origin, who fled from the Chesapeake Tidewater district to join the Midland backwoods population, as the ultimate source of much lawlessness on the frontier.[41] That genetically or culturally based criminality derived from the flight of Scottish wrongdoers and the transporting of English felons lies at the root of the persistently high crime rates of the American highland South is quite plausible, and we find no reason to deny these British influences. We can demonstrate, however, that long before the arrival of felonious Britons on the scene, the original inhabitants of the Delaware Valley, in particular the Finns, had established in the Midland hearth a pattern of disorder, including land squatting, contempt for central authority, lawbreaking, and insurrection. In these ways, New Sweden closely resembled the later Midland frontier.

Further, as described in Chapter 3, this sort of behavior had still earlier characterized the Savo-Karelian districts in northern Europe. Among the backcountry Finns there, beginning even in the Karelian hearth, land squatting was the normal practice, and the right of first occupancy enjoyed widespread acceptance. Land disputes were settled by "the right of the fist" rather than by Swedish or Russian courts and books of law.[42] In interior Sweden, disregard for land titles repeatedly brought Finns into conflict with the Germanic inhabitants and their Teutonic property laws.[43] Crime, too—some of it violent—was common in Savo-Karelian society, as is abundantly revealed in *The Kalevala*, where murder, assault, pillage, theft, rape, and incest are depicted, along with the comforting message that "the marches of Savo are vast enough for a man to hide his wicked deeds."[44] The previously mentioned "Big Jacob," who terrorized Värmland's Finnskog in the seventeenth century, was by no means the only violent criminal among the Savo-Karelians there. Norwegians, Swedes, and fellow Finns alike were harassed, robbed, or murdered by the likes of "Pål the Finn" and "Judge Lars." Finnish squatters on occasion threatened to slash protesting Swedish landowners "into mincemeat" with their felling axes.[45] Lesser transgressions by the Värmland Finns, such as smuggling, tax evasion, and poaching, fill the seventeenth-century court books. So widespread was criminal activity among the burnbeating Finns and so deep the prejudice of Swedes against them that the backhanded compliment "a migratory Finn but nevertheless honest" appears in the early Värmland records.[46]

As previously recounted, many transported Finnish felons, including sundry "malefactors and vicious people," were among the Delaware Valley colonists, and it is not surprising that they brought with them their contempt for Swedish authority and disregard for many laws. While most of the illegal acts perpetrated along the Delaware were minor, some reached Kalevalan proportions. By the end of Swedish rule, in 1655, one settler admitted that "there has been a disorderly and riotous life here," and the new Dutch rulers described some of the local inhabitants as "either troublesome or very dangerous."[47] The Delaware Valley colonial records of three administrations—Swedish, Dutch, and English—are filled with references to smuggling, assault, riot, obstruction of justice, tax evasion, rape, ignoring summons, adultery, army desertion, reckless use of firearms, flight to avoid prosecution, sale of liquor to Indians, murder of Indians, refusal to take an oath, vandalism, killing a neighbor's livestock, horse theft, prostitution, and insurrection on the part of local Finns and Swedes. All of these crimes were committed in a population of less than a thousand persons. The ax was a favored assault weapon, but fists, knives, sticks, guns, and rocks also were used.[48]

Regardless of which Germanic empire tried to rule the Delaware Valley, contempt for central authority remained rampant, finding both subtle and overt expression. For example, one Laars Carelsen, upon being notified by pious Dutch officials in 1662 that his marriage was illegal because he had performed the ceremony himself, indignantly replied that he had simply "followed the same custom which others have followed here."[49] In a Pennsylvania court thirty years later, Hans Peterson could produce no land "tytle but that of mowing it about twenty years," and even into the next century Swedes and Finns in the Delaware Valley still "declared they were men altogether ignorant of the Laws."[50]

On a more serious level, the northern European settlers engaged in repeated mutiny and insurrection. The first of these was an abortive uprising against the tyrannical rule of the Swedish governor of the colony, Johan Printz, following which some of the participants fled into the woods, reaching the Chesapeake Bay in the colony of Maryland.[51] A generation later, in 1669, the Finns rose in rebellion again, this time against the British crown. Led by a certain John Binckson, alias Marcus Jacobson or the "Long Finn," and his cohort and fellow Finn Henry Coleman (Kolehmainen?), the participating colonists were instructed "to fall upon and slay the English" in reprisal for encroachment upon the lands preempted by the old settlers.[52] To read the list of names of the Long Finn's followers is to peruse the "Who's Who" of the Delaware Savo-Karelians.[53] The British crushed the rebellion, banished the Long Finn to Barbados, and fined the other participants.

Six years later, in 1675, another insurrection occurred, involving some of the same men, who balked at an order for communal dike building in a tidal marsh. As a result, local authorities urgently requested "two fyle of soldiers" to crush the "Swedes and Fynnes," who were described as "a sort of people that must be kept under, else they will rebell." The report added that the local Finns were of "the worser sort as by instance the Long Fynne." If the insurrection were not put down, predicted the official, "and a free Court of Law" established, then property and commerce would not be secure.[54] Once again the rising was quelled, but a third of a century later, in 1709, the provincial council of Pennsylvania still categorized the Swedes as "exceedingly Insolent" in their dealings with the government and given to "Invective language."[55]

The rougher element among the Delaware Valley pioneers is perhaps best epitomized in the saga of one Evert Hendricksen, better known as Iver the Finn, an unruly man who arrived in New Sweden as a convicted criminal and laborer with the third royal expedition in 1641, later became a hired soldier, and by the close of Swedish rule, lived as a freeman at Upland (Chester).[56] He participated in the 1653 rising against the governor of New Sweden. During his first twenty years of residence on the Delaware, he acquired the reputation of "an abandoned villain," and in 1662 "the miscreant Iver the Fin" attracted the attention of Dutch officials when he put a knife to the throat of a fellow colonist and threatened "to cut off his head." Trespass by some pigs had sparked this outburst. The following spring, Iver the Finn assaulted the same man with a stick, "with the intention to break his head," and also threatened him with a gun. Neighbors testifying at Iver's trial further accused him of regularly disturbing the peace, engaging in disorderly conduct, discharging firearms in a reckless manner, making "trouble with his axe," stoning canoeists, assaulting fellow colonists with knives and "other things," bigamy, and daily fornication with the wife of a fellow Finn. He was, in brief, "a turbulent man who daily creates trouble with everybody," and for these sins he was banished from his home at Upland and instructed to leave the Delaware Valley. Instead, he drifted down to New Amstel (New Castle), where he threatened Dutch officials, causing them to complain that "we are again molested by this villain." Then, pressed by officialdom, "Evert the Fin fled into the woods and would not make his appearance," only to emerge the next year, after the Dutch government had been replaced by the British, and settle at Everts Hook, near Crane Hook, across the river from the developing Savo-Karelian community around Finns Point. He became a local militia captain and participated in the insurrection of the Long Finn, incurring a stiff fine. Unrepentant, Iver also took part in the 1675 riot against compulsory dike building, helping to lead the armed and drunken mob in New Castle that perpetrated the affair. By 1680, his vitality perhaps sapped by age, he was reduced to mere incitement, attempting "to Incense the people in the River" against the local magistrate by accusing him of saying that "all the Sweads were rebellers against the Government." Iver's descendants are doubtless legion, and the surnames Iverson and Hendrickson continued to be known in the region in later centuries.

Now, Iver the Finn was certainly not a typical resident of the Delaware Valley, nor did all the Finns lead riotous lives or resist central authority. The records leave no doubt, however, that conditions at least as disorderly as those later prevalent on the Midland frontier existed in the valley before the arrival of William Penn and that Finns were the principal instigators. A precedent had been set.

The Church

Just as backwoods pioneers were divided among those who habitually committed crimes and those who merely found central authority repugnant, so also they differed on the matter of religion. Some Midland pioneers simply had no use for or knowledge of Christianity, while others resisted only an organized, powerful church, preferring instead an informal folk faith.[57]

In the former category was a contingent of pioneers encountered in central Texas in the 1850s who were heading "whar the grass grows and the water runs, and the sound of the gospel never comes."[58] A similar attitude on the part of residents in one frontier Illinois community caused a disheartened eastern missionary to admit that he had never seen "a place more destitute of religious instruction," one that offered "a mighty poor chance for a Baptist preaching." He encountered pretty much the same conditions in adjacent Missouri, where in one settlement he met "with so little encouragement in visiting, conversing, and praying . . . that we concluded to pass them by." Moving on to Clay County, Missouri, on the outer frontier in 1824, he found in a population of about two thousand more than a hundred families "entirely destitute of the Scriptures," which led him to conclude that "little or nothing could be effected" to further religion there.[59] Half a century earlier, a fellow missionary visiting northwestern South Carolina learned that even the elderly there had never "seen a minister" before.[60] Western Pennsylvania at that time was in a similarly neglected condition, as backcountry Virginia had been a generation earlier.[61] In the Old Northwest, only about seven percent of the population belonged to churches in 1810, and some remote rural Midland areas preserved the antireligious sentiment of the backwoods into the present century.[62]

Other pioneers retained the Christian faith but favored loosely organized churches that appealed less to intellect than to emotion. Denominations that succeeded among the backwoods folk had to be willing to dispense with parish organization and provide itinerant, circuit-riding preachers; abandon Calvinistic doctrine, accepting in its place free will; discard the seminary and admit untrained ministers; allow worship services and burial in unsanctified places; dismantle central administration and permit unfettered splintering; and approve some truly bizarre emotional behavior on the part of the membership.[63] Methodists and Baptists proved most willing to make these compromises, fostering an atomistic, highly individualistic sort of Protestantism that might be regarded as the logical culmination of the Reformation. Camp meetings and periodic revivals, or reawakenings, also characterized this variety of religion, though such activities were more common behind the frontier, among the secondary settlers.[64]

In searching for precedents for the curious religious condition of the Midland frontier, we once again turn to the so-called "low" Scotch-Irish. Many of those leaving Scotland for Ireland in the 1600s were said to "flee from God" and to be "ungodly."[65] In Ulster, according to some contemporary observers, "little care was had by any to plant religion" initially, and the settlers "cared little for any church," with the result that "on all hands atheism increased, and disregard for God." Eventual preaching of the gospel in Ulster occasionally led to highly emotional conversions, complete with swooning, similar to those witnessed at American revivals.[66] Surely we detect in Ulster much of the future religious institution of the Midland American frontier. It is noteworthy, however, that proper Presbyterianism demanded an educated clergy, served up a rather intellectual fare, and denied free will, while in America only the breakaway Cumberland church abandoned these principles.[67]

"Low" Scotch-Irish influence probably prevailed in the religious sphere of the American backwoods frontier, but the Indian and Savo-Karelian Finn may also have contributed to frontier heathenism. Indians made a substantial genetic and cultural contribution to the Midland population and way of life. It would not be surprising if, in the process, they managed to dilute Christianity. The Savo-Karelians, only superficially Christianized in their isolated European homeland, continued to believe in witches, wizards, water sprites, and forest spirits. Even when living in closer proximity to the Lutheran state church in Sweden after 1570, many backwoods Finns resisted the faith.[68] The Savo-Karelians in Värmland, Medelpad, and other Swedish provinces had little contact with Lutheranism at the time of the American migrations, and according to a recent study, even today nearly all of the old Finnish settlement areas in Sweden continue to be characterized by below-average religiosity. Värmland's Finnskog in 1950 had one of the lowest churchgoing rates in the country, with fewer than ten percent of the population taking Holy Communion and over twenty percent remaining unbaptized.[69]

As might be expected, Savo-Karelian heathenism took root in the Delaware Valley, where close and frequent contacts with the local Indians perhaps reinforced the Finns' animistic views. The valley remained poorly served by churches as late as 1675, and only one house of worship stood on the river above Crane Hook, home of the devout Iver the Finn.[70] The local Lutheranism was chastised in 1697 as "quite irregular," and those Finns who moved back into the New Jersey Pine Barrens escaped all contact with the church and were reported in the 1760s to be "savage heathens" who "knew nothing of Christianity."[71]

However, the case for Savo-Karelian irreligiosity should not be overstated. Some were Christians, even along the Delaware. In 1693, 30 heads of families out of a total of 188 in the valley signed a letter to Sweden, requesting aid in Lutheran religious instruction.[72] Still, a majority apparently had little interest. At the very least, we can say that when the Scotch-Irish encountered the Delaware Finns, the two groups shared pretty much the same religious outlook. Their cultures were compatible in this important societal respect, facilitating an exchange of ideas on other facets of the pioneer way of life.

Education

Religion and education are companion institutions; find the one and you will likely find the other. In Europe, alphabets advanced with the respective churches.

Midland frontier folk were as little concerned with formal education as with organized religion. The backwoods people, often or even generally illiterate, displayed a pervasive anti-intellectualism and a contempt for learning acquired through books. Schools rarely existed in their settlements. Typical, perhaps, was one frontiersman who "could read, but mighty poorly," and "had no use for books or any such trash."[73] By contrast, New Englanders were greatly concerned to provide schools, even in newly settled districts.[74] This Midland/Yankee regional contrast proved to be a durable one, and white literacy rates remained much higher in the northern tier of states than in the American heartland, even after the frontier had passed. Trace the eventual path of the Yankee across the upper Midwest, and you will find that region well supplied with schools and, in the long run, a tradition of first-rate

colleges and universities. Follow the Midlander and you will encounter a far less distinguished educational legacy.

In adaptive terms, the task of woodland pioneering would have
suffered from removal of part of the labor force to the schoolroom,
and the great success of the Midland culture in forest colonization
depended in part precisely on its independence from such cum-
bersome institutions as formal education. The abundant practical
knowledge required for life in the woods was best conveyed ver-
bally and by example. Had schools been essential, the frontier
would have advanced more slowly.

It goes almost without saying that the same groups responsible
for shaping the religious character of the Midland frontier also
dictated its educational nature. Scotch-Irish, Indian, and Finn
alike had little use for the written word, even in Europe. *The Kalevala*, the only substantial written collection of Savo-Karelian
lore, remained merely an oral tradition into the nineteenth century. Illiteracy was the rule in the Finnmarks of Sweden and in the
early settlements along the Delaware.[75] In 1655 three quarters of
the adult male population of New Sweden was illiterate, making
curious Indian-like marks instead of signatures, and no appre-
ciable increase in education or literacy rate could be detected
among them in the following twenty to thirty years.[76] Generations later, many of their descendants, long removed from the
Delaware Valley, also were uneducated and illiterate.[77] Once
again, a societal and institutional precedent had been set at the
very outset in the nucleus of Midland pioneer culture.

Mobility

The weakness of institutions and the ascendant position of the
nuclear family in backwoods society grew in no small measure
out of population mobility, which involved frequent relocations
both within small areas and over considerable distances. The
Midland pioneers, possessed of a "wandering mind which often,
for the slightest motive," prompted them "to emigrate several
hundred miles," led a seminomadic life, moving to a new place
whenever the home region became fairly well settled.[78] This mobility was so common as to constitute "a portion of the variety of
backwoods life and manners."[79]

Local movements were apparently far more common than has
generally been recognized. A recent detailed study of the Sainte
Genevieve area of southeastern Missouri in the period around
1800 revealed that Anglo-American settlers moved locally once
every six years on the average, four times as frequently as the
people of French extraction in the same region. Eighty percent of
all the Anglos relocated at least once in a fifteen-year span, and
one backwoodsman apparently established three different farms
in a single decade. Some moves were so minor that the log house
could be disassembled and dragged to the new site.[80]

Migration over greater distances by Midland backwoods pioneers normally grew out of the so-called "long hunt." Men and

boys became familiar with the destination and route of eventual migration during extended hunting expeditions, then converted the grounds where they sought game into settlements. Such migration to remote places produced the distinctive Midland pattern of frontier expansion, in which isolated homesteads became strewn in the wilderness rather than advancing in a cohesive wave of settlements. For example, in 1769 Daniel Boone found new clearings and cabins fully one hundred miles beyond the outermost settlements in southwestern Virginia. This scattering caused the pattern of new colonization in Midland areas to be extremely fragmented, as is revealed on claim maps for states such as Missouri.[81]

Because backwoods migration derived from the long hunt and involved areas well beyond existing settlements, it could not depend upon roads. Indian trails, traces marked by blazed trees, and animal paths provided the routes, described by early visitors as "bridle-paths that pursued a zigzag course from one cabin to another" and "no more than a single horse path."[82] Normally these old hunting trails could not accommodate wheeled vehicles, and migration was usually accomplished on foot with pack horses.[83] Where vehicular movement was possible, as at one particular place in Illinois, the backwoods family sold out "their crops and claim for an old wagon and yoke of steers," moving some distance away "where a few squatters and bear-hunters had commenced a new settlement."[84] Migration in substantial, German-inspired Conestoga covered wagons—the stereotyped pioneer way—was undertaken almost entirely by secondary settlers. Streams, particularly in the Ohio River drainage basin, provided another common means of backwoods migration.

The seemingly compulsive locational instability of the Midland forest pioneers demands an explanation, for it provides an essential clue to their remarkably rapid westward advancement. The key seems to lie partly in their effective dispersal mechanism, which enabled them to use waterways and mere paths, as well as in their rapid population growth rate, coupled with a cultural resistance to intensification of land use. Selection for large families necessarily led to habitat expansion when offspring reached adulthood, since population density quickly surpassed the low threshold beyond which the extensive land-use system of the backwoods pioneers could not be maintained. The later influx of immigrants directly from Europe and of secondary settlers only hastened the displacement produced by natural increase. Reflecting the problem with overcrowding, diminished hunting was the most common reason given for long-range migration.[85] The backwoods rule of thumb dictating when migration should occur varied from the proverbial "when you see the smoke of a neighbor's cabin" to "when you hear the sound of a neighbor's gun" to when the nearest settler was within "eight or ten miles."[86] The appearance of the proper owner of the land had a similar purgative effect.[87]

The backwoods folk had to choose between intensifying land use and preserving their traditional lifestyle through migration. Some contemporary observers, core Germanic types all, could not understand the motives of those who moved, believing instead that migration "prevented their enjoying the fruit of their la-, bours."[88] But in cultural ecological terms, to remain would have meant to accept a new adaptive strategy, whereas the only long-term payoff in adaptation is to continue to function in the traditional manner for as long as possible.[89] Some, perhaps even a majority, did choose to stay and accommodate a postpioneer society, but a substantial number of backwoods folk, particularly the young, opted to retain the old ways through migration. As in sixteenth-century Finland, a successful woodland pioneering society contained the seeds of its own displacement. Competitive exclusion and fission were inevitably built into the Midland frontier system.[90]

The analogy to Finland is appropriate, for only in northern Europe, among Savo-Karelians, were almost exact duplicates of the several Midland American backwoods relocation practices found. Some Ulster Scots might have been vagabonds or have moved frequently from one tenant farm to another, committed to only one-year leases, but their methods and motives for relocation were fundamentally different from those of the American pioneers.[91] Finns offer much more satisfying prototypes. The shock troops of Savo-Karelian expansion were the previously mentioned *kirves-miehet*, or "ax-wielders," the most mobile element among the eastern Finns.[92] Unencumbered by landownership, they often moved at least short distances every four or five years—the duration of a *huuhta* cycle. A succession of local moves, in which the house logs could be dragged or floated to a nearby *huuhta* site, was followed by a more substantial migration along the route of previous long hunts. The *kirvesmiehet*, like their American counterparts, also detested the sight of smoke from a neighbor's cabin. Paths and waterways directed their migration, as they would in America. Peoples vary greatly in dispersal ability, as cultural ecology tells us, and the ax-wielders of interior Finland, together with the backwoods pioneers of Midland America, had no equals in their ability to scatter as agrarian colonists through a forested environment.[93]

In Sweden, royal authorities quickly learned to distinguish between migratory and sedentary Finns. The former were identified in official records with adjectives such as *ostadige* ("unsettled"), *drifte, dreffse* ("drifting"), *stryk* ("wandering"), or *lös* ("moving"), and as suggested earlier, the Swedes found them particularly troublesome.[94] Migratory Finns formed only a minority of the Savo-Karelian population, particularly after the early years of colonization had passed, but they remained sufficiently numerous and destructive in Sweden to be the subject of roundups and deportations in the 1640s. The ax-wielders were disproportionately represented among the Finns who emigrated to New Sweden.[95]

Mobility in the Delaware Valley

In the American colony, Savo-Karelian mobility persisted. Some local movement involved unauthorized clearings on royal domain or Indian lands, while in other instances the settlers requested official permission to relocate. Even as early as the period of Swedish rule, some freemen in the Upland area sold their "improvements" to the royal company and moved to other land nearby.[96] A bit later, in 1660, several colonists living at Kingsessing, near the Schuylkill River, sought permission from the Dutch to move to nearby Aronameck, about three miles away (Fig. 3.10).[97] Similar early relocations of a local nature were observed in the New Castle area and near Brandywine Creek (Fig. 3.10). Dutch authorities on the Delaware noted with some displeasure that Finns and Swedes had "small parcels of land . . . here and there."[98] In this manner they scattered rather widely through the drainage basin of the lower Delaware, penetrating "tolerably deep" inland along tributaries by 1659 and settling "about a day's journey" from each other.[99] By no means did all of the New Sweden settlers drift about in this manner, but a substantial number apparently did.

Longer-range movements, or true migrations, also occurred. The expansion to former hunting grounds on the eastern shore of the Delaware to establish a second major Savo-Karelian focus, around Finns Point, was described in Chapter 3 (Fig. 3.10). A bit later, in 1669, "Finnes" obtained permission to occupy a presumed earlier hunting ground to the south, along the Appoquinimink River and nearby Blackbird Creek in southern New Castle County, Delaware, but few actually settled there (Fig. 4.1). In fact, "Apoquemene" was described ten years later as a Dutch town.[100] It is nevertheless true that a faint trail of distinctive New Sweden surnames—in particular, Bankston, Justice, and Holston—leads southward down the Delmarva Peninsula all the way to Cape Charles, Virginia.[101] In any case, no major migratory thrust followed this coastal route.

Some early migration proceeded up the Delaware, in the direction of the falls, and by 1675, Finns lived higher on the river than any other whites.[102] However, a request several years later to settle at the falls, around present-day Trenton, was refused (Fig. 4.1). Among those denied permission was one Otto Swansen, who complained that he had "diverse children & but little land."[103] By this decision, the British rulers hindered migration along what might have become a major route of Savo-Karelian expansion— north along the river through the Delaware Water Gap. Though a scattering of Swedish surnames had appeared along this route by 1790, it remained unimportant for their migrations.[104] Earlier, however, under Dutch rule in the 1650s, some Delaware Finns had been invited to move northward to the lower Hudson River area along a route which, even a generation later, remained "but a footpath for men and horses."[105] Some apparently accepted this invitation, for Dutch records mention a certain drifting Finn, Mons Pietersen, who helped found Harlem in 1661 and soon thereafter

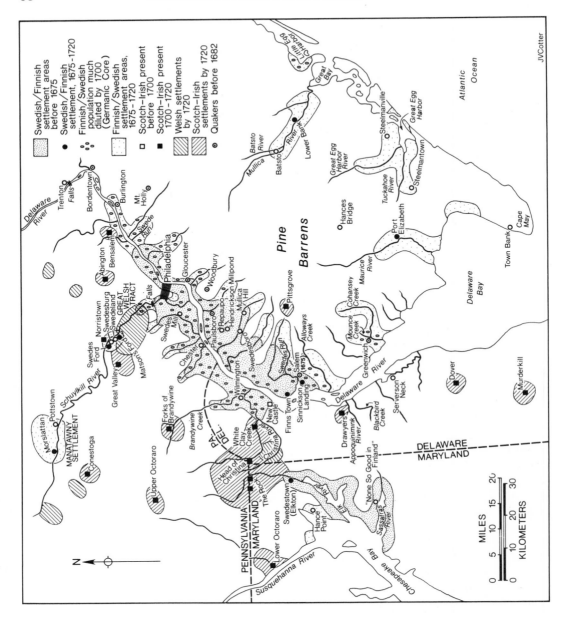

Fig. 4.1. The expanding Midland hearth, 1675–1720. Finns, Swedes, Welsh, and Scotch-Irish—fringe Europeans all—enjoyed close proximity as the Midland culture began rapidly to diffuse away from the Delaware Valley nucleus. (Sources: those listed for Fig. 3.10; and Clement 1893, pp. 84–86.)

colonized Elizabethtown in New Jersey. "Strong drink often made him abusive and violent," however, and eventually prompted his departure from New Netherland.[106]

Beginning in the 1670s, British officials looked more kindly upon those Finns and Swedes who wished to move northwestward up the valley of the Schuylkill River.[107] The presence of their distinctive surnames, such as Rambo, Yokum, Matson, Justice, Holston, and Lykins, as well as suggestive place names like Swedesburg, Swedes Ford, Swedeland, and Matson's Ford along the Schuylkill, document their occupation of the lower valley.[108] William Penn speeded up this Finnish/Swedish dispersal by granting the settlers a large tract above the falls in Upper Merion Township, near Norristown, on the south side of the river (Fig. 4.1). Before 1700, descendants of New Sweden's settlers had advanced beyond the falls of the Schuylkill, both in the lands assigned by Penn and in the Great Welsh Tract.[109] Even farther up the river another Swedish settlement had begun by 1704 in the Manatawny area, around present-day Pottstown (Fig. 4.1).[110] Collectively, the people who settled above the falls became known as the "upper inhabitants."[111] This Schuylkill route soon became one of the major arteries of American migration to the western frontier, connecting the Delaware River core to the Great Valley of the Appalachians.[112] That Swedish and Finnish settlers led the way up this route and stationed themselves along it is highly significant to the evolution of backwoods pioneering. The pivotal importance of the Schuylkill Valley in subsequent westward expansion is suggested by the fact that Daniel Boone and Stephen Holston, both legendary explorers and frontiersmen—and the latter also a New Sweden descendant—spent their formative years there.[113] Moreover, the Schuylkill Valley was a site and route of Welsh and Scotch-Irish settlement and migration (Fig. 4.1).

Most often the Finns and Swedes of the Delaware Valley did not ask permission for their long-range migrations, choosing instead simply to move beyond the jurisdiction of local Germanic authorities in the venerable Savo-Karelian way. Beginning in the early 1650s, Finns and Swedes ascended rivers from the Delaware coast, crossed the narrow neck of the Delmarva Peninsula, and entered the upper Chesapeake Bay region of English-ruled Maryland. There they established another waterside settlement area along the Elk and Sassafras estuaries (Fig. 4.1). The area may have been dominantly Savo-Karelian, for the likes of "Abraham the Finn" and "Marcus the Finn" settled there early, and one local pioneer farm acquired the truthful name "None So Good in Finland."[114] So many people fled away to "skulk" on the Chesapeake, including fifty in a two-week span in 1659, that alarmed Dutch officials reported population decline in the Delaware Valley. In the following several years, many more families of "Fins and Swedes" departed for Maryland.[115] Migration to the head of the Chesapeake Bay region continued for several decades, and even as late as the 1680s, Marylanders recruited Delaware Finns to come to their colony.[116] An account from 1697 suggests that the Elk River settlements retained a "Swedish" character throughout the remainder of the century. By about that time, some Maryland Finns or Swedes had moved farther westward, to the mouth of the Susquehanna (Fig. 4.1).[117]

The head of Chesapeake Bay, in common with the Schuylkill Valley, was strategically positioned to influence later westward migration. Many early eighteenth-century immigrants—in particular, the Scotch-Irish—disembarked at New Castle or Chester, then moved west into the Elk River country and beyond, to the Susquehanna. In so doing, they encountered the Savo-Karelian pioneer lifestyle.

A third major goal of early long-distance migration by New Sweden's population, across New Jersey, proved to be a cul-de-sac that played little or no role in the western frontier epic, but it does illustrate the extraordinary mobility of the old settlers. One route, following the path of earlier long hunts, led waterborne Finns and Swedes southeastward along the Jersey coast in the late 1600s to the outer coastal plain in the lower Cohansey and Maurice river valleys, to Cape May, and to certain other places (Fig. 4.1). As late as 1750, according to tax lists, as much as 40 percent of the Maurice Valley population was of "Swedish" descent. In contrast, some of their kinsmen struck out across the Jersey Pine Barrens and settled along several streams and bays on the east coast—in particular, Great and Little Egg harbors, Great Bay, and the rivers flowing into these inlets. The most prolific Finnish and Swedish families involved in the spread through southern New Jersey were the Mullicas, Steelmans, and Strangs. They left their surnames as toponyms in the area—most notably the Mullica River—and also provided the place name Batsto ("sauna") (Fig. 4.1).[118] Few ever escaped this cul-de-sac to participate in westward expansion.

Most early migration by Finns and Swedes in the Delaware Valley and adjacent areas was accomplished by boat, and their communities were waterside settlements, in the ancestral Savo-Karelian mode.[119] Local use of canoes, which perhaps were inspired by ancestral Finnish dugouts rather than Indian influence, and of boats, which seemingly revealed Swedish traits traceable to Viking times, persisted well into the eighteenth century. In 1732 three New Sweden descendants complained that weirs on the Schuylkill obstructed their canoe access to Philadelphia.[120] But in portaging the Delmarva Peninsula to reach the Chesapeake settlements and in trekking across Jersey, the Finns showed that they could also move overland, skills they had earlier demonstrated in the morainal interfluves of Sweden's Finnmarks. A traveler in 1679 encountered on a path near the falls of the Delaware "a Finland Man well hors'd," and the old inhabitants of New Sweden served as couriers for the Dutch on the trail to New York City.[121] Clearly, these people could migrate both by water and by land.

Genesis of Core and Periphery

The ability and propensity to migrate, in turn, facilitated in the Delaware Valley, well before the end of the seventeenth century, development of the classic pattern of core and periphery that would characterize the Midland cultural area until the frontier vanished two centuries later (Fig. 2.3). The flight of many of the Finnish-inspired old inhabitants of New Sweden before the later-arriving Germanic settlers—in particular, the Dutch, English, and Germans—rather early produced a segregation of sorts. By 1660 the Dutch were residing low on the Delaware, and one had to journey "up the river . . . to the Sweeds Plantations." [122] Decade by decade the Germanic core expanded and the Finnish/Swedish periphery retreated. Dutch officials noted that those settlers "who hold the ground-briefs would willingly dispose of them for a trifle," and such sales began in earnest in the 1660s. Selling out "at a very inconsiderable price," Finns and Swedes on the west bank of the Delaware moved upstream or over into Maryland and New Jersey. [123] Buyers were generally from places such as Hereford-shire in England, while sellers bore Swedish and Finnish sur-names such as Oelsen, Junsen, Colman, Jorissen, and Matsen. In the early 1680s, William Penn purchased the site of Philadelphia from three Swanson brothers, who in exchange were granted land in a more remote place. [124] In this manner, the Delaware west bank from New Castle to Philadelphia became, by 1690, a core region of Germanic, secondary settlement surrounded by a Finnish-based backwoods periphery (Fig. 4.1). The older, more stable, churchgoing element within the Swedish and Finnish population remained and was eventually absorbed into the Germanic postpioneer culture, but the younger, more mobile, volatile element, victimized by competitive exclusion, began a long retreat that would eventually end only at the Pacific. On the New Jersey side of the river, the inevitable displacement occurred later, except around Salem, perhaps in large part because the inferior quality of the land there made it less appealing to the Germanic eye.

Accompanying the core/periphery genesis in the Delaware Valley was a perceived we/they dichotomy. Such sentiment is clearly reflected in contemporary remarks by the Germanic successors concerning the original white inhabitants of the valley. Revealing a prejudice rooted far deeper than in mere ethnicity, one early Pennsylvania German declared that the "Old Settlers" included "many useless persons, the greater part being Swedes," who were "misguided" and habitually drunk. Core thus encountered periphery; stabilizing selection confronted diversifying selection; proper Germanic folk gazed with distaste upon a Finnish pioneer lifestyle. Similar—indeed, almost identical—disparaging remarks would follow the backwoods pioneers across the continent. Ever a subject of contempt and disgust, they would nevertheless open wooded America to the timid, "more civilised race" in the rear. [125]

Long after William Penn's arrival, the process of pioneer dis-

placement in and near the Midland cultural hearth continued. For
a short while, it retained a discernible ethnic stamp. For example,
about 1706 a certain John Hance Steelman, bearing one of the
distinctive New Sweden surnames, sold his "Small Improvement" in the disputed area between Maryland and Pennsylvania
to a British settler, then moved west to the lower Susquehanna in
Maryland, where he once again made "the first small Improvement" and "lived by virtue of his own pleasure," before selling
out again.[126] In short, not only did the old inhabitants of New
Sweden establish a viable woodland pioneering culture in the
Delaware Valley hearth of Midland America, but they and their
descendants established the practice of evacuation to escape the
Germanic secondary settlers. Later immigrants, including the
Scotch-Irish, could choose which of these alternatives—core or
periphery—suited them best, but the pattern was preset.

Community

While the prevalence of mobility, individualism, and the nuclear
family diminished the role of community on the Midland backwoods frontier, social life and mutual cooperation were by no
means eliminated. Indeed, so significant was the need for cooperation that one student of the settlement perimeter spoke, if hy-
perbolically, of the "myth of frontier individualism," and another
described the neighborhood as "one of the most basic associations
of rural frontier life." The early years of colonization witnessed a
high degree of community solidarity, and intermarriage strengthened the ties (Fig. 4.2).[127]

Mutual dependence was reflected in such communal work
gatherings as preparing burned clearings, husking corn, and raising cabins or barns. "They are obliged to have recourse to these
mutual aids and assistances, as they cannot procure sufficient la-
bourers," noted an Ohio traveler in 1797, the result being "a virtue
arising from necessity."[128] Upon completion of the labor, festivi-
ties commenced, though preparatory resort to alcoholic beverages
often began during the work. Many other gatherings were purely
social, with or without a formal excuse such as a wedding. Activities included dancing, drinking, horse racing, barbecues, gambling, sprinting, no-holds-barred fighting, target-shooting, and
tomahawk-throwing, often on a weekly basis.[129] A backwoods
wedding in western Pennsylvania was "a scene of wild and confused merriment," with "dancing to the music of a fiddle" among
a "hospitable and prodigal" people "much addicted to drinking
parties, gambling, horse racing, and fighting."[130]

In part such solidarity derived spontaneously and adaptively
from the chronic labor shortage that is typical of frontiers. Cooperation allowed certain tasks to be accomplished that were beyond
the ability of the individual family to achieve.[131] To a degree, this
communalism probably also grew out of the medieval European
village background. More specific cultural heritages are no doubt
reflected in the boisterous gatherings. Recreational fighting and

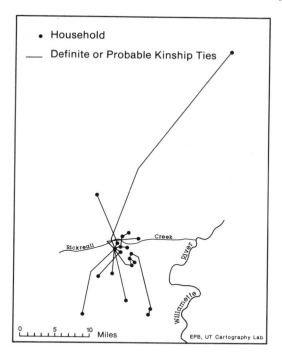

Fig. 4.2. Family clusters in a frontier rural community in the Willamette Valley, Oregon, 1850. (After Bowen 1978, p. 54.)

"striving" contests, in which competitors attempted prodigious feats of strength and endurance, belonged in the Old World tradition of the Scotch-Irish.[132] Communal "log-rollings" and cabin raisings, not to mention boisterous parties, had ample Finnish antecedents. The Kalevalan epic, in its exaggerated way, described how, in interior Finland, "the house is built just right," with "a hundred men ... engaged in raising it, a thousand busy on the roof."[133] In the Savo-Karelian areas in the 1500s, quasi-communal "work associations" arose, though more commonly behind the frontier than in new settlement areas.[134]

In these various ways, then, the American backwoods people preserved the fabric of a society worn thin by the frontier experience. In so doing, they probably drew upon their preadapted ancestral lifestyles in the several fringes of Europe, reinforced by the medieval communalism of the Germanic core.

Mixing and Intermarriage

The Midland American frontier was from the very first a zone of vigorous mixing in which ethnic groups did not long survive. Durable ethnicity was retained some distance to the west among the secondary wave of settlers, but backwoods pioneers, their society atomized, their attachment to place weak, and their choice of marriage partners limited, did not long remain ethnic. Attempts by some scholars to identify the pioneer stock as Scotch-Irish are misguided, for the backwoods culture reflected the sort of blending that perhaps only intermarriage can produce.

Mixing began in the Delaware Valley nucleus of the Midland

while it remained a frontier.[135] Initially, the cultural and genetic exchange in the valley served to collapse the several European ethnic groups introduced by the Swedish crown—Finns, Swedes, Frisians, Jutlanders, and Germans—into a composite group whose members, by 1690, were content to call themselves "Swedes," to speak a Gothic dialect, and to practice a Savo-Karelian pioneer lifestyle.[136] So thorough and firm was this fusing that later descendants of the Holston family, originally Jutlanders from the Dithmarschen area of Holstein, lost awareness of their German origin and referred to themselves as the "Swedish Holsteins."[137] The Yokums, derived from a Schleswig Dane or German, declared their Swedishness for generations by naming their sons "Swan" (Sven).[138] While discernible Savo-Karelian neighborhoods persisted for decades after the 1640s, intermarriage progressed rapidly and blended most of the old settler population into a single group by the end of the century. Representative of the new composite was the Holsteiner, observed near present-day Burlington on the Delaware River in 1679, who lived in a typical small Finnish log cabin with a northern European corner chimney.[139]

A wider mixing began with the arrival of other ethnic groups from Europe. The settlers derived from New Sweden displayed no determination to isolate themselves or to marry within their group.[140] The displacement associated with the formation of a core/periphery pattern in the valley proceeded slowly enough to allow a temporary overlap, so that Swedes for a time lived "scattered among the English and Quakers."[141] In that interval, newcomers married into the Swedish population. Some of the offspring of these mixings stayed to be absorbed into the core Germanic population, while others became "Swedes," or backwoods people. Early records reveal marriages of Delaware Valley Swedes or Finns to English settlers as early as 1644, to Dutch by 1656, Welsh by 1680, Scots by the 1670s, and Huguenots by 1656.[142] A visitor to the Savo-Karelian settlement along Maryland's Sassafras River in 1659 "found Abraham the Fin, a soldier who had run away from Christina [Wilmington] with a Dutch woman."[143] So muddied did the ethnic waters become that the Strang family of southern New Jersey no longer knows whether they were originally Swedish or Scottish, and a 1693 list of self-declared "Swedes" includes surnames such as Koenig, de Foss, Talley, van der Weer, Robertson, and Meyer.[144]

Nor was intermarriage the only device for mixing cultures. Indentured servants in the Delaware Valley often had different ethnic backgrounds than their masters. In the late 1670s and 1680s at Upland (Chester) and other places, for example, Oele Swensen and Lace Cock, both of the Swedish group, had servants named Richard Ducket and Benjamin Goodman, while their fellow Swedes Justa Justassen and John Svenson worked for Englishmen.[145]

One short-run result of contact and mixing was widespread multilingualism in the valley. Some of the old settlers could reputedly speak Swedish, Finnish, English, Dutch, and Welsh.[146]

English had become the local lingua franca by the middle 1670s, but it had absorbed Swedish, Dutch, and Indian loanwords such as *badstow* ("sauna"), *fly* ("marsh" or "meadow"), and *canoe*.[147]

In short, the early emergence of Germanic core and pioneer periphery in the Delaware Valley did not hinder a lively cultural and genetic exchange among the various European ethnic groups. The emerging multiethnic forest colonization culture could draw upon a rich diversity of ideas and practices.[148]

Mixing with Indians

On the Midland frontier, American Indians also participated in the blending of cultures and races. Much of the colonizing success of the backwoods culture rested on the pioneers' ability to absorb Indian ways. That is not surprising, since adaptation in a new land generally requires some accommodation of the aboriginal population. The Indians offered, among other things, new food plants, knowledge of the land, trade, different clothing types, familiarity with the use of wild plants, herbal cures, hunting skills, techniques of warfare, marriage partners, and "novel modes of life that . . . challenged the authority of old traditions."[149] In the final analysis, Indian wars were far less consequential on the American frontier than cultural exchange. The Midland backwoods pioneers, we suggest, were much more active and successful in this interplay than the New Englanders, southern planters, or French Canadians. The Puritans may have shared a first harvest festival with the Indians, and Pocohantas may have consorted with early Virginia planters, but only the Midlanders engaged in large-scale absorption of Indian ways into their adaptive strategy. French *couriers de bois* may have become Indianized, but they did not transfer their acquired traits to the Québec population at large. At the same time, Indians accepted more European artifacts and customs from Midlanders than from any other whites. Cherokees, Creeks, and Choctaws, living in the planters' Charleston hinterland, nevertheless accepted the Midland backwoods pioneers' log cabins.[150]

As a result, Midland whites and neighboring Indians had much in common along their zone of contact in the wooded east. The backwoods pioneers, for their part, exhibited "a half Indian appearance" and were "nearly allied in disposition and manners to an Indian." They took scalps in warfare, adopted corn as their principal food grain, often buried their dead beneath Indian-inspired grave sheds, and treated their ailments with Indian-derived herbal medicines.[151] Economically, trade with the Indians provided one of the lures and rewards of frontier life.

Familiarity and exchange fostered miscegenation on a large scale. References to interracial cohabitation and half-breeds on the backwoods frontier are far too numerous to list, and traders seem to have set the pattern in such undertakings.[152] Moreover, racial mixing was not much stigmatized in the backwoods. The tolerance that encouraged miscegenation is well illustrated in a "get acquainted dance" and dinner given by a white man and his Indian wife in 1861 on the Texas-Oklahoma border. Invitations went out on both sides of the Red River, to Chickasaws and Anglo-Texans alike, and over one hundred people attended. In the Memphis area along the Mississippi, whites by 1797 had "generally married into the Indian families," producing a race of "half-Indians" that was not extraordinary on the frontier.[153]

The results of frontier miscegenation were several. Considerable white blood entered the Indian population, to the extent that there are probably no pure Native Americans left today among the remnants of the eastern woodland tribes. In some other cases, the mixed-bloods assumed an ethnic identity of their own, forming groups such as the famous Melungeons of southern Appalachia.[154] But the most significant outcome of miscegenation was the introduction of partial Indian ancestry into a substantial part of the Midland "white" population (Fig. 4.3). The 1980 United States census revealed for the first time the massive extent of Indian blood among old-stock Anglo-Americans, particularly in the "primary domain" of Midland culture (compare Figs. 1.3 and 4.3). In Tennessee, Kentucky, West Virginia, Arkansas, and Missouri—the heartland of Midland culture—over five percent of the population reported partial Indian ancestry in 1980.[155] We must once and for all discard the myth of American Indian extermination and accept instead the fact that miscegenation was widespread on the Midland frontier and left a permanent mark on the genetic and cultural makeup of Anglo-Americans.

Such frontier mixing was not confined exclusively to Indians. Backwoods tolerance even permitted a black or mulatto wife, though such families were well advised not to be overtaken by the secondary, "better sort" of settlers.[156]

Why was the accommodation of Indian culture and absorption of Indian blood so much greater on the Midland frontier than elsewhere in the United States? Why did not the Puritan or southern planter draw as much upon the aboriginal population as the backwoods pioneer did in adapting to the American setting? Some have suggested that the Scotch-Irish made the crucial difference. The Ulster settlers' "ready adoption of Indian ways" was due in part to "their cultural background and lack of sophistication"— in short, their tradition of diversifying selection—and in part to their previous experience with Irish Catholic "wild natives" in Northern Ireland.[157] There is no doubt a measure of truth in this traditional view, but it is significant that the Scotch-Irish who settled the New England frontier around Londonderry in New Hampshire did not adopt Indian ways or become successful backwoods pioneers.

Instead, we propose, the Midland model for Indian relations was well established long before the Scotch-Irish appeared on the scene, having been accomplished by the old settlers of New Sweden.[158] Later-arriving Germanic immigrants and observers commented that Indians lived among the Swedes, that "the savages and our Swedes are like one people," and "the Swedes themselves

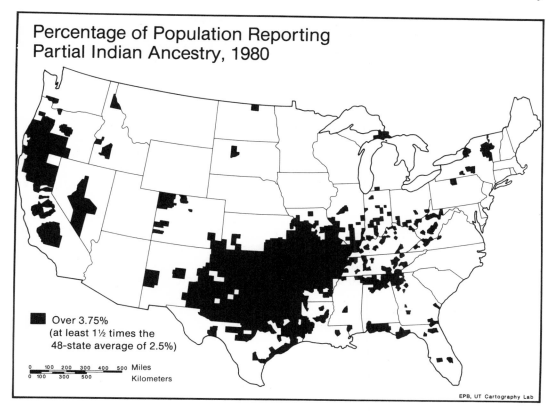

Percentage of Population Reporting
Partial Indian Ancestry, 1980

Over 3.75%
(at least 1½ times the
48-state average of 2.5%)

0   100 200 300 400 500 Miles
0   100   300   500   Kilometers

EPB, UT Cartography Lab

Fig. 4.3.   The Midland, and particularly Upland Southern, concentration of persons, by country, claiming partial Amerindian ancestry in 1980 is at once evident from this map. Clearly, certain other groups known to have Indian blood—in particular, Mexican-Americans and Cajuns—chose to deny such ancestry. (Sources: U.S. Bureau of the Census 1983a, pp. 15–20, 64–68; U.S. Bureau of the Census 1983b, vol. 1, chap. C, pts. 1–51; U.S. Bureau of the Census 1983c; U.S. Bureau of the Census 1983d, Table PA 16.)

are accused, that they were already half Indians, when the English arrived in the year 1682."[159] Similar remarks were later made concerning Midland backwoods pioneers. The local Delaware Indians called the Finns and Swedes *akoores* or *nittappi* ("friend," "fellow tribesmen," or "those who are like us"), acknowledging the similarity, and they had a different collective word, *senaares*, for the English, Germans, and Dutch, whom they properly regarded as alien.[160] No doubt the Savo-Karelians' familiarity with forests, shamanism, hunting, fishing, and slash-and-burn farming helped shape the Indians' view of the Finns as a kindred people. In 1656, when Dutch administrators attempted to block the disembarkation of Finnish immigrants from a ship anchored in the Delaware, local Indians forcibly interceded to allow them to land.[161] This affection and perceived similarity surely assisted cultural exchange between the two groups.

The settlers of New Sweden lived in close proximity to the Delaware Indians for several generations, and bilingualism became common.[162] The Finn Henry Coleman, one of the leaders of the 1669 insurrection, was "well verst in the Indian language,"

and both he and the Long Finn sought refuge among the Delawares when the uprising failed.[163] Various Finns and Swedes
served as interpreters when the English rulers dealt with the
Indians in the 1670s and 1680s. The language they used was a
Delaware-derived pidgin, distinctive to the lower river valley and
presumably partly developed by the Swedes and Finns.[164] Significantly, such pidgins were rare on the Anglo-American frontier,
which suggests that Indian-white cultural exchange was far live-
lier along the lower Delaware River.

More than similarity of lifestyle prepared the Delaware Valley
Finns to interact with the Indians, however. Their European experience with Lapps, or Saami, preadapted them for success in
such relations. For eight centuries before the migration to America, Finns engaged in fur trade with the Lapps, who were their
linguistic kin. The great Savo-Karelian expansion in Finland in
the 1400s and 1500s occurred at the expense of the Lapps, whose
northward retreat continues in the present century. In Sweden,
transplanted Savo-Karelians continued to live on or near the Lapp
frontier (Fig. 4.4). Figuring prominently in *The Kalevala*, Lapps
were alternately feared because of their powerful wizardry and
exploited because of their furs and land, but cultural exchange
and intermarriage were common.[165] Moreover, the Finns and Indians came from opposite ends of a great circumpolar belt of
northern forest shamanism, and their meeting was a confronta-
tion of two like peoples. Far better than the Scotch-Irish, the
Finns were culturally preadapted to life on the Indian frontier.
The Ulster pioneers may have been trained as good Indian haters
and fighters in Northern Ireland, but the Finns excelled in the sort
of cultural interaction with aboriginal people that facilitated successful adaptation.

Perhaps as a result of the close affinity between Indians and
whites in New Sweden, relations were basically peaceful and
Delaware remained forever after a synonym for friendly, acculturated Indians. Only rarely was a Finn or Swede killed by an Indian,
or vice versa, and even thievery was uncommon.[166] A Quaker administration in Pennsylvania assisted the continuation of peaceful relations for a considerable time. The Delaware Valley Europeans had far fewer conflicts with the Indians than did the Dutch,
French, Puritans, and Virginians.[167]

During this peaceful interlude, in the formative years of the
Midland cultural hearth, a vigorous cultural exchange occurred.
The Finns and Swedes acquired from the Indians corn and the
proper methods of its planting and preparation, gourds, pumpkins,
squash, turkeys, furs and skins, sassafras tea, bayberry candles,
herbal medicines, and maple syrup. They adopted wholesale the
Delawares' knowledge of edible and medicinal wild plants, preserving even the Indian names for them.[168] Many of these acqui-
sitions later became permanent fixtures in Midland backwoods
culture. In return, the Indians received livestock, fruit trees,
knowledge of log construction, firearms, liquor, beer, hardwares,
textiles, clothing, diseases, military advisers, and an occasional

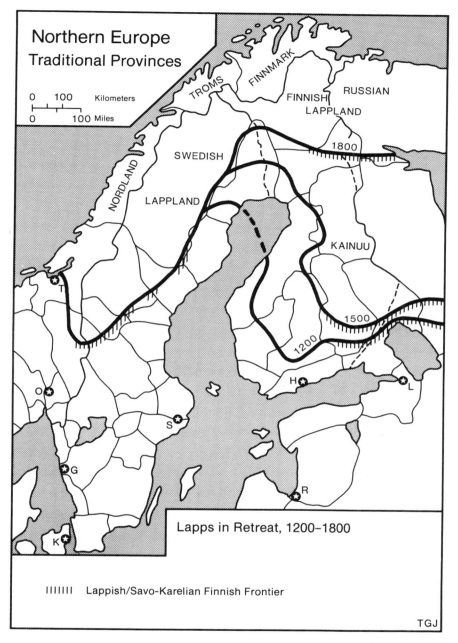

Fig. 4.4. The long-term relationship of Savo-Karelian Finns and Lapps was encouraged by proximity. Note that the most effective displacement of Lapps was accomplished by the Savo-Karelians. (Sources: Itkonen 1947, p. 55; Nickul 1977, fig. 7 following p. 134; Epstein and Valmari 1984, p. 160.)

bothersome Lutheran missionary.[169] Dirck Michielsen, a Finn, and Cornelis Martensen, a Swede, were jailed by the Dutch in 1656 for "having sold beer to the Indians," gaining release only when it became apparent that Michielsen and his companion had consumed most of the beverage in question.[170] William Penn later chided the Swedes, among others, for having "almost debaucht" the Indians with brandy.[171]

One key to the lively exchange between Scandinavians and Indians was a successful trade, carried on both with the Algonquian Delawares and the Iroquoian Susquehannocks behind them to the west.[172] Of crucial importance was the decision of the Swedish crown to permit the freemen among the colonists to trade directly with the Indians.[173] Among the most successful early traders was Jacob Swanson, active along the Delaware in the 1650s. Men derived from the New Sweden colony continued to be prominent in the business for several generations, well into the 1700s.[174] Perhaps the most famous latter-day "Swedish" trader was the previously mentioned John Hance Steelman (1655–1749), who for many years in the early 1700s operated a trading post at Elkton in Maryland, near the head of the Chesapeake Bay.[175]

Cohabitation and miscegenation began at least by the 1670s in the Delaware Valley, though the process was likely slowed by the fairly normal sex ratio in the Finnish population.[176] Later in the century, Indian children are recorded as living in certain Swedish homes on the Schuylkill, most notably the family of Peter Jacom (Yokum).[177] Certain southwestern New Jersey families still claim descent from a mixing of Swedes and Delaware Indians, and further suggestion of miscegenation is the appearance in the eighteenth century of probable Swedish-derived surnames such as Justice and Yokun (a possible corruption of Yokum) in Indian groups as far afield as Tennessee and New York.[178]

It was Finns and Swedes, then, who, well before the arrival of the Scotch-Irish, Welsh, and others, genetically dominated the Midland backwoods population, accepted much-needed cultural contributions from the American Indian, and set the pattern of mutual acculturation, trade, and tolerance that was essential to the piecing together of a successful woodland pioneer culture. The benefits of this mixing awaited the later settlers, who had only to observe the "half Indian" Swedes, positioned strategically on the major routes of migration, and retreat with them beyond the Germanic pale.

Conclusion

Backwoods society, clearly, derived from different sources. Indeed, its practitioners' principal genius may have been their ability to choose from diverse contributions. Our point is that a rudimentary social model for the Midland backwoods culture was fashioned by the first effective occupiers of the Delaware Valley—the people of New Sweden—by 1660, if not earlier. Almost any subsequent observer of the Midland backwoods pioneer would have found a very similar way of life in the early colonial Delaware Valley settlements. In terms of demography, individualism, institutional weakness, disrespect for authority, irreligiosity, mobility, boisterousness, and willingness to marry outside the ethnic group, the early Delaware settlers closely resembled later backwoods pioneers. Secondary Germanic immigrants made the same sort of disparaging remarks about the old settlers of New Sweden that followed the pioneers across the continent. A particular society had emerged along the Delaware—and only there—that was compatible with the later Midland frontier. Yes, the Savo-Karelians and their early neighbors and kinfolk were few in number, but then sparseness of population was itself a frontier attribute and necessity.

Another key to the success of the Midland colonization system lay in its agricultural practices. In Chapter 5 we turn to an analysis of the farming and herding methods of backwoods pioneers.

FIVE

BACKWOODS FARMING

*To fell the clearing he set forth
to a tall backwoods forest.*

Kalevala

The Midland American frontier can be categorized as agricultural, though the backwoods pioneers attained their livelihood through an unspecialized, land-extensive economic system only partly based in farming, a classic example of diversifying selection. Tilling, herding, hunting, fishing, and gathering all yielded some of the necessities of life, and crop raising was not invariably the most important food-producing activity. Reversion to a near-neolithic condition seems to have occurred, in which the cultivation of a small grain field and kitchen garden was left largely to women and children (Fig. 5.1).[1] While not independent of the market system, pioneer agriculture in the backwoods remained basically subsistent in nature.[2] Typical were the settlers of early Missouri, who "made a cornfield of a half-a-dozen acres and a truck patch," or those on the East Texas frontier, who lived in "a cabin in a little clearing where a few acres of corn were making a struggle for existence."[3]

Predictably, visitors from the eastern seaboard Germanic core heaped abuse upon the frontier farming practices. "They neglect, of course, the cultivation of the land," sniffed one New Englander, while another suggested that they "probably understood very little of agriculture" and that a diminutive field of an acre or two, together with the kitchen garden, "was the height of their ambition."[4] Even so, the same observers often concluded that the pioneers lived well. In fact, in some remote, hilly parts of the South, in the primary domain of the Midland culture (Fig. 1.3), many aspects of their agricultural system proved remarkably persistent.[5]

Clearing the Land

The initial settlers in the eastern United States demonstrated a preference for well-wooded country, shunning Indian oldfields and

Fig. 5.1. An early photograph of a pioneer farmstead and garden in Saint Charles County, Missouri, near Saint Louis. (Photo courtesy of the State Historical Society of Missouri, Columbia, with permission, with thanks to James M. Denny, who brought the picture to our attention.)

"openings" as sites for their fields. They often settled near the abandoned clearings of the former Indian residents, but only because those grassy areas provided good range for their cattle and attracted deer. Their colonization system, insofar as tillage was concerned, was geared to the clearing of forest land and to the burst of fertility produced by burning the felled trees. As a result, the essential tool of the backwoods pioneer was the steel felling ax, and skill in wielding it was vital in the task of forest colonization.[6] Axes served many purposes, both in clearing trees and in carpentry. Some pioneers even used the chopping ax to prepare planting holes in rooty ground or, farther west, in prairie sod.[7] They seemed to derive pleasure from wielding their axes to remove the forest, and nearly all apparently felt that clearing woodland was easier than breaking prairie sod.[8] In the final analysis, perhaps the greatest enduring legacy of the backwoods pioneers rests in their initiation of large-scale forest removal in the greater part of the temperate woodlands of North America, opening a wedge for permanent settlement of the land and providing a vehicle for manifest destiny.[9]

How did the Midlanders come by these skills? Certainly they owed little to the American Indians, whose paleolithic axes were inefficient tools for forest removal and placed the natives in a position of technological inferiority.[10] Indeed, steel axes were among the first European trade goods sought by Indians. Nor did Germanic core Europeans have much to offer.[11] The English ax more closely resembled a large hatchet, with a broad edge and narrow handle; it proved to be of little value in American forest clearance.[12] Similarly, the French ax was found to break consistently between the cutting edge and haft hole if used in clearing. Germans from the high Alpine valleys or the eastern Slavic borderlands—the central European areas where abundant woodland remained—were skilled axmen possessing fine tools, but they arrived late on the American colonial scene. Their Rhenish cousins, who preceded them and were neophytes at axmanship, could only wish in vain for Tirolers to help them clear the forests of Pennsylvania.[13] Claims that the Germans first introduced axmanship into the Delaware Valley are simply without substance.[14] The Dutch, even less adept with the ax, preferred to dike and cultivate tidal marshland in the American colony rather than clear forest, as did the Acadian French in Nova Scotia and the early South Carolina rice planters.[15] Incredibly, the Dutch at New Amsterdam in the 1650s actually imported timber from Norway.[16] Other immigrants, unwilling or unable to attack the forests, often settled on grassy Indian oldfields, sites that required manuring since the fertility was already partly exhausted.

The Scotch-Irish were similarly unhelpful. Ulster did retain substantial amounts of timber in the early 1600s, but these forests came under royal or aristocratic protection and were not the scene of colonization projects. Suggestions that the Scotch-Irish were "inured to work hard" with the felling ax in Europe must be rejected as groundless.[17]

In fact, only the Finns and Swedes, from a forested land, arrived in seventeenth-century North America possessing both a satisfactory ax and the ancestral skill to use it to clear woodland.[18] The very name given to the seminomadic Savo-Karelian burnbeaters was, as noted earlier, the "ax-wielders." Forest clearance in the Delaware Valley was begun by the citizenry of New Sweden, and the axmen were often specifically identified as Finns (Fig. 5.2). In 1646 alone, 397 axes were sent over to the colony from Sweden.[19] Dutch and English observers in the Middle Colonies repeatedly acknowledged the superiority of the northern European axmen. In 1683 an Englishman in Pennsylvania recorded his astonishment both at the size of American oaks and that "a Swead will fell twelve of the bigger in a day."[20] Thirty years earlier, a Dutch official in New Netherland declared that "Northerners," or Scandinavians, "are a people adapted to cutting down trees and clearing land, inasmuch as they are very laborious and accustomed to work in the woods."[21] In founding the new colony of Harlem in 1661, the Dutch employed several Delaware Valley Finns and Swedes, including one Cornelius Mathysen, a Finn, who "cut and cleared the primeval forest trees" at the settlement.[22] About the same time, the Dutch also hired "Swedes" to cut masts along the Delaware, and as much as a century later the skilled axmanship of the New Sweden descendants won them jobs as lumberjacks in the New Jersey Pine Barrens. Estate inventories from the early Delaware Valley settlements occasionally distinguish a Swedish type of ax, and one, dated 1673, mentions "2 Old Sweeds axes."[23] We suggest that both the Midland chopping techniques and the

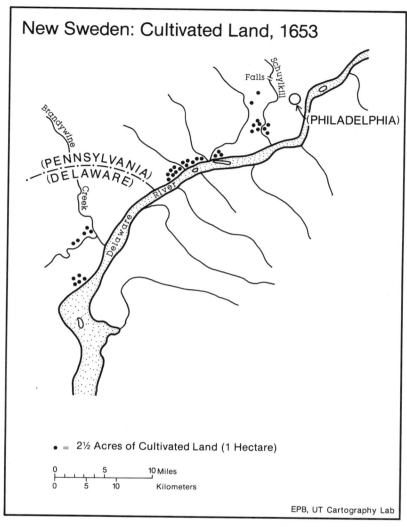

New Sweden: Cultivated Land, 1653

• = 2½ Acres of Cultivated Land (1 Hectare)

EPB, UT Cartography Lab

Fig. 5.2. It is not apparent from the records whether temporary or abandoned clearings are included here. Major agricultural expansion began in 1654, and the amount of cleared land reportedly doubled by the following year, as a large influx of Finns occurred. Data were converted from Swedish *morgen* at the ratio of 1 morgen = 0.63 acre. (Based on data in a 1653 list belonging to Governor Printz, as tabulated in Johnson 1911, vol. 2, pp. 526–27.)

American backwoods felling ax derive from the Savo-Karelian *kirvesmiehet* of New Sweden.

The ax work for a backwoods clearing was usually accomplished by the individual pioneer, working alone or with the help of his sons. A lone chopper could reputedly clear-cut an acre of virgin forest in seven to ten days.[24] Since pioneer fields rarely exceeded five or six acres in size, and were often no larger than one acre, the ax work was not excessively time consuming. Several basic methods were employed in forest removal. The simpler, though inferior, technique involved merely "deadening" the trees by chopping away a girdling strip of bark; the more laborious method required felling. Midland backwoodsmen often employed both techniques, chopping down the "more manageable" trees, under about 12 to 18 inches in diameter, and girdling the thicker trees.[25] Many, however, preferred to clear-cut the forest (Fig. 5.3), and a few relied solely upon the easier but less effective deadening method.[26] Clear-cutters sometimes engaged in "windrow felling," causing the trees to fall parallel in rows. Branches were trimmed from the downed trees and trunks cut into lengths of about 10 to 15 feet.[27]

The dead vegetation was then allowed to dry for several months or longer. In the next step, known as "logrolling," the seasoned timber was collected in heaps, together with underbrush. If some girdling had been done, the logs and brush were piled around the bases of the deadened trees. Logrolling exceeded the labor capacity of the backwoods nuclear family, requiring the assistance of perhaps as many as 18 to 20 neighbors. Fueled by hard liquor, boisterous social gatherings characterized many logrollings.[28]

The "hand-spike" was widely employed at rollings. Cut from a sapling 3 or 4 inches in diameter, the spike was about six feet long and had been shaped with a drawknife to taper toward each end to a diameter of only about one inch. When a log was to be moved to the pile for burning, teams of wielders, consisting of "a man to each end of every hand-spike," lifted and carried it.[29]

Fire, the second essential tool of the backwoods pioneer, was then set to the dried pyres and deadened trees. Alternatively, a preliminary, partial burning, prior to logrolling, could be made, followed a year or so later by a heaping of the remaining wood and a second firing. Burning served both to clear the new field of litter and to produce the ash that guaranteed a burst of fertility. For these reasons, "good burns" were essential to the ecologic restructuring of the clearing. It was at the firing stage that the inferiority of the girdling-only method became most evident, for this method allowed a much less complete rendering of dead wood into ashes. So inefficient was this Indian procedure that fertilizer, in the form of fish, had to be added at the time of planting. Clear-cutting had the added advantages of providing logs for the construction of buildings and fences, and also avoided the problem of dead branches falling on the grain crop. Frequently, however, the fires got out of control and burned deep into the living forest.[30]

Witnesses to the firing of a backwoods clearing were usually impressed by the spectacle. After a day of such burning, the "men looked like a lot of chimneysweeps," and the "log heaps, piles of brush, old stumps and other combustible materials were glowing with heat, and spreading an illumination over the plateau."[31]

So successful was the prevalent Midland system of forest removal, with its abundant reliance upon felling and the steel ax, that it had spilled well beyond the primary domain of backwoods culture by the late 1700s, into the immediate hinterlands of the

Fig. 5.3.   The Midland clear-cut method of land preparation, as seen about 1836 in southern Michigan. Stumps were not troublesome, since plows were not used. Note the worm fence. (From Nowlin 1883, p. 504.)

Yankee and the southern planter, permitting them at last to undertake effective forest colonization. New Englanders, who had initially insisted upon the tedious, slow, Germanic rooting out of forests and later, after about 1700, had adopted the crude deadening method, accepted Midland felling techniques beginning about 1760 in the backcountry of New Hampshire and Vermont.[32] Most likely the Midland method reached the New England frontier when Yankee soldiers who had gone south to fight in the French and Indian War returned, bearing Pennsylvanian ideas.

Abundant regional varieties of the Midland clearing technique are recorded in settler reminiscences and local histories. In interior South Carolina, for example, "the undergrowth was grubbed up and burned; the oaks, maples, dogwood, and hickories were cut down, split up, and hauled to the house for firewood; and the pines were belted or cut round and left to die."[33] In central Indiana, all trees less than a foot and a half thick were cut down, piled around larger, girdled trees, and fired. If the Hoosier did not intend to use the field immediately, he instead girdled the trees and waited until the following year to chop them down, roll the logs, and burn them.[34] The most common method in southern Ontario, where Midland backwoods pioneers formed the first wave of settlers, involved removing the underbrush, clear-cutting the trees, trimming branches, chopping the trunks into shorter sections, logrolling, and burning at a "branding bee."[35] In the New England back country, the recently adopted Midland methods produced, in the late 1700s, a clearing system in which the trees were clear-cut in June, at full leaf, and the opening was fired during the first dry weather of the following spring, usually in May. The larger logs not consumed by the blaze were then cut into shorter lengths, rolled into piles, and burned again. Alternatively, the blackened surviving logs could be split into fence rails.[36] In upstate New York, the clearing process began in May or June. First, underbrush was cut and collected in heaps; then small trees were axed and placed atop the brush piles, together with fallen dead limbs. The larger trees were then felled in windrows and cut into 14- or 15-foot logs. Through the summer months, the cleared vegetation seasoned, and firing occurred at the beginning of autumn. This initial burning only blackened the more sizable timbers, necessitating a sooty logrolling, piling, and second firing. By another Yorker calendar, brush was cut in the autumn, saplings were felled in the early spring, larger trees were cut down at the end of the maple sugar season, and firing was done in May, immediately before planting.[37]

Midland backwoods pioneers did not bother to remove the stumps that their system of clearing inevitably left in the fields (Fig. 5.3). Even in the Delaware Valley, as late as 1750, great stumps were "every where seen on the fields," and similar observations could be made wherever the Midlanders went as pioneers.[38] Stump removal was, rather, an obsession of the tidy, plow-oriented Germanic core folk. Through most of the seventeenth century, New Englanders insisted upon grubbing up every stump, with the result that their settlement frontier barely crawled forward. Even in later years, after they adopted Midland clearing methods and went west, the Yankees did not long tolerate such disorder, holding frontier "stumping bees" as soon as time permitted.[39] Assisted by time and rot, Quakers and Germans—the secondary settlers of the Midland primary domain—also eventually disposed of the stumps, but true backwoods settlers wasted no effort on so unnecessary a chore.

Shifting Cultivation

The clearings so laboriously won from the forest by the pioneers served them at best for three to five years. Crops thrived upon the burst of fertility derived from the ash, and regardless of how natively fertile the soil was, yields fell off rapidly after several harvests. In addition, weeds quickly became a problem that could be controlled only by a large investment in hoe labor. The backwoods pioneers had no ability or interest in restoring the productivity of the soil through manuring, and they refused to submit to a season of hard hoeing. Let their Germanic successors accomplish such intensifications of land use; the Midland pioneers preferred to make another clearing in a different place.

The result was a pioneer system of shifting cultivation, or land rotation. Many of the seemingly compulsive moves of the backwoods people, particularly the local ones, were in fact a perfectly logical outgrowth of the relocation of their fields. They chose to live in the middle of a clearing, unshaded by trees, where they were better able to protect the grain and garden from scavenging animals. If this required dismantling their cabin and dragging the logs to a new site nearby, they willingly did so.

Because the fields were so temporary, forest removal became magnified in importance. Backwoods clearings were small, but the pioneers relocated them so often that considerable acreages of woodland had been destroyed by the time the secondary settlers appeared on the scene. So abundant was land, however, that the backwoods farmers always had ash-richened virgin soil to cultivate and did not have to return to oldfields. Only after the frontier era had passed did the pioneer system of shifting cultivation evolve into a less satisfactory bush-fallow sequence, in which the farmer had to use land "pretty well recovered" from previous cultivation. Such a system was found in parts of the Delaware Valley by the middle of the eighteenth century, but it persisted primarily in the mountain districts of the South.[40]

Most contemporary and modern observers have condemned Midland pioneer shifting cultivation as destructive, the cause of "rapid environmental deterioration," and have branded its practitioners as "land butchers" or "miserable farmers."[41] Even their latter-day kin sometimes joined the chorus of condemnation, calling Tennesseans, for example, "a race of destroyers" who "made no effort to restore the humus to the soil."[42] Backwoods pioneers themselves occasionally acknowledged ruefully the modifications they had wrought. One aged former Texas pioneer, residing on the far western edge of the wooded country, beyond which lay the great prairies, lamented the environmental changes that had occurred since he had first seen the land seventy years earlier. "How beautiful it looked," he recalled, referring to the virgin post-oak forest he had helped colonize in his youth. "Old as I am, if I could hear of another country just like it," a land that "needed to be settled up in the same way, I would go to it."[43] Such criticism and lament miss the point, however. The Midland system of clearance and cultivation facilitated the rapid transformation or restructuring of the forested habitat, thereby providing the key to the sweeping advance of the Anglo-American frontier and opening the way for the secondary settlers. By necessity, the system was destructive, and it makes no sense to apply, retroactively, a twentieth-century conservation ethic to the issue of pioneering.

What was the alternative? We can catch a glimpse of it on New York's early eighteenth-century Mohawk frontier, where a group of German Palatines hung on grimly and "continued to manure & to sew the Land that they might not be starved for want of Corn & food," all the while begging for government assistance.[44] Such Germanic core folk were incapable of pushing the settlement frontier rapidly forward, though their farming techniques were certainly more conservational than those of the backwoods people. Had Palatines, Yankees, or planters led the way, the United States might have remained an Atlantic littoral state, an eastern ethnic enclave like French Québec.

Origins of the System

The beginnings of the Midland backwoods system of fell-and-burn shifting cultivation have been debated for decades. Most likely they were multiple. Prevalent or exclusive use of girdling, as opposed to felling, has almost universally been attributed to American Indian influence, and this claim is surely valid.[45] The eastern woodland tribes produced deadenings in better-drained parts of the forest with their stone hatchets, selecting areas with loose, well-drained, easily worked soils. Relying heavily upon dead brush and leaf mold to fuel their fires, they planted among the skeletons of the trees.[46] Those who adopted the Indian deadening method, including settlers on the English frontier of Virginia, many New Englanders, and a few Midlanders, acknowledged their cultural debt by referring to "tomahawk improvements." Use of the word *tomahawk* suggests Delaware Indian influence, since that loan word is derived from their language.[47] Perhaps most often deadening was employed to meet quickly the minimal requirements of land preemption or, in New England, to produce pasture and meadow rather than cropland.[48] Some scholars have gone so far as to attribute the entire backwoods system of shifting cultivation to the Indians, but such a claim oversimplifies the issue and is incorrect.[49] In particular, it slights the importance of the steel ax, felling, logrolling, and the fuller rendering to ash made possible by clear-cutting. Backwoods farming was more complex, destructive, and productive than the Indian type.

Defenders of the Scotch-Irish have stepped into this breach. Pioneer shifting cultivation, they say, derived from the *runrig* system of the Celtic highlands, in which the cultivated area was divided between a small, continuously cropped, heavily fertilized *infield* and an expansive bush fallow, or *outfield*, only a small part of which was tilled in any given year.[50] The Celtic outfield supposedly provided the model for backwoods land rotation, since the fields there were relocated every three to five years, allowing the land to rest for a decade or more before another crop was planted. In point of fact, however, the Celtic practice bore only a superficial resemblance to Midland pioneer techniques, since it relied very heavily upon the produce of the infield, involved no forest clearance whatever, and brought no virgin land into cultivation.[51] *Runrig* may have preadapted the Scotch-Irish to accept Midland American shifting cultivation, but it provided a largely inadequate model for New World practices.

Recognizing these problems, scholars in a variety of academic disciplines have begun to attribute the more effective Midland clearing techniques to the burnbeating Finns and Swedes of the early Delaware Valley frontier.[52] We certainly agree with this new, if tardy, orthodoxy and suggest that the prototype for backwoods forest clearance and shifting cultivation arose in the New Sweden nucleus of the Midland culture before 1655, drawing heavily upon Savo-Karelian methods. *Huuhta* and *kaski* techniques, from distant Ladoga's shore, assisted American manifest destiny.

In northern Europe, forest clearance and burnbeating were practiced by many Finns and Swedes alike, representing a neolithic survival on the European fringe. It was the Finnish system, however, that more closely resembled the subsequent Midland American type. For the Swedes, shifting cultivation was only one part of an infield/outfield pattern very similar to that of the Celtic lands. The Swedes relied mainly upon the fertilized valley infield, or *inmark*, and used burnbeating principally to create high pasture land in peripheral hilly areas. Indeed, by the 1600s, the outfield, or *utmark*, was rarely used for crops; it had become almost exclusively a zone for pasturage and hay cutting. In contrast, traditional Savo-Karelian Finns derived all of their crops from shifting cultivation and possessed no infield at all.[53] Later generations of Swedes, speaking for the Germanic core of Europe, would refer smugly and contemptuously to the Finnish methods as "primitive."[54]

Finnish burnbeating bore a startling resemblance to the American backwoods type. Clear-cut felling with a steel ax, girdling of larger trees, windrowing, branch trimming, logrolling, and stump retention all were Savo-Karelian practices.[55] Accidental forest fires often resulted from the burning, even though the Finns, like their American counterparts, took care to fell the trees inward, creating a firebreak.[56] Accusations of excessive environmental destruction followed the Finns no less than the American backwoods pioneers.[57] A rapid expansion of the cleared area occurred, in common with the New World pattern . In the Finnish-settled districts of Dalarna Province in central Sweden, about 280 acres of forest per year were removed by the small population of Savo-Karelian burnbeaters between the 1630s and the 1660s. As in America, the clearings possessed a monetary value even when the ax-wielders did not own the land.[58]

Perhaps the essential trait of Finnish burnbeating that facilitated transferal to North America was versatility. Eighteenth-century accounts enumerated no fewer than eight different methods, each bearing a distinctive name and suited to a particular kind of land or vegetative cover.[59] The *huuhta* type, described in Chapter 3, provided a key to the explosive expansion of the Savo-Karelians through interior Finland and Sweden after 1400 and was suited to microthermal coniferous virgin forests. It alone, however, would be an inadequate model for the occupation of mesothermal deciduous woodlands in Midland America, though it probably served well those Finns who drifted east from the Delaware Valley into the New Jersey Pine Barrens (Fig. 4.1). Instead, the previously mentioned *kaski* system, used in northern Europe on virgin deciduous and mixed woodlands and on second-growth deciduous forests 30 to 50 years old, offers a more satisfactory prototype.[60] *Kaski* and Midland American backwoods techniques are very much alike. The *kaski* farmers felled trees in late summer or early fall, lopping off the larger branches, still at full leaf, and spreading them over the new clearing. Firing occurred early the following summer—a far shorter interval than in the *huuhta* system—and flaming tree trunks were rolled over the ground to ignite as much of the leaf mold as possible. Summer grain was then planted. In the following year, incompletely burned logs were dragged and rolled into piles and a second firing was accomplished. Such fields could produce not only rye—the only *huuhta* grain—but also barley and oats, with turnips interspersed, and the *kaski* clearing lasted for three or occasionally even as many as seven or eight years instead of the one or two harvests of the *huuhta* field.

We believe that the Savo-Karelian Finns on the Delaware in the 1640s interpreted the local virgin deciduous woodland as being better suited to *kaski* methods. The very purpose of *huuhta* was to convert coniferous forest to a secondary deciduous woodland, in order that the "normal" *kaski* system could be installed.[61] Even so, the Delaware Valley ax-wielders were unwilling to abandon all *huuhta* practices, in particular their preference for virgin land, the girdling of some larger trees, and their habitual mobility. The resultant mixed system, more *kaski* than *huuhta*, was quite consistent with the proven Savo-Karelian ability to modify their burnbeating system to meet new environmental conditions, and represented an adaptive reward for their well-demonstrated tendency to retain a versatile, diverse set of practices. Nothing in Midland American land preparation was not present in one or another of the ancestral Finnish types of burnbeating. The Savo-Karelians' task along the Delaware involved little more than reaping the benefits of traditional diversifying selection by fashioning a new hybrid system to fit the deciduous virgin woodland. The achievement of this hybrid lay well within the range of their abilities.

Evidence that the Finns did, indeed, develop the new system, and quickly, in the Delaware Valley is provided by colonial records. Their residential mobility, discussed earlier, bore the mark of *huuhta*. Swedish governor Johan Rising reported in 1654 that "a part of the old freemen have requested new lands" a scant decade or even less after establishing their first farms.[62] They desired to sell their existing improvements to newly arrived settlers, but found little market, since the latecomers also were mainly Finns. Even as late as the 1680s, the ratio of improved acreage to total landholding size among the Delaware Valley Finns and Swedes averaged only 1:21, suggesting that they had not yet been forced to clear second-growth forest, but retained the *huuhta* preference for virgin timber.[63] At the same time, the farmers of New Sweden were able to satisfy their craving for the more diverse grain yields of *kaski* and to enjoy the longer productive period of that system. In the 1640s and 1650s, both before and after the Dutch takeover of the colony, local observers recorded that a *kaski* crop regime was being practiced. Mention was made of certain burned clearings planted, in one case, to "rye and barley" and in another to barley alone. Turnips also were raised in the early years. These records must be regarded as conclusive proof that a *kaski* crop association had been established. Similarly, documented references to Finns and Swedes abandoning cultivated clearings in the Brandywine Creek area in the 1660s after harvesting four crops also point to *kaski* rather than *huuhta* as the system being employed.[64]

The devotion of Delaware Valley Finns to the extensive land use and labor minimization inherent in shifting cultivation is suggested by their 1675 uprising against an English edict that they dike the tidal marshes near New Castle.[65] The riot was futile; *kaski* farming had no place in the evolving Germanic core.

Our conclusion, then, is that a diversified northern European adaptive system, implanted through relocation diffusion by a certain ethnic group in one particular segment of the colonial frontier, yielded some essential traits of American backwoods agriculture. Particularistic cultural ecology, linked to a study of ethnicity and diffusion, paves the path to our conclusion. In this context, it is interesting to note that one normative cultural ecologist, viewing precisely the same similarity between Savo-Karelian and Midland American pioneer shifting cultivation, concluded instead that the agricultural colonization of *all* middle- and high-latitude forests would spontaneously and inevitably proceed in this manner.[66] Normative cultural ecologists thus render a universal out of the unique, remain blind to the roles of heritage and diffusion, and reinvent the doctrine of environmental determinism. Our response is that successful adaptation rests firmly upon the base of preadaptation, and the necessary skills cannot simply materialize in response to stress. Fortuitous diffusion, not necessity, provides the key.

Fencing the Clearing

Enclosure of the fired clearing was necessary for protection of the crops from open-range livestock, and fences were built as a normal part of the clearing process. Medium-sized trees suitable for fencing material were spared in the burning of the clearing, cut into suitable lengths, and dragged to the edge of the field. There they were split into "rails," using wedges and employing the blunt side of the ax as a mallet. Depending upon the diameter of the logs, they were split into halves, fourths, or eighths, and about eight hundred rails sufficed to fence an acre. Sometimes whole, unsplit logs from small trees were used to construct worm fences.[67]

The favored and almost universal style for field enclosures was the famous "worm" or "snake" rail fence, consisting of a zigzag stacking, in panels usually six to eleven rails high and meeting at an angle of about 60°. No posts were required, since the worm fence gained its stability from the tripod principle, and the simpler type also contained no lateral supports, depending upon grav-

Fig. 5.4. A stake-and-rider worm fence built of cedar (juniper) bordering a corn field near the community of Bee Cave in the Texas Hill Country near Austin. The scene could well have been in pioneer times. (Photo by T.G.J., 1968.)

ity alone for survival (Fig. 5.3). To add strength, many pioneers placed two diagonal stakes at each joint, set against the ground at about a 45° angle, leaning against the top rail of the fence, and crisscrossed in an X shape. Then an additional rail or two, called "riders," were placed atop the crossed stakes to lock the joint (Fig. 5.4).[68] The resultant worm fence, called a "stake and rider" type, could resist the shoving pressure of livestock and high wind much better than the simpler variety. If round, unsplit logs were used, a slight notching provided the needed lateral strength at the joints, and stakes and riders were not required.

Wherever the Midland pioneers went, even to Ontario, Oregon, and British Columbia, the "usual kind" of enclosure surrounding their fields was this "rough zigzag log fence" (Fig. 5.5). From 1844 to 1986, the seal of the General Land Office of Texas depicted a worm fence. Multiple adaptive advantages of this type of enclosure explained its popularity on the frontier. It was made of an abundant raw material, did not require morticing, hardware, or post holes, and could be erected quickly and cheaply with a minimal expenditure of labor in comparison to other fence types. No gates were needed, since the field was entered "by pulling down a corner of the fence."[69] The rails could easily be disassembled and taken to a new clearing when a field was abandoned. Following a harvest, the worm fence could easily be thrown down in several places to allow stock to forage on straw, husks, and weeds.[70] Rail fences were not too durable and had to be rebuilt, on the average, once every 12 to 15 years, but that hardly concerned the mobile backwoods folk.[71] The pioneer rarely took the trouble to place flat rocks under each joint, a procedure that retarded rotting of the lower rails; instead, such enterprise was left to the secondary settlers.[72]

Backwoods pioneers also built a crude livestock pen using the worm-fence principle. Instead of zigzagging at each joint, the rails or logs were laid in such a way as to form a polygonal enclosure. Some pens of this type still survive in the Rocky Mountains (Fig. 5.6).

The origin of the worm fence has long been debated. Some, completely without evidence, have wrongly attributed it to the American Indian, overlooking the fact that the natives lacked the tools to cut tree trunks to the proper lengths or split them into rails, and ignoring early accounts describing Indian corn fields in the eastern seaboard area as "unfenced on all sides."[73] Some others have fallen back on the tired, if convenient, notion that pioneer innovation explains the worm fence.[74] Even the original regional cultural affiliation has been confused by the popular term "Virginia worm fence."[75] In fact, the documentary evidence points very clearly to a Midland origin, as does a map of the fence's later distribution (Fig. 5.5). The earliest known worm fence dates from 1685 in the Delaware Valley, on Alloway's Creek near Salem, New Jersey, only a few miles from the Savo-Karelian settlement around Finns Point (Figs. 3.10, 4.1).[76] Numerous other documents reveal that rail fences, sometimes clearly identified as the worm type, existed in the Middle Colonies in the 1600s and 1700s.[77]

By contrast, the traditional pioneer fence of New England consisted of massive uprooted stumps laid on their sides, a glorious tribute to the Germanic obsession with tidy fields. Yankee stump fences became an unfailing sign that New Englanders rather than Midlanders inhabited an area. Early Chesapeake planters built woven fences or "rail palings" set vertically in the ground.[78] The pre-plantation Irish in Ulster used portable picket and brush fences to enclose fields, but these offer no viable prototype.[79]

Amandus Johnson, a historian, was the first to approach the correct explanation when he attributed the Midland worm fence to the early Swedish settlers on the Delaware.[80] In fact, the zigzag rail fence is not Swedish, but rather an ancient, archaic Finnic type called *perkka-aita*, vestiges of which remain among the Lapps and Savo-Karelians (Fig. 5.7). In the Finnskog burnbeating areas of Värmland and Hedmark, as well as in interior Finland, archaeological research has occasionally revealed a zigzag tracing on the perimeter of long-abandoned *huuhta* clearings, perhaps the remains of trees felled in an oblique pattern, the so-called "Finn's fence." A field survey of traditional fence types undertaken by Nordiska museet staff in Sweden earlier in this century yielded one respondent from a Finnish parish in Värmland who recalled that zigzag rail enclosures were formerly used there in cases where the fence was frequently relocated, as in the practice of shifting cultivation and the construction of snow baffles.[81] The respondent's sketch leaves no doubt that a worm fence was being

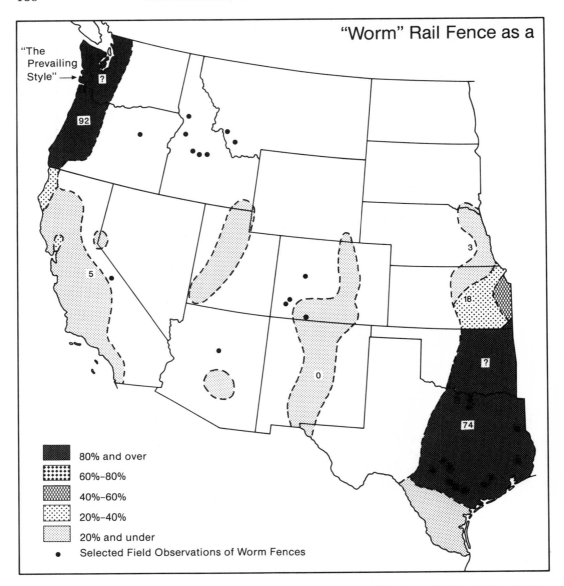

Fig. 5.5. The distribution of the worm fence was remarkably widespread by 1870. Clearly, it had made the transition from the early pioneer culture to the later period. The number shown in each state reveals the statewide proportion of worm fences in 1870 as a percentage of all fences observed. United States data are

described, and as a result a detailed drawing of such an enclosure appeared in the questionnaire subsequently developed by the museum staff.[82] Worm fences made of small round logs have been photographed in Swedish Lappland (Fig. 5.7), and though none survive in the Finnskog or interior Finland, rail-splitting is still practiced there (Fig. 5.8).

The Lapps long used the zigzag fence to direct game during hunts, and the Savo-Karelians may have adopted the idea in their expansion through Savo and Häme. The Lapps and Savo-Karelian Finns also built polygonal enclosures to serve as reindeer pens and

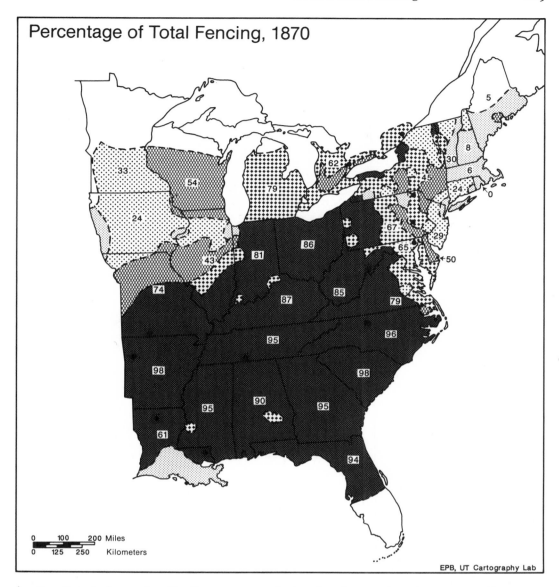

Percentage of Total Fencing, 1870

0 100 200 Miles
0 125 250 Kilometers

EPB, UT Cartography Lab

for 1870; Ontario data are for 1881. Some states were broken down by counties, others were not. Data were liberally interpreted. (Sources: U.S. Department of Agriculture 1872, pp. 498–507; Norris 1982, p. 46; and sundry later field observations.)

tent frames that are essentially identical to the pioneer American type (Fig. 5.9, sketch A).[83]

Stakes and riders also are part of the northern European and Finnish tradition (Fig. 5.9, sketch B).[84] These supports can be applied to types of enclosure other than the worm fence, as for example the minor Midland American type known variously as the "Swede" or "buck" fence, consisting of rails laid at a slant, with one end resting on the ground and the other upon the crisscrossed stakes, where they constitute riders.[85] An identical fence, called *sorkka-aita*, is part of the Savo-Karelian tradition (Fig. 5.9, sketch

Fig. 5.6.   American pioneer polygonal corrals of the round-log, worm type, in Beaverhead County, Montana. Such pens are essentially identical to a traditional Finnic type in northern Europe. (Photo by T.G.J., 1987.)

Fig. 5.7.   The simplest type of round-log worm fence, without stake-and-rider supports. This example is located in the parish of Gällivåre, Swedish Lappland. (Photo courtesy of Nordiska museet, Stockholm, arkiv, no. 424Kak, used with permission.)

Fig. 5.8. Rail-splitting with ax and wedges by Finns in central Sweden, 1912. (Photo by Nils Keyland, courtesy of Nordiska museet, Stockholm, arkiv, no. 15Ag, used with permission.)

B), and the Midland name "Swede fence" commemorates its northern European origin. In addition, stake-and-rider rail fences built as superstructures above low stone walls occur occasionally both in Sweden and in America, though not as a pioneer type.[86] Put briefly, every element of the backwoods worm fence and related minor types is abundantly present in the northern European tradition.

The worm fence is one example of pioneer material culture that survived the frontier era and became part of the landscape of secondary settlement. So common did it remain in the 1870s that it was designated "the national fence."[87] Some examples survive today in the countryside of various states (Fig. 5.4).

Other traditional types of enclosure competed for backwoods acceptance, though none challenged the dominance of the worm fence. Another minor variety was the "log" or "chock and log" fence, built of long spans of unsplit logs notched at each end into short pieces, or chocks, about two feet in length.[88] The chocks met the logs at right angles, looking in every respect like the corners of a log cabin. At their opposite ends, the chocks were notched into the next span of logs, causing the fence to jog back and forth in a crenelated manner. Chock-and-log fences were rarer than rail fences on the frontier, but some can still be observed in

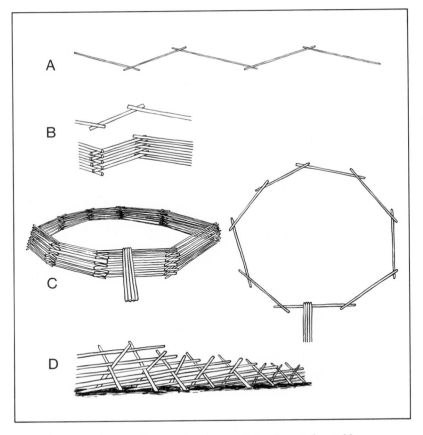

Fig. 5.9. Selected Finnic fences. Key: **A** = traditional type of portable worm fence consisting of round, lightly notched logs, from Gräsmark in the Värmland Finnskog, sketched over fifty years ago from memory; **B** = worm fence in Sweden, labeled type 20c in a Nordiska museet survey; **C** = Lappish worm-fence corral, Inari area, Finland; D = stake-and-rider Savo-Karelian fence from a clearing in the Pieksämäki area, Savo, of the type known in Pennsylvania as a "Swede" or "buck" fence. (Sources: for A and B, Nordiska museet, Stockholm, arkiv, "Hågnader," vol. 1, p. 157, and vol. 2, illus. preceding p. 1; for C, Itkonen 1948, vol. 2, p. 64; for D, Grotenfelt 1899, p. 183, and Fletcher 1950, p. 85.)

the Rocky Mountains, most notably in Beaverhead County, Montana (Fig. 5.10). Fences identical to the American chock-and-log appear widely in Sweden and appear to be more closely related to ethnic Swedes than to Finns.[89]

Ranking second only to the worm fence in the Midland tradition was the "straight-rail fence," also called a "stake and rail" or, in parts of the South, a "post and rider" or "post and rail."[90] The rails were held in place laterally at the joints by two vertical stakes or posts, one on each side (Fig. 5.11). Sometimes the rails rested on withes affixed to each pair of stakes, and a capping was occasionally affixed to the top, connecting the stakes and locking the rails into place. The chief advantage of the straight-rail fence was greater strength, which led pioneers to use it most commonly to

Fig. 5.10. A chock-and-log fence bordering a pasture near the town of Jackson, Beaverhead County, in the Montana Rockies. Never common on the backwoods frontier, this fence type is of Swedish origin. (Photo by T.G.J., 1987.)

Fig. 5.11. A straight-rail or "post and rider" fence enclosing a livestock pen in the Hill Country of central Texas. Wire withes support some of the rails. (Photo by T.G.J., 1984.)

Fig. 5.12. A straight-rail fence with horizontal rails, around a farmyard in Iitti Parish, Häme (Tavastland) Province, Finland. (Photo courtesy of National Museum of Finland, Helsinki, Archives, no. 1945.1, used with permission.)

build cow pens. Though part of Midland American material culture, the straight-rail fence in almost identical form also appears among the French in Québec and in northern Mexico. It may have reached these bordering culture areas by diffusion.

The Midland variety of the straight-rail fence, at least, has roots in the Delaware Valley and appears to be part of the same northern European tradition that provided the worm, Swede, and chock-and-log types. In Europe, Swedes and coastal Finns most often built straight-rail fences out of birch saplings and slanted the rails, so that one end rested on the ground and the other upon a withe. This slanted rail variety seems less directly related to the American type than is a fence common among Savo-Karelian Finns, in which the rails lie horizontally and more sizable timbers are often used (Figs. 3.2; 5.12; and 5.9, sketches C, D).[91] A similar fence appears in some valleys of the Germanic Alps, but not in areas known to have provided immigrants to colonial America.[92] In any case, it is known that the early settlers of New Sweden built straight-rail fences, though all of them had disappeared by 1750.[93]

The kinship and common origin of the straight-rail and worm fences is strongly suggested by an intermediate type found widely in Midland America. Its rails are laid in a zigzag pattern, like the worm fence, but pairs of vertical stakes set in the ground reinforce each joint, as in the straight-rail type.[94] A particularly notable concentration of this fencing survives along U.S. Highway 220 at the border between Highland County, Virginia, and Pendleton County, West Virginia, and others can be seen in the Rocky Mountains. Another, highly significant specimen encloses a hog pen on

Elk Neck, near the Elk River estuary in the old Finnish-Swedish settlement area at the head of the Chesapeake Bay (Fig. 4.1).[95]

In sum, both major and minor pioneer fence types in Midland America seemed to have northern European, largely Savo-Karelian antecedents. Material culture thus provides valuable corroborative evidence concerning the importance of Finnish influence in the backwoods agricultural system. The fences, in common with the techniques of clearing and firing, possessed preadaptive advantages on a forested frontier which facilitated acceptance by the Midland population at large.

Crop Selection

In the small field and garden that occupied the fenced clearing, backwoods farmers raised a simple, adaptable variety of food and feed crops. The field was devoted to grain, almost universally corn.[96] "It is by the culture of Indian corn that all those who form establishments commence," noted an observer among Ohio Valley backwoods pioneers about 1800. "No attention is paid by the inhabitants to any thing but the culture of Indian corn," he added, with some exaggeration.[97] From this versatile crop the pioneers derived roasting ears, boiled corn, bread in the form of "Johnny cakes" or pones, hominy grits, whiskey, and a little feed for horses and poultry.[98] The preeminence of corn as the backwoods grain crop had an ecological basis. It often produced a thousandfold increase, growing prodigiously to a height of 15 feet in minimally prepared ground among the stumps and roots of the newly burned clearing. Corn produced four times as much food per unit of land as wheat from a tenth the seed and came to harvest in a shorter time span. Raised in the usual mound system of cultivation, corn required no plowing or tilling, demanded less labor and no tools in harvesting, could be gathered over a much longer time span than the small grains, and was easily preserved through the winter in its waterproof husk.[99] In short, corn produced more grain for far less labor than its competitors, and as a result has been called one of the three keys to the success of the Midland frontier, together with log construction and the long rifle. Had the Midland pioneers relied upon wheat rather than corn, "it would have taken them a hundred years longer to reach the Rockies."[100] New Englanders, who quickly replaced corn with their traditional Germanic grains, further handicapped themselves as pioneers in so doing.[101]

Even though corn was often the only grain raised on pioneer farms, so that many "had never known what wheaten bread was like," some of the European small grains occasionally found a place in backwoods clearings.[102] In early western Pennsylvania settlements, for example, "a little wheat," oats, and rye competed for space in the new fields.[103] "Monongahela rye" became a frontier currency of sorts in some Midland frontier areas, duplicating a venerable New Sweden custom, and we should not forget that whiskey in the Pennsylvania-Ontario tradition is made from rye rather than corn.[104] Rye, ground "fine with the pole of an axe on a smooth stone," also provided a favored form of frontier ersatz coffee.[105] Wheat and rye were sometimes sown and harvested together on Pennsylvania frontier farms, producing a mixed flour called *meslin*. Bread was occasionally made from a mixture of flour and corn meal called "rye and Injun."[106] In the later hill-farming system of Appalachia, which retained many features of backwoods agriculture, oats, rye, barley, and buckwheat all were raised, though corn was far more important.[107]

Fields were not devoted entirely to grain. A system of intertillage, in which squash, pumpkins, or watermelons were "planted in the corn," was often implemented.[108] Most nongrain crops, though, grew in the kitchen or dooryard garden, located immediately around the cabin, sometimes in a spot where hogs and cattle had been penned in the first winter of settlement (Fig. 5.1).[109] The most common garden crops were squash, cabbage, green beans, cucumbers, gourds, turnips, peas, white potatoes, onions, carrots, radishes, and tobacco. Roasting ear corn, watermelons, and pumpkins sometimes appeared in the garden rather than the field.[110] Potatoes thrived among the stumps in forest clearings, and cucumbers grew well in hoed mounds in the new field or garden. In some colder areas penetrated by the Midland pioneer culture, such as New Brunswick in the Loyalist immigration of the 1780s (Fig. 1.3), potatoes exceeded corn in importance as a pioneer food crop.[111]

Only one European fruit tree, the peach, found a place in the backwoods garden. The unique ecological advantages of the peach were its ability to begin bearing abundantly in only three years, an attribute well suited to the mobile nature of pioneer society, and the fact that it required less care than apples or pears. "The peach is the only fruit tree that they have as yet cultivated," noted an early traveler in the Ohio Valley, adding that it produced "fruit after the second year."[112] Another esteemed quality of the peach was that a passable brandy could be distilled from it.[113] Together with corn or rye whiskey, peach brandy satisfied the enormous appetite backwoods pioneers had for strong alcoholic drink. "A passion for spirituous liquors is one of the features that characterize the country people belonging to the interior of the United States," observed a European visitor.[114]

The genesis of the pioneer backwoods complex of cultivated crops is rather easy to assess, since the origins and diffusion of the various domesticated plants is fairly well known. Obviously, the American Indian made a fundamental contribution to frontier farming, since corn, pumpkins, squash, gourds, tobacco, and certain types of bean are all American domesticates. Without these basic crop adoptions, and particularly corn, the Midland agricultural system would have been far less effective in woodland colonization. The technique of growing crops in separate, raised mounds of roughly square shape, so effective in the burned clearings, also came from the Indians, as did the intertillage of corn, squash, and pumpkins and the preparation of hominy grits, pones, and johnnycakes.[115] It is not an exaggeration to claim that Indian-derived agricultural contributions provided one of the adaptive cornerstones of the backwoods colonization system.

Less obvious is the question of who was responsible for accepting the Indian contributions into Midland pioneer culture. We suggest that these fundamental borrowings were achieved by the Delaware Valley Finns and Swedes as an outgrowth of their close association and harmony with the local Indians, well before the arrival of the Scotch-Irish, Welsh, and most other Europeans upon the scene. That the borrowings did occur in or near the valley is suggested by the Algonquian origin of words such as *pone, succotash,* and *hominy.* The principal scene of this cultural borrowing, we believe, was the area of Passyunk on the lower Schuylkill, now part of Philadelphia, a place where both the Delaware Indians and the colonists of New Sweden had a concentration of farmland (Fig. 4.1).[116]

Before the end of Swedish rule, and even as early as 1644, the colonists had begun raising corn in typical Indian mounds and consuming it as roasting ears, bread, and alcoholic beverages. Some early sources suggested that the people of New Sweden raised "but little Indian corne," and purchase of this grain from the local Delaware Indians remained common for several decades. By about 1660, however, the Finns and Swedes were raising their own corn in abundance.[117] The Finns were uniquely preadapted to accept a bread made from an unfamiliar plant, since in their diversified Savo-Karelian economy in northern Europe they had learned over the centuries to make at least thirteen varieties of "necessity bread" in years of crop failure, using such diverse substances as husks, hulls, moss, bark, willow, bone, grass, chaff, straw, and heather.[118] Even to the present day, Finns in Europe pride themselves on the large variety of breads available in their cuisine. They were also familiar with grits made of oats or barley, which preconditioned them to accept hominy.[119] Other colonial records reveal that Finns and Swedes adopted squash, gourds, and pumpkins from the local Indians, though their tobacco came from the West Indies via the English Chesapeake colonies.[120]

It is also likely that Finns or Swedes were the first to distill liquor from Indian corn. They possessed abundant talent for distilling vodka from rye in Europe, and they imported the needed equipment to New Sweden, where drunkenness became a chronic problem. As early as 1654 the colonists knew how to brew a beer from the darker-colored variety of Indian corn, and they are known to have distilled the peach brandy that later became so popular on the frontier, a practice probably learned from the Dutch.[121]

The watermelon, an Asian domesticate, was probably brought to the Americas by the Spaniards, and it apparently reached New Sweden by way of the West Indies and Virginia, along with light tobacco. By the mid 1650s, watermelons had already found a place in Delaware Valley kitchen gardens among both whites and Indians.[122] How the peach tree reached New Sweden is unclear, though it may have come with the Dutch. Early observers noted the fruit in the colony in the 1650s, by which time the local Indians had adopted it, and elderly northern Europeans living in the valley in 1750 remembered that peaches had been more common there in the frontier period.[123] Rye, barley, buckwheat, oats, flax, cucumbers, peas, cabbage, carrots, and turnips all accompanied the New Sweden colonists on their immigration and were present from the very first in the Midland cultural nucleus. Surpluses of rye from the burned clearings were being sold to the Dutch by 1654, raised by the likes of "Anders the Finn."[124]

Claims have also been made for a Scotch-Irish influence on backwoods American crop selection and dietary preferences. Some of these claims are surely valid. The word *whiskey* derives from the Gaelic, meaning "water of life," and the Ulster folk no doubt massively reinforced the pioneer fondness for hard liquor that had earlier been established by Finns and Swedes. In so doing, they shifted from their favored barley to rye or corn, though they, like the Finns, had known how to distill whiskey from rye in Europe. Oats, the major food grain in Ulster, found little place in backwoods farming. The Scotch-Irish, together with Swiss and Palatine Germans, probably introduced the white potato, newly arrived in Europe from Andean South America, into the Midland culture, but this crop was unimportant in the backwoods.[125]

The gist of many claims of Scotch-Irish influence is that the ancestral crop selection of these people was diverse, preadapting them to accept Indian domesticates; that their traditional spring sowing of grains prepared them for the corn calendar; and that their method of open-hearth baking of breads was similar to the making of cornbread.[126] All of this rings true, and there can be little doubt that the Scotch-Irish reaped the benefits of the diversifying selection they had known in the hardscrabble periphery of Europe. We merely point out that the Scotch-Irish did not adopt Indian crops and methods directly from the natives in America, but instead accepted intact a largely Finnish/Indian pioneer agricultural system that had been developed at least half a century before the massive Ulster immigration began. The Scotch-Irish were preadapted to accept this system, but they had very little to do with shaping it.

When the secondary, Germanic wave of immigration reached the Delaware Valley, the Finnish/Indian farming practices began to be criticized in the same condemning manner that was later directed against backwoods techniques. The old inhabitants were labeled "poor agriculturalists." Some Quakers, though, recognized that "they have lived here 40 years, and have lived much at ease, having great plenty of all sorts of provisions," that they were "the first Christian People that made any considerable Improvement" in the valley.[127] As surely as the trans-Appalachian backwoods pioneer opened the way for the secondary settlers, so the Finns and Swedes prepared the path for the Quakers and Rhenish Germans. Agriculturally, the sequence in the Delaware Valley was no different from that in any other part of the Midland cultural

area. In the Delaware Valley core no less than the outlying parts
of the Midland realm, the Germanic successors criticized the pioneers while at the same time acquiring valuable provisions, structures, cleared land, and even standing crops from them at a trifling
price.

Farming Tools

Backwoods crop-raising required almost no implements other
than the ax. Plowing was both unnecessary, since corn did not
require it, and impractical, given the rooty character of the new
fields. If plowing was attempted, the still pliable roots lashed up
like whips to punish the draft animal and plower. The great majority of pioneers used only a hoe. An Ohio frontiersman recalled
how, in 1801, with his ax he "grubbed and cleared off an acre and
a half, in which I dug holes with my hoe, and planted my corn."[128]
Across Lake Erie, about the same time, another backwoodsman
insisted he "would not live on a farm that required ploughing."[129]
Some few farmers did apparently use a primitive "tree fork" plow,
in which the shorter arm was sharpened to serve as the share and
the longer arm formed the beam.[130]

   If small grains were raised or wild hay was cut, a sickle sufficed
for harvesting, but corn was gathered and husked entirely by hand.
The Indian stump mortar and wooden pestle provided the only
corn-grinding device needed. Wheeled vehicles were usually absent from the pioneer farm, their place taken by a crude land sled,
or drag, used to haul burdens such as harvested grain and firewood
(Fig. 1.2). Some of these hauling devices survived into the present
century as the Appalachian "mountain sled."[131]

   It is tempting to interpret the paucity of agricultural tools and
equipment in backwoods pioneering to Indian influence, particularly since the native method of mound cultivation had been
adopted. However, the Savo-Karelian ax-wielders also had a heritage of plowless grain cultivation, in which seed was simply sown
upon the ashes of the newly burned clearing. The well-known
"Finnish plow," found wherever Savo-Karelians settled in northern Europe, was used not by pioneer ax-wielders but by later generations. Backcountry Finns used a simple sickle in harvesting
and also had a "summer sled" with which to drag grain and
hay back to the farmstead; similar land sleds existed in New
Sweden.[132]

   By contrast, the Ulster Irish were plowers by heritage. They
also practiced a labor-intensive type of spade cultivation, using a
one-sided wooden tool with an iron shoe. Both of these methods
were alien to the backwoods frontier of America.[133]

Livestock

Open-range herding provided another facet of the diversified backwoods livelihood. Swine were by far the most numerous and important livestock, and "hog-meat, dressed and cooked in the most

slovenly and filthy manner" was often on the pioneer table.[134] Archaeological studies of cabin sites typically reveal a high proportion of hog bones, and at one early farmstead in eastern Tennessee, pigs accounted for over 92 percent of all excavated faunal remains of domesticated mammals.[135] Pigs enjoyed an ecological advantage on the frontier, for several reasons. They were well suited to a largely intact mesothermal deciduous woodland, a habitat perhaps not greatly different from the one in which they originally evolved as a wild species, rich in mast and offering the abundant shade required by swine. "These animals never leave the woods, where they always find a sufficiency of food," noted one traveler, adding that they "grow extremely wild."[136] Backwoods pioneers usually shot the hogs at slaughter time rather than try to round them up in a pen. Semiferal types such as the famous Ozark "razorback" survive as examples of the frontier stock.

Adding to the ecological superiority of swine was their ability to take care of themselves on the open range, without herders to protect them from predators, though they were somewhat vulnerable to bears. Moreover, all the meat on pigs was usable. They multiplied far more rapidly than cattle, and since pioneers took few livestock on their longer migrations, rapid proliferation was essential to reestablish the herds. In the short run, livestock were usually in short supply on a new farm.[137] "Domestic animals were so scarce that the possession of any considerable number gave notoriety and name to the possessor," bestowing titles such as "Hog" Mitchell and "Cow" Cooper.[138] For these reasons—foraging ability, self-reliance, totality of meat use, and rapid proliferation—swine attained a position among pioneer livestock that was comparable to the importance corn enjoyed among the crops.

A small herd of cattle also roamed the woods near the pioneer cabin, and the settlers usually kept a couple of calves penned to lure a cow or two back to the farmstead for daily milking in season. Milk, buttermilk, and butter were favored table fare when they could be had.[139] The cattle thrived well enough on grassy Indian oldfields and the settlers' abandoned clearings, in addition to the small prairies, glades, canebrakes, barrens, and balds that dotted the eastern woodlands, but they were far less suited to predominantly forested country than pigs. They could defend themselves quite adequately in the open, forming the classic bovine circle to protect their calves, but they were more vulnerable in the forests and multiplied only slowly there. Beef seems not to have been important in the backwoods diet, and the cattle apparently served primarily a dairy function. The absence of plowing further diminished the role of cattle, since there was then no need for a draft animal.

Farmyard poultry, both chickens and turkeys, inhabited the immediate environs of the pioneer cabin, keeping it devoid of grass and weeds, but their survival was tenuous, given the number of predators lurking in the woods. Chickens often roosted at night in the peach trees. Every farm had a pack of dogs, as well as a horse or two for transportation and dragging the land sled. Wild hay was cut for the horses, and some of the corn crop was fed to them, as well as to the poultry.[140] Sheep and goats, ill suited to forests, unable to protect themselves, in constant need of herders, and slow to multiply, found little or no place in the backwoods livestock system. New Englanders, by catering to the traditional British fondness for sheep, further handicapped themselves as pioneers.

Meats, mainly pork, bear flesh, and venison, if not eaten fresh, were usually preserved by smoking in a meathouse. Dried ham and cured bacon frequently appeared on the pioneer's table. The hog-killing season followed the first hard frost of autumn, and the meat was hung in the smokehouse for curing. Some settlers in areas where maples were common preferred sugar-cured meat, and those living near licks could use salt. Meat was prepared by open-hearth cooking, using such traditional Scotch-Irish fireplace utensils as flesh hook, griddle, frying pan, crane, iron pots, and pothooks.[141]

One is hard pressed to find a European antecedent for the Midland American backwoods livestock system. Certainly Ulster, with its traditional emphasis upon cattle- and sheep-raising and "ancient prejudice against pork," offers little in the way of a prototype, though the Scotch-Irish did have a long heritage of open-range herding and seasonal use of hill pastures, a practice that became widespread in Appalachia.[142] Largely deforested Ireland was so fundamentally different from the thickly wooded Midland frontier that little similarity in livestock raising would be expected. Claims that pioneer open-range herding derived from the remnant English woodlands seem equally unconvincing, particularly since pork was also uncommon in the traditional rural diet of England.[143]

The Savo-Karelian herding system, too, differed substantially from that of Midland America. While the backcountry Finns relied heavily upon open-range herding, far more than, for example, the Swedes, they kept a variety of stock and emphasized cattle.[144] Reflecting this focus, *The Kalevala* includes cattle charms and describes a typical stockraiser who "has creatures roving the backwoods ... seeking out swales, ... a hundred horned cattle."[145] In the Savo-Karelian frontier economy, cattle and dairy products contributed greatly to subsistence, and the ax-wielders placed much more emphasis upon harvesting wild hay from marshes and meadows than American backwoods pioneers did. So attached were the Finns to cattle, reflecting an ancient Karelian emphasis, that some reputedly drove their herds around the head of the Gulf of Bothnia when migrating to Sweden in the 1500s and 1600s.[146] After the frontier era passed in the Savo-Karelian districts of northern Europe, the number of cattle per farm declined significantly.[147]

The livestock holdings of Finns living in Sweden at about the time the Delaware colony was founded are instructive. In 1620, for example, one prosperous Finn in Medelpad Province owned 23 cattle, 15 sheep, 6 pigs, and 2 horses, while a fellow Savo-Karelian there had 13 cattle, 17 sheep, 4 pigs, and 2 horses. At the lower end of the scale, in another of Sweden's Finnmarks, was a Finn with 5 cattle, 7 goats, 4 sheep, a sow, and a horse. In another community, consisting of nine Finnish families, the people owned a total of 35 cattle, 21 sheep, 7 pigs, and 6 horses.[148]

Perhaps the only notable similarity between backcountry Finnish and American practices, aside from the use of open range, involved meat preservation. The Savo-Karelian method was to cure meat by smoking it in the sauna. One could easily imagine a transition from Finnish sauna to Midland smokehouse, particularly since they are architecturally very similar and because the smoking of meat was rarer in the forest-poor Germanic core and Celtic periphery of Europe. Indeed, it is known that the log sauna at early Christina (Wilmington) was also used as a meat smokehouse.[149]

The diverse, cattle-dominated Savo-Karelian livestock system was brought to the Delaware Valley. Cattle were introduced very early and found adequate grass in the forest. The settlers placed great importance upon access to the rich tidal and riverine marshes for cutting wild hay, causing one English observer to mention the "Swamps which the Sweads prize much."[150]

Swine also were brought to New Sweden, as were goats, sheep, and poultry. While they had struggled for survival in the frigid coniferous forests of northern Europe, pigs found a veritable paradise in the deciduous woods along the Delaware and began at once to multiply far more rapidly than the cattle. Some colonists used the east bank as a hog range in the 1650s, preceding the spread of homesteads to that shore of the river. As early as 1663, the 110 farms in the Delaware Valley were stocked with "2,000 cows and oxen, 20 horses, 80 sheep, and several thousand swine."[151] Clearly, sheep were in decline in New Sweden, cattle were holding their own, and hogs were gaining rapidly in the livestock holdings of the settlers. The cattle:sheep:pig ratio in Sweden's Finnmarks had been about 4:3:1, but along the Delaware by 1663 it had changed radically to 1:$\frac{1}{25}$:1. We can assume that this shift continued, with sheep soon being eliminated and hogs gaining numerical dominance. It is a matter of record and personal recollection that the early Swedish and Finnish settlers "had a great increase of hogs," and that the swine "ran about in the woods" semiferal, and had to be shot like wild animals. Meat was smoked and salted, as later on the Midland frontier. The local Delaware Indians adopted the pig from the colonists of New Sweden, while at the same time contributing the turkey.[152]

Apparently, then, the livestock ratios typical of American backwoods herding evolved spontaneously in the Midland nucleus. Darwinian rather than cultural causal factors were at work. Swine took immediate advantage of a highly favorable environmental base and an absence of competition in their mast-eating and rooting niche. Cattle initially remained important, though they were always tempting targets for Indian poachers, but suffered a decline when settlement began spreading up the tributary valleys, away from the hay-producing marshes along the river. They would survive in the backwoods livestock economy, but only as second-class citizens. The Karelian steer had yielded to the American razorback in a survival-of-the-fittest competition, a contest already decided by 1680, if not earlier. In this spontaneous manner, swine took their place, along with corn, the ax, and fire, as one of the four essential elements of backwoods farming.

Rural Settlement Morphology

The American backwoods frontier was dominated by scattered homesteads and individual family farms, a settlement morphology inherently favored in any extensive land-use system. Dispersed habitation could be viewed as an adaptation to plentiful, cheap land.[153] For the initial stage of pioneer settlement, the term "isolated" farmstead may be more descriptive, since backwoods settlers apparently tended to scatter, leaving three to eight or ten miles between dwellings. The individual cabins usually later became the focus of loose family or clan clusters, in which the individual houses stood not more than a mile apart (Fig. 5.13).[154]

Geographer Eugene Wilhelm, in a detailed study of the Virginia Blue Ridge, became convinced that the loose clusters of two or three cabins were created at the very inception of colonization and that isolated farmsteads were rare.[155] Be that as it may, the backwoods cabins did not form a nucleated settlement in the European sense, but stood apart on the individual landholdings. Exactly how much cluster development could occur before the pioneer system of extensive land use began to break down, causing emigration or adaptive adjustment to a more intensive strategy is not clear. No doubt the critical density level varied from one place to another, depending upon the abundance of the resource base. As a general rule, about 300 to 350 acres per capita seems to have been the minimal amount of land needed in the backwoods system, so that a typical family might require around three sections, or approximately 2,000 acres. These demands certainly did not discourage loose clustering, as long as an adequate perimeter remained open.

The causes of Midland dispersed settlement have been vigorously debated by cultural geographers and others for many years. Scholars of a normative bent insisted there was an "American" pattern of dispersal, then proceeded to attribute it to one or another universal cause, such as the breakdown of European communalism and the resultant rise of the nuclear family after about 1500. Others described the European clustered village as the tactic of a landed aristocracy to maximize its control over the rural folk and the components of the settlement fabric.[156] Freed of both communalism and the parasitic nobility, overseas Europeans supposedly gravitated instantly and naturally to dispersed settlement.

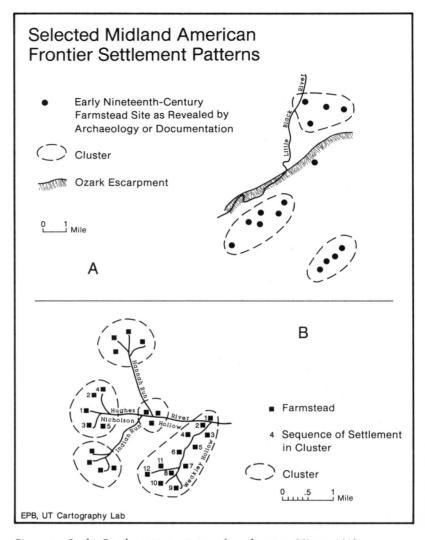

Fig. 5.13. In the Ozark escarpment area of southeastern Missouri (**A**), farmsteads about 1850 generally lay in higher-lying places, while in Virginia's Blue Ridge hollows (**B**), settlement occurred along or near streamcourses. Both areas display farmstead dispersal with a series of loose settlement clusters, probably the dominant type on the American backwoods frontier. (Sources: Price and Price 1981, p. 255; Wilhelm 1978, p. 221.)

To achieve this image of liberated, rational Europeans scattering through the western wilderness, proponents of the normative view have had to gloss over some rather pronounced regional differences in early rural settlement morphology along the colonial eastern seaboard. In point of fact, only the Delaware Valley was characterized exclusively from the very first by dispersed farmsteads. The Dutch in New Netherland doggedly pursued, with partial success, a policy of creating nucleated farm villages, though as early as 1644 some of the Hudson Valley inhabitants, "each with a view to advance his own interest, separated themselves from one another."[157] Not until the advent of English rule in 1664 did dispersed farmsteads begin to gain dominance in New York.

Likewise, the Puritan theocracy of New England sought with considerable success to establish village settlements in Massachusetts and Connecticut.[158] A recent attempt to portray New England as a land dominated from the very first by dispersed farmsteads unjustifiably downplays substantial evidence of quite durable nucleation.[159] A careful reading of the literature reveals a gradual transition from villages to dispersed settlement in New England, a movement that gained momentum in the 1680s but did not run its course until the middle of the eighteenth century. New Hampshire, Vermont, Maine, and western Massachusetts—the periphery of New England—constitute the only section of the Northeast not to have experienced a farm village phase, and the periphery was settled after 1750.[160]

Compared to New England, the estuarine settlements of the Chesapeake English went through a reversed cycle. After the very earliest period, in which villages such as Jamestown were founded, Virginia and Maryland were, indeed, characterized by individual farmsteads scattered in loose chains along the lower river courses. However, as dependence upon indentured and enslaved labor grew, and the plantation system arose, a new phase of clustering developed. Laborers or slaves lived in huts near the planter's house, in a neofeudal arrangement similar to the manorial hamlets and villages of medieval Europe.[161] Only the cataclysm of the Civil War would shatter this settlement form, two centuries later. Farther south, utopian Georgia was initially occupied in village settlements such as Ebenezer, founded by Salzburg Protestant refugees. Albemarle, North Carolina, aped the neofeudal Chesapeake, and the rice planters of South Carolina established a similar set of slave villages based on a Barbadian model. All of the plantation colonies had an inner halo of dispersed farmsteads, but these hardly set the accepted pattern for their respective areas.

Only in the Midland American nucleus was devotion to scattered farmsteads constant throughout the early colonial period. Only there were trial and error unnecessary in developing the most effective form of rural settlement for frontier occupancy. Those who acknowledge this unique morphological attribute of the Midland culture have usually, in seeking an explanation, credited hill Britons with introducing the tradition of dispersed settlement from Atlantic Europe. Some have pointed to the scattered farmsteads of the Welsh Quakers in their tract above the falls of the Schuylkill (Fig. 4.1).[162] In rural Wales, most of the traditional clustered hamlets and villages, with their communal open fields, had given way to scattered freeholdings by the seventeenth century, and we should not doubt that the Welsh, the first Celtic group to arrive in Midland America, founded dispersed settlements similar to those they had known in Europe.[163]

Most, however, have attributed the introduction of the Midland

frontier pattern of scattered farmsteads to the Scotch-Irish.[164]
While the older tradition of both the Scots and the Irish, in common with ancestral Welsh custom, favored communal infield/
outfield farming and nucleated hamlets, called *clachans*, or even
villages, known as *fermtowns* in lowland Scotland, a dispersed
pattern of settlement prevailed in most areas by the late 1600s.[165]
Pockets of traditional Celtic clustering persisted, even into the
twentieth century, but these were relics. In fact, even in ancient
Ireland, freemen had usually occupied *raths*, or scattered farmsteads, while bondsmen inhabited communal *clachans*. In Ulster
during the 1600s, dispersed settlement and enclosed unit-block
holdings were dominant, even though the Articles of Plantation
had stipulated clustered villages.[166] We conclude that the Scotch-
Irish, like the Welsh, were accustomed to dispersed rural settlement before coming to America.

However, we also suggest that the Old World highland British
experience with strewn homesteads did not provide a model for
the Midland frontier, but rather merely served to preadapt the
Scotch-Irish and Welsh to accept a rural settlement form already
established as the dominant type well before their arrival. New
Sweden had set the precedent. At a time when Hudson Valley
Dutch and New England Puritans busied themselves with their
ultimately abortive attempts to transplant the Germanic village
to American soil, in an era when Chesapeake planters were rein-
venting the feudal manor, when French Canadians were creating
chain villages that survive to the present, Finns and Swedes on
the Delaware established the settlement form that would dominate the American frontier.

By the middle 1640s, the stretch of the Delaware above present-
day Wilmington had become the first Midland frontier. Visitors at
that time noted "only few houses and these scattering," situated
"at considerable distance one from the other."[167] The Swedish
toponym suffix *-torp*, meaning a freestanding cottage and farm,
was used in the name of one of the earliest valley settlements,
Printztorp (Fig. 3.10). When the Dutch seized control of New Sweden in 1655, one of their first edicts ordered the scattered population to assemble in Germanic villages of at least 16 to 20 families.
The Finns and Swedes asked that they be allowed to "remain on
the land," stating that they were "not willing to change their place
of inhabitation nor to build in the village, which is to be established."[168] In 1657 the Dutch repeated the order, directing the inhabitants "to concentrate their houses and dwellings and hence-
forth to erect them in [the] shape of a village." Stubbornly
remaining "scattered farmers," the Finns and Swedes again refused, demanding that "each one [be permitted to] remain on his
own place." If the Dutch press the issue, they warned, "then we
shall go away or move to where we may remain living in peace."[169]
Many fled to the upper Chesapeake Bay settlements and into New
Jersey at that time. The Dutch had neither the will nor the power
to enforce their edicts, though they did half-heartedly raise the
issue one more time, specifically in reference to the local Finns.

The government recommended "putting them with the others in one village," rather than "allowing them to settle in scattered places, as is customary with these people."[170] Instead, the decade-long Dutch effort to remodel the settlement morphology along Germanic lines failed utterly, and may have had the reverse effect of causing Finns to scatter even more widely. The English rulers made no attempt to disturb the prevailing settlement pattern, and toward the end of the century an observer noted that "the people live much apart and scattered."[171]

On the New Jersey side, a bit back from the river, a fossilized pioneer settlement form like that of New Sweden survived among the descendants of northern European settlers as late as 1750, when it was described by the visiting scientist, Pehr Kalm. "Now and then you see a single farm, and a little corn-field round it," wrote Kalm, adding that "the farms are most of them single, and you seldom meet with even two together."[172]

A Savo-Karelian Prototype

The reluctance of the Delaware Valley Finns to abandon or modify their pattern of dispersed settlement rested in long ancestral tradition. In the Finnish backcountry, rural settlements since earliest times had been scattered.[173] In the pioneer areas of northern Savo in the 1500s, the ax-wielders lived in isolated farmsteads distant from one another. No more than 230 farms dotted the landscape by the close of the colonization era in the northern half of Savo about 1570, testifying both to the degree of scattering and the large amount of land needed to support a family in the *huuhta* system. Thirty years later, when pioneering came to an end in adjacent northern Häme (Tavastland), only 225 scattered farms had been founded.[174] A similar pattern developed in the various Savo-Karelian Finnmarks of central Sweden (Fig. 5.14). In time, most of these isolated homesteads developed into loose clusters, as sons and daughters established homes nearby (Fig. 5.15). By the early nineteenth century, one scattered settlement in the Orsa Finnmark of Dalarna Province consisted of 11 farms and 70 persons, another of 4 farms with 20 people, and a third of 13 farms and 70 inhabitants.[175] Swedish land reforms of the eighteenth and nineteenth centuries, designed to break up villages, disperse settlement, and unite scattered landholdings into unit-block farms, had almost no impact in Finnish ethnic areas such as western Värmland, since the desired settlement form already existed there.[176]

By contrast, most coastal Finns and the great majority of Swedes lived traditionally either in villages or hamlets, often employing a communal infield/outfield system like that of the Celtic bondsmen.[177] Some Swedes on the peripheries of settlement, in provinces such as Dalsland and Värmland, had adopted dispersed settlement even before the arrival of the Savo-Karelians in central Sweden, but the normal Swedish pattern involved clustering, in keeping with the Swedes' Germanic heritage.[178]

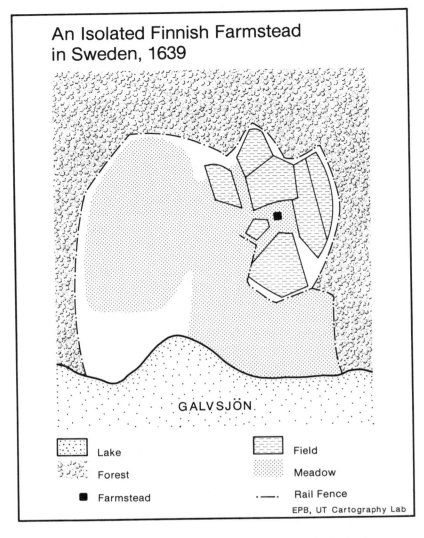

An Isolated Finnish Farmstead in Sweden, 1639

GALVSJÖN

Lake   Field

Forest   Meadow

Farmstead   Rail Fence

EPB, UT Cartography Lab

Fig. 5.14. This farm, named Galfven, lies in Alfta Parish, Hälsingland Province. The rail-fence spur, no longer functional, suggests that the original clearing was smaller. Subdivision of the field implies that the farmer had passed from *huuhta* to *kaski* techniques and was raising several different crops. (Source: Lönborg 1902, p. 396; scale not given.)

All groups, then, arriving in colonial Midland America from the peripheries of Europe—Welsh, Scotch-Irish, and Finns— shared a tradition of dispersed rural settlement. To these should also be added the Alpine German-Swiss, who also inhabited scattered farmsteads in their European homeland. It is not surprising that the fringe Europeans perpetuated this pattern on the American frontier. The crucial point, from the standpoint of the thesis we are testing, is that it was the colonists of New Sweden who established dispersed farmsteads as the prototype for the American frontier.

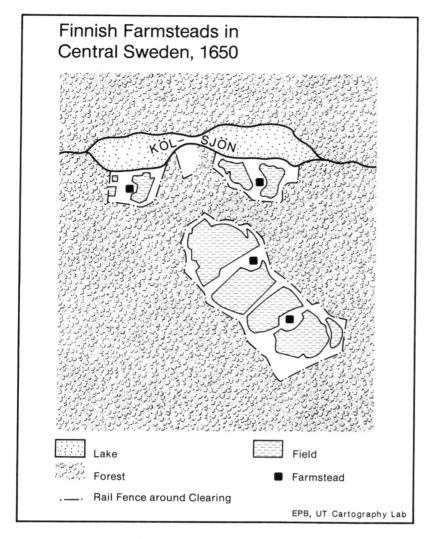

Finnish Farmsteads in
Central Sweden, 1650

	Lake		Field
	Forest		Farmstead
	Rail Fence around Clearing		

EPB, UT Cartography Lab

Fig. 5.15. Four scattered Savo-Karelian farmsteads form a loose cluster similar to those found on the Midland American frontier. This settlement was near Hassela in northern Hälsingland Province. The small clearing with only a partial fence was either new or recently abandoned, its fence rails moved elsewhere. *Kölsjön* means "Keel Lake." (Source: Gothe 1942, pp. 56–57; scale not given.)

Farmstead Site and Layout

On the forest frontier, the typical farmstead lay in the middle of the new clearing, away from the shelter and shade of the woods (Fig. 5.16).[179] This preference puzzled many visitors from Germanic Europe and its evolving eastern seaboard American outlier, who retained romanticized images of the forest. Backwoods pioneers, who labored to open up the clearings, had a rather different outlook. In addition, the dooryard garden thrived best in the abundant sunlight of the clearing's center, and the homestead was more easily defended when surrounded by open ground.

Fig. 5.16. A rare glimpse of a new backwoods farmstead in its clearing. Taken in western Oregon, near the place where Midland frontier expansion ended on the Pacific shore, the photograph nicely captures the image of the new settlement in forested colonial America. (Photo courtesy of the Oregon Historical Society, Portland, Photograph Collection, file no. 198, neg. no. 79130.)

The farmstead so situated consisted of a small number of separate, freestanding log buildings scattered in apparent disorder, paying no tribute to cardinal directions and reflecting no consistent orientation. German settlement geographers long ago labeled this type a *Streuhof*, or "strewn farmstead." The haphazard arrangement makes the individual structures look as if they had been dropped from the sky (Fig. 5.17).

Pioneer farmsteads usually contained no more than three or four buildings, including the cabin (Fig. 5.2). *Barn* reverted to its simpler neolithic Anglo-Saxon meaning of "barley house," or granary, and was represented on the pioneer farm by a mere corncrib. Other structures included a smokehouse or "meathouse," a chicken coop, and a springhouse.[180] If the pioneer remained on one farmstead for five to ten years, the number of buildings grew to as many as seven or more, including a "cookhouse" or freestanding summer kitchen, a horse stable, a root cellar, and possibly even a piggery.[181] The cabin and barn were enlarged to consist of two log units instead of only one, to accommodate a larger family and bigger harvests.

No doubt the danger of fire spreading from one wooden build-

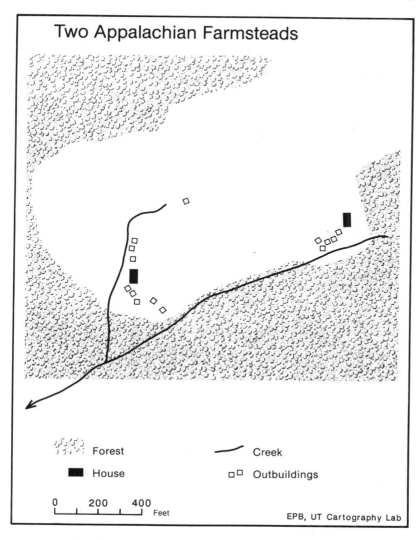

Two Appalachian Farmsteads

Forest

House

Creek

Outbuildings

0   200   400   Feet

EPB, UT Cartography Lab

Fig. 5.17. These farmsteads consist of multiple structures strewn in no apparent order, a Midland American trait. They lie in the Kentucky mountains, near Cumberland Gap. Both are post-pioneer farmsteads, containing more structures than would have been typical in the early years of frontier settlement. (Source: Cox 1978, pp. 62–63.)

ing to another encouraged strewn farmsteads on the American frontier. In addition, log buildings were difficult to splice together, prompting the construction of a separate pen or crib of four walls whenever additional roofed facilities were needed. The strewn farmstead was thus both safer and more practical than other possible types, possessing attributes surely derived from some pre-adapted European prototype.

The Teutonic core of Europe offered few possible models. Palatine immigrants had lived in tightly grouped "Frankish courts," in which the different farm buildings enclosed a central yard.

Most other Germans, as well as the Dutch, had known unitary structures, with dwelling, barn, and stable under a single roof. Swedes had likewise inhabited courtyard farmsteads, even in log-construction areas such as Dalarna, and the English had been accustomed to a loose assemblage of farm buildings around a yard, after royal edict banned unitary farmsteads there in late medieval times.

Europe's Celtic fringe offers better possibilities of a prototypical farmstead. Ireland does, indeed, have a sizable zone where the *Streuhof* prevails, but it coincides with the Erse linguistic refuges of the Catholic west coast rather than the Scotch-Irish lands of the northeast. The most typical Ulster practice was to extend outbuildings in an orderly row along the ridgepole axis of the dwelling.[182] The poorer Irish brought their livestock into their dwelling, in violation of English law.

In fact, only two immigrant groups arriving in colonial America had known both log construction and strewn farmsteads of the Midland backwoods type. Both came from Europe's hardscrabble fringe. Alpine Germans from the high mountain portions of Canton Bern possessed such a heritage, but they began arriving in America well after 1700 and formed only a tiny minority within the Pennsylvania German population. Kinfolk from the Austrian Alps entered the colonies even later, after 1730.[183]

Savo-Karelian Finns inhabited a more satisfactory prototype for the American backwoods strewn farmstead and were, of course, very early present on the Midland scene. Three very different regional farmstead types characterized the Finnish lands in Europe, but only one was transplanted to the Delaware Valley. Russian Karelians lived in large, multistory unit farmsteads with front-facing gable, while many coastal Finns adopted the Swedish courtyard plan. Only the Savo-Karelians consistently occupied formless, strewn farmsteads, to the extent that students of the subject refer to the type as the "Savo" style.[184] They introduced it into their settlements in Sweden after 1570, where it blended rather well with a minority, backcountry Swedish strewn farmstead that was common in newly settled districts (Fig. 3.9).[185]

In the early pioneer period in northern Europe, Savo-Karelian farmsteads consisted of only a few buildings. Records from the sixteenth and seventeenth centuries often mention Finnish farmsteads of only two or three structures—most commonly a log cabin and a stock shelter.[186] The cabin also served as sauna and grain-drying shed in such frontier situations.

As the years passed, the Savo-Karelian farmsteads rapidly accumulated additional structures, since logs were abundant and construction was simple (Fig. 5.18). Half a dozen or so buildings became the average, but postpioneer farms may have had fifteen, twenty, or even more log structures.[187] These included a summer kitchen, sauna, drying shed–threshing barn, barns, hay sheds, horse stables, root cellars, toolhouses, piggery, boathouse, smithy, cowshed, granary, and milking shed.[188] The migratory pioneer ax-wielders never inhabited such large farmsteads.

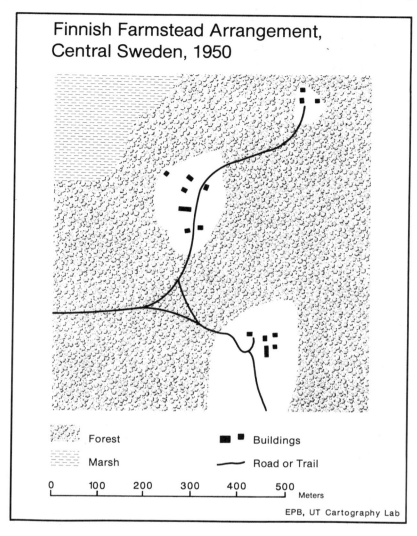

Finnish Farmstead Arrangement, Central Sweden, 1950

Forest　　Buildings
Marsh　　Road or Trail

0　100　200　300　400　500
Meters

EPB, UT Cartography Lab

Fig. 5.18. These three Finnish farmsteads, with typically scattered buildings, are at Honkamakk, near Gräsmark in the Finnskog, Värmland Province. The smallest clearing and farmstead have been abandoned. (Source: sketch map in Nordiska museet, Stockholm, arkiv, item no. EU 42955.)

No pioneer Finnish settlements survive in the Delaware Valley, nor do we have adequate descriptions of the early farmsteads. A German observer accused some of the original inhabitants of having "neither barns nor stables" and of leaving unthreshed grain "lying in the open air." We do know, however, that at least some of the Delaware colonists had saunas, as well as threshing sheds, stables, and granaries. A barn reputedly of "Swedish" origin still stands on the New Jersey side of the river at Greenwich near Cohansey Creek (Fig. 3.10).[189] In all probability the typical Savo-Karelian farmstead of New Sweden contained three to five structures, offering an ideal, practical, and preadapted model for the Midland frontier.

In addition, Finns and Swedes, both in northern Europe and the Delaware Valley, situated their farmsteads in the middle of the clearings, away from the woods.[190] This offers yet another similarity to the pioneer American pattern.

Conclusion

American backwoods farming reflects a blending of ethnic traditions, with the most substantial contributions coming from Finns and Indians. In every case, the characteristics that persisted to become part of Midland pioneer agriculture can be seen to have enjoyed adaptive superiority in an extensive land-use system that provided abundant yield or advantage in return for a minimal expense of labor. The Finns' axmanship, clearing methods, types of fencing, settlement pattern, and farmstead layout each possessed a particular preadapted quality. These techniques and items of material culture were joined to a splendid American Indian crop selection that yielded prolifically in hoed fields and gardens, under the native method of mound cultivation.

Other peripheral European groups, including the Scotch-Irish, added relatively little to backwoods agriculture, but they had known farming methods and rural landscapes sufficiently similar to the Finnish/Indian system to facilitate adoption and participation. Core Germanic immigrants, by contrast, found the pioneer agriculture of the Delaware Valley alien. Rather than accepting, they criticized, choosing instead to install their own, more intensive systems of land use, shunting out the frontier agrarian order.

Closely related to farming, and constituting another aspect of the rural landscape, is folk architecture. Chapters 6 and 7 are devoted to an analysis of pioneer carpentry techniques and building styles, in the hope that these tangible aspects of traditional culture will provide valuable material evidence concerning the genesis of American backwoods pioneering.

SIX

LOG CONSTRUCTION

*[He] raised up a home . . .
shaped the walls in the wilderness.*
Kalevala

The hallmark of the folk building tradition on the Midland American frontier was notched log construction, a carpentry so splendidly suited to forest colonization that it has properly been regarded as one of the preadapted keys to the success of backwoods pioneering. Building with logs allowed utilization of the most abundant raw material of the woodlands in a minimally processed form. This carpentry could be accomplished quickly with only an ax and saw, required no hardware, and allowed the pioneer to be free of dependence upon sawmills, brick kilns, and nail manufacture. The logs not only served as the weight-bearing frame of the structure but also provided at once the outer and inner walls, insulation, and roof support.[1]

Students of American vernacular architecture have long known that log construction was linked culturally to the Midland and its Pennsylvania hearth.[2] British peoples, including the English lowlanders and the Celtic hill folk, knew nothing of this method of construction in Europe, nor did the Dutch or the great majority of Germans. As a result, log buildings were largely or wholly absent from Jamestown and the other Chesapeake Tidewater settlements, from the Massachusetts Bay colonies of the Pilgrims and Puritans, and from the Dutch-ruled Hudson Valley.[3] The English, wherever they settled in colonial America, erected timber-frame houses covered with clapboards affixed by nails. Early Dutch colonists in New York resorted to living in pits dug six or seven feet into the ground and covered with turf roofs.[4] These forms of housing proved far less effective in colonization than the log cabin, helping retard the advance of the frontier in New England, New Netherland, and the plantation South.

Only in the Delaware Valley was log construction present from the very first, and the distinctive Midland American type of carpentry sprang from that colonial hearth. To be sure, certain other American implantments of log carpentry occurred. In the border area between New Hampshire and Maine, in the Piscataqua Valley, a carefully crafted type of notched-log construction arose, apparently derived from a German military garrison house tradition, but this Yankee carpentry never achieved a notable spread and differed fundamentally from the Midland type.[5] The French in Québec also introduced a log-building tradition, which later provided the model for structures erected by the Hudson's Bay Company, but French Canadian carpentry was rather intricate and failed to cross ethnic lines.[6] Similarly, other log-building traditions reached the United States quite early from Russia, via Alaska, and from highland Mexico, into the American Southwest.[7]

None of these rival techniques influenced Midland backwoods log carpentry, and the Pennsylvania tradition can easily be distinguished on the basis of a variety of diagnostic traits. These include distinctive notch types, log-shaping techniques, roof and chimney construction methods, and the practice of leaving cracks, or chinks, between the logs rather than fitting them tightly together.[8] These and other characteristics of Midland carpentry define a simple, crude construction that was well suited to frontier conditions, one that ultimately achieved a remarkably widespread distribution (Fig. 6.1). The rival traditions were all more refined than the Midland type, demanding a higher level of craftsmanship and more time, both of which were disadvantages on the frontier.

Debate concerning the Old World origin of Midland American log carpentry has raged for decades. Some Germanists have argued that it represented a Teutonic tradition implanted in the eighteenth century by German-speaking immigrants from Switzerland, the Black Forest, and the eastern German marchlands in Saxony, Silesia, Bohemia, and Moravia.[9] Recent research has restored and reinforced the more traditional view that Midland log carpentry was derived from Finnish and Swedish practices introduced into the Delaware Valley in the mid 1600s.[10] Scholars have never challenged the claim that the northern European settlers of New Sweden were the first to practice log construction in the Middle Colonies. Abundant documentary evidence establishes this as fact. English Quakers arriving on the Pennsylvania scene in the 1680s marveled at the ability of the "Swedes" to build quickly and effectively with logs.[11] The implantment of northern European log carpentry was not merely the earliest in the Delaware Valley, but as we will demonstrate, provided the model for American backwoods building methods. Finnish and Swedish, not German, roots provide the explanation. Few features of pioneer Midland carpentry lack possible Fenno-Scandian antecedents, and some possess a diagnostic quality permitting northern European origin to be proven.

Log-Shaping

By far the most common Midland American frontier method of construction was to leave logs in their round shape, "just as nature formed them," often with the bark intact (Fig. 6.2).[12] Even dwellings were usually built in this crude manner during the early years of settlement. Barns and other outbuildings among the backwoods pioneers almost universally consisted of round logs. In one Ontario township in pioneer times, 53 of 56 settlers lived in round-log cabins, and a decade later three quarters of the population still occupied such dwellings.[13] Over half of all Cherokee log houses in Georgia were of round-log construction, and in southeastern Pennsylvania the technique remained common long after the passing of the frontier era.[14] In parts of the mountain West, the dominance of unshaped logs in cabin construction can still be observed in the cultural landscape.[15] The advantage of round-log construction lay in its minimization of the amount of labor required to erect a building.

Use of round logs in the Midland carpentry tradition has circumstantial ties to the early Delaware Valley settlements and to the population of New Sweden.[16] Construction with unshaped timbers remains very common among outbuildings in interior Finland and Scandinavia to the present day, while the technique is less common in German-speaking parts of Europe (Fig. 6.3).[17] We believe that Finns and Swedes introduced this crude method into the Midland backwoods woodworking repertoire.

A second, less common American pioneer method involved split-log or half-round construction (Fig. 6.4). Using wooden wedges and the blunt side of the ax as a maul, carpenters split the timbers lengthwise—the same technique they employed in making fence rails. Today, split-log buildings are fairly common in central Sweden, especially Dalarna Province, and documentary evidence suggests that "Swedes" were using this carpentry method in the Delaware Valley in the 1670s and 1680s, building with "trees split through the middle."[18] Even so, half-log construction in Midland America does not prove northern European influence, since, in common with the use of round logs, the technique also appears in some districts of Germanic Europe.[19]

The third Midland shaping method entailed hewing the logs on two sides to produce flattened surfaces for the walls. On both the top and bottom sides, the natural curved surface of the timber was left intact. The crudest and simplest hewing was achieved using only an ax, after the structure had been raised. A Texas backwoodsman, employing this method, "put the logs up round," then some months later "took a chopping ax and hewed the logs down smooth." To achieve such crude, labor-efficient hewing, the carpenter scored the logs in one direction with his ax, then hewed in the opposite direction.[20] Much less commonly on the frontier, logs were hewn prior to construction, a practice normally confined to secondary settlers. After scoring, the carpenter hewed to a chalked line, using either a broadax or, less commonly, a foot adz. Either method left a somewhat irregular face scarred by ax score marks, a diagnostic feature of Midland carpentry (Fig. 6.5).[21] Some hewn-log buildings were found even in the newest frontier settlements, but they became steadily more common

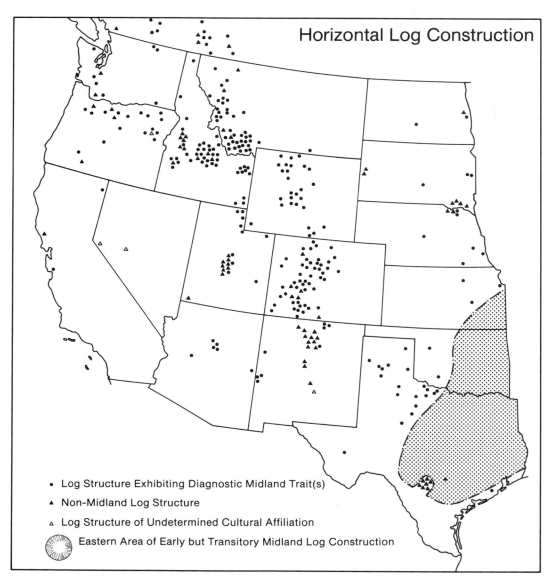

Fig. 6.1. Midland American log construction is easily detected on the basis of the following diagnostic traits: V-notching, diamond notching, half-dovetail notching, chinking, ax-scored hewing, dogtrot house plan, and open-passage double-crib barn. Non-Midland diagnostic traits are double notching, hook notching, false corner timbering, corner posting, medial posting, and chinkless construction. The most controversial findings here are those for New England, New York, and bordering parts of Canada. The sources for the map are so diverse that listing them would be impractical, and only those for the more controversial areas are given. (Sources: Dwight 1969, vol. 2, pp. 82, 84, 90–96, 204, 210, 288, 300, 315, 321–

EASTERN AREA OF GREATEST
AND DURABLE
MIDLAND LOG CONSTRUCTION

0   100   200 miles
0   125   250 kilometers

EPB,UT Cartography Lab

26, 335, 339; vol. 3, p. 125; vol. 4, pp. 35–36, 41, 55, 88; Rempel 1967; Coffey 1984; Coffey and Noble 1986; Candee 1976, chap. 5, esp. p. 267; Hale 1957–60; Kelly 1940; Halsey 1901, p. 136; Arthur and Witney 1972; Séguin 1963, pp. 19–22, 71–76; Mercer 1927; Cummings 1979; Smith 1877, pp. 181, 237, 296, 317–18; Halsey 1902, pp. 98, 102; and the following museums: Adirondack, Black Creek Pioneer Village, Central New Brunswick Woodmen's Museum, Genesee Country Village, Hyde Log Cabin, Kings Landing Historical Settlement, MacLachlan Woodworking Museum, Upper Canada Village, and Point Pelee National Park.)

Fig. 6.2. A barn built of round logs, with open chinks, in Tuscaloosa County, Alabama. The corner-timbering is diamond notched, a Midland type derived from central Sweden. It represents type D in Fig. 6.19. (Photo by Eugene M. Wilson of the University of South Alabama, 1978, used with permission.)

as the years passed.[22] The second, postpioneer phase of Midland carpentry was dominated by hewn-log construction, and the use of round or half-round logs was relegated mainly to outbuildings.

Today, ax-scored hewing is uncommon in Europe, but some vestiges of it survive in Scandinavia and Finland, including the Finnish ethnic areas of central Sweden (Fig. 6.6).[23] In the Delaware Valley, carpenters bearing the distinctive Finnish surnames Mullicka and Laikan are recorded in a 1721 document as "trimming

Fig. 6.3. An outbuilding in Finland showing crude round-log construction with some bark intact and a ridgepole-and-purlin roof. The structure is in the Turkansaaren ulkomuseo near Oulu, Pohjanmaa Province. (Photo by T.G.J., 1985.)

off the walls with an adz" in southwestern New Jersey, which strongly suggests that the Midland hewing method was practiced among the New Sweden descendants before the major immigration of log-building Germans. Moreover, the seventeenth-century Nothnagle House, near the settlement of Repaupo, displays ax-scored, two-sided hewing.[24] Such evidence leaves little doubt about the origin of American ax-score hewing.

Corner-Timbering: The V Notch

The notching of corners is crucial in log carpentry, since it binds the timbers together, prevents lateral slippage, and bears almost the entire weight of the building. At the same time, no other form element of log construction lends itself so readily to diffusionary analysis. In the Midland tradition, only eight notch types occur, none of which lacks a possible northern European prototype.[25] Two of the eight possess particular diagnostic ability in the documentation of Finnish and Scandinavian influence. We will focus upon these two types, known to specialists as "V" and "diamond" notches.[26]

The former is so named because of the inverted V shape of the joint (Fig. 6.5). Two principal subtypes occur, including a round-log variety, in which the logs are allowed to project beyond the corners of the building, and a hewn-log form featuring neatly

Fig. 6.4. An example of half-round log construction identical to the Midland American type, in central Dalarna Province, Sweden. Note the spaces, or chinks, between the logs, another typical Midland trait. The structure stands in Zorns gammelgård at Mora. (Photo by T.G.J., 1981.)

boxed corners (Figs. 6.5, 6.7).[27] In the cruder, round-log type, the apex of the V is often blunted, while the hewn form invariably displays a pointed V.[28] Subtypes intermediate between the two varieties occur frequently, including some slightly hewn forms and an occasional fully hewn specimen that projects beyond the corners instead of being boxed. Some examples are hewn fairly thin, but the majority are left rather thick. In spite of these differ-

Fig. 6.5. Ax-scored hewing, a distinctive feature of Midland carpentry, left marks on this log house in western New York. V-notching was employed, further demonstrating the Pennsylvania affiliation of the structure. The notch represents type H in Fig. 6.12. The house is in the Genesee Country Village Outdoor Museum. (Photo by T.G.J., 1984.)

ences, V-notching has correctly been interpreted as a single type of corner-timbering whose variants possess a common origin.

The geographical distribution of Midland V-notching provides impressive testimony to the importance of Pennsylvania as a cultural hearth (Fig. 6.8). Very common in the Keystone State, it also occurs from Ontario to Florida, from the southern Appalachians

Fig. 6.6.   An ax-scored hewn log wall in central Finland. This structure once stood in the heart of the source region for Finns who migrated to Scandinavia and the Delaware, in the old church district of Rautalampi, Häme traditional province, near the town of Konginkangas. Today it is part of exhibit no. 7 at the Seurasaaren ulkomuseo in Helsinki. (Photo by T.G.J., 1985.)

to northern Arizona, the Olympic Peninsula of Washington State, and British Columbia.[29] Within this huge realm it is the dominant notching form in a wide scattering of localities, including such places as southeastern Ohio, the Shenandoah Valley of Virginia, central Texas, and the Flagstaff area of Arizona.[30] Widely found east of the Mississippi, V-notching is also "a common western form."[31] In Canada, significantly, it is called the "Pennsylvania corner" or "Pennsylvania-Dutch keying."[32] V-notching may be the single best indicator of Midland American log carpentry.

The origin of V-notching has been debated for more than half a century. Henry C. Mercer, who called this type of joint "notched and chamfered," suggested in the 1920s, without supporting evidence, that V-notching came to Pennsylvania from Sweden.[33] Geographer Fred Kniffen and folklorist Henry Glassie, who also lacked any hard evidence, refuted Mercer and accepted an unspecified "local tradition" that V-notching was introduced to Pennsylvania in the 1730s by the Schwenkfelders, a small group of persecuted Silesian German pietists.[34] Subsequent field research in Europe, however, revealed that V-notching did not exist anywhere in German-speaking Europe, including the Schwenkfelder homeland.[35]

Instead, both major types of Midland American V-notching occur in at least proximate form in Scandinavia, and only there (Figs.

Fig. 6.7. Round-log V-notching on a structure in Lake City, Hinsdale County, Colorado. The V notch is well represented in the mountain West, a stronghold of surviving Midland American backwoods material culture. (Photo by T.G.J., 1987.)

6.9, 6.10). The prototype occurs in one small region overlapping the border of Sweden and Norway (Fig. 6.11). Included is the Finnskog region of western Värmland, which is noteworthy as the main source of Delaware Valley Finns.

While Finns apparently brought V-notching to the Delaware, they did not invent this type of corner-timbering. Nor did the Swedes. Our field research also carried us into most other provinces of Sweden, as well as the source regions of the Finnskog

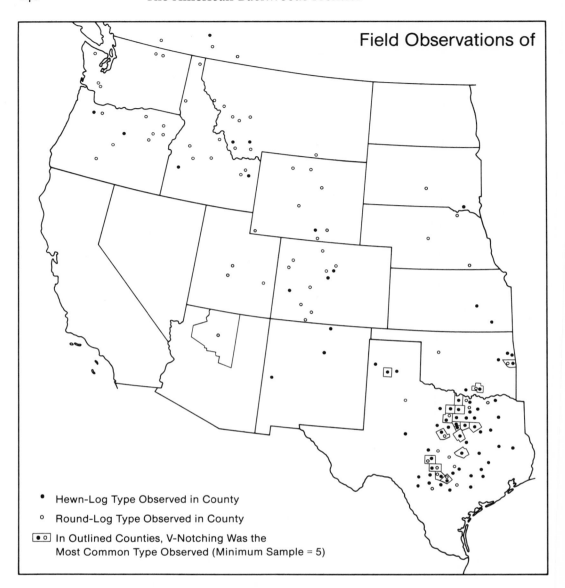

Field Observations of

- Hewn-Log Type Observed in County
- Round-Log Type Observed in County
In Outlined Counties, V-Notching Was the
Most Common Type Observed (Minimum Sample = 5)

Fig. 6.8. This map of V-notching startlingly reveals the extent of the Midland cultural area, or Pennsylvania extended, as measured by one element of material culture. At the same time, it suggests the influence of New Sweden and, ultimately, the Värmland source region. (Most of the sources are listed in Jordan, Kaups, and Lieffort 1986–87b, pp. 22–23. Additional sources include Miller 1977, pp. 7, 33, 73;

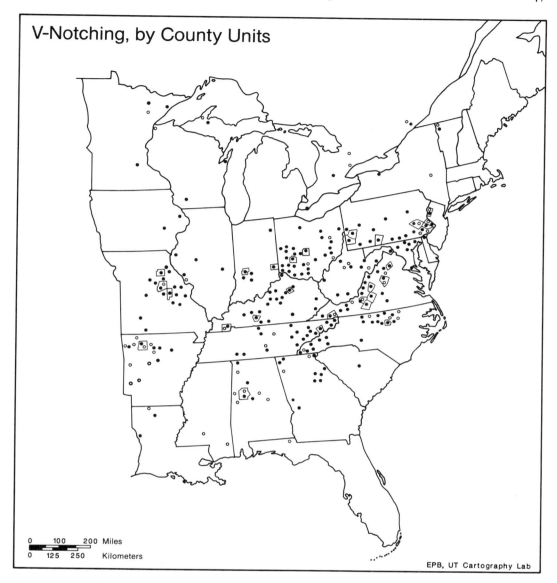

V-Notching, by County Units

Hutslar 1986; Williams and Dockery 1984, pp. 36, 95, 98, 112–13; Flanders 1984, app., p. 29; Clinton and Lofton 1981, pp. 10, 11, 16; Heikkenen and Edwards 1983; Elbert and Sculle 1982, p. 4; Langsam and Johnson 1985, pp. 70, 79, 116, 126, 132, 136, 148, 151; Torma and Wells 1986, pp. 21–72; Fort Steele Heritage Park; Fort Missoula Museum; Calgary Heritage Park; and Point Pelee National Park exhibit.)

Fig. 6.9. V-notching with a blunt apex on an outbuilding in a Finnish farmstead near Rödjåfors, Värmland Province, Sweden, in the Finnskog source region of the Delaware Valley colonists. It represents type C in Fig. 6.12. The crowns on the butt ends of the logs have deteriorated, revealing the notch structure. (Photo by T.G.J., 1985.)

Fig. 6.10. V-notching with a sharp apex on a building from Tången in Långelanda, Eda Parish, Värmland Province, Sweden, dating from the late seventeenth or early eighteenth century. The structure is now at the Sågudden Open-Air Museum in Arvika. The notch best represents type G in Fig. 6.12. (Photo by T.G.J., 1985.)

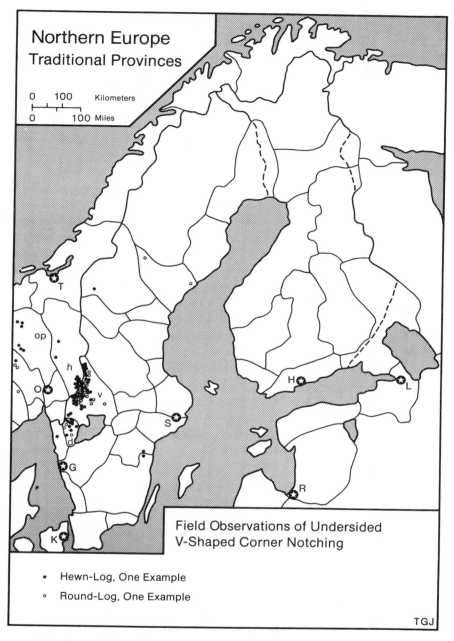

Fig. 6.11. Key to abbreviations: **d** = Dalsland Province; **G** = Göteborg; **H** = Helsinki; **h** = Hedmark Province; **K** = København; **L** = Leningrad; **O** = Oslo; **op** = Oppland Province; **R** = Riga; **S** = Stockholm; **T** = Trondheim. Buskerud Province borders Oppland on the southwest. (Sources are listed in Jordan, Kaups, and Lieffort 1986–87b, p. 28.)

settlers in Finland, but nowhere else did we encounter V-notching. By contrast, southern interior Norway offered abundant examples—in particular, Hedmark, Oppland, Buskerud, and bordering portions of adjacent provinces. Deeper into Norway, the age

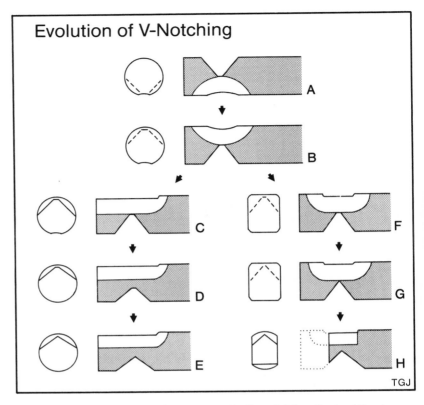

Fig. 6.12. Key: **A** = medieval Norwegian, Gudbrandsdalen, Oppland Province; **B** = medieval and postmedieval Norwegian, as in exhibit no. 58 at the Norsk folkemuseum; **C** = late-medieval Norwegian, as in the exhibit at Hallingdal folkemuseum; **D** = Midland American, as in Figs. 6.7 and 6.13; **E** = Midland American, ubiquitous; **F** = Finnskog district in Värmland and Hedmark provinces, ubiquitous; **G** = Värmland Swedish, as in the Sågudden hembygds museum exhibit from Tången in Långelanda, Eda Parish; **H** = Midland American, ubiquitous. In type H, note how the Midland hewn form of V-notching has had the typical Scandinavian crown removed, producing a curious asymmetry. (For sources, see Jordan, Kaups, and Lieffort 1986–87b, p. 31, nn. 19–27.)

of the oldest surviving specimens of V-notching increased, yielding a noteworthy fourteenth-century example from the Hallingdal in Buskerud and a late-sixteenth-century building from the Hamar area of western Hedmark.[36] Even Swedish ethnographers interpret V-notching in Värmland and neighboring provinces as Norwegian.[37] At one outdoor museum in the Finnish part of Värmland, V-notching is described in the building guide as "norsk."[38] In fact, the Norwegian word *laft* was long used in western Värmland for "notch," instead of the proper Swedish word *knut*.[39]

The ancestral V notch was common in parts of medieval Norway and is one of the oldest documented forms of Norwegian carpentry. The round-log type is, predictably, the oldest, and the earliest specimens of it are inverted, with the V cut in the top of the log (Fig. 6.12).[40] The Gudbrandsdal in Oppland Province is perhaps the original source of V-notching in its primitive inverted form.[41] Still in medieval times, Norwegians began cutting the V-type notches on the underside of the log, a style that more closely resembles the later American type. Most V-notching in Scandinavia retains a crown at the end of the log which conceals the structure of the joint (Fig. 6.12), but some Nordic carpenters began fairly early to carry the V shape all the way to the butt end. Significantly, V-notching with crowning intact is encountered fairly frequently in the mountain West of the United States and Canada, a zone that preserves much Midland backwoods material culture (Fig. 6.13).

Apparently the immigrating Finns, who occupied Finnskog heights and hills between the valley-dwelling Norwegians and Swedes, accepted items of material culture from both neighboring groups. The adoption of V-notching likely occurred by 1620, and the Finns may have acquired it from Värmland Swedes rather than directly from Norwegians. A generation later Finnskog Finns transferred the notch to New Sweden.

Crucial additional support for this view is provided by the round-log V-notching found on the well-known "Lower Swedish Cabin" in Clifton Heights, Pennsylvania (Fig. 6.13). Recently dated by dendrochronology as being constructed in 1697, the Lower Swedish Cabin provides irrefutable evidence that American V-notching derives from New Sweden. Also, the reputedly seventeenth-century "Swedish" granary at the Cumberland County Historical Society Museum in Greenwich, New Jersey, displays round-log V-notching mixed with the related saddle notching.[42]

Diamond Notching

Another diagnostic characteristic of Midland American carpentry is diamond notching, named for the pared, or "necked," diamond-shaped projection, up to a foot in length, that forms the notch and carries through to the crown or butt end. As with V-notching, both round-log and hewn subtypes occur (Fig. 6.2, 6.14).[43] In neither is the crown allowed to project much, if any, beyond the corner of the structure. The actual notch, V-shaped to accommodate one apex of the diamond, is cut into the pared projection. Most diamond notching is *oversided*, or cut into the top side of the projection, but a minority of specimens display *undersided* notching (Fig. 6.15). Clearly, these several forms have a common origin, though the undersided variant may have been influenced by V-notching.

Diamond notching is the least common Midland type and occurs principally in one rather confined area of North Carolina and adjacent southern Virginia, along and on both sides of the axis of the Fall Line, in the inner Coastal Plain and eastern Piedmont (Fig. 6.16). Individual outliers in Georgia and Alabama have been found close to the Fall Line, suggesting diffusion in part along the old road linking Richmond, Raleigh, Columbia, Augusta, Colum-

Fig. 6.13.   Round-log V-notching with crowning intact on a nineteenth-century structure in the Fort Steele Heritage Park, British Columbia. Retention of the typically Scandinavian crown on many V-notched buildings in western North America, where pioneer material culture remains common, suggests that the practice was once common in Midland backwoods carpentry and firms up the genetic link to northern Europe. The notch illustrated resembles type B in Fig. 6.12. (Photo by T.G.J., 1987.)

bus, and Montgomery (Fig. 6.2).[44] In the interior South, diamond notching is rare, confined to several isolated examples observed in Tennessee and Kentucky. Documentary evidence is likewise uncommon, limited to a single 1779 reference to a courthouse in

Fig. 6.14.   Round-log V-notching on the Lower Swedish Cabin, Creek Road, Clifton Heights, Pennsylvania, in the territory of the New Sweden colony. Dendrochronology reveals that the house was erected in 1697. The walls are chinked. This structure firmly links Scandinavian and Midland V-notching. (Photo by T.G.J., 1988.)

eastern Tennessee with "diamond corners."[45] The notch failed to attain a notable western diffusion; no examples have been found beyond the Mississippi River.[46]

The connection of diamond notching to Pennsylvania and the original Midland hearth is suggested by its occurrence on hewn-

Fig. 6.15. Diamond notching with hewn logs at Fort Gaddis, Fayette County, Pennsylvania, dating from ca. 1770. The carpentry represents type F in Fig. 6.19. Note the awkwardness where the outer ridge of the diamond projects beyond the hewn wall surface. Mud chinking seals the cracks between the logs. (Photo by the Western Pennsylvania Architectural Survey, Carnegie Library of Pittsburgh, no. F1-107d, used with permission.)

log Fort Gaddis, also called the Gaddis blockhouse, dating from about 1770 and located near Uniontown in Fayette County. This is the only known example of diamond notching in Pennsylvania (Fig. 6.14).[47] The fort was established by Thomas Gaddis, who came from Frederick County, Virginia, in the Great Valley of the Appalachians. Many other early settlers of Fayette County also came, via the Catawba Trail, from the northern Virginia backcountry and adjacent Berkeley County, West Virginia.[48] These currents of migration suggest that diamond notching reached Fayette County from southeastern Pennsylvania via a detour down the Great Valley, rather than from the Virginia Piedmont and inner Coastal Plain. Genealogy and Fort Gaddis tell us to look to the Delaware Valley for the origin of diamond notching. Clearly we find today a mere remnant of the former distribution of this cornering technique.

In the North Carolina–Virginia concentration, diamond notching appears most often on outbuildings, particularly tobacco barns, and the round-log variety prevails on such structures.[49] We believe round-log diamond cornering was linked, along with round-log V-notching, to the early pioneer stage of construction,

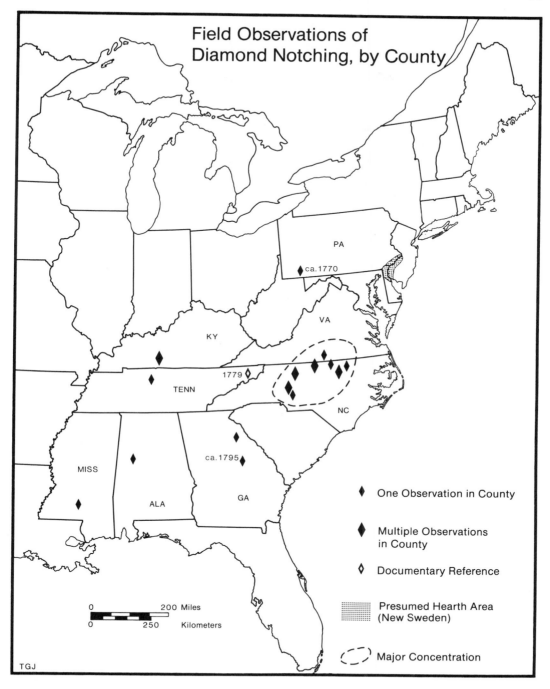

Fig. 6.16. The distribution of diamond notching revealed here is clearly relict. (For sources, see Jordan, Kaups, and Lieffort 1986–87a, caption for Fig. 3; Cooper, letter to T.G.J.; and nn. 44, 45, and 47 of this chapter.)

Fig. 6.17. The awkward projecting ridge inherent in hewn-log diamond notching has been planed away on some logs of this Franklin County, North Carolina, structure. (Photo by T.G.J., 1983.)

a stage best preserved, in eastern seaboard states at least, on out-buildings. Transition to the more refined postpioneer carpentry stage proved difficult, and hewn specimens of diamond notching often appear awkward, with the outer side ridge of the diamond projecting beyond the surface of the flattened wall (Fig. 6.14).[50] In some instances, this visually offensive ridge was planed off, pro-ducing a more aesthetic corner lacking the distinctive diamond shape (Fig. 6.17). Such evidence reveals that hewing did not occur in the prototypical form of the notch.

Few students of American material culture have addressed the question of the diamond notch's origin. Some have proposed that it "seems" to be or "is likely" an Americanism, derived from V-notching.[51] Indeed, the diamond shape does approximate a doubled V notch, and in some individual structures both of these types of notch appear. Kniffen and Glassie first suggested the possibility of northern European origin, declaring that the diamond notch "bears a superficial and probably accidental similarity" to certain Scandinavian types.[52] Our own field research in northern Europe establishes that the similarity comes closer to being striking, rather than superficial, and is anything but accidental.[53]

The prototype of American diamond notching is Swedish. It is a joint variously called there, in its evolutionary progression, a *rännknut* ("groove notch"), *gotisk* ("Gothic") *rännknut*, or *sexkantsknut* ("hexagonal joint") (Fig. 6.18).[54] In common with American round-log diamond notching, the Swedish type is shaped only toward the ends of the log, displaying a double necking virtually identical in appearance to the Midland form (Fig. 6.19). The only essential difference between the Old and New World types lies in the flattening of the top and bottom of the Swedish notch, yielding a hexagon rather than a diamond. This flattening facilitated the common tightly fitted Scandinavian style of log construction and would have been without purpose on American Midland walls, where chinks were left between the logs.

The evolution of the Swedish hexagonal notch has been carefully studied by northern European ethnographers. Medieval specimens, the oldest surviving examples, were necked only on the underside of the log (Fig. 6.19, sketch A), in a manner identical to the prototypical V-notching; but in the late Middle Ages, necking of the top side developed, initially "on the head and later also on the body of the log inside the notch" (Fig. 6.19, sketch B).[55] Initially the hexagonal shape occurred only within the notch, and a crown retaining the natural round shape of the log was left at the butt (Fig. 6.19, sketch B).[56] By the end of the Middle Ages, craftsmen were carrying the hexagonal shape to the end of the log, and one Swedish ethnographer has referred to this as the "Renaissance notch" (Fig. 6.19, sketch C).[57]

Many such postmedieval Swedish groove notches have an almost perfect diamond, rather than hexagonal, shape. Even as late as the end of the sixteenth century, notching with quite minimal flattening at log top and bottom remained common, particularly in Dalarna Province (Fig. 6.18).[58] Then, in the 1600s, the trend was to steepen the sides of the notch, while at the same time broadening the base and top. In this manner the diamond gave way to a true hexagon and ultimately to an altogether different notch form.[59] Abundant examples of the older, diamond-shaped type of Swedish groove notch survive, and some continued to be made even in later centuries (Fig. 6.20).[60] Surely American dia-

Fig. 6.18.   Diamond-like hexagonal notching dating from 1574, Dalarna Province, Sweden, now in the Skansen museum, Stockholm. It represents type C in Fig. 6.19. (Photo by T.G.J., 1985.)

mond notching derives from this archaic postmedieval variety of groove notching. Nearly all of the Swedish examples are oversided notches, in common with most of their American counterparts, but undersided specimens have been found (Fig. 6.20).[61]

Hexagonal and diamond-shaped groove notching occur principally in a rather confined region of central Sweden (Fig. 6.21). Dalarna is the focus of this area, and the densest concentration of such notching is found around Lake Siljan, in the middle of that

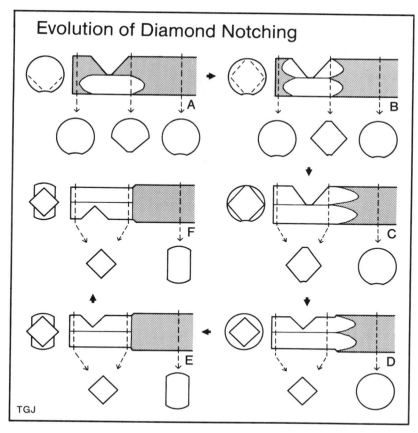

Evolution of Diamond Notching

TGJ

Fig. 6.19. Key: **A** = medieval, Sweden and Norway; **B** = late Middle Ages, Sweden; **C** = Renaissance hexagonal notch, Sweden; **D** = oversided round-log diamond notch; **E** = oversided hewn-log diamond notch; **F** = undersided hewn-log diamond notch. Types A, B, and C are Scandinavian; types D, E, and F are Midland American. (For sources, see Jordan, Kaups, and Lieffort 1986–87a, caption for fig. 10.)

province. Adjacent Härjedalen and nearby Jämtland also offer numerous examples. The oldest specimens are found in Dalarna and bordering western Hälsingland.[62]

Without question, the northern European diamond or hexagonal groove notch is most common in Sweden, though it is conspicuously absent from the Finnish-settled parts of that country. The notch occurs in Norway, though less commonly.[63] Hexagonal groove notching, often with a near-perfect diamond shape, is also occasionally found in Finland. Similar corner-timbering has reputedly been present in southwestern Finland since the 1400s and is said to prevail in some areas there today. It may represent a Swedish introduction. However, the prototypical groove notch, necked only on the underside (Fig. 6.19, sketch A), is also apparently a venerable Karelian Finnish type.[64] To the south, in Estonia, hexagonal notching is known both as the "old Estonian corner" and the "Swedish corner."[65]

Fig. 6.20.   Diamond-like undersided hexagonal groove notching, dating from the nineteenth century, in Kilvåmsbodarna, Tåsjö Parish, Ångermanland Province, Sweden. (Photo by John Granlund, 1932, courtesy of Nordiska museet, Stockholm, arkiv, item no. EU17202 and photo no. 150Kaj, used with permission.)

These East Baltic occurrences aside, Sweden is the most likely source of American diamond notching. We believe that the post-medieval or Renaissance groove notch spread from Sweden to the Delaware Valley colony, most likely brought over by an ethnic Swede. The person or persons responsible probably came from Dalarna, but possibly from Jämtland or the valley of the Klarälven in Värmland Province. Emigrants from Dalarna and Jämtland, as well as Värmland of course, including both ethnic Swedes and Finns, did help colonize the Delaware Valley (Fig. 3.1).[66] In any

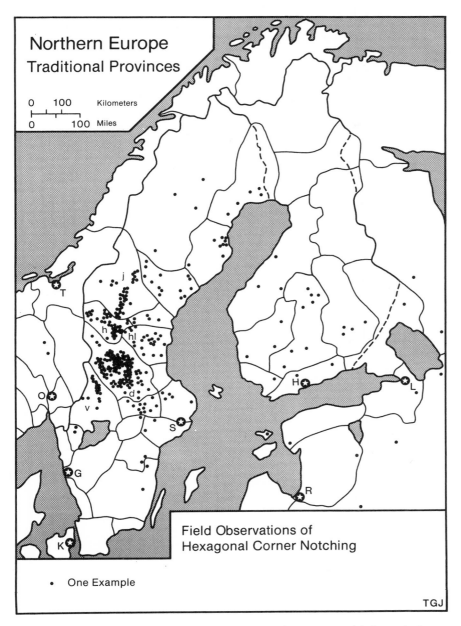

Fig. 6.21. Notching of a type ancestral to the diamond variety most likely reached New Sweden from the Dalarna concentration. Key: **d** = Dalarna; **G** = Göteborg; **H** = Helsinki; **h** = Härjedalen; **hl** = Hälsingland; **j** = Jämtland; **K** = København; **L** = Leningrad; **O** = Oslo; **R** = Riga; **S** = Stockholm; **T** = Trondheim; **v** = Värmland. (For sources, see Jordan, Kaups, and Lieffort 1986–87a, caption for fig. 13.)

case, the diamond notch provides yet another obvious link between the American and Scandinavian log-carpentry traditions.

Diamond notching lacks any particular adaptive value, because it is more difficult and labor consuming to fashion than certain cruder forms such as V-notching. This deficiency helps explain its failure to attain widespread acceptance on the Midland frontier, and it also suggests that Swedes were less important than Finns in shaping American pioneer carpentry. However, the lack of adaptive value itself becomes diagnostic. The presence of such incidental aspects of northern European carpentry in Midland America weakens any case for independent invention and virtually proves the diffusion from Sweden. In this sense, the unnecessary double-pointing to produce the diamond shape falls in the same category as artistic decoration, becoming all the more potent as a key to diffusion precisely because of its superfluousness.

Chinking

Almost universally, Midland backwoods carpentry utilized "chink" construction. Adjacent logs in the wall did not touch, because a crack, or chink, from half an inch to several inches wide, was left between them, a practice distinctive to the Midland woodworking tradition in North America and one of its diagnostic features (Figs. 6.2, 6.7). Even today, chink construction can be observed wherever Midland building techniques spread, from Pennsylvania to Texas and British Columbia.[67] Conversely, the careful shaping of logs to fit them tightly together in the wall is an almost unfailing indicator that the structure does not belong in the Midland tradition (Fig. 6.1).[68] The adaptive advantage of leaving chinks rests in ease of construction.

On outbuildings, particularly haybarns and corncribs, the chinks usually remained open, to facilitate ventilation, and even some pioneer dwellings were similarly exposed to the weather.[69] Normally, however, cabins, as well as smokehouses, among the American backwoods folk had the cracks between the logs filled with "chinking" and were made airtight with some sort of "daubing."[70] Chinking material, which varied considerably, included boards, thin slats of split wood, rails, heartwood billets, poles, moss, and small rocks.[71] Backwoods pioneers normally employed ordinary mud or clay as daubing, sometimes mixing it with grass, straw, or hair as a binder (Fig. 6.14). A lime-and-sand cement also could be used for daubing, but frontier carpenters rarely took such trouble.[72] One Texas settler, a typical backwoodsman, recalled that he "cut chinkin' out of little poles mostly," then "chinked the cracks and plastered them over with mud."[73]

Both chink construction and chinking belong in the older northern European log-carpentry tradition and were implanted very early in the Delaware Valley (Fig. 6.13). Two surviving seventeenth-century log buildings in the area of New Sweden have chinked walls, and early observers mentioned structures having "sand and stones filled up betwixt the logs," and "crevices stopped up with clay."[74] At the same time, some surviving log buildings associated with New Sweden's settlers are of rather refined chinkless construction. Most likely, chink carpentry was introduced by the Finns, while the tightly fitted structures were built by Swedes. Since the chinked wall was easier to construct, it proved better preadapted to the frontier and became the Midland norm. The more refined, chinkless technique never progressed beyond the banks of the Delaware.[75]

The proposed connection between chink construction and Finns becomes clear if the pattern of distribution in northern Europe is considered (Fig. 6.22). In areas settled by Finns, particularly the Savo-Karelian and Lappish districts, open-chink construction remains very common on outbuildings (Figs. 6.3, 7.16). Northern Savo and Häme, the principal source regions of the Värmland and Delaware Finns, retain abundant open-chink structures today, particularly haysheds. By contrast, areas settled or influenced by Swedes contain far fewer instances of such carpentry. Indians had for centuries stored corn in ventilated structures, and the Finnish open-chink meadow hayshed proved admirably preadapted to this same purpose of corn storage when introduced to the Delaware Valley.[76]

Finns also have a very old tradition of filling the cracks between logs with some form of chinking, a practice that was especially common among the Karelians and the Värmland Finns (Figs. 6.22, 6.23, 7.19). Moss was the most common chinking material, and *The Kalevala* refers to a "moss-caulked house" (Fig. 3.8).[77] Archaeological finds suggest that clay may also have been used as chinking in Finland, as far back as prehistoric times, though a Finnish visitor to the Delaware Valley about 1750 was surprised to find the New Sweden descendants using clay chinking instead of the usual moss.[78] Analysis of a chinking sample we removed from an abandoned structure in northern Finland, near the border of Lappland, revealed reindeer moss (actually a lichen), sawdust, sand, and hair clippings (Fig. 3.8).[79] Another Finnish chinking method utilized poles (*neulahirsi*) or small boards. This remains the favored Värmland practice and is similar to several Midland American methods (Fig. 6.23).[80]

Ethnographers regard chink construction as the most ancient and primitive type in northern Europe, and its survival in Finnish areas is best regarded as a relic distribution rather than a venerable ethnic affiliation. As the centuries passed, the more refined and time-consuming chinkless log carpentry spread, and the older, primitive method was increasingly confined to outbuildings or structures for summer use and banished to the remoter interior districts of northern Europe.[81] Clearly, chink construction characterized the Savo-Karelian frontier and in that capacity reached the Delaware Valley.

Missing, however, from the Fenno-Scandian chinking tradition was daubing, unless the few prehistoric fragments of clay chinking that have been found can be considered as such. Instead, the Finns left the chinking material exposed, at least on the exterior. Perhaps in earlier centuries, when chinked dwellings were still common, greater care was taken to make the wall weathertight, but all surviving chinked structures that we observed in northern Europe lack daubing. It may be that the Scotch-Irish experience

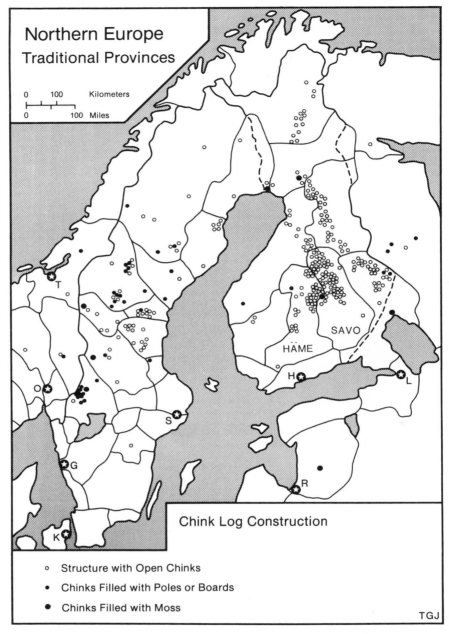

Fig. 6.22.   The concentration of chink construction is particularly notable in Savo-Karelian areas. Compare Fig. 3.5. (Sources: principally field research; notable examples are contained in the following open-air museums: Jamtli, exhibits no. 8, 13, 14; Lycksele hembygdsgård; Tröndelag folkemuseum, exhibit no. 10; Norsk folkemuseum, exhibit no. 76; Arvidsjaur Lappstaden; Valdres folkemuseum; and Latvijas etnogrāfiskais brīvdabas muzejs. See also Nordiska museet, arkiv, especially photos no. 13Yj, 22Dak, 24Fy, 29Ak, 43Bå, 85Eah, 106Das, 157Pl, 16Aaj, 186Caf, 189Ch, 238Lac, 257Kz, 270Ln, 370Hah, 409In, 431Daz, 431Daå, 467Faf, 468Då, and item no. EU45460; National Museum of Finland, Archives, especially photos no. 2576.16, 2631.47, 3031.54, 3210.169, 3490.960; Sirelius 1909, pp. 27–28; Sirelius 1911, p. 116; and Levander 1943–47, vol. 3, p. 79.)

Fig. 6.23. A Finnish single-crib log haybarn with slats and poles as chinking, in the Finnskog, Värmland Province, Sweden, near Lekvattnet. Such chinking is common among the Värmland Finns. (Photo by Nils Keyland, 1916, Nordiska museet, Stockholm, arkiv, no. 29Ar, used with permission.)

with chimney daubing or the Germanic practice of wattle-and-daub construction provided the prototype for the American frontier practice.

Others have attributed Midland chink carpentry, together with chinking and daubing, to log-building Germans, who emigrated to colonial America from Silesia, Saxony, Bohemia, and Moravia.[82] These claims were made in the absence of any field data, and it is not difficult to see how such a conclusion might be reached on the basis of photographs in secondary sources. The eastern German structures display the same striped pattern—dark logs alternating with light daubing—as those in Midland America. Close field inspection, however, revealed to us that most of the German buildings in question are not examples of chink construction. Instead, the logs touch in the center of the wall, so that chinking is not required, and the daubing merely fills the indentations left by the natural curvature of the logs. The Finnish methods are much closer to the Midland American backwoods techniques. Moreover, the eastern German immigrants in question arrived after 1730, long after the earliest references to chinked-log construction in the Delaware Valley, and in any case the adoption of the New Sweden chinking techniques by the Scotch-Irish was documented by an eighteenth-century visitor.[83]

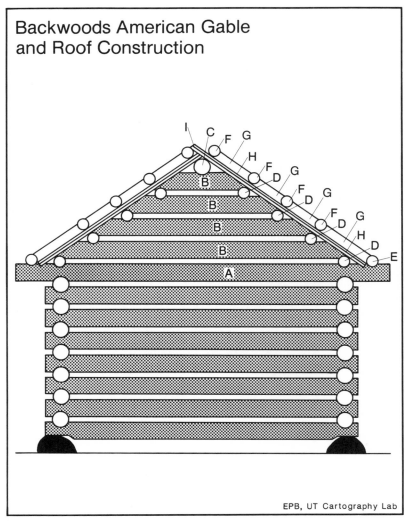

Backwoods American Gable
and Roof Construction

EPB, UT Cartography Lab

Fig. 6.24. Key: **A** = eave beam; **B** = trap logs (trapping); **C** = ridgepole;
D = purlins (rib poles); **E** = butting poles; **F** = weightpoles; **G** = knees;
H = clapboards; **I** = capping. (After Hutslar 1986, fig. 123.)

Building the Gables and Roof

The most prevalent form of gable- and roof-building by Midland
backwoods pioneers was known as "ridgepole and purlin" construction (Fig. 6.24). Gables, in common with the lower walls,
consisted of logs, into which were notched a ridgepole and parallel
purlins, also called "rib poles," which ran the length of the building from one gable to the other and easily bore the weight of the
roofing material (Fig. 6.25). The timbers that formed the gables
were known as "trap logs." The pitch of a ridgepole-purlin roof
was low, generally between about 20° and 25°, but ranging as low
as 5° or 10° and as steep as 30°. In postpioneer times, after the
frontier era had passed and the backwoods people had moved

Fig. 6.25. A typical American backwoods low-pitched, ridgepole-and-purlin roof structure, on a squatter's cabin in Taney County, Missouri. Such roofs largely disappeared with the passing of the frontier era in the eastern United States. Note that the ridgepole and purlins are notched into the trap logs of the gable wall, providing solid, substantial support for the roof. (Photo by Lynn Morrow, 1985, Firm of Kalen and Morrow, Forsyth, Missouri; used with permission.)

west, a steeper, raftered roof containing board gables and lacking a ridgepole replaced the earlier log type.[84] The link between pioneering and the ridgepole-purlin roof becomes clear from a reading of contemporary settler accounts. In the first decade of colonization in southern Michigan, for example, "it is doubtful if there was a cabin with rafters and board gable in Cass or Van Buren counties, and for years after you could distinguish the eastern [secondary] settler from the [backwoods] southerner by the board gable with rafters."[85] Few ridgepole-purlin roofs survive in the eastern United States today, but the plains and mountains of the West, where the frontier imprint remains more vivid, form a last stronghold of the pioneer roof (Fig. 7.21).[86] A particularly low-pitched ridgepole-purlin type is so common beyond the hundredth meridian as to be called the "Anglo-western roof."[87] The adaptive advantage of the ridgepole-purlin roof on the frontier was based in part on the greater ease with which it could be constructed. The raftered roof with board gables required more work and a higher level of craftsmanship.

Finns and backcountry Swedes in northern Europe knew no gabled roof type other than the ridgepole-purlin, and there is no reason to doubt that they introduced it to New Sweden.[88] Even today, the great majority of log buildings in Scandinavia and Finland exhibit such gables and roofs (Figs. 6.3, 6.23). In Savo-

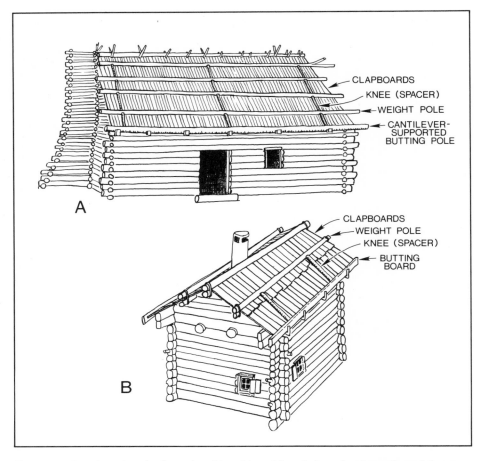

Fig. 6.26. **A** = American backwoods cabin with weightpole-knee-butting-pole roof, from a 1791 sketch, probably in frontier Georgia. **B** = portion of a house from the Karelian Isthmus (now part of the Soviet Union), on display at the Seurasaaren ulkomuseo in Helsinki; note that it, too, has a weightpole-knee-butting-board roof. (Sources: Swanton 1946, pl. 58; Valonen 1963, p. 45.)

Karelian areas, measurements of roof pitch yielded figures normally ranging between 13° and 27°, consistent with most Midland American specimens. Some duplicated the extremely low pitch of the Anglo-western roof.[89] The gentle pitch of the roof, coupled with the great strength achieved by the notching of ridgepole and purlins into gable logs, offered yet another adaptive advantage in northern Europe. Snow could easily accumulate on the roof, providing much-needed insulation in the winter season. The gentle pitch had one additional virtue, both in Europe and frontier America: roofing remained in place largely by the force of gravity, requiring no nails or pegs as fasteners. The raftered roof was not as strong and could not as readily accommodate a gentle pitch.

In the Alps, where winters are as bitter and snowy as those in northern Europe, the ridgepole-purlin roof also occurs on log buildings.[90] Alpine Germans may have accomplished a second introduction of this roof type into colonial America after about

Fig. 6.27.   The ridgepole-and-purlin roof with butting pole (here a board), weightpoles, knees, and clapboards on the Abraham Lincoln birthplace cabin, Hodgenville, Kentucky. Compare it to Fig. 6.28. (Photo by W. L. McCoy, Hodgenville, Kentucky; used with permission.)

1710, but the earlier Finnish-Swedish diffusion was in all probability the crucial one for Midland backwoods carpentry. Moreover, the most common Germanic roof in Europe was precisely the steep, raftered type associated with secondary settlement in Midland America. As before, we observe an apparent link between Finn and frontier on the one hand, between Germanic folk and secondary settlement on the other.

The roof covering employed by American backwoods carpenters further demonstrates the connection to Finnish material culture. In the Savo-Karelian areas of northern Europe and on the Midland frontier, a most unusual and distinctive wooden roofing prevailed, offering virtual proof that the Finns of the Delaware Valley exerted an influence on American forest pioneer culture. Because this roofing method constitutes very important diagnostic evidence in support of our thesis, we describe and illustrate it in some detail here.

Construction of the Midland pioneer roof began with the last log below the gable in each end wall. These two logs, called "eave bearers" or "eave beams," were allowed to project as cantilevers "a foot or eighteen inches" on both ends (Fig. 6.26).[91] Into the projecting beams, on each side of the building, were notched "butting poles" or "butt logs," which ran the length of the eave, parallel to the purlins and ridgepole. In the words of an Ohio pioneer,

Fig. 6.28. A Finnish roof with clapboards, capping, weightpole, knees, and butting board, from Kaukola, near Käkisalmi on the Karelian Isthmus (now part of the Soviet Union). The house is part of exhibit no. 20 at the Seurasaaren ulkomuseo, Helsinki. Such roofs are the almost exact prototype for the American backwoods type. (Photo by T.G.J., 1985.)

"The eave bearers are those end logs which project over to receive the butting poles."[92]

The next step was to select a straight-grained tree three to four feet in diameter, usually an oak or an ash, and, using a frow, split clapboards from it measuring three or four feet in length, one half to three fourths of an inch in thickness, and five to eight inches in width.[93] The first "course" of clapboards, also called a "range" or "tier," was then placed loosely on the lower purlins, resting at the lower end against the butting pole. To help hold the clapboards in place, a substantial "weightpole" was then laid atop the first course, usually directly above one of the purlins (Fig. 6.27). To keep the weightpole from sliding or rolling down the roof, heartwood spacers called "knees" were inserted perpendicularly between it and the butting pole.[94] Sometimes the weightpole and purlin below it were tied together at each end to add still more stability. A second course of clapboards overlapped the first, in shingle fashion, often resting at its lower end against the weightpole, as did a second set of knees, which in turn supported yet another weightpole higher on the roof.[95] The number of courses depended upon the size of the roof and the length of the clapboards. At the ridge, boards on the windward side were allowed to project six inches or so beyond the crest to serve as "capping."

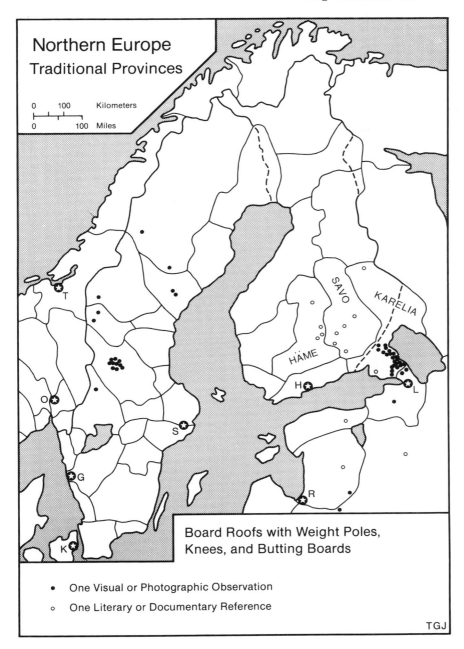

Fig. 6.29. The distribution of this roof type coincides with that of Savoan and Karelian settlement shown in Fig. 3.5. (Sources: National Museum of Finland, Archives, photos no. 3.1, 985.7, 1069.17, 1069.21, 3321.6, and photos in the 3490 series; Nordiska museet, arkiv, photos no. 39Ev, 42Cg, 43Bå, 44Jå, 48Jm, 108Iac, 108Iz, 149Aad, 150Nab, 191Ek, 414Qu, 450Uar; Zornsamlingarna, arkiv, photo no. 57 and photos in Toresen and Rot skans files; Seurasaaren ulkomuseo, exhibit no. 20; items cited in nn. 98, 99, 100, and 101 of this chapter; Bielenstein 1907, pp. 24–32; Wallin 1892–93; Lagus 1893, p. 13; Hämäläinen 1930, p. 259; Paulaharju 1906, p. 45.)

Fig. 6.30.   A double-pen Karelian house with typical roof, including ridgepole, purlins, butting board, weightpole, knees, and clapboards. The central passage, once open, is enclosed as a hall. Compare the roof to American examples in Figs. 6.26 and 6.27. The house is near Lahdenmaa, Kirvu Parish, on the Karelian Isthmus, now part of the Soviet Union. (Photo by U. T. Sirelius, 1908, courtesy of National Museum of Finland, Helsinki, no. 985.7, used with permission.)

This most unusual roof covering accompanied Midland pioneers wherever they ventured in the eastern forests. Examples can be documented from Pennsylvania, Georgia, Texas, Indiana, Virginia, Iowa, Michigan, and many other states.[96] Settler accounts clearly indicate that clapboard-weightpole-knee roofing was the dominant pioneer type, and it continued to be employed in new settlements in the Appalachians as late as the 1890s. The lack of need for nails or pegs to hold the roofing in place was an adaptive advantage in frontier conditions. Shingling, a German tradition, came to dominate Midland structures only in the secondary stage of settlement.[97]

The precise prototype of the American pioneer roofing technique occurred in northern Europe, mainly among Savoan and Karelian Finns (Fig. 6.28).[98] The use of clapboards, called *liiste* in Finnish, which rest against a butting beam at the eaves, of weightpoles positioned above purlins, knees as spacers, and capping on the windward side, was once fairly widespread east of the Baltic, from Latvia and the Novgorod area northward into Karelia (Fig. 6.29).[99] Such roofing is venerable there, and was linked to the forest pioneering activities of the Savo-Karelians in interior Finland.

Fig. 6.31.   A roof with butting board, weightpole, and knees, in Tännäs Parish, Härjedalen Province, Sweden. Note how the roof boards project beyond the ridge crest as capping, in the American manner. The use of weight stones is not typical, but the practice occurs occasionally in interior Sweden. (Photo, 1927, courtesy of Nordiska museet, Stockholm, arkiv, no. 191Ek, used with permission.)

It is commemorated in a reference in *The Kalevala* to a cabin with a "planked roof." The Finnish clapboard roof with weightpoles, knees, and butting board survived into modern times on the Karelian Isthmus (Fig. 6.30).[100] It also spread with the Savo-Karelians to Sweden, where some examples can still be seen (Figs. 6.29, 6.31).[101]

Independent invention of this highly distinctive roofing method could hardly have occurred. Instead, we feel certain that it spread with Finns to the New Sweden colony, where it became the model for the American frontier roof. Indeed, one could hardly ask for a more convincing demonstration of the validity of our main thesis. Because of its several, previously mentioned advantages, Savo-Karelian roofing proved more suitable on the American frontier than other, competing types introduced from Europe. German shingling required more and finer splitting work, as well as nails. Dutch thatching, introduced into the Hudson Valley, was both tedious and time consuming, with the result that it never became common in America.[102] British roof types, likewise, were rejected by the Midland backwoods settlers.[103]

Other Carpentry Features

Many, perhaps most, pioneer cabins had floors of earth or packed clay. A traveler among Midland backwoods pioneers in Missouri visited cabins in which "the floor was the earth, and filthy in the extreme"; similar references for other areas are abundant.[104] A minority of frontier dwellings, though, boasted "puncheon" floors, made of thick rived-and-hewn boards about four to six feet in length. The puncheons reached only from one floor joist to the next and were heavy enough to rest loosely, rather than being fastened down.[105]

Earthen floors occurred widely in seventeenth-century European rural dwellings, both in the British Isles and in the subarctic north, as well as among eastern woodland American Indian tribes. The origin of the Midland pioneer practice may well be multiple. Backcountry Finns knew both earthen and loose-board floors. In common with American pioneers, Finns stored items of food below the floor, simply lifting boards when access was desired. In addition, the shipbuilding tradition in northern Europe, as far back as Viking times, featured loose puncheon decking.[106]

The American backwoods dwelling usually also lacked a ceiling and windows (Fig. 6.25). "A cabin has commonly no windows at all," noted an early traveler in western Pennsylvania, and later observers in other frontier areas echoed his complaint.[107] Sometimes, though, a small window was present, "protected with a kind of clarified raw-hide that admitted light," "greased paper," or only a clapboard shutter held by leather hinges.[108] Though lacking ceilings, many cabins had a sleeping loft covering as much as half the room. Another favored sleeping place was a one-legged bed quickly fashioned by driving a forked pole into the earthen floor near a corner of the cabin, placing rails that reached from the fork to the wall chinks in two directions, adding rived slats, and stretching a hide over the top.[109]

A windowless stone cabin with sleeping loft was a common Celtic type in Europe. The American pioneer dwelling no doubt reflects some British influence in these respects, but traditional Finnish log houses of the interior districts also usually lacked ceilings and had both sleeping lofts and one-legged corner beds.[110] In some parts of northern Europe, cabins once had small, parchment-covered apertures, but the most common Savo-Karelian window, closed by a sliding board that ran in a groove, did not gain acceptance on the American frontier, though it had been introduced to New Sweden.[111]

While some pioneers were satisfied with mere smoke holes for ventilation, most insisted upon proper chimneys and fireplaces. On the Midland frontier, chimney construction was normally achieved through carpentry rather than masonry (Fig. 5.1). At the midpoint of one gable wall, the pioneer sawed out a hole for the fireplace, "then took short logs, notched them down good [to diminish the chinks], and built a [small] pen with three sides around that hole," notching the logs into the gable wall. This

firebox extended to about mantle height, then tapered down to a
freestanding chimney built of notched sticks, reaching above the
level of the roof ridge (Fig. 6.26). The firebox then acquired a lining
of flat rocks, and the interior wooden surfaces were thickly plastered with mud.[112] Such chimneys, "made of wood and Lath'd &
filled with Clay" existed in the Delaware Valley nucleus of the
Midland culture.[113]

The American backwoods fireplace and chimney owe only
their notched log construction to the Finns and Swedes. In all
other respects—exterior position, central placement in a gable
wall, shape, dimensions, and arrangement—they display British
features. Even the daubing or plastering was probably derived from
the English or Scotch-Irish.[114] By contrast, the Finns had never
developed a satisfactory method of ventilating their home fires.
The interior walls of the Savo-Karelian dwelling bore a blackening
of soot, causing Swedes to call the Finnish dwellings "smoke cabins." A low open hearth of clay and stone stood in one corner of
the dwelling, and at best a hollow tree trunk guided smoke up
toward a small hole in the upper wall or roof. Only in the nineteenth century did proper chimneys diffuse through the Finnish
backcountry. The crude, inadequately ventilated Savo-Karelian
corner hearth reached the Delaware Valley, but gave way there to
the British fireplace and chimney as the Midland pioneer culture
coalesced.[115]

In northern states, at least, the exterior British-style chimney
represented yet another transitory symbol of the frontier. Secondary settlers there preferred masonry chimneys built inside the
wall of the house. One Michigan settler later recalled that the
pioneer cabin could easily be identified by its exterior chimney.[116]
In the South, the chimney remained outside the wall in postpioneer times, but log-and-stick construction gave way to stone
or brick masonry in most areas.

Cabin versus House

The preceding description and analysis of Midland log carpentry
demonstrates that in various ways the backwoods pioneer dwelling was distinct from the log house of the secondary settlement
phase. Contemporary observers clearly recognized this contrast,
employing the terms "cabin" and "house" to distinguish the two
traditions. One traveler journeying west of the Appalachians
about 1800 reported that "the temporary buildings of the first settlers in the wilds are called *Cabins*," characterized by "unhewn
logs," a roof "covered with a sort of thin staves . . . fastened on by
heavy poles," and rail chinking "daubed with mud." By contrast,
"if the logs be hewed, if the interstices be stopped with stone and
neatly plastered, and if the roof [be] composed of shingles nicely
laid on, it is called a *log-house*."[117] Countless other observers,
both earlier and later, restated this dichotomy.[118] In sum, pioneer
cabins displayed crude carpentry, with round logs projecting at
the corners, small size, low height, earthen or puncheon floors,

ridgepole-purlin-weightpole roofs, mud-sealed chinking, exterior daubed wooden chimneys, and minimal fenestration. Erected by amateur laborers, they had a limited lifespan.

Students of American folk architecture have, justifiably, accepted this traditional classification of log carpentry in their research on states as diverse as Alabama, Oregon, and Utah.[119] The dichotomy hardly represents an overstatement. Previous sections of the present chapter further demonstrate that backcountry northern European carpentry prevailed in the American frontier cabin stage.

In Finland and Scandinavia, Savo-Karelian pioneer log structures "were poorly made and did not last long."[120] As a result, relatively few buildings of this type survive in northern Europe, a problem compounded by the tendency of most curators to select only the best-crafted carpentry specimens for preservation and display at the scores of outdoor folk museums. In our field research, however, we found enough examples of crude, cabin-style carpentry in Finland and Scandinavia—mainly in northern regions and remote mountain pastures—to verify that construction techniques compatible with those of the Midland American frontier had formerly been abundant among the Savo-Karelian Finns (Figs. 3.8, 6.3, 6.23).[121]

If the primitive Midland backwoods carpentry tradition was essentially Finnish in origin, then a question must be addressed concerning the quite different, far more refined log construction techniques introduced by Finns into the upper Midwest between about 1880 and 1920.[122] The distinctive North Woods Finnish carpentry in Michigan, Wisconsin, and Minnesota can easily be recognized as alien to the Midland tradition. It displays notch types unknown to the Pennsylvania-derived builders, as well as chinkless walls. Can both traditions be Fenno-Scandian? The answer is yes, for several reasons. First, most Finns who settled the upper Midwest were not Savo-Karelians, but instead came largely from the coastal provinces of Finland, especially Pohjanmaa (Fig. 3.1). The cultural contrasts between coastal and interior Finns, described in Chapter 3, are fundamental. Swedish influence, which remains strong in the Finnish littoral, has had profound effects on carpentry. Second, the Finnish migration to the Lake Superior region occurred a quarter of a millennium after the Delaware Valley colonization. During those two and a half centuries, the more primitive carpentry associated with Savo-Karelian expansion became largely relict, retreating to the northern and upland refuges, where vestiges of it survive today. Indeed, a diligent Swedish field researcher seeking architectural traces of the older Savo-Karelian tradition about 1880 penetrated far into the Finnish interior before finding examples.[123]

To accept the Midland American cabin/house dichotomy and the Fenno-Scandian origin of cabin carpentry is not to deny northern European influence in the later house stage. As described earlier, both V- and diamond notching made the transition from round-log to hewn-log construction, as did chinking. The Germanic imprint was greater on the secondary carpentry phase, but by no means did Finnish and Scandinavian contributions disappear. In fact, Swedish techniques may have been more important than those of the Germans in postpioneer log carpentry. Some of the carefully crafted, hewn, dovetailed log dwellings erected by Swedes in the Delaware Valley still stand, and they could well have provided a model for second-generation Midland construction techniques. New Sweden received both the crude, backcountry Finnish methods and the more refined Swedish methods.[124] In terms of carpentry, periphery and core were represented from the first in the Delaware colony by two distinct ethnic woodworking traditions.

Diffusion and Distribution

The crudely fashioned Finnish carpentry gained acceptance by other frontier ethnic groups in the Midland cultural hearth precisely because of its simplicity, which allowed neophytes to acquire the methods without undue difficulty, and because of its several preadapted advantages, described earlier. Finns and Swedes in the Delaware Valley, extending help to new arrivals such as the Quakers, both "assisted them to build . . . dwellings" and sold existing houses to them.[125] By 1700, long before the arrival of log-building Germans from Switzerland and the Slavic borderland, settlers of diverse ethnic backgrounds along the Delaware lived in log structures. As early as the 1670s some English colonists there had log houses, as did Holstein Germans.[126] Many Welsh followed their example in the following decade, as did some other British settlers.[127] Even the Dutch at New Castle occasionally had log structures built by hired carpenters.[128] By the middle of the eighteenth century, the later-arriving Scotch-Irish occupied chinked log cabins similar to those of the earlier Swedish and Finnish pioneers.[129]

Some very rapid diffusion of Delaware Valley log carpentry to other areas apparently occurred. By the 1660s the technique had reached the Maryland Eastern Shore, and by about 1680 at least one "house made of Logs, such as the *Swedes* in *America* very often make," stood in the Albemarle Sound region of northeastern North Carolina.[130] These early references are compatible with known and possible dispersals of fugitive settlers from New Sweden.

Eventually, Midland log carpentry, revealed by its array of distinctive construction features, not only spread through the primary domain of the culture but also diffused into the immediate hinterlands of the coastal-based New Englanders and southern planters (Fig. 6.1). As early as 1728, in the area between the Dismal Swamp and Albemarle Sound, along the Virginia–North Carolina border not far from the Atlantic, "most of the houses" were log structures covered with board roofs.[131] The diffusion into backcountry New England, especially Vermont and New Hampshire, began about 1760, coincident with the spread of Midland forest clearance methods, at the close of the French and Indian War. Yankee troops returning from service in Pennsylvania probably acted as the agents of diffusion. By 1790, typical Midland round-log construction with clay-and-moss chinking prevailed among pioneers in upcountry New Hampshire, and some houses displaying the diagnostic Midland V-notching still stand in northern Vermont.[132] In the inner coastal plain of the South, log construction remained important in postpioneer times, even after the plantation system displaced the yeoman farmer, but in New England, log buildings almost completely disappeared during the secondary phase of settlement, obscuring the transitory Midland backwoods cultural influence there.

To the west, cabin-type carpentry reached all of the Midland secondary domain and zone of penetration (Figs. 1.3, 6.1). Individual specimens can even be found in some areas of the West that were largely untouched by Midland culture. The Rocky Mountains and other forested ranges of the West today offer examples of some of the best surviving backwoods Midland carpentry. Regrettably, the log buildings of the West remain largely unstudied, their abundance having yielded neglect.[133]

A carpentry method can be applied to many different architectural styles. Potentially, at least, building technique stands independent of floor plan and design. In fact, however, Midland backwoods carpentry was applied to an equally distinctive and diagnostic folk architecture, a style we will consider in Chapter 7.

SEVEN

BACKWOODS FOLK ARCHITECTURE

A house is looming up yonder . . .
Whose house indeed is it,
What good-for-nothing's home . . . ?

Kalevala

American backwoods log architecture encompassed a small number of simple, efficient, and interchangeable house and barn plans, a complex that possessed adaptive value in the woodland frontier setting (Fig. 7.1). The basic dwelling unit was a rectangular "pen" consisting of four log walls, which could be doubled in several distinctive ways to accommodate enlargement. If the structure served as an outbuilding instead of a house, "crib" rather than "pen" was used to describe the basic unit. Universal concepts of pen/crib construction and enlargement accompanied the Midland backwoods pioneers in their diffusion through the American forests.[1]

The Dogtrot Cabin

At least one of the Midland backwoods dwelling types, the so-called dogtrot or open-passage house, is so distinctive as to possess diagnostic qualities. A wide house consisting of two full-sized pens of equal or roughly equal size separated by an open-air breezeway in the center and covered by a single span of roof with side-facing gables, the dogtrot was normally of single or one-and-a-half story height (Fig. 7.1, sketches F, G; Fig. 7.2).[2]

The common folk early recognized this as a highly distinctive floor plan and applied to it names such as "double log house," "double-pen," "two-pens-and-a-passage," "three-P," "dogrun," "possumtrot," "saddlebag," "dingle," and "East Texas house."[3] Though the plan was very common in frontier areas, numerous travelers felt compelled to describe the dogtrot type in their journals. A typical observer, in Oklahoma, explained how "two square pens are put up with logs" and the "space between the pens is covered in and serves for eating-place and depository of harness, saddles, and bridles."[4] Another early traveler, in 1828, noticed that almost all of the "forest houses in the interior of the state of

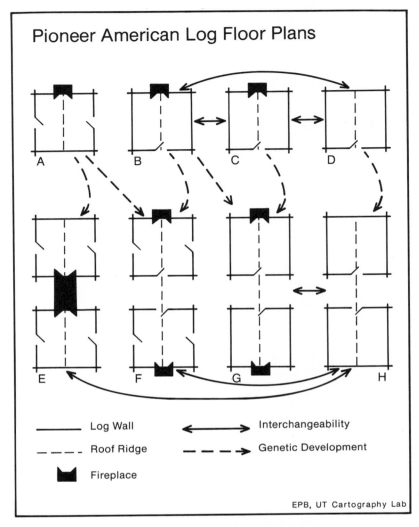

Fig. 7.1. Key: **A** = single-pen cabin, English plan; **B** = single-pen cabin, Finnish plan; **C** = freestanding kitchen; **D** = single-crib barn, smokehouse, or corncrib; **E** = saddlebag double-pen house; **F** = dogtrot double-pen house with British eave doors; **G** = dogtrot double-pen house without eave doors; **H** = open-passage double-crib barn. The plans are to a remarkable degree interchangeable.

Georgia consist of two divisions, separated by a wide, open passage, which extends from the front to the back of the building."[5]

In spite of its distinctive appearance and obvious diagnostic potential, the dogtrot plan is burdened by a clouded cultural history. Until recently, attempts to explain its origin and diffusion produced mainly controversy.[6] Even famous men of letters had their say on the subject of dogtrot genesis. Herman Melville facetiously attributed the partitioned plan to "some architect affiliated with a quarrelsome family."[7] Folklorist Henry Glassie proposed that the dogtrot evolved in the Upland South as an Americanism, relatively late. Altering somewhat a suggestion by

Fig. 7.2. A single-story dogtrot log cabin at Brownsville, near the western border of Pennsylvania. Note the roof weightpoles, wooden chimney, and worm fence. (Source: Smith 1854, illus. facing p. 232.)

Fred Kniffen, Glassie supported an origin in eastern or southeast-ern Tennessee about 1825, when "some clever individual(s)" modified the British central-hall, gable-chimneyed house of the American southern Tidewater district by converting the passage into a breezeway.[8] Students and associates of Kniffen and Glassie have, with minor modifications, accepted this view.[9]

Glassie pointed to the Tidewater district from North Carolina to Georgia, from Pamlico Sound to the vicinity of Savannah, as the likely hearth area of the enclosed-hall prototype, but others favor the Virginia and Maryland Chesapeake shore.[10] Some schol-ars feel that the dogtrot evolved earlier, in the eighteenth century, probably in Virginia and presumably from the same New World British prototype (Fig. 7.3).[11] The Georgian-inspired symmetry of the British central-hall house was supposedly influential in guid-ing development of the dogtrot.[12]

In tracing the genealogy of the British prototype to Europe, pro-ponents of this viewpoint fell into mild disagreement. Some fa-vored the ancient Welsh and southwestern English longhouse, a Germanic type that originally sheltered people and livestock on different sides of the passage. Equipped with front and rear doors to provide access to the central hall, the longhouse by 1600 had become exclusively a dwelling. Others championed the very sim-ilar enclosed "through-passage of the north-west Ulster house."[13] In any case, the gable-chimneyed central-hall house was wide-spread in the British Isles. English, Welsh, and Scotch-Irish all

Fig. 7.3. A story-and-a-half dogtrot house on the New River in Giles County, western Virginia, reputedly built in 1783 and no longer extant. It was situated near the Great Valley of the Appalachians, a major route of Pennsylvania migration. Note the worm fence. (Source: Johnston 1906, illus. facing p. 398; see also pp. 396–98, 448.)

knew the type. A similar trisected house plan, lacking gable placement of the hearth, occurred across much of Europe.[14]

Etymology offers additional, if somewhat confusing, evidence of British influence. The term *double house,* often applied to the dogtrot type, apparently derives from England. However, the original British meaning did not suggest the presence of a central hallway, nor did a passage necessarily exist in houses to which the term was applied in America. In England, as in the colonial United States, a double house was often simply a two-room dwelling. William Penn did not further elaborate upon the "double brick house" he observed in Philadelphia in 1685, suggesting that it was a type known to him in England. Similar references in eighteenth-century New England and Virginia do not imply the dogtrot plan.[15] Moreover, similar cognates such as the Swedish *dubbelhus* and German *Doppelhaus* cloud the issue.[16] No doubt an etymological clue is also contained in the use of the vernacular term *saddlebag house* to describe both a double-pen dwelling with a chimney wedged between the two rooms and a dogtrot house taller than one story.[17] Structurally, these two types are very similar, which helps account for the confusion while at the same time suggesting a genetic link between them (Fig. 7.1, sketch E; Fig. 7.4).

Certain other scholars have noted the striking similarity of the

Fig. 7.4. A massive chimney and double fireplace stand between the two log pens of a "saddlebag" house at Fort Washita in southern Oklahoma. The possible kinship to the dogtrot plan is obvious. (Photo by T.G.J., 1981.)

Fig. 7.5. An open-passage double-crib log barn in the Texas Hill Country near Austin. The similarity to the dogtrot house plan is readily apparent. (Photo by T.G.J., 1984.)

dogtrot house to American log double-crib barns with open wagon runways, a widespread barn type often found in the same farmsteads with dogtrot dwellings (Fig. 7.5). The two are probably genetically related, since log houses in Midland America were often later demoted to the status of barns, reflecting a remarkable level of structural interchangeability. Possible derivation of the dogtrot by inspiration from an Alpine hay-meadow open-runway double-crib log barn introduced into Georgia by Salzburg Protestants in the 1730s has been proposed.[18]

Despite the similarity of dogtrots to certain British dwellings or Alpine hay barns, and regardless of the etymological evidence, the fact remains that no house type displaying the single most distinguishing hallmark of the dogtrot—the open central breezeway—occurs anywhere in the British Isles or Germanic lands, or for that matter in the American southern Tidewater.[19] This troublesome absence forced the anglophiles to accept pioneer innovation as the key and to ignore the well-documented conservatism of folk cultures and the rarity of invention on the American frontier.[20] The Germanists face the even less palatable prospect of demanding that a barn served as the model for a house, an unlikely and perhaps unprecedented sequence.

These difficulties prompted some other students of American folk architecture to seek the origin of the dogtrot house elsewhere. A few among them believe that the dogtrot derived from northern Europe, the only region in which double-pen log houses displaying open, central breezeways occurred. They credit the Swedes and Finns who settled in the colonial Delaware Valley with introducing the dogtrot type, a proposal that has met with widespread disapproval.[21]

Dogtrot Cultural Affiliation

The difficulty in resolving this problem of origin rests in a failure to establish cultural and ecological context. Our first task, then, is to verify the Midland affiliation of the dogtrot house. In this respect, many of the previous studies are confusing. On the one hand we read of Tidewater roots, while on the other we are asked to accept an innovative modification embarrassingly far removed from the coast, beyond the boundary between the Tidewater and Midland cultural regions. Nearly all who have addressed the subject ask us to accept the dogtrot as a *southern* type, leaving the lowland/upland dichotomy somehow to be finessed. Origin is variously placed in Tennessee, North Carolina, Georgia, or Virginia, and the proposed British or Alpine prototypes are positioned on the outer southern coastal plain.

It seems to us that the cultural affiliation of the dogtrot house can best be ascertained from that most geographical of undertakings—mapping its occurrence (Fig. 7.6). Remarkably, such a project has never before been attempted on more than a statewide level. Claims of "southern" or Midland affiliation, in the absence of such a map, are without foundation.[22] In compiling the map, we did not rely exclusively upon field observation of the relic specimens still standing. Present distribution is not necessarily representative of past distribution, and "the survival of dog-trots . . . would appear to have little to do with original occurrence."[23] In our search we also used local historical sources and contemporary accounts from past centuries.

Richard H. Hulan was the first to suggest that, when field and documentary evidence of dogtrot distribution was collected, it would reveal a pattern and chronology incompatible with southern origin.[24] While Hulan took only the first tentative steps toward an accurate plotting of dogtrot distribution and diffusion, presenting no map, he intuitively reached the correct conclusions—the dogtrot was far older as an American type than was consistent with upland southern origin, and the several paths of diffusion of the open-breezeway house, when backtracked, led to Pennsylvania, not the Chesapeake or the southern seaboard. The trace has gone somewhat faint, but the Pennsylvania connection seems incontestable.

Indeed a reasonably well documented 1698 log dogtrot house built by a Finnish family still stands near the banks of the Delaware (Fig. 7.7). The remarkable Boulden-Stubbs house, built no later than 1750 near the head of Chesapeake Bay, offers another splendid example of an early dogtrot dwelling near the Midland cultural hearth.[25] Far-flung eighteenth-century log dogtrot specimens from northern New Jersey, northwestern Pennsylvania, Toronto, the western Virginia Ridge and Valley country, the Georgia Fall Line, the area near Natchez on the Mississippi, eastern and central Kentucky, and perhaps even Buffalo, New York, support the logic of Midland origin (Fig. 7.6).[26] Still today, a few surviving specimens occur along some of the presumed major diffusionary paths—the Delaware and Susquehanna rivers, leading into upstate New York and, beyond, toward Ontario; the road from Lancaster to the forks of the Ohio and on down Zane's Trace; the Great Valley, with its low passes eastward onto the Piedmont and west through Cumberland Gap to the Kentucky country; the Ohio and Mississippi river system; and others. Aside from the main paths, migratory eddies or cul-de-sacs in valleys often yield the best surviving specimens (Fig. 7.8).

Aged documents and sketches, sometimes preserved in county histories, yield an even greater harvest than field research. For example, a log house built about 1792 in far northwestern Pennsylvania is clearly revealed to be a dogtrot in a nineteenth-century sketch, and the attached county history traces the builder's migration to the area from the Wyoming Valley, via the Susquehanna and Venango trails.[27] Often the evidence is merely suggestive. We learn, for example, that the first dwelling built in Hagerstown, Maryland, in 1739, consisted of "two large log pens far enough apart to constitute a hall," or that the crude log habitations of the planters in the Maryland backcountry in the 1770s contained "an

Fig. 7.6. These observations of dogtrot-type houses display an obvious link to Midland culture in America. (Sources: field observations; the items listed in nn. 11, 23, 26, and 34 of this chapter; the items listed in Jordan and Kaups 1987; and, particularly for the more controversial areas, Bowman 1971, pp. 63, 76, 170–72; Bracey 1977, pp. 142, 156, 169; Sherman and Sherman 1969, p. 22; Whitwell and Winborne 1982, p. 42; Gregorie 1954, pp. 17, 71; Winberry 1974, p. 68; Howe 1898–1902, vol. 1, p. 700; vol. 2, pp. 192, 327, 465–73, 542, 570; Riedl, Ball, and Cavender 1976, pp. 99–100; Tebbetts 1978, pp. 46–47; Hoover and Rodman 1980, p. 45; Torma and Wells 1986, pp. 3, 29, 64; Williams and Dockery 1984, pp. 12, 20, 38, 67, 88, 119; Lewis 1984, p. 140; Linley 1972, pp. 23, 25, 28–30, 39, 102; Zelinsky 1953, p. 188; Taylor 1981, pp. 138, 148; Little-Stokes 1979, pp. 14, 16, 107, 112; Lounsbury 1980, pp. 18, 100; Swaim 1981, p. 59; Madden 1974, pp. 61, 74; Lancaster 1961, pp. 9, 44; Johnston and Waterman 1941, pp. 7, 16, 19; Clinton and Lofton 1981, pp. 15–21; Freeman 1958, following p. 16; Rohe 1985, pp. 86–91, 102–3; McDowell and

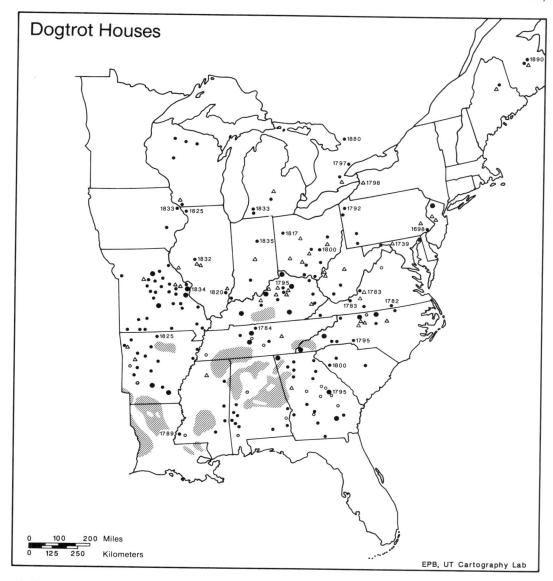

Dogtrot Houses

Abell 1986, pp. 72–73; Central New Brunswick Woodmen's Museum, outdoor exhibits; Groefsema 1949, pp. 309–10; Wilson 1984, pt. 1, pp. 64, 66; Longyear 1915, p. 362; Kniffen 1936, pp. 184, 190–91; Kerkhoff 1962, pp. 122–23; Kentucky Heritage Commission 1979, pp. 83, 88; Marshall 1981, pp. 54–57; Michael and Carlisle 1979, pp. 81–91; Merrill 1985, pp. 16–18; Potter 1907, pp. 396–97; Rothert 1913, pp. 169, 173, 181; Stewart 1883, p. 324; van Ravenswaay 1977, pp. 131–39; *Umatilla County* 1981, p. 128; Hayes 1922, p. 386; Horton 1974, p. 133; Johnson 1912, p. 28; *Historic and Architectural Resources* 1977, app. J, pp. 5:12, 26:21; Moore, letter to T.G.J.; Brown, letter to T. G. J.; Biggs and Mackoy 1951, p. 10; Bowman 1965, p. 112; Douglass 1922–23, p. 51; Federal Writers' Project 1937, p. 22; Copley 1912, p. 641; Wilson 1969, pp. 73–98; Hutslar 1977, pp. 25–29, 36–44; Yeager 1977, pp. 14, 28, 31–33, 36, 39, 47, 53–56, 77; Darby Pioneer Heritage Museum; Boulden-Stubbs house; Morton House Museum.

Fig. 7.7. The dogtrot house of a New Sweden family near the Delaware River in Prospect Park, Pennsylvania, reputedly dating from 1698. The trot was enclosed much later. (Photo by T.G.J., 1980.)

apartment to sleep in, and another for domestic purposes."[28] Such explicit and suggestive accounts provided much of the data base for Fig. 7.6.

Chronology, as revealed in such documents, tells us that the dogtrot house moved with the Midland frontier as a pioneer dwelling. Modern field research demonstrates that subsequently it largely disappeared or underwent fundamental modification in every area where it had been implanted by the pioneers, save only parts of the South.[29] Most likely an accidental preadaptation to the humid subtropical climate explains the persistence of the dogtrot house into postpioneer and even modern times there. Elsewhere, as in the Rocky Mountains, only occasional surviving specimens of the Midland dogtrot can be found (Fig. 7.9).

The American distribution of the open-passage double-crib log barn also demonstrates undeniable Midland cultural affiliation (Fig. 7.10). Such a correlation strongly suggests that the dogtrot house and double-crib barn traveled in company and are genetically related.

The Cultural/Ecological Context of the Dogtrot

The fact that pioneer American log construction emanated from southeastern Pennsylvania and is, with certain minor regional exceptions, universally regarded as evidence of Midland influence in material culture, should long ago have instructed us that the

Fig. 7.8. A flimsy partition of recent construction encloses the dogtrot of a house on Highway 18 in Jordan Mines, Allegheny County, Virginia. The site, in a cul-de-sac valley to one side of the Great Valley of the Appalachians, is just the sort of place where pioneer dogtrot houses are most likely to survive. (Photo by T.G.J., 1984.)

Fig. 7.9. A derelict dogtrot cabin built of V-notched round logs in Jackson County, Colorado. The dogtrot plan occurs occasionally in the Rockies. Note the ridgepole-and-purlin roof covered with boards and the exposed splicing of the two pens. Note also the similarity to Figs. 7.2 and 7.19. (Photo by T.G.J., 1987.)

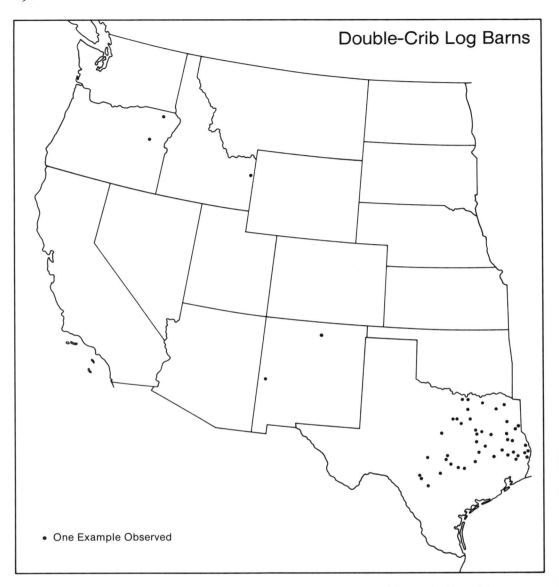

Fig. 7.10. Surviving examples of the open-runway (lacking doors) variety of the log double-crib barn are widespread in the Midland American cultural region. (Sources: primarily field research, in addition to items cited in footnotes in Jordan and Kaups 1987, pp. 54–55; Martin 1984, p. 59; Roberts 1976a, p. 13;

log dogtrot house was part and parcel of the preadapted American pioneer culture. The small Midland repertoire of interchangeable floor plans, including the dogtrot, is splendidly adapted to forest colonization. Houses, barns, and other outbuildings could easily evolve from the simpler one-room units into double-pen or double-crib structures (Fig. 7.1). The single-pen or one-room cabin had a floor plan similar or nearly identical to that of a smoke-house, single-crib barn, or freestanding kitchen. Indeed, original cabins often or even generally later made the transition to another such function. Larger cabins, frequently achieved by adding a sec-

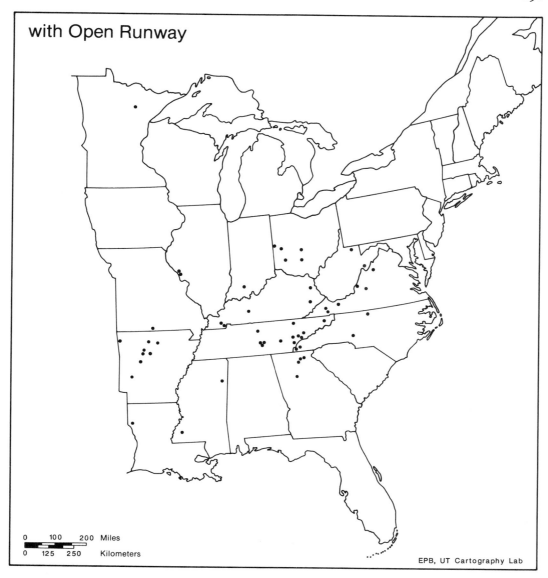

with Open Runway

0 100 200 Miles
0 125 250 Kilometers

EPB, UT Cartography Lab

Wright 1956, p. 94; Kaplan 1981, pp. 243, 254–55, 294, 303, 305; Terrell 1970, p. 15; Carlisle and Ferenci 1978; Williams and Dockery 1984, pp. 103, 113; Riedl, Ball, and Cavender 1976, pp. 214–17; Lyle 1970–74, p. 11; Hutslar 1986; Moffett and Wodehouse 1984.)

ond room to an existing dwelling, in turn displayed floor plans scarcely distinguishable from double-crib barns. The adaptive value of such interchangeability is obvious. It minimized the number of structures that had to be constructed.

Significantly, the dogtrot house plan and the related open-runway double-crib barn represent the *simplest* way to enlarge from single-pen/single-crib size, an attribute that greatly enhanced their adaptive value. It is tedious and time consuming to splice log walls, particularly if the first pen was constructed earlier. A separate, second unit of four walls is far easier to build. If the second pen is situated eight to ten feet from the first, the skids normally employed to hoist logs into place in the upper wall can be employed. The point is that if a structure of two log rooms was desired, the easiest solution was to build independent pens and space them apart in the manner of a dogtrot.[30] The passage could be left open as a breezeway or it could be filled with a chimney, thereby producing the saddlebag plan. Once introduced into the Midland pioneer architectural complex, then, the double-pen plans enjoyed a natural appeal and adaptive value based partly in ease of construction and enlargement.

In pioneer times, dogtrots normally resulted from the addition of a room to an existing single-pen house. Charles Martin's remarkable study of material culture in an upper valley of eastern Kentucky, where woodland pioneering persisted into the late nineteenth century, provides a valuable documentation of house evolution in a frontier setting. One log dwelling recorded by Martin began as a single-pen in 1890, was enlarged to become a dogtrot in 1905, and had its passage enclosed as a hall in 1929.[31] An enlarged dwelling was normally needed in the frontier setting, since selection in woodland colonization favors a high birthrate and large families. "Their little corn-patch increases to a field, their first shanty to a small log house, which, in turn, gives place to a double-cabin," noted an early observer on the Illinois frontier.[32]

Moreover, houses are, as has been said, "public occasions." Even in a folk cultural setting, a dwelling provides a visible statement about its inhabitants. The larger the house, the greater the status of its occupants. In spite of the ease of construction, the dogtrot plan, in a frontier setting, was one way publicly to announce prosperity, a matter of no small social importance, since even backwoods pioneers were partially enmeshed in the market economy. For example, one early Texas settler described double-pen types, both dogtrots and saddlebags, as the houses of "vain" people, while a traveler on the same frontier placed them among "the better sort" of log dwellings.[33]

Yet another adaptive advantage of the dogtrot plan was its remarkable versatility. Not only could it serve the needs of a large frontier family, but a second room set apart from the first was well suited to serve as an inn, summer kitchen, tavern, office, classroom, chapel, or jury quarters.[34] The breezeway was not only a fine place in which to sit or sleep in warm weather, but it also made a convenient tackroom or a practical tollgate. Firsthand accounts of the Midland frontier reveal that these diverse uses of the plan were common.

In sum, viewed in cultural and ecological context, the dogtrot becomes more than simply a house type. Its construction, versatility, size, status, and interchangeability endowed it with attributes well suited to the forested frontier. Splendidly adapted, it survived selective pressures as long as pioneer conditions prevailed, and it persisted even later where it enjoyed climatic advantages.

The Northern European Parallel

In seeking the origin of the breezeway plan, these contextual and adaptive characteristics must not be forgotten. We suggest that the proponents of northern European origin are correct, not only because open-passage dwellings occur nowhere else in Europe, but more importantly because some such houses in Scandinavia and Finland fit into a cultural context very similar to that of Midland America and enjoyed identical selective advantages as their counterparts on the New World frontier.

In northern Europe, two rather distinct open-passage dwelling types occurred (Fig. 7.11). The first was a seasonally occupied far-pasture structure found among Germanic Scandinavian folk. The surviving relics of this type are concentrated in the border area between Sweden and Norway—from Hedmark and Dalarna provinces northward to Norrland and the Ångermanälven, on the borders of Lappland—though the distribution was formerly more widespread, reaching even into southern Norway.[35] In these structures one log pen normally served as a dwelling, while the other functioned as a milk shed and often had a cheese cellar beneath it (Fig. 7.12). The second pen could also be used for storage, as a woodshed, as a dormitory for hired hands, or as the residence of a second family. Such open-passage double-pen *seter* or *fäbod* houses perhaps originated in eastern Norway, where they have been built since at least 1700.[36]

The Norwegian seasonal house is an unlikely prototype for the Midland American dogtrot, since both cultural and ecological contexts were different. Moreover, no notable migration occurred in colonial times between these highlands and North America. It is true, however, that some dogtrot log houses, located above 5,000 feet in the Great Smoky Mountains of North Carolina and Tennessee, served as summer cabins for cattle herders seeking pasture in the Appalachian balds.[37]

The second, and more promising, northern European double-pen type was a traditional farmhouse found particularly in Finland, mainly in Savo-Karelian areas (Figs. 3.7, 6.30).[38] A relic form of a venerable folk house found in eastern Baltic lands, it occurred among Novgorod Russians, Livonians, and Lithuanians as well as Finns (Fig. 7.11). This open-passage farmhouse seems also to have been known among certain late-medieval Swedes and Norwegians.[39] Savo-Karelian pioneers probably carried the type northwestward in the course of their remarkable agricultural colonization of interior Finland between about 1500 and 1700, and by that time it had become closely linked to their Finnish subculture. The house then spread with them to central Sweden (Fig. 7.13). The folk architectural tradition of the Savo-Karelians is still abundantly displayed in the lake-strewn interior of Finland, and it can also easily be detected in modern Scandinavia. In significant ways, the Savo-Karelian architecture is distinct from that of the coastal Finns, Russian Karelians, Swedes, and Norwegians, especially in its simplicity.[40]

To a much greater extent than their neighbors, Savo-Karelians erected structures similar to those of Midland American backwoods pioneers. Their houses began as examples of the single-pen *pirtti*, with a gable-end entrance and a chimneyless corner fireplace (Fig. 3.6). Enlargement to the open-passage double-pen plan followed some years later, and many dogtrots remained open as late as the 1800s (Fig. 7.14). Some older Savo-Karelian houses display clear evidence that the passage, or *läpikulku*, was enclosed long after the original construction (Fig. 7.15).[41] The second pen of such dwellings, often unheated, served a variety of functions,

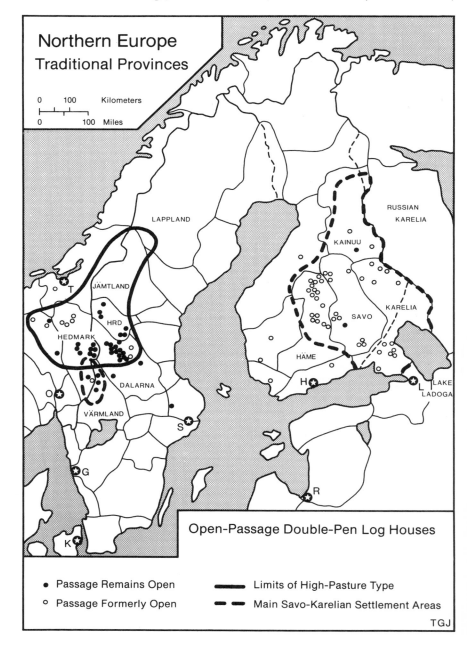

Northern Europe
Traditional Provinces

0   100   Kilometers

0   100   Miles

LAPPLAND

RUSSIAN
KARELIA

KAINUU

JÄMTLAND

T

KARELIA

HRD

SAVO

HEDMARK

HÄME

DALARNA

H

LAKE
LADOGA

L

O

VÄRMLAND

S

G

R

K

Open-Passage Double-Pen Log Houses

• Passage Remains Open   ▬▬▬ Limits of High-Pasture Type

○ Passage Formerly Open   ▬ ▬ Main Savo-Karelian Settlement Areas

TGJ

including guest room, parlor, storage room, bedroom, sauna, and summer kitchen.[42]

The context of the Savo-Karelian open-passage double-pen structure was virtually identical to that of the Midland American dogtrot. Both served a highly mobile, rapidly expanding woodland colonization culture based in hunting, gathering, and slash-and-burn grain-farming. Both housed the abundant children of a prolific pioneer population, and both largely vanished with the passing of the frontier era. The Finnish architectural context also bore a startling resemblance to that of Midland America. Savo-Karelians, too, possessed a small repertoire of simple, interchangeable log buildings of single- and double-pen size (Fig. 7.14). Included were the dogtrot plan and apparently the open-runway double-crib barn as well, abundant examples of which can still be seen today in interior Finland, though their antiquity is uncertain (Fig. 7.16) The original cabin was often subsequently demoted to the status of freestanding kitchen, granary, or sauna. Enlargement of the dwelling to double-pen size, encouraged by the abundance of children, was nonetheless seen as a status symbol among the Finns, a worthy home for a family that had prospered by selling furs and surplus grain. Indeed, Finnish houses in the hills of Swedish Värmland were typically larger than those of the nearby Germanic valley folk.[43] In short, the same adaptive features that led to the success of the dogtrot and related plans on the Midland frontier also worked among the Savo-Karelian Finns. Placed in forested colonial America, the Finnish floor plans were splendidly preadapted.

Additional material evidence supporting the Savo-Karelian origin of the American dogtrot plan is provided by a distinctive pattern or progression of roof construction. In building a single-pen or single-crib log unit that was later to be enlarged, both Savo-Karelian and Midland American carpenters often left the ridgepole and purlins projecting by seven to ten feet as cantilevers on

---

Fig. 7.11.   Key: **G** = Göteborg; **H** = Helsinki; **HRD** = Härjedalen; **K** = København; **L** = Leningrad; **O** = Oslo; **R** = Riga; **S** = Stockholm; **T** = Trondheim. (Sources: field research and the items cited in footnotes in Jordan and Kaups 1987, pp. 65, 67, 69; Norsk folkemuseum, exhibit no. 75 and Wilse photograph collection, vol. 64, no. 16215, and vol. 129, no. 21618; Nordiska museet, arkiv, photos no. 14Ey, 23Bo, 23Ea, 24Hl, 33Eå, 39Iaf, 47Jag, 48Ji, 52Dv, 70Gn, 71Cu, 71Dac, 72Ij, 149Ac, 178Ht, 494Uä, 494Vi, and item no. EU18991; Museum of Soviet Ethnography, displayed photo of "Tatar House"; National Museum of Finland, Archives, photos no. 985.7, 985.15, 1069.21, 1213.2, 1427.26, 1429.2, 1482.4, 1482.10, 1513.28, 1513.39, 1560.30, 1929.416, 1956.2, 2097.9, 2105.122, 2288.1, 2288.5, 2690.71, 2796.78, 2804.2, 2914.7, 2994.74, 3156.79, 3161.14, 3184.455, 3184.785, 3184.1061a, 3184.1375, 3184.1422, 3195.51, 3195.263, 3210.77, 3281.5, 3490.566, 3490.866, 3538.368, 4878.243, 4878.463; Seurasaaren ulkomuseo, exhibits no. 20, 25, 29, 30; Zornsamlingarna, Zorns museet, photo no. 1932.29; displays at regional and local museums, including Tröndelag folkemuseum, Meldal House; Finnetunet; Jämtlands län museum, special exhibit on *fäbod* life; Pielisen museo, exhibits no. 14–17, 39–41; Karjalainen kotitalo-ulkomuseo; Lepikon torppa; Vesannon torpparimuseo; Pienmäen talomuseo; Laukaan kotiseutumuseo.)

Fig. 7.12. A seasonally occupied high-pasture dwelling in the Tännäs District of Härjedalen Province, Sweden, near the Norwegian border, 1920. Displaying the dogtrot plan typical of summer herder cottages in this region, it consists of a living room on the left, *svale* (open passage) in the center, and a *kove* (cow shelter) on the right. (Photo by Nordiska museet, Stockholm, arkiv, no. 70Gn, used with permission.)

one of the gable ends (Figs. 7.17, 7.18). These subsequently provided support for the roof of the dogtrot or runway when the structure was enlarged to double-pen or double-crib size (Fig. 7.19).[44] Often, roofing was not immediately applied to the cantilevered supports, and the single-pen log unit was temporarily left in an awkward and unusual construction stage.

Finnish-Plan Single-Pen Cabins in America

If the American dogtrot plan displays Savo-Karelian influence, surely the Finnish-type single-pen cabin from which the open-passage dwelling evolved in the Old World, the *pirtti*, must also be present in the Midland cultural area. As described in Chapter 3, the Finnish single-pen plan can easily be recognized by its lone, gable-end door, a feature alien to the British folk architectural tradition, in which eave entrances are almost universal (Fig. 7.14, sketches A, B, C, D; Figs. 3.6, 7.17).[45] A common American dogtrot house consists of two Finnish-plan single-pen cabins facing across a passage, without front or rear doors (Fig. 7.1, sketch G).

The gable-entrance single-pen cabin that characterized the Savo-Karelian migrations was an ancient type among the Finnish

Fig. 7.13. A story-and-a-half double-pen Savo-Karelian log house in Norwegian Hedmark, a few miles from the Swedish border. Double doors, front and rear, now enclose the central passage, which also contains a stairway. The room on the left is a kitchen, and on the right is the living room. Now the centerpiece of Finnetunet Open-Air museum, the house is no longer inhabited. (Photo by T.G.J., 1985.)

people and possessed certain adaptive advantages. In northern European pioneer settings, the *pirtti* was a low structure, sometimes even a dugout built into a hillside, and a gable-end entrance avoided the problem of the inhabitants' having to duck under the low eave and butting pole when entering the cabin.[46] An eave door in effect permitted the walls of the structure to be at least two rounds of logs lower, while still offering an adequately tall entrance, thereby minimizing the labor of construction and providing adaptive advantage. Then, too, an eave-side door would have been undesirable both in the subarctic winter, when winds blew snow down from the roof to collect below the eaves, and in the following spring, when meltwater dripped from the roof for weeks. Placing the door in a gable end also permitted a cantilevered roof shelter to be built above the entrance, supported by the projecting purlins and ridgepole described earlier.[47] Many Finnish *pirtti* had such porches.

In America, the Finnish-plan single-pen cabin found ample representation in the Midland architectural tradition (Fig. 7.1, sketch B). Its surviving occurrence, however, is mainly western, in areas beyond the Mississippi River that received Midland influence relatively late (Fig. 7.20). Past the one hundredth meridian, the Finnish plan, called the "Anglo-Western cabin," spread with early miners, trappers, ranchers, farmers, and lumberjacks as a common frontier type, spilling over into adjacent parts of Canada and Mexico. The most common western type lacks a projecting porch, but many of these cabins do possess such a cantilevered addition and have misleadingly been labeled the "Rocky Mountain cabin"

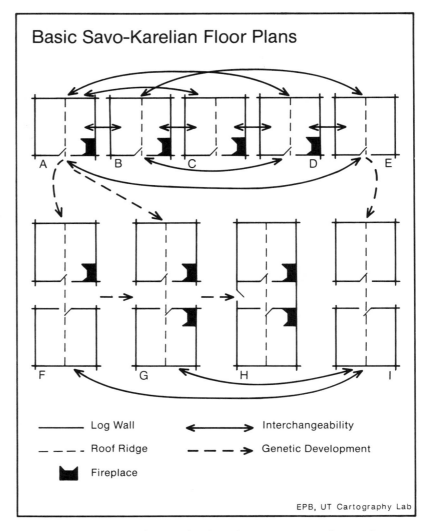

Fig. 7.14. Key: **A** = single-pen cabin (*pirtti*); **B** = sauna; **C** = freestanding kitchen; **D** = grain-drying crib; **E** = single-crib granary or hayshed; **F** = double-pen house with open passage and one fireplace; **G** = double-pen house with open passage and two fireplaces; **H** = double-pen house with enclosed hallway; **I** = double-crib barn with open runway.

(Fig. 7.21). A taller subtype, in which an attic is present above the projecting porch, also occurs in the mountain West and startlingly resembles certain Savo-Karelian *pirtti* in northern Europe (Figs. 7.22, 7.23).[48] Both in the Rocky Mountains and on the Great Plains, a semidugout variety of the Finnish-plan cabin served as a dwelling for many pioneer ranchers, miners, and farmers (Fig. 7.24). It, too, closely resembles a traditional Savo-Karelian type of structure.

Why should the present distribution of the Finnish-plan cabin in North America be so dominantly western? In part, the answer probably lies in the heavier snowfall of the mountain districts,

Fig. 7.15. Crude enclosure of the hallway in a former open-passage double-pen log house of Savo-Karelian affiliation in Häme traditional province, Finland. The older room, on the right, dates from 1744, and the second pen was constructed in 1780. Today the house is in the Laukaan kotiseutumuseo. (Photo by T.G.J., 1985.)

which causes the same adaptive advantages enjoyed by the gable-end entrance in northern Europe to come into play. More crucial to our thesis, however, is whether the western concentration rules out a diffusionary link to the colonial Delaware Valley. We think not. Instead, evidence suggests that the Finnish-plan cabin once existed abundantly in the East but, in the manner of the ridge-pole-purlin roof, subsequently, in postpioneer times, gave way to rival types. In other words, the western concentration should be viewed as the relict, the West as the displaced East.

A former eastern presence of the gable-entrance single-pen dwelling can be documented. Savo-Karelians introduced the plan into New Sweden, and at least one seventeenth-century specimen apparently survived until very recently in southeastern Pennsylvania.[49] Diffusion to the Midland pioneer population at large was achieved. Sketches and other early illustrations reveal that Finnish-plan cabins, sometimes with projecting gable porch or bare cantilevered purlins, were present on the frontier in Ohio in 1831, southern Indiana in 1828, western Tennessee in 1848, southern Wisconsin about 1835, the lower peninsula of Michigan in 1826, Illinois in the 1830s, southern Ontario in the early years of its settlement, and the Minnesota lumbering camps in 1867 (Fig. 7.25).[50] In Illinois, the Finnish-plan log dwelling was reputedly a "typical early pioneer's cabin," and, for what it is worth, Currier

Fig. 7.16. An open-runway double-crib log meadow barn in the Savo-Karelian settlement area surrounding Lake Oulu, near the border between Pohjanmaa and Kainuu provinces, Finland. The barn stands near the town of Pyhäntä, in a marshy region. (Photo by T.G.J., 1985.)

Fig. 7.17. A single-pen Savo-Karelian cabin at Pertunmaa, west of Mikkeli, in southern Savo Province, Finland. Note the projecting ridgepole and purlins awaiting a second pen. This dwelling can be regarded as an embryonic Finnish dogtrot. Compare it to Fig. 7.18. (Photo by Albert Hämäläinen, 1929, National Museum of Finland, Helsinki, Archives, no. 1560.18, used with permission.)

Fig. 7.18. This crude pioneer house in Minnehaha County, South Dakota, exhibits the same projecting purlins and ridgepole as the Finnish cabin in Fig. 7.17. (Copied from Bailey 1899, p. 833.)

Fig. 7.19. The recent joining of two log cribs to form this Finnish barn in the Finnskog District of Värmland Province, Sweden, illustrates how the projecting purlins of the older crib, on the right, formed the roof for the open runway of the enlarged barn. The same process occurred in the enlargement to dogtrot plan in both Finnish and American settings. Note the chinking in the right-hand crib. (Photo by Nils Keyland, 1916, courtesy of Nordiska museet, Stockholm, arkiv, no. 29Cx, used with permission.)

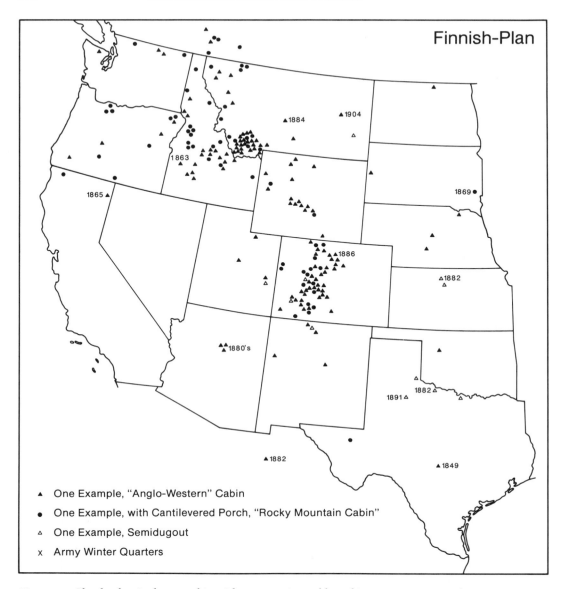

Finnish-Plan

▲ 1884   ▲ 1904

1863

1865 ▲

1869 ●

▲ 1886

△ 1882

▲▲ 1880's

1891 △   1882 △

▲ 1882

▲ 1849

▲ One Example, "Anglo-Western" Cabin

● One Example, with Cantilevered Porch, "Rocky Mountain Cabin"

△ One Example, Semidugout

x Army Winter Quarters

Fig. 7.20. Clearly, the single-pen cabin with entrance in a gable end is most common in the western United States and Canada. All Forest Service structures have been excluded. (Sources, aside from field research, are too numerous to list in full, but representative ones include those cited in nn. 49–53 of this chapter; Wilson 1984, pt. 1, p. 55; Weis 1971, pp. 152, 204, 260, 286; Hughes-Jones and Gettys 1981, fig. 5; Davidson 1977; Welsch 1980, p. 316; Groefsema 1949, pp. 302, 317, 387; Kimball 1954, p. 69; Russell 1971,

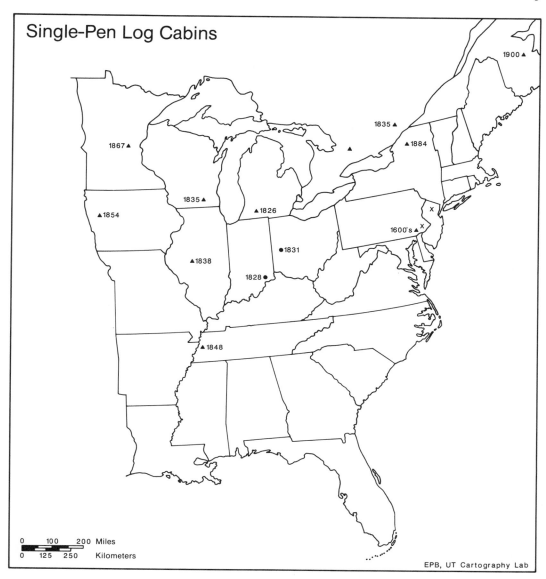

Single-Pen Log Cabins

1900 ▲

1835 ▲

1867 ▲   ▲ 1884

▲ 1854   1835 ▲   ▲ 1826   X

                                1600's ▲ X

                ▲ 1838   ● 1831

                1828 ●

                ▲ 1848

0   100   200 Miles
0   125   250   Kilometers

EPB, UT Cartography Lab

p. 440; Cody Old Town Open-Air Museum; Fort Missoula Museum; Calgary Heritage Park; Fort Steele Heritage Park; Florin 1970, pp. 339, 406, 456; Kennedy 1964, p. 126; Platt 1978, pp. 36–37, 84; Remington 1961, illus. following p. 52; Chapin 1931, illus. following p. 142; Freeman 1958, illus. following p. 64; Ward 1983, pp. 88, 91; Oregon Historical Society, photo collection.)

Fig. 7.21. A Finnish-plan log cabin with projecting ridgepole-and-purlin roof in Beaverhead County, Montana. The gable entrance and porch helped prevent snowmelt and drifting at the door. (Photo by T.G.J., 1987.)

Fig. 7.22. The so-called Rocky Mountain cabin, distinguished by its cantilevered porch sheltering the gable entrance, at Wyle's Ranch, Payette National Forest, Idaho. Compare it to the Finnish example in Fig. 7.23. (Photo from Mary Wilson 1984, pt. 1, p. 42, used with permission and kindly provided by Jerry Wylie of the Intermountain Region Office, U.S. Forest Service, Ogden, Utah.)

Fig. 7.23. A Savo-Karelian cabin from the Finnskog region of Värmland Province, Sweden. It strikingly resembles the Rocky Mountain cabin in Fig. 7.22. (Source: sketch by Nils Keyland, Nordiska museet, Stockholm, arkiv, no. 303Be, used with permission.)

Fig. 7.24. A Finnish-plan semidugout log cabin with crude ridgepole-and-purlin roof in the Rocky Mountains of Gunnison County, Colorado. Note the board chinking. (Photo by T.G.J., 1987.)

Fig. 7.25.   A Finnish-plan single-pen cabin with ridgepole-and-purlin roof at the site of Kalamazoo, Michigan, in 1826. Such sketches reveal that the gable-entrance plan, now confined largely to the West, existed in the frontier era in the East. (Source: Hoyt 1907, p. 144.)

and Ives chose the gable-entrance type for their well-known print *A Home in the Wilderness.*[51] Some specimens of the Finnish-plan cabin survive to the present day in the Adirondack Mountains, southern Ontario, and central New Brunswick.[52]

Another persistent use of the gable-front log cabin in the East was as winter housing for soldiers in wartime. In both the Revolutionary and the Civil War, crudely built, low, round-log Finnish-plan huts housed many enlisted men. During the Civil War, "the predominant form of winter house was the single-room log hut . . . with a single doorway set in the gable end or the side wall."[53] We suggest that, in conditions of war and stress, such as at Valley Forge, the Midland folk reverted to one of the most primitive forms of log housing in their architectural repertoire, to an almost forgotten pioneer type.

Other vestiges survive in the East. Perhaps one of the most common fates of Finnish-plan cabins in the eastern states was to become absorbed into dogtrot houses (Fig. 7.1, sketches B, G). Even more often, the original backwoods cabin was later demoted to a lesser function, reflecting the interchangeable character of plans. The most typical eastern Midland single-crib barn, corncrib, freestanding summer kitchen, and smokehouse all feature a gable entrance, and the latter structure usually even has a projecting gable on the entrance end (Fig. 7.1, sketches B, C, D; Fig. 7.26). All may derive from the Finnish front gable plan, as has recently been suggested for the corncrib, and it is probably not accidental

Fig. 7.26. A single-crib log barn in the Hill Country of central Texas. Such typical Midland barns perpetuate the plan of the pioneer Finnish cabin throughout the primary domain of the Midland culture. (Photo by T.G.J., 1984.)

Fig. 7.27. A Finnish summer kitchen, or *kota*, in Röjden, Finnskog, Värmland Province, Sweden. The Midland American freestanding kitchen was very similar. (Photo by E. G. Rådberg, 1890, courtesy of Nordiska museet, Stockholm, used with permission.)

that the Midland log kitchen is almost identical in plan to its Finnish equivalent, the *kota* (Fig. 7.1, sketch C; Fig. 7.14, sketch C; Fig. 7.27).[54]

In any case, one should not regard the present, western-dominated distribution of front-gable cabins as a reflection of their former pattern in the United States. If the Finnish-plan cabin had never existed in the East, it would be difficult to explain how it diffused so widely, among such a diverse pioneer clientele, through the western plains and mountains. Where could it have originated, if not in the Midland cultural hearth along the Delaware, and still have gained such a scattershot distribution in the West? The most satisfying explanation, we feel, is to accept the decline, demotion, and disappearance of the Finnish-plan cabin east of the Mississippi. We view today merely the ascendant position of Germanic secondary settlement in the East, not the original cultural order that prevailed on the now-vanished eastern frontier. The West better preserves, in this case, a Midland pioneer form that was once also common in the East, just as the South better preserves the dogtrot.

British Architectural Influence

While the pioneer folk architecture of the Midland American frontier bore a practical, preadapted Finnish imprint, British immigrants also exerted an influence. An "English plan" single-pen cabin, distinguished by side-facing gables, front and rear doors centered in each eave wall, and square shape, with each wall between 15 and 16 feet in length, became the most common type on the backwoods frontier, even though it possessed fewer adaptive advantages than the Finnish-plan cabin (Fig. 7.1, sketch A). The Scotch-Irish introduced a similar eave-entrance plan for the single-pen cabin which differed from the English type only in being somewhat elongated, with eave walls five or six feet longer than the gabled sides. The doors of the Scotch-Irish cabin were positioned off-center, producing an asymmetry that was absent from the English plan.[55]

The English cabin, unlike the Scotch-Irish type, shared with the Finnish plan an ease of enlargement to double-pen size, though a third door, in the gable end opposite the fireplace, had to be cut to accommodate the dogtrot plan (Fig. 7.1, sketch F). Three doors unnecessarily weakened a log structure, and as a result the Finnish plan enjoyed adaptive advantage and preference if such an enlargement was envisioned (Fig. 7.1, sketch G). However, if a chimney was to be placed in the space between the two pens, forming a saddlebag house, the English single-pen plan offered the best solution (Fig. 7.1, sketch E; Fig. 7.4). Indeed, ample British precedent existed for such a central-chimney plan, and the saddlebag folk house can probably be regarded best as representing English influence.[56] British, too, was the enlargement to double-pen size by positioning a second room abutting the first, with no passageway or chimney between, a Midland American type known as the "Cumberland" house (Fig. 7.28). Essentially two English-plan cabins built side by side, the Cumberland type was most easily constructed all at once as an elongated single-pen house with a central partition wall of logs, since the use of skids to raise timbers into place was difficult when pens abutted. The Cumberland, in common with the dogtrot and saddlebag plans, satisfied an ancient British preference for side-gable, linear "longhouses." In fact, the similarity of the Savo-Karelian dogtrot to British longhouses may help explain its successful diffusion through the Midland pioneer population.[57]

Perhaps the most obvious British influence on Midland backwoods cabin plans involved chimney placement, as we suggested in Chapter 6. All of the pioneer dwelling types in question displayed English chimneys centrally positioned in a gable wall, a concept alien to the northern European tradition.[58]

In sum, the architecture of American backwoods dwellings and outbuildings was, in many important respects, consistent with Savo-Karelian pen and crib plans that had evolved in a forest colonization setting. The small number of simple, interchangeable building types enjoyed proven preadaptive attributes in new wood-

Fig. 7.28.   A Cumberland-plan log house in Middle Tennessee built as an elongated, partitioned single-pen dwelling. The Cumberland house type almost certainly reveals British influence. (Photo by T.G.J., 1978.)

land settlements, while at the same time bearing sufficient resemblance to traditional British buildings as to be compatible with the preferences of the majority population group. Diffusion of Finnish architectural forms on the American frontier can be understood best in these cultural-ecological and syncretic contexts.

The previous three chapters have, to one degree or another, dealt with agriculture. In Chapter 8, we turn to two other major components of backwoods livelihood—hunting and gathering—which were essential to the adaptive success of Midland American pioneer life.

EIGHT

HUNTING AND GATHERING

He crushes wolves with his fingers,
lays bears low with his hands.

Kalevala

For the backwoods pioneers, native fauna and flora formed a resource base at least as important as the soil. Wild animals and
plants rivaled domesticated species in providing food, clothing,
and marketable produce, causing hunting and gathering to equal
or surpass farming and herding as sources of frontier livelihood.
The rifle has correctly been listed as one of the three adaptive keys
to Midland American forest colonization, and hunting as an essential element in the diversified, unspecialized economy of the
backwoods people (Fig. 8.1).[1]

Hunting

On the eastern seaboard in colonial times, hunting prowess remained largely a Midland cultural trait. Citizens of most colonies,
from Québec to the Carolinas, dealt heavily in the fur and skin
trade, but only in the Delaware Valley did European settlers actually perform much of the hunting and regularly rely upon it for
part of their subsistence. Elsewhere, the Europeans served merely
as middlemen in the trade, while the task of hunting remained in
the hands of Indians. As late as the Proclamation of 1763, the
British crown was concerned to protect and preserve Indian territorial rights in the North American interior, in order not to dis-
rupt the fur trade.

The failure of most New World colonists to engage even in subsistence hunting is not surprising. Core Europeans, including English, French, Dutch, and German immigrants, came from lands
where commoners had long been denied the right to hunt and
bear arms. Even highland British folk, such as the Scotch-Irish
and Welsh, had ceased to be hunters by the 1600s. The remnant
forests of the British Isles, Holland, France, and Germany, together with their decimated fauna, had come under royal protection, and hunting was a privilege of the titled class. German peas-

ants had little besides the ancient story of Hubertus to remind them of their former hunting skills, and the English countrymen could only recite the tales of Robin Hood, who had long ago poached in the royal forest.

From whom, then, did the Midland backwoodsmen acquire their hunting skills? Only two apparent possible sources exist. American Indians, for whom wildlife utilization constituted one of the most important economic activities, could have passed their hunting techniques to the Midlanders. Such is the traditional explanation given for the backwoods pioneers' hunting ability. No doubt the European settlers in the Delaware Valley learned a great deal from the Indians about local fauna, which differed in some ways from that of the Old World. Midland Algonquian, often Delaware, names such as *opossum*, *skunk*, and *raccoon* were adopted for unfamiliar animals, suggesting the native contribution, and the backwoods settlers came to relish the meat of the coon and possum as much as the Indians did.[2] However, if

Fig. 8.1. The long hunter of the American backwoods. (Source: *Davy Crockett's Almanack* 1837, cover illus., reproduced from the copy at the Harry Ransom Humanities Research Center, The University of Texas at Austin.)

Indians offered the model for the cultural complex, then Europeans should have become adept hunters along the entire colonial eastern seaboard, not just in the Pennsylvania hearth area. Moreover, the success of Midland hunting rested largely upon the rifle, a tool completely unknown to the Indians.

In point of fact, the only European commoners who possessed a preadapted skill at rifle hunting upon arrival in colonial America were the Finns of New Sweden, a people who had always depended heavily upon the chase for their livelihood.[3] Traditionally, before the development of *huuhta*-type farming, hunting had been the principal activity of the backcountry Finnish people, and when Savo-Karelians colonized Värmland and other Swedish provinces, hunting once again provided much of their livelihood in the years before the new clearings could be planted.[4] The emigration of Savo-Karelians from Sweden to the American colony was prompted in part by their habitual violation of royal, Germanic game laws, which had been instituted in an attempt to curtail the large-scale hunting the Finns had brought to Scandinavia.[5] While seventeenth-century core Europeans could only recite venerable folk tales about a vanished hunting era, Finns still lived the life of the chase. After the Dutch seized rule of the Delaware Valley, they were accused of continuing to recruit colonists from the Kingdom of Sweden because such people "are more conversant with, and understand better than any other nation, . . . hunting and fowling."[6]

It is our thesis that an important, preadapted component of Midland backwoods rifle hunting derived from the Savo-Karelian Finns of New Sweden. In this chapter we will demonstrate various parallels between Midland American and Finnish hunting techniques and material culture.

The Importance of Hunting

For the earliest backwoods settlers in a region, hunting constituted the "chief occupation," providing for the pioneers "the greater amount of their subsistence."[7] In Ohio, for example, early Midland frontiersmen "lived mainly by hunting, raising, however, a little corn, the cultivation of which was left, in a great measure, to their wives."[8]

The most basic purpose of backwoods hunting was to provide food. Venison and bear meat frequently found a place on the pioneers' dinner table, as did the flesh of smaller game such as squirrel, raccoon, wild turkey, and opossum.[9] The backwoods folk were said to prefer bear "to all other kinds of meat," and during the winter it accounted for a substantial part of their diet. Bear grease took the place of oil.[10] Pioneers usually distinguished between meat and venison, regarding the flesh of the deer as less substantial. One Kentucky woman apologized to a group of hungry travelers that she "had not *meat* to give us, but we were welcome to as much *venison* as we could eat," whereupon the transients were led to the carcass of a buck hanging in the fireplace jambs. They cut their own steaks, threw them on the coals of the fire to cook, added a sprinkling of hard salt, and ate the venison hot from the fire.[11] Squirrel, too, was regarded as inferior fare, and they were so plentiful and easily hunted that the backwoods people ate only the choice parts—the hams and back.[12]

The hunt also provided much of the pioneers' clothing. Deerskin seems to have been the almost universal choice for garments, and a traveler in the Virginia backcountry about 1750 reported that "the clothes of the people consist of deer skins," an observation repeatedly made by visitors to the Midland frontier.[13] In the early Missouri backwoods, garments reputedly included "not a particle of cloth of any kind." Moccasins and caps also were of deerskin, and Texas pioneers wore "rude caps made of green deerskin," some so inadequately cured that coyotes regarded them as food.[14] The coonskin cap associated with the Davy Crockett myth apparently has no basis in fact.

The skin clothing of the American backwoods folk has been regarded as a borrowing from the Indians, as is suggested by the Delaware Algonquian loan word, *moccasin*.[15] It is noteworthy, however, that the Savo-Karelian Finns had a long tradition of skin clothing and moccasin-type shoes, and some of the descendants of the New Sweden colonists continued to wear buckskin as late as the middle of the eighteenth century, even in the immediate environs of Philadelphia.[16] Most likely, Midland backwoods attire developed in the Delaware Valley as a blending of Finnish and Indian styles and techniques, an exchange facilitated by the basic similarity of the two traditions. At the very least, the New Sweden colonists were preconditioned to accept Indian clothing.

On a commercial level, hunting provided the most important link between the American backwoods and the market economy of western Europe and the eastern seaboard. In this respect, the Midland frontier was enmeshed in the von Thünenian world city as the outermost zone of economic activity by white people (Fig. 2.1). As a result, skins and furs served as the currency of the backwoods; from the earliest decades, from the Delaware Valley hearth to the edge of the Great Plains, Midland pioneers payed taxes with pelts. Cash was rare in almost all newly settled areas; "pelts of any kind passed current and constituted the principal medium of exchange."[17] Backwoodsmen traded skins and pelts for better weapons, gunpowder, ammunition, steel traps, coffee, liquor, salt, knives, and other items. In western Pennsylvania, early settlers acquired "whiskey and clothes" in exchange for skins.[18] Savo-Karelian Finns had also used pelts for cash in northern Europe, and the Finnish word for money, *raha*, originally meant "fur."

Some backwoodsmen participated in purely commercial hunts, trekking in large groups deep into the eastern forests in search of furs and hides. Kentucky became a major early goal of such ventures in the 1760s. Sizable parties of hunters assembled in such places as Rockbridge County in the Great Valley of Virginia or the Yadkin Valley on the Piedmont of North Carolina, then went west to spend long seasons beyond the mountains. Pelts and hides, packed in bales, were marketed as far afield as Spanish New Orleans.[19] These commercial ventures helped provide a prototype for the later buffalo hunters of the Great Plains and the Mountain Men of the Rockies.

Aside from achieving the goals of commerce and subsistence, backwoodsmen pursued hunting because they enjoyed it. For many of them, the chase offered the greatest pleasure in life. One early participant, who lived in the Virginia backcountry, captured the appeal of hunting in his reminiscences. "As soon as the leaves were pretty well down and the weather became rainy, accompanied with light snows," he wrote, the backwoodsmen became irritable and discontent at home. "I have often seen them get up early in the morning at this season, walk hastily out and look anxiously to the woods and snuff the autumnal winds with the highest rapture, then return into the house and cast a quick and attentive look at the rifle." The hunting dog, "understanding the intentions of his master, would wag his tail and by every blandishment in his power express his readiness to accompany him to the woods." Not long afterward, a day was appointed for "the march of the little cavalcade" to the hunting camp deep in the forest.[20]

Backwoodsmen took far more pleasure in hunting than in farming. One Tennessean, left behind by the frontier and faced with the prospect of tilling land that "is very hilly and will kill any man to work it," hired a letter written to a kinsman in the Ozarks, asking "wheather I could do any better their killing Deer, bair, and turkeys than to stay heir to work these hills."[21] Needless to say, he opted for the Ozarks. Indeed, as previously suggested, this fondness for and reliance upon hunting proved a fatal flaw that prevented Midland pioneer culture from maintaining its hold on any area, since its methods were destructive and even modest increases in population density ruinously upset the hunting ecology. Heavy dependence upon the hunt, coupled with an unwillingness to abandon such livelihood, quickly made these settlers victims of competitive exclusion. An early Ohio frontiersman, whose "happiness depended upon a life in the woods," lamented the day when "my neighbors became too numerous and my hunting-grounds were broken in upon by the axe of civilization," causing game to become "scarce and hard to take."[22]

Preferred Game

Surviving accounts leave little doubt that American backwoodsmen took greatest delight in bear-hunting, not only because the animal was a worthy, dangerous adversary that preyed upon the settlers' livestock, but also because of their fondness for bear steaks. Late autumn through the winter was the season for bear-hunting, when the animals were fattest and most lethargic.[23] In 1749 a visitor to one settlement in backcountry Virginia at that time of year found "most of the men were away hunting bears," and half a century later in the same area the males reportedly went "every winter to hunt bears" in the mountains.[24] This fas-

Fig. 8.2.   A Scandinavian bear hunter. (Source: Norsk folkemuseum, Oslo-Bygdøy, Norway, archives, item no. L87.622, used with permission.)

cination persisted even into the early twentieth century in remnant bear ranges such as the Appalachians.[25]

Only deer rivaled bears as objects of backwoods hunts. The season for deer began early, in autumn, and extended through the first part of winter. Valuable supplies of venison and hides provided only part of the motivation for killing deer, however, since these animals, along with raccoons, could greatly damage crops and gardens.[26] A variety of other animals were hunted, but the Midland complex clearly had a bear/deer focus and was more specialized than American Indian hunting.

The emphasis on bear and deer had an almost precise parallel in the bear/moose concentration of northern Europeans (Fig. 8.2). Finns hunted bears for the same basic reasons American backwoodsmen did, and in *The Kalevala,* abundant concern for the killing of open-range cattle by bears is displayed. Lengthy Kalevalan charms served to protect hunters from bears, since the undertaking was especially hazardous before the advent of the rifle, when Finns still used spears, bows, and traps in the hunt.[27] No other game animal is as honored in the Finnish epic as the bear. Moose, like American deer, were attracted by the grainfields and abandoned grassy clearings surrounding Finnish settlements in northern Europe, and they were the most common game sought by Savo-Karelian hunters.[28] Still, it would be incorrect to regard the Finns or their American counterparts as highly specialized hunters. The Finns also went after wolves, reindeer, beavers, squirrels, foxes, wild geese, and various other game. Squirrels constituted a moderately important food source for them and for Midland backwoods pioneers as well.[29] Even so, the honored great hunters of northern Europe and frontier America were those who killed many bears, moose, or deer.

In the colonial Delaware Valley, the settlers of New Sweden perpetuated the northern European hunting tradition, focusing particularly upon bear, deer, and waterfowl. The Swedish and Finnish colonists prepared bear flesh as they did pork, and reputedly had a great fondness for it. Bears in New Sweden, smaller and less fierce than those in northern Europe, did not molest the cattle herds very much, but they did prey upon hogs. For that reason, efforts were made to exterminate bears in the vicinity of the Delaware Valley settlements, though descendants of the New Sweden colonists were still hunting bears in 1750, along the Maurice River in southern New Jersey (Fig. 3.10). Venison was a main food in the New Sweden diet, and it is possible that the importance of deer hunting in New Sweden derived from the Delaware Indians, for whom this animal was the principal winter game.[30]

Hunting Grounds

Much hunting by American backwoodsmen was "resident," involving the shooting or trapping of game in the immediate vicinity of the homestead. Such local activity served to protect fields and herds, while at the same time supplementing the daily diet. Resident hunting constituted a year-round activity and was often performed by boys. Most kills were small game, such as squirrels, raccoons, and opossums, but deer were frequently taken in this manner, and occasionally even bears. While the supply of most local game diminished after a few years, the number of deer often increased, because of the practice of shifting cultivation. Destruction of the climax forest and the subsequent abandonment of old fields encouraged the growth of grass, a modification that allowed deer to multiply.[31]

The more important and commercialized type of hunting was "transient," involving a seasonal "long hunt" in distant grounds, away from the settlements. Game was more abundant there, though the backwoodsmen had to compete directly with Indians in these settings. Because of the danger of encountering Indians, "long hunters" often moved in large parties, though they broke up into smaller groups of three or four for the actual hunting.[32]

Backwoodsmen often roamed far afield on their long hunts, driven by curiosity and a sense of adventure, remaining away from home for extended periods. These excursions could far outdistance the usual fall or winter hunt, particularly if there were grown children back at the farmstead to help with the crops. On one occasion, Daniel Boone left his Yadkin Valley residence in North Carolina in May for a long hunt and did not return until two years later. However, according to the principles of cultural ecology, the location of hunting should maximize production while minimizing transportation, so most backwoodsmen chose the nearest abundant ground, connected to their settlement by a stream or trail.[33]

Most typical, certainly, were long hunts involving several days of travel, consisting of a relatively small number of neighbors, and occurring in the nonagricultural half of the year. Representative was the 1792 excursion by two Ohio backwoodsmen who "prepared themselves with a light canoe, with traps and ammunition, for a fall hunt" up the Big Sandy River valley, in search of beavers and otters.[34] Regardless of the range or duration of the long hunt, pathfinding skills were essential.

As discussed earlier, the route to the hunting grounds normally became a path of subsequent migration. Some of the larger long hunt groups even founded a "station" as their base of operations in the wilderness, and these usually developed into permanent settlements as the migration process unfolded.[35] The early western lobe of Midland expansion in Kentucky and Tennessee was once dotted with "station" toponymic suffixes, and a few of these, such as Thompsons Station south of Nashville, survive today.

The backwoods long hunt to distant grounds has usually been interpreted as a borrowing from the American Indian, and the natives of the eastern woodlands did, at least occasionally, undertake such expeditions.[36] We should not doubt that the Indians exerted such an influence, and their trails, together with their knowledge of the geography, provided the basis for much backwoods pathfinding. However, the ancestral Savo-Karelian practice of the long hunt also could have contributed to the evolution of the Delaware Valley hunting complex in the formative decades before 1660 and 1670. The long hunt occurred from the early years in New Sweden, and colonial records refer to "a small creek which comes from the hunting country" west of New Castle on the Delaware and to a variety of other hunting grounds (Fig. 3.10).[37] There is no reason to doubt that these prototypical Midland long hunts, in the hearth of the cultural area, owe at least a partial debt to Finnish influence.

One of the greatest of the eighteenth-century Appalachian long hunters, Stephen Holston, was descended from a New Sweden family and bore a surname unique to that group. Born in the "Swedish" settlement area above the falls of the Schuylkill, Holston by 1746 lived in western Virginia along the river named for him. By midcentury, he and a few hunting companions had journeyed down the Holston, Tennessee, Ohio, and Mississippi rivers as far as Natchez, helping to initiate the famous trade link between the Appalachians and New Orleans. After returning east, Holston continued to drift from one place to another, settling near the Cherokees in the Saluda country of western South Carolina in 1753 and later in eastern Tennessee. Some of his children or grandchildren, who had heard him tell of his long hunts, eventually migrated to the Natchez area, settling on nearby Sicily Island in Louisiana. By the 1820s, his descendants had reached southeastern Texas.[38] We suggest that Holston perpetuated and dispersed not merely a New Sweden surname but also an ancestral Finnish fondness for the long hunt and an ability to use waterways.

The Long Hunter's Shanty

Stephen Holston provides a genealogical link between New Sweden and the backwoods long hunt, but material cultural evidence of the connection also exists. Savo-Karelian influence is strongly suggested by the form of the temporary log shelters American long hunters erected at the hunting grounds. These crude structures consisted of three log walls and a single-pitch, lean-to roof. The fourth, tallest side, facing the campfire, remained completely open. Pairs of stakes driven into the ground stabilized the side walls, while at the rear the side logs were notched into the lower, rear wall. Variously called a "half-faced cabin," "three-faced camp," "open Logg Cabbin," and "open-faced shanty," these shelters remained surprisingly warm, even in the coldest weather.[39]

To our knowledge, no examples of the hunter's shanty survive in Midland America, not even in museums, but contemporary descriptions of them are numerous. One backwoodsman in late-eighteenth-century western Pennsylvania "cut some small trees and put up three sides of a small cabin, leaving the front open, and having our fire on the outside." His shanty measured only nine or ten feet square, and most were not more than three or four feet tall at the rear.[40] A more detailed description from the Virginia backcountry mentions that the back side of the half-faced cabin "was sometimes a [single] large log," and at a distance of eight to ten feet from it two pairs of "stakes were set in the ground a few inches apart," in the manner of a straight-rail fence, "to receive the ends of the poles for the sides of the camp." Above, "the whole slope of the roof was from the front to the back" and made of "slabs, skins, or . . . the bark of hickory or ash trees." To complete the shanty, "the cracks between the logs were filled with moss."[41]

The half-faced hunting cabin accompanied the spread of the Midland frontier, even achieving diffusion, with chinked-log construction, into northern New England after the Revolutionary War.[42] It also served some Midland pioneers as a first crude dwelling at a new settlement site, a logical development since the backwoods people often converted their former hunting grounds into farms. As a boy of seven, Abraham Lincoln lived in such a shanty when his family moved to southern Indiana in 1816.[43]

The precise prototype of the open-faced shanty, down to the last detail, occurred among the Savo-Karelian Finns in northern Europe, who used it for exactly the same purposes as the Midland American pioneers (Figs. 3.3, 8.3).[44] Even the moss chinking was the same. An ecological analysis of the structure helps explain why, once introduced by the New Sweden settlers, the shanty would have achieved acceptance by other groups. It benefits from the principle known to physicists as the "heat reflector oven," as

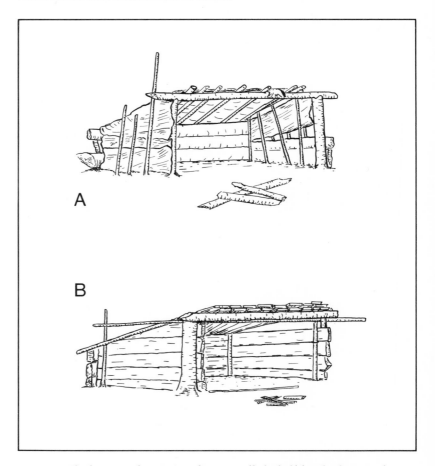

Fig. 8.3. The hunter's shanty, "or what was called a half-faced cabin; . . . the back part of it was sometimes a large log; at the distance of eight or ten feet from this, two stakes were set in the ground a few inches apart, and at the distance of eight or ten feet from these, two more, to receive the ends of the poles for the sides. . . . The whole slope of the roof was from the front to the back. The covering was made of slabs, skins, or . . . the bark of hickory or ash trees. The front was left entirely open. The fire was built directly before this opening." While the description above is from frontier Virginia, the shanties shown are from Karelia. **A** = Repola, Russian Karelia; **B** = Pielisjärvi, northern Finnish Karelia. (Sources: Sirelius 1909, p. 19; Doddridge 1824, p. 124.)

the campfire's warmth is reflected downward from the underside of the single-pitch roof and trapped. This natural heating efficiency, derived from the configuration of the shanty, lent it an ecological advantage on the winter hunt. The open-faced shanty thus joins the V notch, diamond notch, and weightpole-knee-butting board roof as substantial, well-nigh irrefutable material evidence of northern European influence on the Midland American forest frontier.

Less commonly, the backwoods shanties could be provided with a fourth, front log wall, while retaining the single-slope roof. These, too, served as hunters' camps or crude first dwellings. Such shanties served as Confederate troop quarters in the Civil

Fig. 8.4. A four-walled log shanty used as a haybarn in northern Finnish Karelia. American pioneers also built such shanties, one of which is illustrated in Howe 1898, vol. 1, p. 680. (Photo by Lars Pettersson, 1945, National Museum of Finland, Helsinki, Archives, no. 2576:14, used with permission.)

War. Later, most four-walled shanties were converted to cribs or hog houses and, remarkably, some survive to the present day in Appalachia.[45] This more elaborate shanty, too, has an almost exact Fenno-Scandian counterpart, which has undergone a parallel demotion to such functions as calf shed (Fig. 8.4).[46]

Weapons and Paraphernalia

American backwoodsmen by and large hunted with rifles, though some use was made of shotguns and traps. Even as late as 1900, a few Appalachian folk employed bows and arrows.[47] Contrary to the popular image, the famed Kentucky long rifle, an excellent weapon in its time, was not the typical gun of the backwoods. Its cost was beyond the means of most pioneers, unless they were heavily involved in commercial hunting. For example, the Midland backwoods rabble that assembled to fight for Texas independence in 1836 brought only a few good Kentucky long rifles, one of which is on display at the Alamo museum in San Antonio. The majority of the combatants possessed only worn, nondescript weapons such as "little dobble barrels shot guns" or a "Harpersferry yauger" with "the stock and barrel . . . tide to geather with buckskin strings" and "the lock tied on with a buck skin string."[48] An observer among the backwoodsmen in the Ohio Valley about 1820 was astonished by "how well they shoot with even a bad rifle."[49] A generation earlier, a traveler in the southern Appalachians described the local hunting weapon as a "carabine," a short-barreled, lightweight firearm.[50] Perhaps the majority of these guns were one or another type of long-barreled rifle equipped with a flintlock.[51] The longer the barrel, the greater the accuracy of the shot.

The paraphernalia associated with the flintlock rifle hung from a leather "shot pouch strap" worn, if one was right-handed, across the left shoulder (Fig. 8.5). According to an account from central Indiana, about 1830, the attached equipment included (1) the *powder horn*, made from a cattle horn that had been scraped out and polished until thin and partially transparent; (2) the *shot pouch*, six to eight inches square, made of deerhide and hung below the powder horn, to hold bullets and "patchin," the metal jackets for the shot; (3) the *powder charge*, a measuring cup to assure the proper amount of gunpowder was used for each shot, made from the tip of an antler and hung from the strap on a short leather thong; and (4) the *scabbard*, containing a butcher knife and placed on the strap above the powder horn.[52] Other attachments to the shot pouch strap could include a flint whet, an oil horn for lubrication, an awl for moccasin repair, and a hatchet, though the latter tool was usually carried at the waist.[53] The hunter's "rifle shirt," of deerskin or linen, reached below the hips, and "Indian leggings," also called "leather stockings," completed the attire.[54] One Texas backwoods hunter reportedly "wore a buckskin hunting shirt, pantaloons, and moccasins, and had hanging to his person a hatchet, knife, shot-pouch, and powder-horn."[55]

The Savo-Karelian Finns, while still in northern Europe, had become rifle hunters using flintlock weapons. An account of a January 1649 long hunt in the Fryksdal area of Finnish-settled Värmland mentions two rifles used for moose in a party of twelve.[56] The local Finns were known to manufacture their own rifles, and one *Finnbössa*, or "Finnish rifle," in the Värmlands Museum measures about six feet in length.[57] Another museum, in the Finnskog, contains flintlock long rifles dating from as early as 1610, and in Dalarna Province, seventeenth-century rifle manufacture was centered in the town of Evertsberg.[58] Old Finnish log buildings in Europe are often scarred from target practice, and have numerous pits where bullets were dug out with a knife for reuse.[59] Museums in the Finnish districts of Sweden, as

Fig. 8.5. An Appalachian hunter of the middle nineteenth century with his long rifle and his leather strap hung with paraphernalia. He represents well the traditional Midland American backwoods hunter. (Source: Crayon 1858, p. 180.)

well as in Finland, contain hunting straps, powder horns, shot pouches, oil horns, powder charges, flint whets, and other traditional rifle hunting equipment, some dating from about 1600 (Fig. 8.6).[60] Such paraphernalia remained in use until recent times in Lappland, though flint firing had been replaced by percussion caps (Fig. 8.7).[61]

Virtually all of these northern European weapons and related equipment would be recognized instantly by an American backwoodsman, for they were virtually identical to his own. Now, to a certain extent, hunting paraphernalia were similar wherever flintlock rifles were used in Europe and America, but the parallels between Fenno-Scandian and Midland backwoods equipment extended even to the position of the various items on the shoulder strap.

In short, the Finns and their Swedish companions arrived in the Delaware Valley already familiar, as commoners, with the weapons and equipment that later characterized the Midland frontier. More than that, they knew how to manufacture rifles and shotguns at isolated forest forges, to mold their own bullets, and to mine surface deposits of iron ore. Once in New Sweden, they

Fig. 8.6. A Finnish powder horn, dated 1714, and attached powder charge (measure) made from a cowhorn, from the Mangskog area in the southern part of the Finnskog, Värmland Province, Sweden. A small pouch for fire-making equipment accompanied these items, but is not pictured here. (Source: Sågudden hembygdsmuseum, Värmland, Sweden, item no. 2089; photo by T.G.J., 1985.)

Fig. 8.7. An American backwoodsman would be familiar with most of this gear. Key: **1** = powder strap or shot pouch strap (Swedish *rem* or *kruttyg*); **2** = powder horn (*kruthorn*); **3** = the "screw iron" (*skruvjärn*), with which one positioned the charge in loading; **4** = small powder charge (*rypmått*), for bringing down smaller animals; **5** = bullet or shot pouch (*kulpung* or *kulpåsan*); **6** = large powder charge (*tyädarmått*), to bring down bears and other larger animals; **7** = percussion cap container (*knallhattdosa* or *knallhatthorn*), used after flintlock rifles became obsolete; **8** = yarn pouch (*strypåsan*), containing a coarse, saturated yarn used to clean the rifle. These paraphernalia are from the Stensele area of Swedish Lappland, and were sketched by Nils Eriksson in 1930. They belonged to a man born in 1839. (Source: Nordiska museet, Stockholm, arkiv, etnologiska undersökningen files, "Jakt," vol. 1 [1928–36], p. 127, used with permission.)

continued to hunt with firearms, initially using "long French guns" and fowling pieces, some of which were made over by local blacksmiths and fitted with flintlocks.[62] Why should we not attribute the continuity of the Midland American hunting experience and tradition to these colonists of New Sweden?

Hunting Techniques

American backwoodsmen employed five basic hunting methods: still, trap, torch, drive, and encirclement. Still hunting demanded the greatest skill, for it required expertise in woodcraft. The hunter needed to know the habits of the game, to be familiar with their range, to recognize tracks, and to use such information to

stalk or lie in wait for the animals. Commonly, the rifleman engaged in still hunting positioned himself in a "stand" along
known paths of game movement, but he also often employed
calls, imitating wild turkeys, bleating fawns, or marsh geese. Salt-
ing assisted him in hunting deer, and decoys helped lure waterfowl. American Indians, in particular, excelled at still hunting,
since their lack of rifles made it necessary for them to move quite
close to the intended prey, and they perfected various calls, dis-
guises, and decoys. We may assume that backwoodsmen learned
much about still hunting from the Indians.[63]

Trap hunting, elaborately and imaginatively represented in the
traditions of both American Indians and northern Europeans, suffered a decline with the advent of the rifle. Even so, backwoodsmen never completely abandoned this passive hunting method,
and the development of steel spring traps ultimately, in the nineteenth century, led to its revival. The often ingenious traps of folk
design, Indian and Finnish alike, never gained much acceptance
on the Midland frontier, however.[64]

Torch, or fire, hunting required at least two persons and was
performed at night, preferably after a rain, so that fallen leaves
made little noise underfoot (Fig. 8.8). The light of the torch
"shined" the eyes of the prey, usually deer, causing the animal to
remain motionless and easily visible while the rifleman took aim.
If the shot was not immediately fatal, the "track dog" was loosed
and ran the wounded deer to ground. Hunting dogs were an essential part of most backwoods methods of seeking wild game, and
"every well regulated family" on the frontier "kept a number of
savage dogs." Davy Crockett reportedly hunted deer with eight
large dogs.[65] Both Indians and Finns had abundant experience
using hunting dogs, but the northern European methods, involving greater training, seem to parallel more closely American backwoods practices.[66]

Hunting in the dark was hazardous, and there were reported
instances when imprudent riflemen, aiming at shined eyes, shot
their own saddle horse or a track dog being held firmly in check
between the knees of a fellow hunter. Quite aside from the danger,
some, particularly the gentry of the postpioneer period, regarded
torch hunting as unsportsmanlike. Backwoodsmen, more concerned to put food on the table or harvest skins for market, lacked
such scruples. Even the most famous of the backwoods hunters,
Daniel Boone, torch hunted occasionally. Delaware Valley Indians
are known to have used the method, and it is probably correct to
attribute the importance of torch hunting in the backwoods to
Indian influence.[67]

Drive, or chase, hunting was usually done on horseback with
packs of dogs. The wild animal was flushed and pursued through
the forest until the dogs had cornered or treed it. In the southern
Appalachians about 1800, backwoodsmen hunted bears "with
great dogs, which, without going near them, bark, teaze, and
oblige them to climb up a tree, when the hunter kills them." Alternatively, if the habitual paths of game flight were known, one

Fig. 8.8. Torch hunting in the American backwoods. (Source: Thorpe 1858, p. 613.)

party of hunters flushed and drove the game while others, having taken stands along the path, waited for the animals to run by.[68] Finns and Swedes knew well the techniques of drive hunting, called *drevjakt* in Swedish, using both dogs and rifles. The Finns habitually entered the hibernation dens of bears and tried to kill them there, but often the roused animal fled, prompting the chase.[69] While American Indians in various parts of the United States also drive hunted, sometimes using fire to flush the game, the backwoods technique more closely resembled the northern European method.[70]

Encirclement hunting was similar to the drive, but required larger bands of men and was far more effective in killing game. The simpler form, called "round up" hunting in Tennessee, involved surrounding a large tract of forest, then noisily driving an-

Fig. 8.9.   Contemporary sketch of a fire encirclement (*inringning*) bear hunt in Tuna Parish, Dalarna
Province, Sweden, in January 1722. The parish is notable as a Savo-Karelian settlement area. Four bears are
shown trapped in the middle of a fire ring about "1,600 steps" in circumference. Very similar fire hunts
were carried out by American backwoodsmen. (Source: Nordiska museet, Stockholm, arkiv, photo no.
307Eö, used with permission.)

imals toward the center, where riflemen waited. The other
method, sometimes also called "fire hunting," required setting
the woods ablaze in a circle, then letting the flames force game to
flee toward the middle. Such fire encirclement hunting, highly
destructive, was observed among backwoodsmen on the frontier
of western Pennsylvania and in many other areas.[71]

The Delaware Indians of New Sweden, as early as the 1650s,
made a "fire huntt by making a Ring," using both rifles and bows,
and the "surround" was reputedly a common Indian hunting
method.[72] However, both methods of encirclement, using noise or
fire, were also venerable customs among Finns and Swedes in
northern Europe. Noise encirclement, called *skalljakt* in Swedish, was usually employed to rid neighborhoods of troublesome
predators, either bears or wolves, and adjacent parishes or settlements often cooperated in the venture. An excellent illustrated
report of a fire encirclement hunt in a Savo-Karelian district of
Dalarna Province, Sweden, in 1722 survives (Fig. 8.9). Conceiva-
bly, the Delaware Indians could have learned fire encirclement
from the settlers of New Sweden at the same time they acquired
rifles. Recent studies indicate that the use of fire by pre-contact

Indian hunters in the eastern forests was much less extensive than previously believed. Indeed, the only firsthand description of early Indian fire-driving is from the Delaware Valley in 1655, after Finns had been hunting there for fifteen years.[73] Most likely, both the Finns and the Delawares knew the method prior to contact, encouraging and facilitating acceptance of fire encirclement in the syncretic pioneer culture that evolved in the Midland hearth area.

Regardless of which hunting method was used, the game, hides, or salted meat had to be transported. Most backwoods hunters used two or three horses equipped with packsaddles, both to carry supplies on the way to the hunting grounds and to haul pelts and meat on the way home. Commercial hunters packed pelts in bales weighing 50 to 100 pounds, two of which could be carried by each horse. On local hunts, the kill could be brought home slung over the saddle in front of the rider.[74]

Lack of Conservation

The roots of America's ecological crisis have been variously sought. Some blame the nation's Judeo-Christian tradition, with its teleological separation of a man-God-nature trinity and divine-granted human dominion over earth, flora, and fauna. Others fault Protestantism in particular for tolerating interest-bearing loans, thereby stimulating capitalism, and for its work ethic based in the proposition that accumulation of personal wealth is a sign of divine approval. Still others blame the original superabundance of land and other resources in America for undermining the long tradition of careful land stewardship that formed part of the heritage of immigrating Europeans. We see an additional cause for the disregard of conservation inherent in the Midland frontier culture responsible for the colonization of much of the continental United States.

In the period prior to the industrial revolution in America, no clearer example of habitual environmental destruction could be found than in backwoods hunting practices. By almost any standard, Midland pioneer hunting was highly wasteful of faunal and, given the extensive use of fire, floral resources. Firearms made destructively huge kills possible, and the European-based market network provided an economic justification.

In American backwoods society, great hunters were highly esteemed, as might be expected. Their skill was measured largely by the magnitude of the kill, and boasting became the legitimate right of the great hunter. For example, pioneer Texan Martin Bailey, "known the country round as *the* deer hunter," acquired his reputation by killing 1,500 deer in but four years, "only saving their skins."[75] Davy Crockett boasted of killing 58 bears in a single fall and winter.[76] Hunting mishaps that led to heroic hand-to-paw struggles with bears became part of the backwoods great hunter mystique. In frontier Missouri, one pioneer proudly described "a contest he had with a wounded bear. . . . He had broken the barrel of his rifle over the head of the enraged animal, and while one arm and his side were at the mercy of the bear, he was successful in wresting his hunting knife from its sheath and plunging it into the heart of his assailant."[77] Numerous accounts of such "bear wrestling," many no doubt embellished, appear in the American frontier literature.[78]

What heritage underlay such an attitude toward hunting, in which careless heroism and huge, meat-wasting kills capable of exterminating species of game were the cardinal virtues? Surely it did not derive from the American Indians, who felt at one with nature and killed only what they needed for food and clothing. We propose that the destructive Midland backwoods hunting culture was introduced from northern Europe, where commercialism had flourished as early as the time of Novgorod, and the introduction of the rifle about 1600 had greatly increased the killing power of hunters in the interior districts, upsetting the balance of traditional methods.

By the 1630s, Savo-Karelian Finns roaming the forests of central Sweden had already drawn the wrath of royal officials by shooting moose for their hides alone, leaving the carcasses to rot.[79] Great hunters, basing their reputations on the size of the kill, arose among the Finns in Sweden, and even after the fauna was much reduced, in the 1800s, one Värmland Finn acquired widespread fame by killing 48 bears and 30 moose.[80] At the same time, the rifle had made bear-hunting far less dangerous and heroic, causing the backcountry folk of northern Europe to glorify the occasional mishaps that led to mortal close-hand combat with bears (Fig. 8.10). Surviving such contests greatly enhanced the reputation of the rifle hunter among the Scandinavians and Finns.

In short, a model for the wasteful, boasting American backwoods hunter existed among the Savo-Karelians in northern Europe. Indeed, the Finns' lack of conservation in hunting contributed to their deportation to the American colony. Not surprisingly, the same practices immediately took root in New Sweden. Along the Maurice River in southern New Jersey (Fig. 3.10), for example, the colonists were reputed "to kill the Geese in great numbers, for their Feathers, leaving their Carcasses behind them," and one Delaware "Swede" boasted that he had "killed twenty-three ducks at a shot."[81] In the 1700s, a Swedish descendant living along the Egg Harbor River in New Jersey, and Mauntz Rambo, living near Swede's Ford, above the falls of the Schuylkill, both bore the title "celebrated hunter." Rambo had "killed numerous deer in the neighbourhood" and once "shot a panther" (Fig. 4.1).[82] The great hunters of New Sweden provided the most likely prototype for Midland backwoods practices and perhaps helped lay the foundation of America's ecological crisis.

Fishing and Gathering

Fish apparently played only a small role in American pioneer subsistence. Bearers of an inland culture, based in well-drained coun-

Fig. 8.10. Mortal combat with a bear in Norway's Finnmark Province, ca. 1770. Both in northern Europe and on the American frontier, such accidental combat enhanced the reputation of hunters and entered the folklore. (Source: engraving by Charles Eisen, courtesy of Norsk folkemuseum, Oslo-Bygdøy, Norway, archives, item no. NF.7406 (L.55.558), used with permission.)

try, Midlanders lacked access to the sea and abundant lakes. Some fishing occurred in freshwater streams, usually with poles and baited hooks, but occasionally employing trotlines, gigs, and seines.[83] Contemporary accounts suggest that fishing in the backwoods was usually an inconsequential leisure activity, left largely in the hands of boys and old men. In this sense, the Midland pioneer diet departed from the ancestral traditions of the eastern woodland Indians and the Savo-Karelian Finns, possibly reflecting Scotch-Irish tastes. The ease of rifle and shotgun hunting rendered fishing unnecessary, perhaps helping explain its unimportance on the American frontier. The Finns did introduce trap fishing and other techniques along the abundant waterways of the Delaware estuary and upper Chesapeake Bay, but when the Midland culture spread inland, away from the New Sweden nucleus, fishing dwindled in significance.[84]

By contrast, the gathering of products from wild plants and trees assumed an important place in the backwoods livelihood. Midland pioneers gathered walnuts, pawpaws, plums, berries, hickory nuts, pecans, wild grapes, crabapples, persimmons, maple sap, celandine, sassafras, purslane, tawkee, nettles, ginseng, and many other foods and herbs. They raided bee trees for honey. Contemporary references to such dietary items as "spice-bush tea," "juice of the maple," and "dried venison sopped in honey" are representative.[85] In part, gathering activities were ecologically enhanced by the colonization process itself. Berry growth, for example, was stimulated by the destruction of the climax forest, and abandoned fields yielded a considerable harvest for gatherers.[86]

Honey and maple syrup seem to have been particularly important because they supplemented the standard diet with high-energy food at a sensitive and vulnerable time of the year, the spring. Pioneers often drank unboiled maple sap as a beverage, and many acquired it from trees that were to be cut down immediately afterward to make a clearing. Others set up "sugar camp settlements" consisting of several "sugar cabins" for collectors and boilers, often distant from the settlements.[87] A degree of commercialism even entered the maple-sap-gathering economy in some localities. Beyond the maple forests, the importance of honey was paramount. Some Missouri pioneers were said to subsist largely on "animal food and wild honey," and bee-tree lore was abundant among the backwoods people.[88]

The traditional view is that the gathering activities of Midland American pioneers derived in great part from the Indians, and there seems to be no reason to dispute the claim. Recent ethnobotanical studies of rainforest Indian groups in South America indicate that they utilize 80 to 100 percent of the native vegetation for some economic purpose, and there is no reason to doubt that the eastern woodland tribes in North America had achieved a similar level of adaptive success. Midland frontier folk annexed this extensive Indian knowledge of edible and medicinal plants, a body of information acquired during centuries or millennia of residence in the eastern forests. Adoption of Indian loan words such as *pokeberry, pecan, tawkee,* and *pawpaw* essentially prove the native contribution, as do backwoods folk cures based on obscure herbs and roots.[89]

We suggest that the transferal of such knowledge from Indian to European began in earnest on the New Sweden frontier and was largely accomplished by the Finns and Swedes before the arrival, in force, of other ethnic groups in the Delaware Valley. Algonquian loan words are disproportionately represented in the Midland folk floral vocabulary, even in the South. When a European naturalist visited the Delaware Swedish descendants about 1750, he found many Indian plant uses and related loan words, preponderantly Delaware Algonquian, among them. By that time, the local tradition of using wild plants was quite venerable, clearly linked in the minds of the older settlers he interviewed to the early frontier period in New Sweden. The naturalist found, for example, that both the Swedish descendants and the local Indians ate the seeds of the arrow arum, a plant they called by the corrupted Delaware Algonquian name *tawkee*.[90] Subsequently, *tawkee* became the general Midland folk dialect term for the arrow arum. Also firmly established as early as the time of New Sweden was the importance of honey in the Midland pioneer diet. "Bees thrive and multiply exceedingly," wrote a newly arrived Welshman, and "the Sweeds often get great store of them in the Woods, where they are free for any Body."[91]

The adoption of Indian gathering practices and plant uses in colonial New Sweden was, in turn, facilitated by a rich, preadapted northern European gathering tradition, a heritage exhibiting some close parallels to Indian practices. Lengthy passages of *The Kalevala* are devoted to bee charms, honey, or herbal cures, and the rural folk of interior provinces, Finns and Swedes alike, were accustomed to birchbark tea, various necessity breads made from trees, moss, or heather, and many other foods, drinks, and ointments derived from the local flora.[92]

In conclusion, we propose that, while the hunting and gathering livelihood of the American backwoods pioneers was based to a considerable extent upon Indian practices, Finns and Swedes achieved most of these borrowings in the colony of New Sweden before 1660, while at the same time introducing into the Midland cultural complex from northern Europe such characteristics and noteworthy elements as the flintlock rifle and its related paraphernalia, the great hunter mystique, wasteful methods, the bear/deer emphasis, the hunter's log shanty, and perhaps also the long hunt. The existence of a preadapted tradition of hunting and gathering, particularly among the Savo-Karelian Finns, in northern Europe greatly assisted the incorporation of Indian knowledge after the early emigrants arrived in the Delaware Valley. On no other part of the colonial American frontier was such rapid and comprehensive acceptance of Indian expertise in hunting and gathering achieved, as is reflected in the disproportionate presence of Algonquian, and particularly Delaware, loan words for flora and fauna in American English. We believe that the syncretic Midland system of hunting and gathering owed its existence to the early meeting of Indian and Finn along the Delaware. It was in place, awaiting the later settlers, long before the great Ulster and German immigrations.

NINE

BACKWOODS FRONTIER EXPANSION, 1725-1825

> *I will recite my words
> to the backwoods.*
>
> Kalevala

The years 1720 to 1725 marked the beginning of an explosive expansion of the Midland American backwoods frontier, a rapid diffusion that would reach the Oregon country in only a century and a quarter. The first hundred years or so of this remarkable dispersal, during which the backwoods pioneers set America unalterably upon the path of manifest destiny, are the subject of the present chapter.

The previously described spread of the Midland frontier in the fourscore years before 1720 was modest, serving to establish bases on the upper Schuylkill in Montgomery and Berks counties, Pennsylvania, and at the head of the Chesapeake Bay, east of the lower Susquehanna, that would serve as jumping-off points in the phase of rapid expansion (Fig. 4.1). If we break that earlier period down into two parts, we see that the Midland backwoods culture was formed in the decades 1640–1680, drawing principally upon preadapted northern European traits and borrowings from the American Indian. Then, between 1680 and the 1720s, vigorous ethnic mixing and intermarriage allowed the infant backwoods culture to escape its earlier ethnic identity and spread through the entire Midland periphery, surrounding the rapidly developing riverine Germanic core in the Delaware Valley.

All that was needed to set the backwoods culture into rapid westward motion was a sizable population base that would both provide more frontier pioneers and speed the growth of the Germanic core, thereby displacing more pioneers. This missing demographic component fell into place when the mass immigration of Scotch-Irish and Germans began about 1720. By and large, the Ulster folk, from Europe's hardscrabble fringe, flocked to the Midland frontier, where an essentially Finnish-Indian adaptive system was already in place, while most of the Germans helped enlarge the Midland core, producing the Pennsylvania Dutch landscapes that endure to the present day.[1] The sudden addition of such large

233

numbers of people to the frontier zone, coupled with the vigorous, displacing growth of the Germanic core, required a rapid, continuous expansion of backwoods settlement. Given the vulnerability of the pioneer adaptive system to increased population density, the spread of the Midland frontier was thus guaranteed to continue until the pioneers reached the Pacific.

Pathways West

The routes of American frontier expansion in the century after 1725 are so well known and have been charted so often as to require scant attention here (Fig. 9.1). Suffice it to say that from the frontier bases on the Schuylkill River and at the head of Chesapeake Bay, Midland pioneers probing westward in Pennsylvania almost immediately encountered the Appalachian Mountains.[2] Gaps and breaks in the easternmost ridge permitted easy access into the Lebanon and Cumberland valleys of Pennsylvania, both of which are parts of the remarkable topographic feature called the Great Valley of the Appalachians, a broad and fertile trough stretching the length of the range, from New York to Alabama.[3] From the upper Schuylkill in Berks County, Pennsylvania, the Lebanon Valley beckoned, leading to the Susquehanna River at Harrisburg. Settlers near the head of Chesapeake Bay could either move up the Susquehanna to Harrisburg or arc west through York and Gettysburg to enter the Great Valley near Hagerstown in Maryland. The first great Scotch-Irish concentration in the Great Valley lay in Cumberland County, just west of Harrisburg.[4]

Once the Midland backwoods pioneers entered the Great Valley, the orientation of the terrain deflected the major migratory thrust southwestward, into the Virginia backcountry. So pronounced was this deflection that the primary domain of the Midland cultural area became centered in the Upland South, a hinterland that latitude would have awarded to the planters of the Chesapeake and coastal North Carolina. West of the Great Valley, an orderly succession of smaller, elongated valleys and intervening parallel ridges duplicated the northeast-southwest alignment and reinforced the deflection. Backwoods pioneers moved rapidly down the Great Valley in the mid eighteenth century, reaching eastern Tennessee by the 1750s. So great was the swarming that many settlers spilled eastward through gaps in the Blue Ridge onto the Piedmont of Virginia and the Carolinas, preempting the very backyard of the coastal planters (Fig. 9.1).

Others preferred to move westward from the parallel ridge-and-valley sector of the Appalachians to the lands west of the mountains. To do so, they had to pass through the formidable east-facing wall known as the Appalachian front, beyond which lies an extensive, dissected plateau in which the soils are far inferior in fertility to those in the ridge-and-valley country. The easiest access through the front was offered by Cumberland Gap, which provided a route to the superb Bluegrass Basin of Kentucky, beyond the mountains. More difficult roads led westward to the

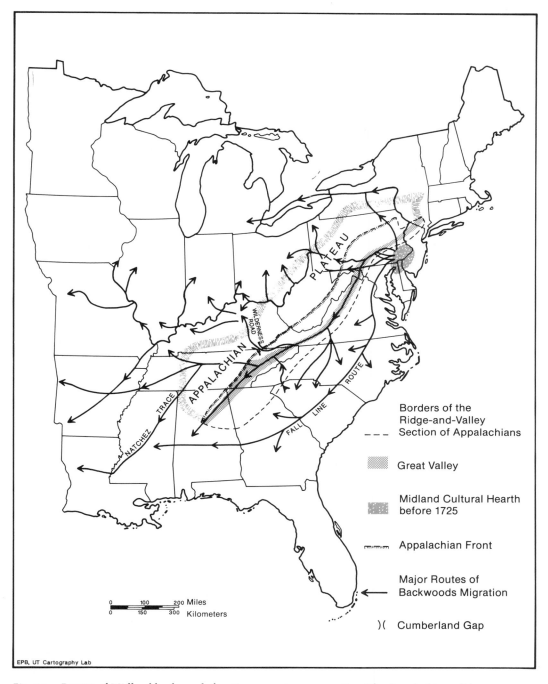

Fig. 9.1. Routes of Midland backwoods frontier expansion, 1725–1825. The Appalachians did not act as a barrier, but they did channel migration along certain paths.

forks of the Ohio at Pittsburgh, beyond which the river provided a fine transportation route. Smaller numbers crossed the plateau by moving north along the Delaware and Susquehanna rivers, entering upstate New York.

Still other Midland pioneers remained east of the mountains, moving southwestward along the axis of the Fall Line as far as Georgia and Alabama. They encountered fellow Midlanders spilling eastward through the Blue Ridge gaps, and together they solidified the Pennsylvanian claim to the Piedmont and the inner Atlantic Coastal Plain.

Through these major routes and many lesser paths, the Midland pioneers forged their way west. A map of Scotch-Irish settlements by the time of the American Revolution, fifty years after the great dispersal of backwoods pioneers began, indicates their achievements as forest colonizers (Fig. 9.2).

The Genetic Heritage of New Sweden Westward

What role did the progeny of New Sweden play in the expanding Midland frontier after 1725? A definitive answer is impossible. Any attempt to reconstruct the ethnic heritage of America's colonial population, including its backwoods component, by analyzing surnames in the 1790 census schedules or similar lists is futile and has, with little exaggeration, been called "a fool's errand."[5] For example, one scholar, inspecting the 1790 schedules for North Carolina's white population, concluded that Scotch-Irish made up 13.5 percent of the total, while others, using the very same schedules, reckoned the Ulster proportion at 41 percent.[6] The "Swedish"-descended population of late-eighteenth-century New Jersey has variously been placed at 1.1, 2.9, and 3.9 percent, based on tax lists.[7]

Persons of highland British ancestry, including Scotch-Irish, Welsh, Scots, and English settlers derived from hill areas such as Cornwall and the Pennines, probably formed a majority of the population on the Midland American frontier, though some claims of their numbers and proportions seem excessively high.[8] By comparison, the genealogical legacy of New Sweden on the frontier has scarcely been mentioned or even considered, though historians of the western states have occasionally acknowledged the northern European presence. In West Virginia's population, "we find reminders of New Amsterdam and New Sweden"; Ohioans are said to have "a tincture of Swedish and Hollander blood"; Kentucky's early settlers are labeled a "heterogeneous mixture" that includes those descended from "Scandinavia" or "Swedes"; and among the backwoods pioneers who were peopling the frontier in western North Carolina, "one group was the Swedes."[9] Most often, though, New Sweden's seed has gone undetected beyond the Delaware Valley.

We cannot begin to provide an accurate estimate of the proportion of Finnish and Swedish descendants in the Midland frontier population. Too much intermarriage occurred, even before 1700; too many northern European surnames were Anglicized; too often the seventeenth-century colonists had changed their surname each generation, in the old Swedish manner, thus hope-

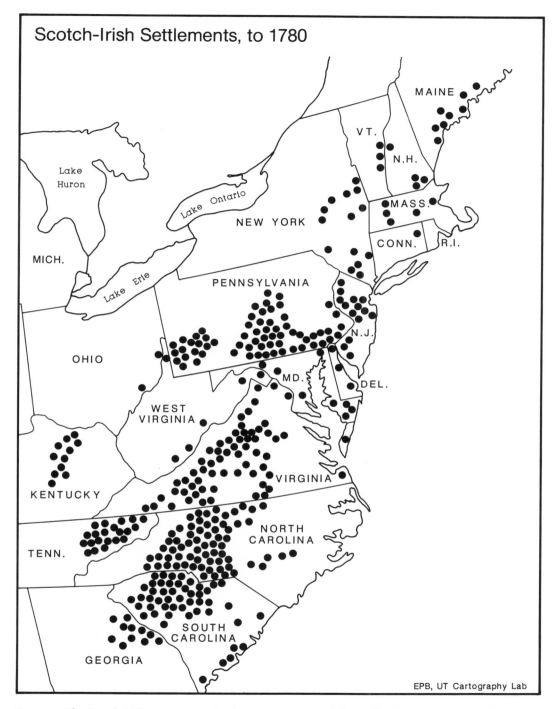

Scotch-Irish Settlements, to 1780

EPB, UT Cartography Lab

Fig. 9.2. The Scotch-Irish were present in almost every sector of the Midland American frontier by 1780. However, their ethnic identity had become greatly weakened through intermarriage. (Sources: Hanna 1902, frontispiece; Mitchell 1966, p. 296.)

Table 9.1   Twenty-two Colonial American Surnames Derived
Exclusively from the New Sweden Colony

Major American Variants	Original Form
Bankston, Bankson, Pinkston	Bengtsson[x]
Bartleson, Partleson	Bertilsson
Clemson	Clementsson, Clemmenson
Dalbo, Dalbow	Dahlbo
Derrickson	Didricsson
Eustace, Justice, Justis	Göstasson
Holston, Holsten	Holstein**
Longacre	Långåker
Lykins, Likens, Laican	Laikkonen*, Laukkainen?*
Mecum, Meekim	Mekonen?*[x], Mäkinen?*
Mink	Minkinnen*, Mankinen*[x]
Mullica	Mulikka*[x]
Olson, Oldson	Olsson
Rambo, Rambow	Rimbo?, Rombo?, Romppainen*[x]?
Seneker, Senecca	Sinikka*
Stallcup, Stalcop	Stalkop**
Steelman, Stilman	Stille
Sturkon	Stör----?
Swanson	Swensson
Tussey, Tossa	Tossavainen*[x], Thoresson
Vanneman, Veinom, Veinon	Veinom*[x], Viainen?*[x], Van Neman***, Vainoinen?*[x]
Walraven	Wallrafen**, Wallraven**

Sources: Nordmann, 1888, pp. 107–8, 140; Craig and Yocom, 1983, p. 251; Acrelius, 1874, p. 156; the sources listed in Chapter 9, n. 11; Olovsson, 1979; Nordström, 1986; Kalm, 1929, p. 219.
  *Of unquestionable Finnish origin.
  **Of German or probable German origin, absorbed into the Swedish/ Finnish group by 1690.
  ***Of Dutch origin, absorbed into the Swedish/Finnish group by 1690.
  [x]Common among Värmland Finns in Sweden.

lessly tangling many genealogies.[10] We can, however, demonstrate that many of New Sweden's families scattered with the frontier. Through laborious genealogical research, we have been able to identify 22 American surnames that apparently remained unique to the New Sweden progeny as late as 1825, a century after the explosive Midland expansion began (Table 9.1).[11] These family names are diagnostic of descent from the very group we claim practiced the original backwoods culture. Regrettably, many other surnames associated with some of the most prolific of the New Sweden families, such as Matson, Ericson, Yokum, Anderson, Thomason, Hanson, Everson, Huling, and Paulson, could not be included in our list, because later colonial immigrants of different ethnic origin introduced the same family names.[12]

After about 1725, and even earlier in some cases, bearers of many of the diagnostic surnames, as well as other families whose genealogical connections to New Sweden are proven, became identified with various parts of the Midland frontier, leading the way west. Some began the westward trek by skirting the head of Chesapeake Bay. For example, in 1700 John Hance Steelman lived in the old Finnish-Swedish settlement area on the Elk River in northeastern Maryland, but by 1710 he had found his way to the lower Susquehanna, and by 1740, to Adams County, Pennsylvania, far to the west, at the foot of the Appalachians. He was reputedly the first white settler west of the Susquehanna.[13] Others, including the Holstons and Rambos, moved from the upper Schuylkill settlements into the Great Valley, reaching Virginia's Shenandoah Valley shortly after 1730.[14] Later in the century, Swain Paulson, still bearing a corrupted Swedish given name, departed the Virginia backcountry, crossed through Cumberland Gap, and became one of the first settlers in the Salt River country of Mercer County, Kentucky.[15] Edward Swanson belonged to a band of nine that formed, in 1779, the initial expedition to middle Tennessee, where he became the first inhabitant of Williamson County.[16]

Still others remained east of the mountains, settling even on the coastal plain as they dispersed southwestward from New Sweden. A certain Swan Swanson reached eastern North Carolina by 1714. Bankstons were among "the first pioneer settlers" of Washington Parish in eastern Louisiana in 1812, and by about the same time the Eustis family was already represented at Natchitoches, on the frontier of western Louisiana.[17]

If we map all of the 22 diagnostic New Sweden surnames on the basis of the 1820 census schedules, the scattering of the Delaware Valley descendants in the first century of rapid Midland expansion is strikingly revealed (Fig. 9.3). The great western bulge of the Midland frontier, so evident in 1800, is shown to have been liberally sprinkled with New Sweden descendants (Fig. 1.6). Clearly, they were well represented in the backwoods population.

Maps showing the diffusion of individual, representative diagnostic surnames during the century 1725–1825 are equally revealing. An example is the Rambo family, descended from Peter Gunnarsson Rambo, who arrived in New Sweden from a village near Göteborg (Fig. 9.4).[18] His descendants entered the American interior via the upper Schuylkill–Great Valley route, reaching both the Upland South and the Ohio Valley. Eventually they followed the Oregon Trail to the Pacific Coast.[19] Rambos are listed among

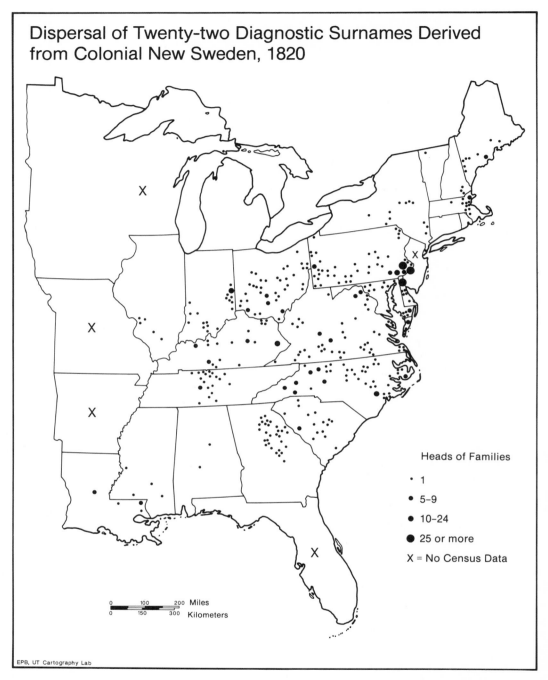

Dispersal of Twenty-two Diagnostic Surnames Derived from Colonial New Sweden, 1820

Heads of Families

· 1

● 5–9

● 10–24

● 25 or more

X = No Census Data

0 100 200 Miles
0 150 300 Kilometers

EPB, UT Cartography Lab

Fig. 9.3. Distribution, by county units, of the heads of families bearing the 22 diagnostic surnames derived from New Sweden (see Table 9.1). For Alabama, Georgia, Illinois, Indiana, Louisiana, Michigan, North Carolina, and Tennessee, substantial parts of the census population schedules are missing. For Arkansas, Florida, Missouri, and New Jersey, there are no surviving census records. (Sources: Georgia Historical Society 1969; Gillis and Gillis 1963; Heiss 1966; Jackson 1981a, 1981b, 1981c; Jackson and Schaefermeyer 1976; Jackson and Teeples 1974, 1976; Jackson, Schaefermeyer, and Teeples 1974, 1976a–h, 1977a–d; Ohio Library Foundation 1964; Potter 1974.)

Fig. 9.4. The Rambo family spread with the Midland American frontier, following both the Great Valley and the Ohio Valley routes. (Sources: Dye and Dye 1983–85; Rambo 1948; Rambo 1983; Hulan 1980b; Hulan 1981; *Pennsylvania Archives*, 1st ser., vol. 1, pp. 213–14; *Archives of Maryland*, vol. 37, p. 402; U.S. Bureau of the Census 1908a–l; Fothergill and Naugle 1978; Norton 1973; De Valinger 1954; Stryker-Rodda 1972; *Substitutes for Georgia's Lost 1790 Census* 1975; Heinemann 1965; Stemmons 1972; Creekmore 1980; items cited in caption for Fig. 9.3; and U.S. Geological Survey, "Geographic Names Information System.")

the earliest settlers in various areas, including the interior districts of Pennsylvania.[20] Thanks to a recent series of highly popular motion pictures, the name "Rambo" has become an American idiom, which unintentionally commemorates the rough-and-ready Midland backwoodsmen who carried the surname across the United States.

Another representative dispersal was achieved by the Lykins family (Fig. 9.5). Descended from a Finnish immigrant who probably arrived on the Delaware after Swedish rule had ended, the Lykins accomplished a classic Midland diffusion by 1825, following the Great Valley and Ohio Valley routes.[21]

The spread of the Bankston/Pinkston family illustrates the importance of the Fall Line route of expansion east of the Appalachians. As early as 1653, Mats Bengtsson fled the rule of Governor Printz in New Sweden, helping to establish the Finnish/Swedish settlement area of northeastern Maryland on the upper Chesapeake Bay, though he may not be a progenitor of the family. The later Bankstons and Pinkstons spread along the Piedmont and the inner Coastal Plain, all the way to the "Florida parishes" of eastern Louisiana. Others may have reached the South by way of the Delmarva Peninsula (Fig. 9.6). The Bankston migration closely paralleled the main diffusion of diamond notching (compare Figs. 6.16 and 9.6). Bengtsson was a common Finnish surname in Värmland during the seventeenth century, and the American Bankston/Pinkston family may well be of Finnish descent.[22]

The dispersal of New Sweden descendants to the American interior can also be demonstrated by plotting the distribution of specific place names that include one or another of 22 diagnostic surnames. The primary domain of the Midland cultural region is dotted with toponyms such as Rambo Hollow (Marshall County, Tennessee), Stalcup Bend (Jackson County, Arkansas), Swanson Cove (Towns County, Georgia), Lycans Ridge (Wayne County, West Virginia), Steelman Chapel (Gibson County, Indiana), Pinkston Branch (Tishomingo County, Mississippi), and Justus Gap (Union County, Georgia) (Fig. 9.7).[23] Such place names are all the more revealing because they typically commemorate the first settlers in an area.

A curiosity of the toponym map is the elongated cluster of diagnostic New Sweden surnames in the heart of the southern Appalachians, reaching from the Kentucky–West Virginia border area due south as far as the northern fringe of Georgia (Fig. 9.7). Probably the cluster is merely coincidental, but it does correspond to an area where many aspects of Midland backwoods culture survived into the present century. Just possibly, the cluster might be a clue and reminder of New Sweden's role in the genesis of American woodland pioneering. If so, it is no accident that in the Big Sandy country along the Kentucky–West Virginia border, the Finnish-descended Lykins family had developed their major concentration by 1825 (Fig. 9.5) and that "one is almost sure to find a Justice at every turn of the road."[24]

Spread of the Surname Lykins (and Variants), 1725–1825

Implantment of Surname in Seventeenth Century

● Surname Present in County before 1775

• Surname Present in County 1775–1825

▲ Toponym Containing Surname

← Known or Presumed Major Routes of Diffusion

0   100   200 Miles
0   150   300 Kilometers

EPB, UT Cartography Lab

Fig. 9.5. Throughout its first century of dispersal, the Lykins family retained an upper southern distribution, using both the Great Valley and the Ohio Valley routes of migration. Variants of the name include Likens, Laican, and Lykens. The puzzling outlier in the backcountry of New England remains unexplained, but may have resulted from troop movements in the Revolutionary or French and Indian War. (Sources: those listed in the captions for Figs. 9.3 and 9.4; Boyd 1962–71, vol. 1, p. 246; Kozee 1973, pp. 28, 131, 162.)

Spread of the Surname Bankston/Pinkston
(and Variants), 1725–1825

Implantment of Surname
in Seventeenth Century

Surname Present in
County before 1775

Surname Present in
County 1775–1825

Toponym Containing
Surname

Known or Presumed
Major Routes of Diffusion

0   100   200 Miles
0   150   300 Kilometers

EPB, UT Cartography Lab

Fig. 9.6.   More than one original New Sweden family may be involved in the spread of this surname. To a
remarkable degree, the Bankston/Pinkston family remained east and south of the Appalachians. (Sources:
those listed in captions for Figs. 9.3 and 9.4; Vacher 1947; Gillis 1963; *Colonial and State Records of North
Carolina,* vol. 4, p. 709; vol. 22, p. 501; vol. 23, p. 819; *Index to the Headright and Bounty Grants of
Georgia* 1970; *Index to the Wills of Charleston County, South Carolina* 1950, p. 13; Ardoin 1970–77.)

Toponyms Bearing One of the Diagnostic Surnames Derived from New Sweden

- One Example

X State Excluded due to Lack of Index

- - - Borders of the Midland Culture Primary Domain

0 100 200 Miles
0 150 300 Kilometers

EPB, UT Cartography Lab

Fig. 9.7. The diagnostic surnames mapped here are listed in Table 9.1, with the exception that all "Mink" and "Seneca" toponyms were deleted, owing to possible confusion with faunal and Indian names. An effort was made to detect and eliminate toponyms derived from the nineteenth-century Scandinavian immigrations, especially in the upper Midwest. The curious cluster of New Sweden surname-toponyms in the middle of the southern Appalachians, shown within the light dashed line, is intriguing and possibly significant. In New England, fully 60 percent of the toponyms shown are Eustace/Justice names, which suggests either an undetected problem with the diagnosticity of the surname or an early splinter migration in that direction. (Sources: Adams and Keller 1969; Holmes 1962, pp. 31, 45; Kuethe 1936, p. 163; Rennick 1984; Romig n.d.; U.S. Geological Survey, "Geographic Names Information System.")

Ethnicity and Westward Expansion

Finnish and Swedish ethnicity played no notable role in the westward expansion of the Midland frontier after 1725. While a few northern European ethnic pockets survived in the sandy cul-de-sac of migration in southern New Jersey, even into the latter half of the eighteenth century, the New Sweden descendants who went west were quickly absorbed into a composite backwoods population. Only occasionally did Swedish- or Finnish-derived given names, such as Swain (Sven), Lassey (Lasse), Banks (Bengt), Mounce (Måns), and Matty (Matti), remain linked to diagnostic surnames, even early in the westward expansion. A certain Banks Meekum resided in the South Carolina backcountry in 1790, and Swain Stalcup was listed among the pioneers of Sumner County, Tennessee, in 1802, but these instances were unusual.[25] It is futile and wholly unnecessary to seek a western transplanting of Fenno-Scandian ethnicity.

We would do better to look upon the Midland backwoods frontier as a place, to use the words of *The Kalevala*, "into which a people has vanished, a staunch folk sunk down."[26] Rather than cling to a dying seaboard ethnic enclave, many New Sweden families went west and simply disappeared into the population at large. The price they paid for joining the diaspora was the loss through intermarriage of the last vestiges of their ethnic identity, becoming a progeny largely ignorant of their northern European roots. Their reward, though they could not know it, lay in the incidental transfer of a substantial part of their traditional Finnish forest pioneer culture to the greater Midland backwoods population, completing a diffusion begun well before 1700 in the Delaware Valley cradle.

The Finns and Swedes in colonial Midland America, then, while few in number, displayed a propensity to live among and marry people not of their kind, and subsequently to scatter westward on the backwoods frontier without regard for the preservation of their ethnicity. These attributes, attitudes, and tendencies led to the transfer of much of their splendidly preadapted culture to a much larger community.[27]

TEN

CONCLUSION

Do you remember anything more,
or has your foolish talk
now come to an end?

Kalevala

We have offered an explanation for the development of the highly successful American backwoods settlement frontier through an analysis of both its cultural and ecological components, by linking ethnic diffusion to adaptation in a formative colonial stage. The Midland pioneer culture was unique, and for that reason our explanation had to be particularistic. We rejected normative models, including environmental, economic, and societal determinism, as inadequate to explain a culture that arose at a single moment of colonial history in one unremarkable valley on the eastern seaboard. The acultural generalizations of Turner, Webb, and von Thünen cannot explain what happened in the seventeenth-century Delaware Valley, nor can the models of the normative cultural ecologists.

A particular preadapted immigrant European culture, practiced by Savo-Karelian Finns, was, by pure chance, placed in the mesothermal forests of North America, where it was joined to the indigenous culture of certain eastern woodland Indians, most notably the Delawares, to yield all the essential ingredients of a syncretistic Midland American colonizing system. The Scotch-Irish subsequently supplied the largest single genetic input to the backwoods population, setting the colonization machine in rapid westward motion, but the material culture and techniques that allowed successful forest colonization were largely of Finnish and Indian origin.

The Midland backwoods culture arose in the lower Delaware Valley. Very early its position became peripheral to an evolving, expanding Germanic core, and the process of westward displacement began. Those who seek the origins of the culture in the west, on the Scotch-Irish frontier of 1720–1780, mistake child for parent, purveyor for inventor.

The Essential Diffusionary Evidence Restated

Our conclusions rest upon societal, economic, and architectural evidence, part of which is diagnostic (Table 10.1). The essential characteristics of the Midland American colonization system can be simply restated: steel ax, rifle, log construction, corn, hog, worm fence, scattered settlement, mobility, and shifting cultivation. All of these can be derived from a combination of seventeenth-century Finnish and Indian cultures, and all were well established in the Midland nucleus prior to the arrival of the Scotch-Irish, who were in any case ignorant of many or most of these vital characteristics.

That backwoods American log carpentry and architecture were derived in part from the interior and peripheral districts of northern Europe is proven by the diagnostic character of V-notching, diamond notching, open-passage house, weightpole-butting board-knee roof, and hunter's shanty. The Fenno-Scandian contribution to Midland axmanship, clearing techniques, and shifting cultivation is revealed in the diagnostic value of the split-rail worm fence. American Indian gifts to the system are, similarly, proven diagnostically.

The remaining evidence of diffusion from Finnish northern Europe is circumstantial, since more than one origin is possible, but when considered in conjunction with the diagnostic characteristics, it gains added legitimacy. The whole matter is somewhat akin to high biblical criticism. If the critic proves one error or inconsistency in the Holy Scriptures, then all books and verses cease to be divine. If you accept the Finnish origin of just one American feature—the weightpole-butting board-knee roof, for example—then the possibility or even the likelihood of Finnish influence in other aspects of the Midland pioneering system cannot be dismissed. When *seven* diagnostic characteristics of northern European origin are accepted (Table 10.1), then logic demands approval of a considerable Fenno-Scandian role in the shaping of Midland frontier colonization culture. Singly, a Finnish-like trait in backwoods America could be dismissed as chance independent invention, but complexes of multiple, interrelated, diagnostic northern European traits, such as those that exist in carpentry and architecture, simply cannot be cast aside. Coincidentally, the parallel circumstantial evidence of Finnish influence gains added weight.

Evidence of diffusion, even if diagnostic, remains nonexplanatory.[1] A transatlantic movement is proven, as is a merger with Indian and other cultures, but still missing is the explanation of how so small a group could have been so influential and why the fusing occurred. To be sure, part of the answer lies in the fact that the Finns and Swedes, while not numerous, nevertheless formed a significant proportion of Delaware Valley rural inhabitants through the last half of the seventeenth century, the crucial time of contact and fusion. That is, during the early period of interaction with British and other immigrants, the northern Eu-

Table 10.1 Summary of Seventeenth-Century Ethnic Evidence

Selected Midland American Frontier Characteristics	Savo-Karelian Finns	Swedes	Hill Britons	Lowland English	Germans	Dutch	Eastern Woodland Indians
Free peasantry	●	○	○	x	x	x	—
Poorly churched	●	○	●	x	x	x	●
Weakly developed classes	●	x	○	—	—	—	●
Mobility	●	—	x	—	—	—	●
Crude log carpentry	●	○	—	—	x	—	—
Interchangeable floor plans	●	x	—	—	—	—	○
Open-passage house	●	○	—	—	—	—	—
Exterior chimney at gable	—	—	●	●	—	—	—
V-notch	●	○	—	—	—	—	—
Diamond notch	x	●	—	—	—	—	—
Weightpole-knee roof	●	x	—	—	—	—	—
Shifting cultivation	●	○	○	—	—	—	●
Axmanship	●	●	x	—	x	—	x
Plowless farming	●	—	—	—	—	—	●
Worm fences	●	—	—	—	—	—	—
Corn, squash, pumpkins	—	—	—	—	—	—	●
Peaches	—	x	x	●	●	●	—
Scattered farmsteads	●	○	●	○	○	○	—
Distilled alcoholic drink	●	●	●	○	○	○	—
Hogs	○	●	○	●	●	●	—
Untended open-range stock	●	x	○	—	—	—	—
Hunting skills	●	○	x	—	○	—	●
Rifle	●	●	●	●	●	●	—
Hunter's shanty	●	x	—	—	—	—	—
Long hunt	●	○	—	—	—	—	●

Key: ● = common; ○ = occasional; x = rare; — = absent; *italicized words* = diagnostic traits.

ropeans constituted a high enough percentage of the total farm population to make a major impact on the resultant syncretic rural culture. A count of surnames from the 1677 tax lists in the New Castle area, for example, suggests that Finns and Swedes accounted for between 20 and 25 percent of the population.[2]

These proportions do not, however, address the question of *why* the later immigrants, who formed the majority, adopted Finnish traits, or why, at an earlier period, Swedish settlers accepted an essentially Savo-Karelian lifestyle. We have tried to demonstrate in the preceding chapters that cultural ecology provides the elusive explanatory mechanism.[3]

Explanation

Our main point has been that the Finns were preadapted for life in the American backwoods and that they enhanced their fitness by accepting from the Delaware Indians certain other adaptive elements that were of value in the eastern deciduous woodlands. Contemporary accounts reveal that Dutch and British administrators in the Middle Colonies clearly recognized the unique fitness of the Finns for forest colonization, as Swedish royal authorities had earlier concluded, and that the same officials also understood that Hollander and English immigrants were poorly suited to the task.[4] Less environmental stress was placed upon the Savo-Karelian adaptive strategy because it had developed in a forest colonization setting, while the strategies of the English, Dutch, Palatines, and Celts had not.[5] It is not accidental that those Scotch-Irish who came to the Middle Colonies, gaining exposure to the Fenno-Indian adaptive strategy, became notably successful backwoods pioneers, while fellow immigrants from Ulster who settled parts of interior New England, failed to become effective forest colonizers.

Isaiah Bowman, in a much earlier geographical study of settlement frontiers, stressed the importance in such situations of the Emersonian principle, "Let one man in a company be wise, and all are wise, so great is the contagion."[6] In the early Delaware Valley settlements, the Finns possessed the pioneering wisdom. Selection has been called "a mechanism for bringing about highly improbable events," and in that particularistic way, following the Emersonian principle, a small group of Finns instructed an emerging nation in the art of forest colonization.[7] Their complex of preadapted traits diffused to the Midland backwoods population at large because it worked far better than any competing system.

What, precisely, endowed the Finnish cultural complex with superiority? First, their individualistic tradition of diversifying selection, as well as the basic similarity of their lifestyle to that of the forest Indians, preconditioned them to accept new ideas possessed by the natives, in particular the Delawares. While the Finnish culture was to a remarkable degree preadapted, its bearers had to cope in America with a somewhat different flora, fauna, soil, and climate. For this vital information, they relied extensively and almost immediately upon the ecological wisdom of the local Indians. Successful adaptation usually requires such exchange or deculturation, the adoption of elements from another population's ecological strategy, and immigrant groups possessing a heritage of diversifying selection are culturally prepared for the necessary borrowing.[8] In addition, the fewer and more tenuous the linkages to the parent state in colonial settings, the greater the stimulus for adaptation, and the Finns were pretty much left to their own resources along the Delaware.[9] The net result was a rapid response time on the part of the Savo-Karelians in America, which allowed them to adapt quickly to the new set of environmental conditions and to accommodate change.[10]

Quickly formed, the syncretic Fenno-Indian adaptive strategy offered (1) a method for restructuring the wooded environment for economic use rapidly and at a minimal expenditure of labor; (2) techniques for producing food, shelter, and clothing that were both labor efficient and, due to their diversity, accompanied by little risk of failure; and (3) a socioeconomic structure that could function in the virtual absence of a network of central places. In short, the Fenno-Indian strategy accomplished the goals of forest colonization with the least possible effort, risk, and outside help—hallmarks of a successful adaptive system.[11]

Each major Midland American backwoods characteristic illustrated adaptive advantage. Mobility and the scattered settlement pattern offered both an effective dispersal mechanism and a perpetuation of the adaptive strategy of extensive land use. Skilled wielding of the steel ax, coupled with plowless cultivation in fired clearings, provided the most labor efficient method of restructuring the ecosystem and converting biomass into nutrients for domestic plants. Corn yielded more food per acre than any other grain crop and permitted a gradual harvest, while the peach tree bore fruit at a younger age than other orchard trees. Untended open-range hogs proved remarkably prolific and self-reliant in the oak-rich eastern woodlands, producing abundant meat high in energy-yielding fat at a trifling expense of labor.

Crude chink-log carpentry and the building of split-rail worm fences both utilized the most abundant raw material in minimally processed form and produced structures that could easily be relocated, thereby minimizing labor input. Interchangeable floor plans reduced the number of buildings that had to be erected, and the open passageway in double-unit log houses and barns offered the easiest method of enlargement. The Finnish-plan cabin possessed climatic advantages, placed the door in the wall with greatest headroom, and could most easily be converted into a double-pen plan. A ridgepole-and-purlin roof structure, covered with boards and secured by weightpoles and knees, enjoyed ease of construction, utilized a ubiquitous raw material, and required no nails. The three-faced hunter's shanty uniquely took advantage of the heat-reflector-oven principle, and the long hunt maximized the availability of game, while simultaneously providing the information base for future migration.

Each of these characteristics offered adaptive advantages and probably could have withstood the diffusionary process singly, but in fact many of them were strongly interlinked, forming an adaptive package. Such clusters or complexes possess a durability and stability that individually diffused traits do not enjoy. It is the package, not the constituent parts, that faces selection. When bearers of such a preadapted complex additionally accomplish the first effective settlement of an area, as was true of the Delaware Valley Fenno-Indian system, then the package acquires almost invulnerable staying power in the face of later, alien immigration. In fact, the doctrine of first effective settlement becomes understandable precisely in cultural ecological terms; the successful adaptation or preadaptation of cultural complexes explains effective colonization.

Thus, later-arriving immigrant groups did not significantly alter the established colonization technology of the frontier population. They influenced tastes, but not techniques. Groups such as the Scotch-Irish and the Alpine Germans contributed significantly only to those aspects of backwoods culture that were unrelated to adaptation. From the Germans, for example, came the yodel of country western music, the "good old boy" nickname "Bubba," and vernacular terms such as *to gobble up* food, but frontier adaptive strategy was not reshaped along Alpine lines. Similarly, the much more numerous Scotch-Irish, while reinforcing many vital aspects of the earlier-established pioneer adaptive strategy, placed their distinctive mark mainly upon societal and cultural matters of taste in the backwoods. Emotional, atomistic dissenter Protestantism was likely their doing, as were blood feuds, British ballads, and the bagpipe-like squealing of Appalachian fiddles. In terms of forest colonization techniques, however, the Midland American frontier was most assuredly not Ulster extended.

Simplification

The simplification of European culture in the New World is also linked, in part, to adaptation. To be sure, Finnish culture began to be simplified at the point of departure, in northern Europe, when disproportionate numbers of migratory Savo-Karelian *kirvesmiehet* were sent to the Delaware Valley colony. But simplification continued at the destination, along the Delaware, where many introduced elements of Finnish culture withered and died, without becoming part of the Midland American pioneer culture. These discarded elements included the sauna; Finnish language; incipient Lutheranism; belief in sorcery; birchbark basketry and shoes; emphasis on cattle-herding; corner hearths without chimneys; ceiling-height, gable-to-gable "summer beams" in dwellings; emphasis on fishing; preference for rye bread; sleighs; and beer.

Some of these characteristics were discarded as maladaptive in the new environmental setting, but the majority simply possessed no particular adaptive advantage and were rejected by the non-Finnish majority. Why should the Scotch-Irish, Germans, or English have learned the Finnish language or adopted sauna bathing? These features amounted to matters of cultural taste and had nothing to do with the success or failure of the forest colonization system. In such matters, the traditional tastes of the Celtic and Germanic majority prevailed. The rapid disappearance of these superfluous Finnish traits suggests that minority groups, even if they arrived early, can hope to make a lasting contribution to fused colonial cultures only in adaptive strategy, in techniques and technology. A different diffusionary mainspring, clearly non-ecological and more responsive to the will of the majority, governs matters of taste.

Legacy

How important, in the final analysis, was the Midland backwoods culture? It is easy, we feel, to overstate, as Turner did, the durability of frontier influence in American life, though certain elements do seem to have survived into postpioneer times, often becoming maladaptive in the process.[12] Wanton environmental destruction in North America may be at least in part a legacy of the backwoods frontier, as was suggested in Chapter 8.

We should not, however, seek many relics of the frontier in our modern way of life. Periphery rarely exerts much influence on core, and the peripheral culture in question vanished a century ago. The adaptive process that created the American woodland pioneering system was opportunistic, favoring immediate advantage over eventual gain, and when the opportunity for colonization ended on the Pacific shores, the frontier culture did not long endure.[13] Succeeding generations have been little affected.

The pioneer legacy is less cultural or ideological than geographical. If the Germanic core ultimately overwhelmed and absorbed the Fenno-Indian-Celtic frontier, the backwoods folk facilitated that expansion by accomplishing the initial settlement of the land. The historical geographer Ellen C. Semple discerned the true backwoods legacy when, commenting upon the achievement of a Mississippi River boundary by the fledgling United States in a 1783 peace treaty, she attributed it to "the presence in these western lands of a vigorous people who had made good their title by axe and plough and rifle." Pioneer occupancy "constituted a more solid claim to the debated territory than the yellow parchments of dead monarchs or living potentates."[14] Today we are a transcontinental nation rather than a littoral state. We obeyed a manifest destiny. That is the true legacy of the Midland backwoods folk and their Finnish teachers.

NOTES

Chapter 1. A Backwoods Culture

Epigraph: Lönnrot 1963, p. 10 (poem 2, lines 133–34).
1. Michaux 1805, p. 111; Harpster 1938, p. 195; *Pennsylvania Archives*, 1st ser., vol. 1, pp. 213, 216, 217; vol. 2, pp. 213, 289, 521, 697, 771.
2. Harris 1805, p. 59; Peck 1965, pp. xxxv, 101, 103; Harpster 1938, p. 134.
3. Hinke and Kemper 1903–4, vol. 11, p. 123; Guillet 1963b, vol. 1, p. 246.
4. Dwight 1969, vol. 2, pp. 439–40.
5. Peck 1965, p. 145; Baily 1969, p. 104.
6. A somewhat similar list appears in Newton 1964, p. 152.
7. Harpster 1938, pp. 134, 195–97.
8. Fiske 1897, vol. 2, p. 312.
9. Harpster 1938, pp. 196–97.
10. Peck 1965, pp. xxxv, 101, 106, 144, 149.
11. Turner 1921, p. 16.
12. Harpster 1938, p. 197; Peck 1965, pp. xxxv, 146. See also Bowman 1931, p. 8.
13. Smithwick 1983, pp. 47, 166.
14. Harris 1805, p. 58.
15. Howe 1898–1902, vol. 2, p. 401.
16. Guillet 1963b, vol. 1, p. 304.
17. Guillet 1963b, vol. 1, p. 303.
18. Michaux 1805, p. 113; Peck 1965, p. xxxvi; Guillet 1963b, vol. 1, p. 303; Dwight 1969, vol. 2, pp. 439–40.
19. Meinig 1972, p. 160; Gulley 1959, p. 66.
20. Peck 1965, p. 150.
21. Smithwick (1983, pp. 1–18) provides a fine personal account of a man from the older settlements learning the backwoods way of life in early Texas.
22. Darby 1956; Mikesell 1960, pp. 66–67.
23. Gulley 1959, pp. 85–88.

24. The terminology for this regional classification is borrowed, with slightly modified definitions, from Meinig 1965, pp. 213–17.
25. Turner 1962, p. 164; Evans 1969, p. 73.
26. Newton 1974, pp. 147–48; Mitchell 1978, pp. 67, 73, 75; Turner 1962, p. 164. See also Meinig 1957–58, p. 21.
27. These types of diffusion follow the Hägerstrand model, discussed in Jordan and Rowntree 1986, pp. 13–16.
28. Fiske 1897, vol. 2, pp. 317, 321.
29. Pillsbury 1983, pp. 59–69; *Pennsylvania Archives*, 1st ser., vol. 2, pp. 12–13.
30. Gerlach 1976, p. 14; Turner 1962, p. 168.
31. Michaux 1805, p. 113.
32. Peck 1965, pp. 144, 149.
33. Meinig 1957–58, p. 21; Clark 1970, pp. 335, 352, 355.
34. See Dodge 1942, map following p. 436, and p. 437.
35. Dodge 1942, pp. 438–39.
36. Cronon 1983, p. 119; Lockridge 1970, pp. 168–69; Gates 1968, pp. 43–44.
37. Dodge 1942, p. 435.
38. Turner 1962, pp. 93, 96.
39. Jordan 1981, pp. 25–157.
40. Turner 1962, p. 184.
41. Turner 1962, p. 208.
42. Arthur and Witney 1972, pp. 36–53.
43. An excellent geographical analysis of the Russian frontier is Gibson 1976. See also Mikesell 1960, p. 67.
44. A good geographical treatment is Harris 1966. See also Mikesell 1960, p. 69.
45. Campbell 1937, p. 123.
46. Sauer 1941, p. 23.

Chapter 2. In Search of a Mainspring

Epigraph: Lönnrot 1963, p. 338 (poem 50, lines 612–14).
1. A splendid interdisciplinary analysis of many such models and theses is found in Lewis 1984, pp. 8–27.
2. Meinig 1976, p. 34; Wynn 1983, p. 366.
3. Sauer 1930, p. 284; Leyburn 1935, pp. 5–6; K. Lewis, in Green and Perlman 1985, pp. 252–55.
4. Hardesty 1980–81, p. 68.
5. Hudson 1984, p. 22.
6. Sauer 1930, p. 283.
7. Harris 1977, pp. 469, 472; Keller 1947; Foster 1960, p. 13; Hartz 1964, p. 3. See also Zelinsky 1973, p. 5; Mitchell 1978, p. 67; and Meinig 1976, pp. 31–34.
8. Buffington 1939, pp. 276–86.
9. Zelinsky 1973, p. 13; Kniffen 1965, p. 551.
10. Zelinsky 1973, p. 13.
11. Kniffen 1965, p. 551.
12. Kniffen 1965, p. 551.
13. Mitchell 1978, pp. 67, 69.
14. Evans 1966, pp. 77–79; Wertenbaker 1938, p. 303; Mitchell 1978, p. 69.
15. Zelinsky 1973, p. 6.

16. Wells 1973, pp. 6, 8–10; Hallowell 1957a, 1957b.
17. Harris 1977, p. 474.
18. Newton and Pulliam–Di Napoli 1977, p. 378; Newton 1974, pp. 145–48.
19. McDonald and McWhiney 1980a, pp. 11–15; McDonald and McWhiney 1980b, 1095–118; McWhiney and McDonald 1983, pp. 89–102; McDonald and McDonald 1980, pp. 179–99.
20. Gerlach 1984, p. 47.
21. Vlach 1978. See also Vlach 1976.
22. Berthoff 1986; Akenson 1984.
23. Duncan 1980.
24. G. Pierson, in Taylor 1972, p. 74; Wynn 1983, pp. 354, 356.
25. R. Billington, in Turner 1962, p. vii.
26. G. Pierson, in Taylor 1972, p. 94; Pierson 1940, p. 454.
27. Billington 1977, pp. 20, 22.
28. G. Pierson, in Taylor 1972, p. 79.
29. Billington 1977, p. 20; G. Pierson, in Taylor 1972, p. 74; L. Hacker, in Taylor 1972, p. 52.
30. Gulley 1959, p. 65.
31. L. Hacker, in Taylor 1972, p. 52; Mikesell 1960, pp. 62–64.
32. Turner 1962, p. 207.
33. Webb 1931.
34. Webb 1931, pp. 5, 8, 140–41.
35. Hardesty 1980–81, p. 71.
36. Semple 1903, pp. 64, 68, 73.
37. Semple 1903, pp. 61–62.
38. Semple 1903, p. 78.
39. Leyburn 1935 p. 187.
40. Bowman 1931, p. 1
41. Von Thünen 1966.
42. Chisholm 1962; Peet 1969; Peet 1970–71; Jordan 1981, pp. 18–22.
43. Peck 1965, p. 150.
44. See, for example, Paynter 1982, pp. 4–5, 15.
45. Webb 1951.
46. Webb 1951, pp. 36–44.
47. Lewis 1984, pp. xxiii, 25–27.
48. Lewis 1984, pp. 2, 20–21, 26, 113.
49. Mitchell 1977.
50. Mitchell 1977, pp. x, 3, 4, 230.
51. Mitchell 1977, pp. 3–4; Wynn 1983, p. 364.
52. Lewis 1984, p. 1.
53. Harris 1977.
54. Lemon 1972.
55. Kirch 1980, pp. 102, 104–5; Durham 1976, pp. 89–121.
56. Hardesty 1980–81, pp. 69, 71; Green 1979, p. 69; Hess 1979, pp. 123, 136; Diamond 1977, pp. 249–50.
57. Lewis 1984, p. 12; Hardesty 1980–81, pp. 72–73; Casagrande, Thompson, and Young 1964, p. 283.
58. Margolis 1977, pp. 43, 58–60; Hardesty 1980–81, p. 77.
59. Hardesty 1980–81, p. 77; Diamond 1974, p. 805.
60. Hudson 1951, p. 575; Margolis 1977, p. 59.
61. Sahlins and Service 1960, pp. 75–76.
62. Prigogine, Nicolis, and Babloyantz 1972a, pp. 24–26, 28; Prigogine, Nicolis, and Babloyantz 1972b, pp. 36, 40–41; Hardesty 1986, p. 15.
63. D. L. Hardesty, in Lewis 1984, p. xx.

64. Butzer 1982, pp. 282–83; Denevan 1983, p. 401; Kirch 1980, pp. 103–5.
65. Denevan 1983, pp. 400–401; Kirch 1980, p. 129.
66. Kirch 1980, p. 127.
67. Green 1979, pp. 74, 83, 84, 87.
68. Diamond 1977, pp. 253, 258–59; Hardesty 1986, pp. 12–14. It is regrettable that many cultural ecologists reject the particularistic approach; see, for example, Rhoades and Thompson 1975.
69. Newton 1974.
70. Newton 1974, p. 147.
71. Paschall 1912, p. 254; Brodhead 1853–58, vol. 4, p. 274.
72. Miller and Savage 1977, p. 125.
73. Butzer 1982, p. 284; Denevan 1983, p. 402; Newton 1974, pp. 146–47; Zelinsky 1973, p. 6; Kirch 1980, pp. 122–23.
74. Sahlins and Service 1960, p. 52; Lewis 1984, p. 11.
75. Diamond 1977, pp. 255, 259.
76. Denevan 1983, p. 403; Butzer 1982, pp. 123, 284.
77. Butzer 1982, pp. 284, 285; Denevan 1983, pp. 400, 402.
78. Denevan 1983, p. 402; Lewis 1984, p. 13.
79. Diamond 1977, p. 259.
80. Evans 1967, p. 234.
81. Keller 1947; Sahlins and Service 1960, pp. 51–52.
82. Brodhead 1853–58, vol. 2, p. 210.
83. See, for example, Stone 1973; and Ehlers 1967.
84. Jordan 1985.
85. Sauer 1930, p. 284; Stilgoe 1982, pp. 175–77; Linderholm 1976; Johnson 1955.
86. Wertenbaker 1938, p. 26; Glassie 1972, p. 49; Kniffen and Glassie 1966, p. 58. See also Zelinsky 1973, p. 21.
87. Zelinsky 1973, p. 20.
88. The spokesman for the Scotch-Irish are legion; see, most notably, the works listed in the bibliography by E. Estyn Evans, Russel L. Gerlach, Forrest McDonald, and Grady McWhiney. Their cause has also been repeatedly promoted through the Ulster-American Heritage Symposia, the most recent of which was held at Western Carolina University in 1986.

Chapter 3. Eastern Finnish Culture and Its Spread to Colonial America

Epigraph: Lönnrot 1963, p. 164 (poem 23, line 793).
1. Mead 1959, p. 145; Meitzen 1895, vol. 2, pp. 172, 189–90; Retzius 1885; Grotenfelt 1899, pp. 15–16; Valonen 1971; Talve 1973–74, p. 95; Vuorela 1976, pp. 1–149; Korhonen 1985, pp. 411–13; Sirelius 1923.
2. Valonen 1971; Geographical Society of Finland 1925, maps 7, 9, 18; Aaltonen 1952; Renqvist 1952; Kujala 1952.
3. Soininen 1959, pp. 153–55, 164–65; Soininen 1961, pp. 139–44; interviews with P. M. Tvengsberg; Jutikkala 1963, pp. 19–21; Jutikkala 1980, pp. 70, 207–9; Kortesalmi 1969, pp. 309–50; Åström 1978, pp. 27–29; Talve 1979, pp. 51–52; Keränen 1984, p. 75; Korhonen 1985, pp. 362–63; Vilkuna 1948; Kulturhistorisk leksikon 1956–75, vol. 7, col. 683; vol. 14, cols. 556–57; vol. 17, cols. 489–91.

4. On Finnish burnbeating, see also the classic work by Grotenfelt (1899).

5. Soininen 1959, pp. 152–53; Soininen 1961, pp. 137–54; Jutikkala 1963, p. 20; Jutikkala 1980, pp. 66–70, 200–210; *Kulturhistorisk leksikon* 1956–75, vol. 17, cols. 487–88; Åström 1978, pp. 27–28; Talve 1979, pp. 51–52; Korhonen 1985, pp. 361–63.

6. Soininen 1961, pp. 155–59; Lönnrot 1963, pp. 228–29 (poem 32, lines 33–116); Jutikkala 1963, p. 24.

7. Boat exhibits at Ylä-savon kotiseutumuseo and Konneveden kotiseutumuseo; Jutikkala 1963, pp. 30–37; Jutikkala 1980, pp. 54–66, 197–202; Vuorela 1975, pp. 21–24; Åström 1978, pp. 25–26; Talve 1979, pp. 68–70; Soininen 1961, pp. 29–56; Keränen 1984, pp. 35–36, 54–60; Korhonen 1985, pp. 371–77.

8. Sirelius 1909, p. 19; Soininen 1961, pp. 49–53, 428–29; *Kulturhistorisk leksikon* 1956–75, vol. 4, cols. 39–45; vol. 16, cols. 88–89; Vuorela 1975, p. 23.

9. Jutikkala and Pirinen 1974, p. 15

10. Soininen 1959, pp. 160, 162, 165–66.

11. Retzius 1885, pp. 62–68, 75–79; Sirelius 1909, pp. 24–25, 109; Heikel 1888, pp. 206–7; Meitzen 1895, vol. 2, p. 206; Vuorela 1975, pp. 304–6; Jokipii 1961, pp. 40–48.

12. Soininen 1961, pp. 56, 429.

13. Diamond 1977, p. 251; Hardesty 1986, pp. 14–16; Vilkuna 1960, pp. 47–48, 52.

14. Auer and Jutikkala 1941, p. 58.

15. Auer and Jutikkala 1941, pp. 58, 72; Talve 1973–74, pp. 100–101; Korhonen 1985, p. 413; *Kulturhistorisk leksikon* 1956–75, vol. 8, cols. 279–80.

16. Soininen 1959, pp. 150–51; Soininen 1961, p. 435; *Kulturhistorisk leksikon* 1956–75, vol. 15, cols. 47–49.

17. Soininen 1961, pp. 211–66, 434.

18. Soininen 1961, pp. 243–50, 265–66, 434; Jutikkala 1980, pp. 46–50, 66.

19. Lönnrot 1963.

20. Retzius 1885, pp. 89–102, 110; Heikel 1888, pp. 232, 237; Kolehmainen and Laine 1979, pp. 74, 399; Ailonen 1980, p. 13; Talve 1979, pp. 32, 36–37, 44–48; Korhonen 1985, pp. 352, 356–57.

21. Sirelius 1911, pp. 91–93, 98–99.

22. Kaups 1981, pp. 140–44; Dmitrieva 1982–83, p. 41; Heikel 1888, pp. 112–22, 213, 231–32; Sirelius 1909, p. 34; Retzius 1885, p. 70; Karjalainen kotitalo-ulkomuseo; Laukaan kotiseutumuseo; Vesannon torpparimuseo; Vuorela 1975, pp. 306–9; Talve 1979, pp. 38–41; Korhonen 1985, p. 352.

23. Sirelius 1909, pp. 27–28, 70–71; 1911, p. 116; Vuorela 1975, pp. 407–8; Valonen 1977, p. 29; Talve 1979, pp. 33–34.

24. Soininen 1961, pp. 168, 432; Meitzen 1895, vol. 2, pp. 187–88; *Kulturhistorisk leksikon* 1956–75, vol. 8, col. 423.

25. Soininen 1961, pp. 163–90.

26. The definitive study of the colonization of northern Savo is Soininen 1961, esp. pp. 125–36. See also *Suomen asutus* 1973, pp. 19–20 and the map entitled "Savolaisasutuksen leviäminen 1560-luvulla."

27. Jutikkala and Pirinen 1974, pp. 13, 62–63; Vilkuna 1953, pp. 10–11; Hämäläinen 1930, p. 14; Soininen 1959, pp. 150–51; Soininen

1961, pp. 125–36, 428; Rikkinen 1977, pp. 19–25; Keränen 1984, pp. 74–104; Veijo Saloheimo, in Huovinen 1986, pp. 7–22.

28. Soininen 1961, pp. 191–210.
29. Sømme 1960, p. 150.
30. Soininen 1959, pp. 151, 155; *Kulturhistorisk leksikon* 1956–75, vol. 15, col. 48.
31. Bibliographical sources on the Finnish settlement of Sweden are Koivukangas and Toivonen 1978, pp. 53–63; and Eklund 1953.
32. Broberg 1967, p. 97; Falk 1921, pp. 229–35; Nilsson 1950, p. 53; Jutikkala and Pirinen 1974, p. 82; Hämäläinen 1945, p. 9.
33. General sources on the Finnish settlement of Sweden include Nordmann 1888; Lönborg 1902; Broberg 1967; Linderholm 1974; and Segerstedt MS.
34. Gothe 1942, pp. 31, 37–38, 43, 46; Gothe 1950, pp. 493–95; Gottlund 1931, pp. 79, 105, 145, 197; Lönborg 1902, pp. 67–70; Nordmann 1888, pp. 6–7; Østberg 1935, p. 272; Soininen 1959, p. 151; Hämäläinen 1945, pp. 9–10; Segerstedt MS, vol. 1, pt. 1, pp. 29, 63, 487; Värmlands museum files, "Värmlands Finnarna," vol. 1, pt. 1.
35. Keyland 1954; Bromander 1901; Reponen 1934; Lönborg 1901, p. 231; Tvengsberg 1961, 1982; Østberg 1935, p. 272; Hämäläinen 1945; Broberg 1953; Jacobsen 1985, pp. 91–105; Talve 1982, pp. 178–88.
36. Åkerhielm 1907, pp. 191, 193–95.
37. Interview with O. Koehler.
38. Detailed maps of Finnish settlements in Sweden are found in Campbell et al. 1957, vol. 1, p. 49; Lönborg 1902, p. 83; Segerstedt MS, vol. 1, pt. 1, map following p. 740; Montelius 1960, p. 286; and Broberg 1981, pp. 35–37.
39. *Sweden: Official Standard Names* 1963, pp. 197–99.
40. Falk 1921; Rydberg 1929; Bill 1982; Palmqvist 1953; Nilsson 1950; Broberg 1967, pp. 95, 98; Broberg 1973, p. 25; Nordmann 1888, p. 17; Eklund 1953; Huovinen 1986.
41. Gothe 1942, 1945, 1948, 1950.
42. Østberg 1931–32; Nordmann 1888, pp. 133–43; Broberg 1967, p. 94; Matson 1902–8.
43. Wiklund 1902; "Suomalais-ugrilaisten kansojen," map following p. 135; Djurklou 1873; Magnusson 1877.
44. Nilsson 1938, pp. 12, 17.
45. Montelius 1960, p. 288; Broberg 1967, p. 97; Nilsson 1938, pp. 26–27.
46. Broberg 1967, p. 97; Bromander 1901, p. 141.
47. Hämäläinen 1945, pp. 15–16; Broberg 1967, p. 97; Kortesalmi 1969, pp. 297–309.
48. Falk 1921, pp. 256–57; Bromander 1902; Talve 1953, pp. 35–40.
49. Erixon 1962–63, vol. 1, p. 52; Nilsson 1950, p. 155; Falk 1921, pp. 243–53; Tvengsberg 1961, p. 127; Lönborg 1902, pp. 376, 379, 381, 396; Nordmann 1888, p. 92; Hämäläinen 1945, pp. 39, 45, 64, 173; Jacobsen 1985, pp. 91–114.
50. Ward 1930, p. 103; Nordmann 1888, app. 4, pp. xv–xviii; Hämäläinen 1945, p. 25.
51. Bromander 1902, p. 284; Broberg 1953.
52. Magnusson 1877, p. 153.
53. Magnusson 1877, p. 152; Johnson 1911, vol. 1, pp. 126, 147–48, 239, 243.

54. Falk 1921, pp. 244, 261–63, 279; Axelson 1852, p. 73; Magnusson 1877, pp. 134–35, 150–53; Soininen 1961, p. 431.
55. Magnusson 1877, pp. 149–50.
56. Nordmann 1888, p. 115.
57. Falk 1921, pp. 257–58; Broberg 1981, pp. 50–62.
58. The best general source on New Sweden is Johnson 1911. See also Acrelius 1874; Arfwedson 1909; Carlsson 1971; Clay 1858; Linderholm 1976; Odhner 1879; Sprinchorn 1883–84; and Ward 1938.
59. Printz 1912b, p. 121; Rising 1912a, p. 149; Schwartz 1982, p. 103; Bridenbaugh 1976, p. 149.
60. Johnson 1911, vol. 2, pp. 634, 667; Sprinchorn 1884, p. 249; Brodhead 1853–58, vol. 2, pp. 211–12; Gothe 1945, p. 125.
61. Paschall 1912, pp. 251–52; Penn 1912a, pp. 237–38; Fernow 1877, pp. 647–49; Ferris 1846, p. 129.
62. Thomas 1912, p. 316.
63. Jordan 1983, pp. 59–61.
64. Sources on the Finns in New Sweden include Wuorinen 1938; Ilmonen 1916; Louhi 1925; Kerkkonen 1969–70; Bill 1983; Dunlap and Moyne 1952; Nordmann 1888, pp. 144–56; and Koivukangas and Toivonen 1978, pp. 103–5.
65. Dunlap 1954, pp. 35, 38, 39.
66. Linderholm 1974, p. 58; Johnson 1911, vol. 1, p. 147; Nordmann 1888, p. 145.
67. Johnson 1911, vol. 2, pp. 517, 524, 535, 547, 708, 713–20; Dunlap and Moyne 1952, pp. 81–83.
68. Fernow 1877, pp. 169, 191, 285, 298, 307, 366, 406, 451; Brodhead 1853–58, vol. 2, pp. 210–12, 242, 605, 608; Holm 1834, p. 65.
69. Thomas 1912, p. 316; Paschall 1912, pp 251–52; Penn 1912a, p. 237; Penn 1912b, p. 260; Edmundson 1715, p. 95; Brodhead 1853–58, vol. 3, pp. 113, 182; Fernow 1877, pp. 536, 647–49.
70. Johnson 1911, vol. 1, pp. 149–52, 239, 243; Odhner 1879, p. 406; Louhi 1925, p. 52.
71. Nordmann 1888, p. 147; Johnson 1911, vol. 1, p. 267.
72. Louhi 1925, pp. 57, 82–83; Magnusson 1877, p. 132; Gothe 1945, p. 127; Johnson 1911, vol. 2, pp. 633, 724–26.
73. Rising 1912a, p. 149.
74. Bridenbaugh 1976, p. 149; Wuorinen 1938, pp. 51, 79; Dunlap and Moyne 1952, p. 85.
75. Dunlap and Moyne 1952, p. 85.
76. Brodhead 1853–58, vol. 3, p. 343; Lindeström 1925, pp. 89–90.
77. Johnson 1911, vol. 2, p. 634.
78. Brodhead 1853–58, vol. 2, pp. 211–12, 242; *Pennsylvania Archives*, 2nd ser., vol. 5, p. 470.
79. Johnson 1911, vol. 2, pp. 650–52; Wuorinen 1938, p. 79; Arfwedson 1909, pp. 25–26; Gothe 1945, pp. 126–29; Sprinchorn 1884, p. 249; Nordmann 1888, p. 150; Bill 1983, p. 39.
80. Gothe 1945, p. 125.
81. Edmundson 1715, p. 95.
82. Johnson 1911, vol. 1, pp. 239, 243, 267; vol. 2, pp. 708, 712; Dunlap and Moyne 1952, p. 82; Louhi 1925, pp. 39, 42; Lindeström 1925, pp. 125–26.
83. Rauanheimo 1921, pp. 36–40.
84. Rauanheimo 1938, pp. 37–39.
85. Linderholm 1974, p. 58; the parish was misread as Sun*d* in Johnson 1911 (vol. 1, pp. 147, 267) and Nordmann 1888 (p. 145).

86. Axelson 1852, p. 75; Magnusson 1877, p. 132; Linderholm 1976, p. 47; Johnson 1911, vol. 1, pp. 149–50, 239; vol. 2, pp. 633, 724–26; Louhi 1925, pp. 82–83; Nordmann 1888, pp. 145–46, 150.

87. Falk 1921, pp. 245–46.

88. Gothe 1945, pp. 125–26; Odhner 1879, p. 405; Johnson 1911, vol. 1, p. 239; vol. 2, p. 711; Linderholm 1976, p. 47; Bill 1983, p. 39.

89. Arfwedson 1909, pp. 25–26; Gothe 1945, p. 126.

90. Johnson 1911, vol. 1, pp. 239, 243; Dunlap and Moyne 1952, p. 82.

91. Heckscher 1954, pp. 85, 97, 116.

92. Bromander 1902, p. 290.

93. Odhner 1879, p. 406.

94. Falk 1921, pp. 245–46.

95. Odhner 1879, pp. 405–6.

96. *Pennsylvania Archives*, 2nd ser., vol. 5, map following p. 232; Fernow 1877, pp. 307, 646–49; Danckaerts 1913, p. 100; Ferris 1846, p. 133; Acrelius 1912, p. 69; Holm 1702, p. 75; Kerkkonen 1969–70, p. 40; Nordmann 1888, pp. 147–48; Lindeström 1925, p. 173; Dunlap and Moyne 1952, pp. 82, 84.

97. Kalm 1972, pp. 170, 308; Muntz 1959, pp. 11–24; Skottsberg 1960, pp. 230–32.

98. Bjarnson 1976, pp. 240–41; Clement 1893, pp. 83–87; Wacker 1975b, pp. 165, 169–70; *New Jersey Archives*, vol. 21, pp. 576, 646; vol. 30, pp. 413–14; Federal Writers' Project 1938a; Federal Writers' Project 1938b, pp. 58–64; *Pennsylvania Archives*, 1st ser., vol. 1, pp. 32, 57; Dunlap and Moyne 1952, p. 85; Leiby 1964, pp. 91–92; 101–2; Brodhead 1853–58, vol. 2, p. 53.

99. *New Jersey Archives*, vol. 21, p. 553; Bjarnson 1976, pp. 242–43.

100. Kalm 1972, p. 213; Federal Writers' Project 1938a; Leiby 1964, pp. 92–93; *Pennsylvania Archives*, 1st ser., vol. 1, p. 35; Armstrong 1860, p. 80.

101. Kalm 1972, pp. 170–71, 193, 210; Wacker 1975b, pp. 171, 281; Muntz 1959, pp. 11–24; Kerkkonen 1938, p. 97.

102. Brodhead 1853–58, vol. 2, p. 210; Holm 1834, pp. 102, 164–66.

103. Fernow 1877, p. 143; Kalm 1972, p. 99; *Pennsylvania Archives*, 2nd ser., vol. 5, p. 249.

104. Kalm 1972, p. 228.

105. Kalm 1929, pp. 222–23; Kalm 1972, p. 260; See also Kerkkonen 1938, p. 109.

106. Jordan 1985, pp. 67–70.

107. Horner 1971; Dunlap and Moyne 1952, p. 87; Kalm 1929, p. 222; Kerkkonen, 1938, p. 109.

108. Armstrong 1860, p. 70.

109. *Pennsylvania Archives*, 2nd ser., vol. 5, p. 104; Kalm 1929, p. 102; Kalm 1972, p. 171; Holm 1834, p. 102.

110. Kalm 1972, pp, 87–88.

111. Thomas 1912, p. 349.

112. Armstrong 1860, pp. 74–75; *Pennsylvania Archives*, 2nd ser., vol. 5, p. 579.

113. Martin 1969–70; *Colonial Records [of Pennsylvania]*, vol. 1, pp. 93–96.

114. *Pennsylvania Archives*, 2nd ser., vol. 5, p. 597; Kalm 1972, p. 255; Kerkkonen 1938, p. 104.

115. Edmundson 1715, p. 95.

116. Armstrong 1860, p. 70.

117. Brodhead 1853–58, vol. 3, p. 186; Fernow 1877, pp. 126, 214, 425–26; Ferris 1846, pp. 119–20.
118. Kalm 1972, p. 213.
119. Penn 1912b, p. 260.
120. Lindeström 1925, p. 87; Brodhead 1853–58, vol. 2, p. 76, vol. 3, pp. 113, 182; Fernow 1877, pp. 292, 349–50; Rising 1912a, p. 137.
121. Weslager 1967; Johnson 1911, vol. 2, p. 709; Ferris 1846, p. 55.
122. Danckaerts 1913, pp. 96, 98, 105; Myers 1912, p. 344.
123. Penn 1912b, p. 260.
124. Leyburn 1962, p. 197.
125. Fernow 1877, p. 145; Federal Writers' Project 1938a, p. 2.
126. Levick 1893; Becker 1984, pp. 7–10; Jones 1912, pp. 451–52; *Pennsylvania Archives*, 1st ser., vol. 1, pp. 108–9.
127. Armstrong 1860, p. 167; Fernow 1877, pp. 490–92; Strang 1970, pp. 111–12.
128. Leyburn 1962, pp. 185, 248–49; Ford 1915, pp. 212, 262–64; Hanna 1902, vol. 2, pp. 14, 61–62, 94–96, 102–7; Pastorius 1912, p. 397; Dankers and Sluyter 1867, p. 211.
129. Leyburn 1962, pp. 157, 169, 185.
130. Johnson 1911, vol. 2, p. 714; Danckaerts 1913, p. 98; Paulsen 1972, pp. 267–68; Evjen 1916, pp. 151–220; Kalm 1929, p. 219.
131. Johnson 1911, vol. 2, pp. 703, 706, 711, 713, 716, 720; Pastorius 1912, pp. 400, 407.
132. Federal Writers' Project 1938a, pp. 1–2.
133. Schwartz 1982, p. 99.
134. Leyburn 1962, p. 256; Evans 1969, pp. 73, 77, 86.
135. Hallowell 1957a, 1957b; Jacobs 1973.

Chapter 4. Backwoods Society in Midland America

Epigraph: Lönnrot 1963, p. 107 (poem 17, lines 313–14).
   1. Wells 1973, pp. 6–15.
   2. Peck 1965, p. 203.
   3. Harris 1805, p. 59.
   4. Peck 1965, p. xxxvi; Baily 1969, p. 103.
   5. Peck 1965, p. 149.
   6. Green 1979, p. 85.
   7. Peck 1965, p. 149.
   8. Odhner 1879, p. 409; Holm 1702, p. 61.
   9. Penn 1912a, pp. 237–38.
  10. Klepp 1982, p. 489.
  11. Ferris 1846, pp. 305–7.
  12. Fernow 1877, pp. 646–47.
  13. Kirch 1980, pp. 120–21.
  14. Klepp 1982, p. 510.
  15. Peck 1965, pp. 145–46.
  16. Peck 1965, pp. 102, 145, 149.
  17. Guillet 1963b, vol. 1, p. 246.
  18. Taylor 1972, pp. 52, 80.
  19. Bowen 1978, p. 55.
  20. Johnson 1911, vol. 2, p. 634.
  21. Duncan 1980, pp. 181–98.
  22. Hardesty 1986, pp. 12, 14, 15; Hess 1979, p. 136.

23. Pohl and Hardin 1985–86, pp. 271, 275–76.
24. Taylor 1972, p. 80.
25. Jordan 1988, fig. 1.9; Spenser 1970, p. 1; Nickels, Kallas, and Friedman 1973, p. 302; Harris 1805, p. 59.
26. Leyburn 1962, p. 191.
27. Soininen 1961, pp. 432–33; Heckscher 1954, pp. 36–38; Hanna 1902, vol. 1, p. 545; Conzen 1983, map A-25.
28. Harpster 1938, pp. 120–21; Campbell 1921, pp. 92–93.
29. Sauer 1920, p. 150; Peck 1965, p. 136; Baily 1969, p. 104.
30. Semple 1901, p. 600; Peck 1965, p. xxxv.
31. *Pennsylvania Archives*, 1st ser. vol. 2, p. 474; Peck 1965, p. 136.
32. Hanna 1902, vol. 1, pp. 59–60; Smithwick 1983, p. 108; Peck 1965, p. 138.
33. Smithwick 1983, p. 47; Harpster 1938, p. 137.
34. Taylor 1972, p. 80; Brown 1963; Brown 1975, p. 21; Leyburn 1935, pp. 215–23; Gard 1949.
35. Hanna 1902, vol. 2, p. 83.
36. Horsman 1970, p. 127; Brown 1963, p. 112; Brown 1975, p. 23 and chaps. 3, 8; Smithwick 1983, p. 60.
37. Peck 1965, p. 155; Montell 1986.
38. Hanna 1902, vol. 1, pp. 60–61; Leyburn 1935, p. 215.
39. Evans 1969, p. 84.
40. Ford 1915, pp. 101–5; Hanna 1902, vol. 1, pp. 551–58; Leyburn 1962, p. 191.
41. Fiske 1897, vol. 2, pp. 317, 321.
42. Meitzen 1895, vol. 2, pp. 185–88; Soininen 1961, pp. 431–32.
43. Magnusson 1877, pp. 134–35; Bromander 1902, p. 290.
44. Lönnrot 1963, pp. 85, 200–201, 223–24, 247–50, 254–55, 280–81.
45. Axelson 1852, pp. 73, 123; Bromander 1902, p. 290.
46. Falk 1921, p. 281.
47. Lindeström 1925, pp. 125–26; Fernow 1877, p. 121; Acrelius 1912, p. 42.
48. Fernow 1877, pp. 38, 126, 129, 131, 214, 305–8, 340, 425–26, 451, 535; Brodhead 1853–58, vol. 1, pp. 88–89; *Colonial Records [of Pennsylvania]*, vol. 2, p. 477; Armstrong 1860, pp. 47, 50–55, 60, 69–75, 110, 176–77, 180; Keen 1883a, p. 220; Lindeström 1925, pp. 125–26; Watson 1830, p. 254.
49. Fernow 1877, pp. 366–67.
50. *Colonial Records [of Pennsylvania]*, vol. 2, p. 481; *Pennsylvania Archives*, 2nd ser., vol. 19, p. 42.
51. Rising 1912a, p. 136; Rising 1912b, p. 157; Johnson 1911, vol. 2, pp. 497, 513; Lindeström 1925, pp. 125–26.
52. Keen 1883a, pp. 219–20; Fernow 1877, pp. 463–72; Brodhead 1853–58, vol. 3, pp. 182, 186; *Pennsylvania Archives*, 2nd ser. vol. 5, pp. 582–87; Ferris 1846, pp. 120–21; Louhi 1925, pp. 134–38; Acrelius 1874, p. 116.
53. Fernow 1877, pp. 469–70.
54. Fernow 1877, pp. 535–37; Gehring 1977, pp. 64, 85–87.
55. *Colonial Records [of Pennsylvania]*, vol. 2, pp. 480, 482.
56. The story of Iver the Finn, also called Evert Hendrickse Eck, is told in Fernow 1877, pp. 425–26, 439–40, 470, 535, 649; Keen 1878a, vol. 2, pp. 329–30; Keen 1879b, p. 353; Keen 1879c, p. 463; Collin 1936, p. 289; Gehring 1977, pp. 91–92, 299, 308; and Johnson 1911, vol. 1, pp. 151, 462–63; vol. 2, pp. 517, 518, 704, 705, 711, 719.
57. Horsman 1970, p. 137; Peck 1965, pp. xli, 85–90.

58. Smithwick 1983, p. 240.
59. Peck 1965, pp. 70, 101, 149–50, 203; see also pp. 144–45, 161, 186.
60. Campbell 1921, p. 154.
61. Hinke and Kemper 1903–4, vol. 11, p. 117; Harpster 1938, p. 120.
62. Semple 1901, pp. 614, 616; Horsman 1970, p. 137.
63. Taylor 1972, pp. 79–80; Campbell 1921, p. 158; Leyburn 1935, pp. 193–95, 200; Peck 1965, p. 124; Horsman 1970, pp. 132, 134–35.
64. Leyburn 1935, p. 196.
65. Hanna 1902, vol. 1, p. 551.
66. Ford 1915, pp. 103, 110, 112; Hanna 1902, vol. 1, p. 552.
67. Horsman 1970, p. 136; Leyburn 1935, p. 192.
68. Broberg 1953, pp. 67–99; Magnusson 1877, p. 152.
69. Gothe 1945, pp. 176–86; Gustafsson 1957, pp. 20, 145.
70. Armstrong 1860, pp. 152–53; Leiby 1964, p. 101; Ward 1930, p. 103.
71. Holm 1834, p. 99; Leiby 1964, pp. 96–97.
72. Ferris 1846, pp. 305–7.
73. Smithwick 1983, p. 5; Peck 1965, pp. 101, 122, 145, 149; Campbell 1921, p. 260.
74. Horsman 1970, p. 141.
75. Gothe 1945, p. 183.
76. *Pennsylvania Archives*, 1st ser., vol. 1, p. 93; Fernow 1877, pp. 107, 158, 539; Klepp 1982, p. 511.
77. *Pennsylvania Archives*, 1st ser., vol. 2, p. 336; Wacker 1975b, p. 170.
78. Michaux 1805, pp. 52–53, 111, 114; Sauer 1920, pp. 102–3, 151–52. For similar statements on mobility, see Guillet 1963, vol. 1, p. 303; Harpster 1938, pp. 196–97; Leyburn 1962, p. 199; Smithwick 1983, pp. 173, 215; Peck 1965, pp. 122, 145.
79. Peck 1965, p. xxxvi.
80. Schroeder 1986. See also Peck 1965, p. 145; and Schroeder 1983, pp. 1–10.
81. Doolittle 1973, p. 37; Moize 1985, pp. 820–21; Rice 1975, p. 26; Shortridge 1980, p. 69. On long-distance migration, see Peck 1965, p. 122; and Smithwick 1983, p. 173.
82. Harpster 1938, p. 120; Peck 1965, p. 144.
83. Peck 1965, p. 102.
84. Strong 1914, Peck 1965, p. 103.
85. Guillet 1963b, vol. 1, p. 304; Peck 1965, p. xxxv; Harpster 1938, p. 133; Michaux 1805, pp. 111–12.
86. Flower 1882, p. 67; Smithwick 1983, p. 173.
87. Sauer 1920, p. 151; Peck 1965, p. 145.
88. Michaux 1805, p. 113.
89. Kirch 1980, p. 130.
90. Hess 1979, pp. 129, 135; Green 1979, pp. 76, 99.
91. Ford 1915, p. 102.
92. Soininen 1961, p. 432.
93. Broberg 1981, p. 49; Diamond 1977, p. 253
94. Odhner 1879, p. 405; Nordmann 1888, p. 43; Falk 1921, pp. 244, 281; Montelius 1953, p. 49.
95. Montelius 1960, pp. 285–88; Falk 1921, pp. 245–46; Odhner 1879, pp. 405–6.
96. *Pennsylvania Archives*, 2nd ser., vol. 5, p. 249; Johnson 1911, vol. 2, pp. 517–18.
97. Fernow 1877, p. 300.
98. Fernow 1877, pp. 306, 384; Ferris 1846, p. 109; Gehring 1977, p. 264.

99. Brodhead 1853–58, vol. 2, p. 71; Westman 1931, vol. 2, p. 38.

100. *Pennsylvania Archives*, 2nd ser., vol. 5, p. 579; Fernow 1877, p. 464; Dankers and Sluyter 1867, pp. 209, 212.

101. Jackson 1981c; Jackson, Teeples, and Schaefermeyer 1977b; *Archives of Maryland*, vol. 45, p. 67.

102. Edmundson 1715, p. 95.

103. Fernow 1877, pp. 586–87, 636; Armstrong 1860, pp. 61, 74–75.

104. American Council of Learned Societies 1932, pp. 393, 397; Purvis 1982, p. 28; Norton 1973; Stemmons 1972; Stryker-Rodda 1972; U.S. Bureau of the Census 1908h.

105. Danckaerts 1913, p. 95.

106. Evjen 1916, pp. 341–44.

107. Armstrong 1860, pp. 62, 71, 87–88, 115.

108. *Pennsylvania Archives*, 1st ser., vol. 1, pp. 213–14; Sandel 1906, pp. 296–97; Holstein 1892, pp. 14, 19; Rambo 1948, pp. 1–19; Day 1843, p. 485; American Council of Learned Societies 1932, p. 394; Becker 1984, p. 171.

109. Gibbons 1968, pp. 1–10; Rawle 1884, pp. 103–5.

110. *Pennsylvania Archives*, 1st ser., vol. 1, p. 173; Day 1843, pp. 481, 485; Sandel 1906, pp. 296–97.

111. Clay 1858, p. 80.

112. American Council of Learned Societies 1932, p. 392.

113. Williams 1936, pp. 26–29; Moize 1985, pp. 814, 817, 818. Daniel Boone's homestead, for example, is located just east of Reading, near Baumstown, Pennsylvania, on the Schuylkill River.

114. *Archives of Maryland*, vol. 1, pp. 205, 400; vol. 51, p. 479; vol. 54, pp. xxi, 31; Fernow 1877, pp. 109, 336; Russell 1978, pp. 203–10; Carlsson 1978, pp. 13–14; Rising 1912b, p. 157; Scisco 1930, p. 259; Ryden 1930, pp. 54–55; Hall 1910, pp. 315–16; Brodhead 1853–58, vol. 2, pp. 64, 89; Johnson 1911, vol. 2, pp. 497, 513; Hulan 1984, pp. 4–9; American Council of Learned Societies 1932, p. 392.

115. Fernow 1877, pp. 249, 254, 299, 306, 308, 336; Brodhead 1853–58, vol. 2, p. 82.

116. Hall 1910, p. 438; Fernow 1877, pp. 308, 336.

117. Sandel 1906, pp. 445–46; *Pennsylvania Archives*, 1st ser., vol. 2, pp. 22, 25; Ferris 1846, p. 156; Holm 1834, pp. 98, 101.

118. On the expansion in New Jersey, see Wacker 1975b, pp. 170–71; Bjarnson 1976, pp. 241–44; Sandel 1906, pp. 295–98, 445; U.S. Bureau of the Census 1909, pp. 16, 119–20; American Council of Learned Societies 1932, pp. 392–97; Leiby 1964, pp. 95–97; Strang 1970, pp. 111–19; Federal Writers' Project 1938b, p. 61; Federal Writers' Project 1938c, bull. 4, p. 1.

119. Hulan 1986, pp. 63–69.

120. *Pennsylvania Archives*, 1st ser., vol. 1, p. 315; Fernow 1877, p. 330; Kalm 1972, pp. 87–88.

121. Edmundson 1715, p. 95; Fernow 1877, p. 140.

122. *Pennsylvania Archives*, 2nd ser., vol. 5, pp. 613–14.

123. Armstrong 1860, pp. 103–4, 116–19, 135, 141, 146–50; Brodhead 1853–58, vol. 2, p. 53; Fernow 1877, pp. 586–87, 636; Kalm 1972, p. 261; Dunlap 1954, pp. 36–37.

124. *Pennsylvania Archives*, 1st ser., vol. 1, p. 173; Paschall 1912, pp. 251–52; Kalm 1972, p. 25.

125. Pastorius 1912, pp. 369, 383, 386; Baily 1969, p. 103.

126. *Pennsylvania Archives*, 1st ser., vol. 2, pp. 22, 25; Craig and Yocom 1983, pp. 254–56.

127. Boatright 1941; Bowen 1978; pp. 53–54; Doolittle 1973, p. 40.
128. Baily 1969, pp. 96–97.
129. Strong 1914; Smithwick 1983, pp. 25, 28; Ford 1915, p. 275; Horsman 1970, pp. 124, 128.
130. Harpster 1938, p. 123; Hanna 1902, vol. 2, p. 82.
131. Thompson 1972–73, p. 17.
132. Evans 1969, p. 81.
133. Lönnrot 1963, p. 181.
134. Soininen 1961, pp. 163–90, 432–33; Green 1979, p. 90.
135. Schwartz 1982, p. 115.
136. Evjen 1916, pp. 151–220; Danckaerts 1913, p. 108; Dankers and Sluyter 1867, p. 180; Johnson 1911, vol. 2, p. 714.
137. Holstein 1892; Kalm 1929, p. 219.
138. Stemmons 1972, p. 680.
139. Dankers and Sluyter 1867, p. 175; Collin 1936, p. 217.
140. Schwartz 1982, p. 99; Sutherland 1936, p. 152; Fernow 1877, pp. 349–50; Brodhead 1853–58, vol. 2, p. 76; vol. 3, p. 182; Lindeström 1925, p. 87; Paschall 1912, p. 251; Ferris 1946, p. 129; Becker 1984, pp. 26–27.
141. Arfwedson 1909, p. 25; Danckaerts 1913, p. 105; Swanson 1930, pp. 11–12; Brodhead 1853–58, vol. 3, p. 113.
142. Fernow 1877, pp. 145, 156; Armstrong 1860, pp. 167, 172; Printz 1912a, p. 116. See also Sandel 1906, pp. 290, 292; Federal Writers' Project 1938b, p. 79; Keen 1878b, pp. 226–28.
143. Brodhead 1853–58, vol. 2, pp. 88–89.
144. Strang 1970, p. 111; Ferris 1846, pp. 305–7; Klepp 1982, pp. 504–5.
145. Armstrong 1860, pp. 51–52, 89, 102, 179; Keen 1883c, p. 106.
146. Edmundson 1715, p. 95; Ferris 1846, p. 109; Paschall 1912, p. 252; Swanson 1930, p. 12.
147. Armstrong 1860, pp. 58, 70; Edmundson 1715, p. 94.
148. Evans 1969, p. 73; Klepp 1982, p. 505.
149. Hess 1979, p. 136; Hallowell 1957b, p. 201; Evans 1969, p. 82.
150. Pillsbury 1983; Williams and Dockery 1984, p. 14; Jordan 1985, p. 22.
151. Guillet 1963b, vol. 1, p. 246; *Pennsylvania Archives*, 1st ser., vol. 2, p. 772; Jordan 1982, pp. 34–38; Harpster 1938, pp. 134, 195–97; Baily 1969, p. 116.
152. See, for example, Kenny 1913, p. 7; Harpster 1938, p. 121; Campbell 1937, pp. 180, 184, 217, 224–25; Williams and Dockery 1984, p. 14.
153. Gunter MS, p. 3; Baily 1969, p. 142.
154. Price 1951, pp. 256–71.
155. U.S. Bureau of the Census 1983a, pp. 16–20, 46–50, 64–68.
156. Smithwick 1983, pp. 163–66.
157. Leyburn 1962, pp. 257, 266; Hanna 1902, vol. 1, p. 163; Evans 1965, p. 47.
158. Weslager 1957; Westman 1931, vol. 2, pp. 16–17.
159. Kalm 1972, pp. 217, 256; Arfwedson 1909, p. 28; Holm 1834, p. 100.
160. Holm 1834, pp. 100, 146; Lindeström 1925, p. 223; Goddard 1971, p. 15; Acrelius 1874, p. 47.
161. Fernow 1877, p. 126.
162. Paschall 1912, p. 252; Kalm 1972, p. 256.
163. *Pennsylvania Archives*, 2nd ser., vol. 5, p. 579; Fernow 1877, p. 463.
164. *Pennsylvania Archives*, 1st ser., vol. 1, pp. 35, 67; Goddard 1971, p. 15; Gehring 1977, p. 231; Acrelius 1874, p. 55.
165. Auer and Jutikkala 1941, p. 76–79; Jutikkala and Pirinen 1974, p.

14; Lönnrot 1963, p. 14, 33, 69–70, 77–78, 189, 219, 243; Grotenfelt 1899, p. 15.

166. Kalm 1972, pp. 256–57; Johnson 1911, vol. 2, p. 708; Printz 1912a, p. 103; Fernow 1877, pp. 305, 345, 357; Holm 1834, p. 75.

167. Wacker 1975b, p. 76.

168. Kalm 1972, pp. 102–3, 178, 248–50; Printz 1912a, p. 99; Armstrong 1860, p. 156; Johnson 1911, vol. 2, p. 568; Watson 1830, pp. 470–71; Ferris 1846, p. 136; Jessee 1983, pp. 42–44.

169. Budd 1685, p. 29; Fernow 1877, p. 129; Kalm 1972, p. 257; Carlsson 1971, p. 12; Ferris 1846, p. 136; Jessee 1983, pp. 33–38, 47–48; Arfwedson 1909, p. 28.

170. Fernow 1877, p. 129.

171. *Pennsylvania Archives*, 1st ser., vol. 1, p. 69.

172. Jennings 1984, pp. 113–14, 119–20; Jessee 1983, p. 33.

173. Fernow 1877, pp. 73–74; Johnson 1911, vol. 2, p. 500.

174. *Pennsylvania Archives*, 2nd ser., vol. 5, p. 747; Brodhead 1853–58, vol. 3, p. 342.

175. Springer and Springer 1952–55, vol. 5, p. 275; *Pennsylvania Archives*, 2nd ser., vol. 16, p. 523; Craig and Yocom 1983, pp. 248, 254–58.

176. Danckaerts 1913, p. 149.

177. Keen 1878b, p. 226.

178. Johnson 1921–53, vol. 10, pp. 601–2; Armstrong 1931, vol. 1, p. 42; Trigger 1978, p. 291.

Chapter 5. Backwoods Farming

Epigraph: Lönnrot 1963, p. 226 poem 31, lines 261–62.

1. Howe 1898–1902, vol. 2, p. 65; Otto and Anderson 1982, p. 95; Otto 1983, p. 31; Newton 1974, p. 152.

2. Price and Price 1981, p. 241.

3. Smithwick 1983, p. 69; Peck 1965, p. 144.

4. Harris 1805, p. 59; Peck 1965, pp. 122, 132–33; Sauer 1920, p. 151.

5. Otto 1983, p. 36.

6. Petersen 1960, illus. following p. 500; Pittman 1973, p. 65; Peters 1973, pp. 18–20.

7. Thomas 1900, p. 534; Nowlin 1883, p. 489.

8. Strong 1914; Guillet 1963b, vol. 1, p. 304.

9. Michaux 1805, p. 113; Guillet 1963b, vol. 1, p. 303.

10. Green and Perlman 1985, p. 118; Fletcher 1950, p. 35; Haines 1888, p. 11; Kalm 1972, pp. 220, 257.

11. Stilgoe 1982, pp. 171–72.

12. Geike 1864, p. 42; Guillet 1963b, vol. 1, p. 303; Kalm 1972, p. 261.

13. Pastorius 1912, p. 397.

14. Lemon 1966, p. 479.

15. Fernow 1877, p. 429; Danckaerts 1913, p. 147.

16. Brodhead 1853–58, vol. 1, p. 572.

17. Evans 1965, p. 47; Ford 1915, p. 115.

18. Lloyd 1870, p. 367; Montelius 1953, pp. 42, 51; Bridenbaugh 1976, p. 150; Sauer 1930, p. 284; Federal Writers' Project 1938c, bull. 2, p. 3.

19. Armstrong 1860, p. 89; Rising 1912b, p. 163; Fernow 1877, p. 384; Johnson 1911, vol. 1, p. 255.

20. Paschall 1912, p. 253.

21. Brodhead 1853–58, vol. 1, p. 370.
22. Evjen 1916, pp. 338–44.
23. *Pennsylvania Archives,* 2nd ser., vol. 5, p. 288; Brodhead 1853–58, vol. 2, p. 16; Leiby 1964, p. 95; Gehring 1977, p. 52.
24. Jones 1965, p. 44; Guillet 1963b, vol. 1, p. 312.
25. Johnson 1978, p. 13; James 1916, p. 232; Hutslar 1986, fig. 14, p. 144; Reynolds 1938, p. 76; Srygley 1891, p. 127.
26. Various techniques are described in Howe 1898–1902, vol. 1, pp. vi, 103, 318; vol. 2, p. 195; Belknap 1812, pp. 97–100; Johnson 1978, pp. 13–15; Primack 1962, p. 485; Cronon 1983, pp. 108–18; Williams 1982, p. 14; Dwight 1969, vol. 2, pp. 82–84, 325–26; Guillet 1963a, pp. 274–75; Guillet 1963b, vol. 1, pp. 310–11; Peck 1965, pp. xxxv, 134; Campbell 1921, p. 252; Martin 1984, p. 107; Wilkie 1834, pp. 173–76; Muntz 1959, pp. 90–91.
27. Jones 1965, pp. 43–44; Guillet 1963a, pp. 274–75; Guillet 1963b, vol. 1, pp. 310–11.
28. Soper 1900, p. 402; Geike 1864, pp. 45–46; Doddridge 1824, p. 169; Fletcher 1950, p. 64; Guillet 1963a, p. 280; Wilkie 1834, p. 173.
29. Srygley 1891, pp. 127–30.
30. Geike 1864, pp. 49–51; Guillet 1963b, vol. 1, p. 320; Mahr 1955, pp. 216–17.
31. Peck 1965, p. 153; Guillet 1963a, p. 277.
32. Dwight 1969, vol. 2, pp. 325–26; Belknap 1812, pp. 97–98.
33. Gregorie 1954, p. 18.
34. Johnson 1978, pp. 13–16.
35. Guillet 1963b, vol. 1, pp. 310–11.
36. Belknap, 1812, pp. 97–99; Dwight 1969, vol. 2, pp. 84, 325–26.
37. Jones 1965, pp. 43–45.
38. Kalm 1972, pp. 90, 254.
39. Michaux 1805, p. 110; Hoffman 1835, vol. 1, p. 184; Geike 1864, p. 58; Wilkie 1834, p. 226; Campbell 1937, illus. following p. 80; Guillet 1963a, pp. 282–83; Guillet 1963b, vol. 1, pp. 15, 319, 325; Cronon 1983, p. 120; Stilgoe 1982, p. 172.
40. Kalm 1972, p. 99; Otto 1983, p. 31; Otto and Burns 1981, p. 176; Martin 1984, pp. 107–8; Hart 1977; Campbell 1921, pp. 251–52; Semple 1901, pp. 601–2; Kephart 1916, p. 36.
41. Evans 1969, p. 74; Guillet 1963b, vol. 1, p. 303.
42. Taylor 1909, pp. 281–82.
43. Strong 1914.
44. Brodhead 1853–58, vol. 5, p. 554.
45. Stilgoe 1982, pp. 172–73; Primack 1962, p. 485; Belknap 1812, p. 97; Evans 1965, p. 48; Semple 1901, p. 600.
46. Kalm 1972, pp. 220–21; Fletcher 1950, pp. 34–37; Muntz 1959, pp. 31–40 and fig. 10; Konrad 1986.
47. Day 1843, p. 342; Holm 1834, p. 147.
48. Belknap 1812, pp. 97, 100.
49. Meinig 1957–58, p. 9; Otto and Burns 1981, pp. 179–80.
50. Evans 1966, p. 73; Evans 1969, p. 80; Hart 1977, pp. 150–51.
51. Otto and Burns 1981, p. 179.
52. Primack 1962, p. 485; Muntz 1959, pp. 61–62, 90; Otto and Anderson 1982, p. 92; Stilgoe 1982, pp. 175–77; Cox et al. 1985, p. 10.
53. Falk 1921, pp. 264–65; Montelius 1953, pp. 44–45, 48–49; Montelius 1960, p. 285; Lindgren 1939, pp. 76, 133.
54. Grotenfelt 1899.
55. Soininen 1959, pp. 154, 158; Keyland 1954, pp. 88–89; Montelius

1953, p. 42; Levander 1943–47, vol. 1, p. 337; Nordiska museet, arkiv, "Jordbruk" file, "svedjebruk" folder; Kuopion museo, "ryt-könen" exhibit; Vilkuna 1953.

56. Retzius 1885, p. 45; Montelius 1953, pp. 42, 51.
57. Heckscher 1935–49, vol. 1, pt. 2, p. 400; Bromander 1902, p. 296.
58. Montelius 1953, p. 51.
59. Soininen 1959, pp. 151–52; Grotenfelt 1899, pp. 37–38; Soininen 1974, p. 449.
60. Data on *kaski* farming are from Soininen 1959, pp. 152–53; Soininen 1974, p. 450; Montelius 1953, p. 43.
61. Soininen 1974, p. 450.
62. Rising 1912a, p. 139.
63. Keen 1883c, pp. 106–7.
64. Lindeström 1925, p. 180; Kalm 1972, p. 256; Fernow 1877, p. 143; Gehring 1977, p. 264; Printz 1912a, pp. 99, 107–8.
65. Gehring 1977, pp. 85–87.
66. Green 1979.
67. Howe 1898–1902, vol. 1, p. 103; Fletcher 1950, p. 85; Jones 1965, pp. 44–45.
68. Meredith 1951, pp. 135, 137, 139, 144, 147; Riedl, Ball, and Cavender 1976, pp. 260–61, fig. 56, types A, B; fig. 57, type A; Geike 1864, pp. 52–53; Browne 1929, p. 184; Raup 1947, pp. 3–4; U.S. Department of Agriculture 1872, pp. 500, 504.
69. Kalm 1972, pp. 228–29; Withers 1950, pp. 225–31; Wright 1956, pp. 133–35; Norris 1982, pp. 41, 44, 46; Hewes 1982, pp. 301–2, 304–5, 325, 331; Campbell 1921, illus. preceding p. 73; Bowen 1978, p. 74; Draper 1842; Pocius 1977, pp. 10–14; Clemson 1974, pp. 11–12, 52; Long 1961, pp. 31–33; Michaux 1805, p. 58; U.S. Department of Agriculture 1872, p. 507.
70. Draper 1842.
71. Humphrey 1916, p. 7.
72. Riedl, Ball, and Cavender 1976, p. 260, fig. 56, type B.
73. Raup 1947, p. 3; Zelinsky 1959, p. 15; Brodhead 1853–58, vol. 1, p. 182; *Pennsylvania Archives*, 2nd ser., vol. 5, p. 78.
74. Stilgoe 1982, p. 190; Via 1962, p. 34; Zelinsky 1959, p. 15.
75. Meredith 1951, p. 144.
76. Albert C. Myers Collection, at the Historical Society of Pennsylvania, Philadelphia, as quoted in Raup 1947, p. 3. Unfortunately, Raup mistook Salem, N.J., for Salem, Mass., and concluded erroneously that worm fences existed in early New England. Others have unquestioningly copied this lamentable mistake; see, for example, Zelinsky 1959, p. 15.
77. See, for example, Becker 1984, p. 101; Kalm 1972, pp. 228–29.
78. Meredith 1951, pp. 141–42; Raup 1947, p. 1; Norris 1982, p. 43; Cronon 1983, p. 120; Via 1962, p. 34.
79. Robinson 1984, p. 30.
80. Johnson 1955, pp. 6–7, 29.
81. Interview with P. M. Tvengsberg; interview with E. Jauhiainen; Nordiska museet, arkiv, "Etnologiska undersökningen" files, "Hågnader 1929–1937," vol. 1, p. 157 (doc. EU7503); Levander 1943–47, vol. 1, p. 342.
82. Nordiska museet, arkiv, "Etnologiska undersökningen" files, "Hågnader 1929–1937," vol. 2, illus. preceding p. 1, type 20c.
83. Itkonen 1948, vol. 2, p. 64; Sirelius 1909, p. 58; Nordiska museet, arkiv, photo collection, no. 424Kah.

84. Grotenfelt 1899, p. 183; Nordiska museets arkiv, "Etnologiska undersökningen" files, "Hågnader 1929–1937," vol. 2, illus. preceding p. 1, type 25.
85. Fletcher 1950, p. 85; Via 1962, p. 35.
86. Meredith 1951, p. 140; Nordiska museet, arkiv, "Etnologiska undersökningen" files, "Hågnader 1929–1937," vol. 2, illus. preceding p. 1, type 25.
87. U.S. Department of Agriculture 1872, p. 506.
88. Campbell 1937, illus. following p. 80, example no. 4; Fletcher 1950, p. 86; Noble 1984, vol. 2, p. 120; specimen on display at Upper Canada Village museum, Morrisburg, Ont.
89. Specimen on display at Södra Råda ödekyrka museum, Värmland, Sweden; Nordiska museet, arkiv, photo collection, nos. 82Eb, 82Eq, 424Kaj.
90. U.S. Department of Agriculture 1872, p. 503; Meredith 1951, p. 149; Sloane 1955, p. 30; Via 1962, p. 34; Riedl, Ball, and Cavender 1976, p. 260, fig. 56, type D. Raup (1947, pp. 4–5) calls this a type 1 post-and-rail fence. It should not be confused with the post-and-rail fence of the northern states, which has holes cut in the posts to accommodate the rails.
91. Grotenfelt 1899, pp. 184, 259, 309, 311; Levander 1943–47, vol. 1, p. 342; Hämäläinen 1930, p. 47; Valonen 1963, pp. 17, 93; Gothe 1945, p. 45; "Värmland" 1955, illus. following p. 1136; Jordan 1985, p 84. See also National Museum of Finalnd, Archives, "Aita" file, photos 1463.38, 1495.16, 2121.26, 2576.16, 3156.43a; Norsk folkemuseum, archives, Wilse photo collection, no. 288; Nordiska museet, arkiv, photo collection, nos. 53Haf, 163Faa, 258Gao; Nordiska museet, arkiv, "Etnologiska undersökningen" files, "Hågnader 1929–1937," vol. 2, pp. 45, 275; vol. 3, p. 347; specimen on display at Julita gård museum, at the "knektstugan" (soldier's cottage).
92. Swoboda 1975–78; vol. 1, pp. 36, 55.
93. Kalm 1972, pp. 228–29; Federal Writers' Project 1938a, pp. 26–27. Johnson 1911, vol. 2, illus. following p. 518, is an old map of Fort Christina which, if viewed with a magnifying glass, reveals a Swedish-style straight-rail fence with slanted rails.
94. Sloane 1955, p. 30; Riedl, Ball, and Cavender 1976, p. 260, fig. 56, type C; Vaughan and Ferriday 1974, p. 253.
95. R. Hulan, letter to T.G.J., April 20, 1983, and attached xerox of photograph.
96. Hoffman 1835, vol. 1, p. 221; Evans 1969, p. 81; James 1916, p. 232; Price and Price 1981, pp. 244–45.
97. Michaux 1805, pp. 109, 178.
98. Peck 1965, p. xxxv, 103, 122, 132; Hinke and Kemper 1903–4, p. 123; Michaux 1805, pp. 110–1; Hoffman 1835, vol. 1, p. 144; Sauer 1920, p. 151; Hilliard, 1972, pp. 150–60.
99. Howe 1898–1902, vol. 1, pp. 289–90; Michaux 1805, p. 110; Hoffman 1835, vol. 1, p. 144; Fletcher 1950, p. 149; Wilhelm 1965, p. 18; Brooks 1916, p. 134; Roe 1988, p. 3.
100. Doolittle 1973, p. 35; Brooks 1916, pp. 134–35.
101. Cronon 1983, p. 117.
102. Smithwick 1983, p. 8.
103. *Pennsylvania Archives*, 1st ser., vol. 2, p. 738; 2nd ser., vol. 4, pp. 557–58; Harpster 1938, pp. 134–35.
104. Gehring 1977, p. 97; Hall 1985, p. 51.
105. *Pennsylvania Archives*, 2nd ser., vol. 4, p. 558.

106. Fletcher 1950, p. 151.
107. Campbell 1921, illus. preceding p. 253; Semple 1901, p. 602.
108. Snoddy MS.
109. Hoffman 1835, vol. 1, p. 155.
110. Strong 1914; Peck 1965, pp. xxxv, 103, 144; Evans 1969, p. 83; Bowen 1978, p. 74.
111. "What Did Early Settlers Grow?" 1984, p. 10.
112. Harris 1805, p. 58; Michaux 1805, p. 110; Horsman 1970, p. 113; Kalm 1972, p. 45.
113. Michaux 1805, p. 111; Harris 1805, p. 58.
114. Michaux 1805, p. 40. See also Harpster 1938, p. 133; and Horsman 1970, p. 120.
115. Fletcher 1950, pp. 34–39; Evans 1969, p. 83; Sauer 1930, p. 284.
116. Holm 1834, p. 78; Mahr 1955, pp. 227–28.
117. Lindeström 1925, pp. 179–80; Kalm 1972, pp. 173, 255–56; Armstrong 1860, p. 76; Printz 1912a, pp. 98–99; Rising 1912b, p. 163; Holm 1834, p. 121; Fletcher 1950, pp. 43, 149; Johnson 1911, vol. 2, pp. 531, 535–36; Paschall 1912, p. 252.
118. Axelson 1852, pp. 112–13.
119. Nordmann 1888, p. 104; Vuorela 1976, p. 103.
120. Armstrong 1860, p. 156; Kalm 1972, p. 178; Lindeström 1925, p. 178.
121. *Pennsylvania Archives,* 2nd ser., vol. 5, p. 597; Edmundson 1715, p. 95; Kalm 1972, pp. 255–56; Jones 1912, p. 456; Fletcher 1950, p. 149; Leiby 1964, pp. 96–97; Bromander 1902, p. 284; Retzius 1885, pp. 113–14; Holm 1834, p. 102.
122. Lindeström 1925, pp. 181, 183, 223; Holm 1834, p. 43.
123. Lindeström 1925, pp. 177, 223; Kalm 1972, pp. 44, 256–57.
124. Armstrong 1860, p. 76; Paschall 1912, p. 252; Kalm 1972, pp. 93, 255–56; Fletcher 1950, p. 43; Carlsson 1971, p. 11; Meinig 1957–58, p. 9; Graves and Colby 1986, p. 109; Montelius 1953, pp. 49–50; Printz 1912a, pp. 99, 107–8; Nordmann 1888, pp. 13, 148; Suomen maantieteellinen seura 1960, pl. 23-11; Lindeström 1925, p. 180; Johnson 1911, vol. 1, p. 462.
125. Hall 1985, p. 51; Leyburn 1962, p. 264; Storrie 1962, pp. 98, 100; Robinson 1984, p. 179.
126. Evans 1969, pp. 81–83.
127. Thomas 1912, p. 316; Printz 1912b, p. 121; Fernow 1877, p. 300; Paschall 1912, p. 251; Pastorius 1912, p. 397; Fletcher 1950, p. 44; Retzius 1885, p. 113.
128. Howe 1898–1902, vol. 2, p. 459; Flower 1882, p. 72.
129. Guillet 1963b, vol. 1, pp. 305–6.
130. Semple 1901, p. 602.
131. Ford 1915, p. 283; Horsman 1970, p. 114; Campbell 1921, p. 98 and photo preceding p. 97; Draper 1842.
132. Retzius 1885, pp. 43, 48; Vuorela 1976, p. 33; Østberg 1935, p. 285; Lönborg 1902, p. 398; Keyland 1954, pp. 21, 85–86; Levander 1943–47, vol. 1, pp. 342–43, 379; Campbell et al. 1957, vol. 1, p. 19; Johnson 1911, vol. 1, pp. 364–65.
133. Robinson 1984, pp. 30, 31, 179.
134. Peck 1965, pp. 122, 132; Michaux 1805, pp. 109, 191; Hoffman 1835, vol. 1, p. 145; Bowen 1978, p. 87; Hilliard 1969, pp. 461–80.
135. Price and Price 1981, p. 244; Smith 1980, p. 63.
136. Michaux 1805, p. 191.

137. Harpster 1938, p. 134; Howe 1898–1902, vol. 1, pp. 289–90; Flanders 1985, p. 9.
138. Smithwick 1983, p. 8.
139. Michaux 1805, p. 109; Harpster 1938, p. 134; Peck 1965, p. 103.
140. Flower 1882, p. 72; Horsman 1970, p. 118; Peck 1965, p. xxxv.
141. Michaux 1805, p. 109; Evans 1969, p. 80.
142. Leyburn 1962, p. 262; Buchanan 1973, p. 606; Evans 1969, p. 80.
143. Otto and Burns 1981, p. 181.
144. Montelius 1953, p. 53; Montelius 1960, p. 290; Gothe 1942, pp. 86–88; Gothe 1945, pp. 143–52; Soininen 1974, pp. 453–54; Soininen 1961, pp. 155–59; Laukkanen 1982, illus. following p. 209; Talve 1953, p. 54–64; Segerstedt MS, vol. 1, pt. 1, p. 34.
145. Lönnrot 1963, pp. 153, 228–32.
146. Gothe 1945, p. 144.
147. Soininen 1961, p. 432; Bromander 1901, pp. 122–51.
148. Nordmann 1888, pp. 70–71; Gothe 1945, pp. 148, 150; Talve 1953, p. 54.
149. Vuorela 1976, p. 115; Johnson 1911, vol. 2, p. 536.
150. *Pennsylvania Archives*, 1st ser., vol. 1, p. 175; Paschall 1912, p. 254; Armstrong 1860, pp. 43, 60; Printz 1912b, p. 121; Kalm 1972, pp. 78, 176, 253; Danckaerts 1913, p. 105.
151. Brodhead 1853–58, vol. 2, p. 210; *Pennsylvania Archives*, 2nd ser., vol 5, p. 227; Johnson 1911, vol. 1, p. 202.
152. Kalm 1972, pp. 111, 255, 257–58; Johnson 1911, vol. 1, p. 202.
153. Lewis 1984, pp. 83–84; Price and Price 1981, pp. 242, 244, 249, 254; Doolittle 1973, p. 40; Mitchell 1977, p. 239; Jordan 1976, pp. 84–88.
154. Wilhelm 1978, p. 221; Price and Price 1981, pp. 254–55.
155. Wilhelm 1978, pp. 207–8.
156. Paynter 1982, p. 232.
157. Brodhead 1853–58 vol. 1, pp. 150, 367–68; Trewartha 1946, p. 583.
158. Trewartha 1946, pp. 570–72; Scofield 1938, pp. 652–63; Meinig 1986, vol. 1, p. 104; McManis 1975, pp. 53–59.
159. Wood 1982, pp. 333, 336.
160. Lockridge 1970, p. 94; Clark 1970, pp. 198, 206–19, 358; Dwight 1969, vol. 2, pp. 230–31; vol. 3, p. 271; McManis 1975, p. 63.
161. Trewartha 1946, pp. 585–94.
162. Becker 1984, pp. 164, 255, 474.
163. Jones 1973, pp. 437–38, 453, 471–73; Davies 1973, pp. 480, 528.
164. Evans 1965, p. 42; Evans 1966, p. 72; Evans 1969, p. 84; Meinig 1957–58, p. 6; Sauer 1930, p. 284.
165. Uhlig 1961, pp. 286–94; Leyburn 1962, p. 263; Proudfoot 1959, pp. 111, 114–17; Buchanan 1973, pp. 584–87; Whittington 1973, pp. 532–43, 554–67, 576; Fairhurst 1960, pp. 67, 70–71; Evans 1939, pp. 27–28, 30, 35.
166. Proudfoot 1959, p. 116; Buchanan 1973, pp. 603–5; Evans 1939, p. 28; Hanna 1902, vol. 1, p. 558; Robinson 1984, pp. 158–61, 165.
167. *Pennsylvania Archives*, 2nd ser., vol. 5, p. 104; Fernow 1877, p. 29.
168. Fernow 1877, pp. 115, 139.
169. Fernow 1877, pp. 191, 300, 312.
170. Fernow 1877, pp. 336–37.
171. Arfwedson 1909, p. 25; Holm 1834, p. 102.
172. Kalm 1972, pp. 210, 214; see also pp. 180, 254, 288.
173. Retzius 1885, pp. 89, 110; Meitzen 1895, vol. 2, p. 183.

174. Soininen 1961, pp. 110–13, 430; Soininen 1959, p. 151.
175. Nordmann 1888, pp. 12 and 24 and app. pp. iii–xv; Gottlund 1931, pp. 96, 98, 163; Axelson 1852, p. 69; Soininen 1961, pp. 73, 430; Falk 1921, pp. 243–53; Gothe 1945, pp. 199, 205, 208.
176. Lundén 1981, p. 130.
177. Nilsson 1950, pp. 30, 55; Lindgren 1939, p. 196; Erixon 1961, pp. 58, 65–67, 73–74; Meitzen 1895, vol. 3, pp. 329–31, 335–38, 521–23, 526–27; vol. 4, figs. 100, 142, 144; Retzius 1885, p. 89.
178. Magnusson 1877, pp. 130–31; Erixon 1961, p. 62; Lindgren 1939, p. 81.
179. Meinig 1986, vol. 1, p. 441.
180. Wilhelm 1978, p. 233; "What Did Early Settlers Grow?" 1984, p. 10.
181. Meinig 1986, vol. 1, p. 441; Becker 1984, p. 256; Cox 1978, pp. 62–63; Carlisle 1978, p. 33; Dovell 1952, vol. 1, p. 434; Bollaert 1956, p. 117; Stewart-Abernathy 1985; Peck 1965, p. xxxv.
182. Gailey 1984, p. 233; Erixon 1947, p. 320.
183. Jordan 1985, pp. 86–87.
184. Heikel 1888, pp. 232–37, 244; Hämäläinen 1945, pp. 18–23; Valonen 1963, p. 462; Lönborg 1901, p. 231; Retzius 1885, pp. 89–101; Kolehmainen and Laine 1979, pp. 36, 74, 118–20, 137, 399.
185. Nilsson 1950, p. 157; Segerstedt MS, vol. 2, pt. 1, fig. iii; von Schoultz 1951, pp. 23–26, 169; Hämäläinen 1945, pp. 170–76; Levander 1943–47, vol. 1, p. 146; vol. 3, p. 27; Reponen 1934, pp. 55–77.
186. Nordmann 1888, p. 12; Falk 1921, p. 247.
187. Tvengsberg 1961, p. 127; Hämäläinen 1945, p. 19; Soininen 1974, p. 456; Skråkarberget hembysgården tomta museum.
188. Lönborg 1902, p. 392; Heikel 1888, p. 237; Nilsson 1950, p. 155; Ailonen and Kinnunen 1980, pp. 12–13; Retzius 1885, p. 89; Hämäläinen 1945, pp. 19–20.
189. Pastorius 1912, p. 397; Armstrong 1860, pp. 116–17, 172; Bealer and Ellis 1978, pp. 155–56; Horner 1971, pp. 23–28; Johnson 1911, vol. 1, pp. 364–65; Cumberland County Historical Society Museum.
190. Lloyd 1870, p. 364; Kalm 1972, p. 210.

Chapter 6. Log Construction

Epigraph: Lönnrot 1963, p. 180 (poem 25, lines 474, 481).
1. Lewis 1984, p. 140; Newton 1974, p. 152; Srygley 1891, p. 131.
2. Jordan 1985, pp. 7, 14–39.
3. Shurtleff 1939; Robinson 1984, p. 137.
4. Danckaerts 1913, pp. 96–97; Brodhead 1853–58, vol. 1, p. 368.
5. Candee 1976.
6. Hale 1957–60.
7. Winberry 1974; Gritzner 1971.
8. Jordan 1985, pp. 14–23.
9. Wertenbaker 1938, pp. 298–303; Kniffen and Glassie 1966, pp. 58–63; Glassie 1972, p. 49.
10. Mercer 1927b, p. 63; Kimball 1922, pp. 6–8; Weslager 1969, chap. 7; Jordan 1983; Jordan 1985, pp. 41–85, 146–50; Cooper 1986, p. 228.
11. Paschall 1912, pp. 250–51.
12. Jordan 1985, p. 105.

13. Coffey 1984, p. 72.
14. Swank 1983, p. 25; Schiffer 1976, p. 245; Pillsbury 1983, pp. 65–66.
15. Attebury 1976, p. 37; Davidson 1977.
16. Jordan 1985, pp. 44–45, 55; Wacker 1968, pp. 77–79; Wacker and Trindell 1968, pp. 254–55; Bealer and Ellis 1978, pp. 155–56.
17. Jordan 1985, pp. 44–45, 88–89, 126, 147; exhibits at Funäsdalen hembygdsgård, Vemdalen hembygdsgård, Valdres folkemuseum, Konneveden kotiseutumuseo, Skansen, and Latvijas etnogrāfiskais brīvdabas muzejs.
18. Dankers and Sluyter 1867, p. 174; Paschall 1912, pp. 250–51; Jordan 1985, pp. 44–46; Nordiska museet, arkiv, photos 494Tay, 801Kaq (EU29590); Zornsamlingarna, museet, documents on Hedbodarna/Älvdalen.
19. Jordan 1985, pp. 88–89.
20. Strong 1914; Jordan 1978, p. 106; Srygley 1891, pp. 139–41.
21. Jordan 1985, pp. 15–17.
22. Coffey 1984, pp. 72–73.
23. Exhibits at Ransäter hembygdsgård; Julita gård; Jokkmokk hembygdsgård; Lycksele hembygdsgård; Konneveden kotiseutumuseo; Seurasaaren ulkomuseo, exhibits 3, 7; Ockelbo hembygdsgård; Fagersta hembygdsgård; Torp hembygdsgård; Sågudden hembygdsmuseum; Gunnarskog hembygdsgård; Dalby hembygdsgård; and Rikenberg friluftsgård.
24. Federal Writers' Project 1938a, p. 118; Nothnagle Log House.
25. Jordan 1985, pp. 18–21, 147.
26. Jordan, Kaups, and Lieffort 1986–87a, 1986–87b.
27. Kniffen and Glassie 1966, pp. 53–54.
28. Jordan 1985, pp. 53–54.
29. Rempel 1967, pp. 15, 37, 49; Clemson 1974, pp. 17, 19, 25, 31; Black 1976, p. 9; Russell 1971, p. 455; Davidson 1977; Wright 1956, p. 74; Schiffer 1976, pp. 89, 92, 120, 177–79; Kaups 1983, p. 8; C. S. Daly, letter to T.G.J., June 4, 1985.
30. Jordan 1978, pp. 65–66; Whitwell and Winborne 1982, p. 14; Hutslar 1977, p. 247; Lyle 1972, p. 30; Attebury 1976, p. 39; Pitman 1973, pp. 73–74.
31. T. Carter, letter to T.G.J., October 12, 1984.
32. Mann, Skinulis, and Shanoff 1979, p. 15; Rempel 1960, illus. following p. 16.
33. Mercer 1927a, p. 17; Mercer 1927b, pp. 52, 55, 57.
34. Glassie 1963, p. 10; Kniffen and Glassie 1966, p. 59; Rempel 1960, p. 241.
35. Jordan 1983–84, p. 110; Jordan 1980, p. 159; Jordan 1983, pp. 65–69.
36. Exhibits at Hallingdal folkemuseum and Hedmarksmuseet og Domkirkeodden.
37. Erixon 1937, pp. 40, 45; interview with I. Skre; interview with L. Roede.
38. Skråckarberget hembysgården tomta.
39. Erixon 1962–63, vol. 1, p. 68.
40. Sandvig 1947, p. 7; Boëthius 1927, p. 284, fig. 327, sketch 1; interview with L. Roede.
41. Visted and Stigum 1951, vol. 1, p. 44; Sandvig 1947, p. 7.
42. Lower Swedish Cabin museum; Cumberland County Historical Society Museum.
43. For more detail, see Jordan, Kaups, and Lieffort 1986–87a, pp. 70–

78. See also Kniffen and Glassie 1966, pp. 54–55; Jordan 1985, p. 21; and Swaim 1981, pp. 54–55.

44. Glassie 1963, p. 11; Kniffen and Glassie 1966, pp. 61, 63; Linley 1982, p. 20; Clinton and Lofton 1981, pp. 10–11, 14; E. M. Wilson, letter to T.G.J., June 5, 1984.

45. Hulan 1975, pp. 39, 40; Library of Congress, H.A.B.S., records on the Belle Meade estate, Davidson Co., Tenn.; Yeager 1977, pp. 12–13; Patrick and Tomlan 1981, p. 16.

46. J. M. Denny, letter to T.G.J., December 20, 1985; Jordan 1978, p. 51.

47. Michael and Carlisle 1976, pp. 42–45; Stotz 1966, pp. 35, 41; Sipe 1931, p. 758; *Fort Necessity and Historic Shrines* 1932, pp. 140–44.

48. Day 1843, p. 340; Mulkearn and Pugh 1954, pp. 219–20; *Fort Necessity and Historic Shrines* 1932, p. 140.

49. Hood 1983.

50. Stotz 1966, p. 41.

51. Kniffen and Glassie 1966, p. 56; Glassie 1963, p. 11; Kniffen 1969, p. 3.

52. Kniffen and Glassie 1966, pp. 54, 56, 58–59, 63.

53. Jordan 1985, pp. 53–54, 59, 147; Jordan, Kaups, and Lieffort 1986–87a, pp. 70–78.

54. Arnstberg 1976, pp. 96, 99, 141; Erixon 1957, pp. 76–77; Boëthius 1927, p. 60.

55. Erixon 1937, pp. 16, 19; Erixon 1957, pp. 76–77; Arnstberg 1976, pp. 97, 99; Homman 1964, p. 46.

56. Erixon 1937, p. 19, fig. 5.

57. Boëthius 1927, p. 60, fig. 43, sketch D; Erixon 1937, pp. 15–16.

58. Boëthius 1927, p. 60, fig. 43, sketch E.

59. Erixon 1937, p. 16.

60. Nordiska museet, arkiv, photo no. 150Kaj; Skansen museum, exhibit on Dalarna (Mora).

61. Nordiska museet, arkiv, item no. EU16029.

62. Homman 1964, pp. 46–49; Erixon 1937, p. 19.

63. Interview with L. Roede; Boëthius 1927, p. 284, fig. 327, sketch 4, and pp. 298, 304; Erixon 1937, pp. 19–21.

64. Vuorela 1975, p. 408; Valonen 1958–59, p. 25; Erixon 1937, pp. 15, 21.

65. Habicht 1977, p. 13; Tihase 1974, p. 54.

66. Johnson 1911, vol. 1, pp. 149–50, 239, and map following p. 2; vol. 2, p. 711; Louhi 1925, p. 41; Keen 1878b, p. 225.

67. Mercer 1927a, pp. 16–17; Jordan 1985, p. 17; Hudson 1975, pp. 10–11; Clemson 1974, pp. 3, 21, 25, 77; Attebury 1976, p. 37; Weis 1971, pp. 109, 260.

68. Carter 1984, pp. 60, 66, 68; Mercer 1927a, pp. 5–12.

69. *Pennsylvania Archives*, 1st ser., vol. 1, p. 413; Peck 1965, pp. 144, 149; Jordan 1978, p. 158.

70. Hunter 1925, p. 415; Srygley 1891, pp. 132–33.

71. Harpster 1938, p. 224; Doddridge 1824, p. 137; Mercer 1927a, pp. 16, 17; Mercer 1927b, p. 52; Hutslar 1986, figs. 103, 106–7, 110–11, 130; Attebury 1976, p. 37; Thomas 1974, p. 791; Carlisle 1983, pp. 533, 541.

72. Carlisle and Ferenci 1978, p. 19; Carlisle 1983, pp. 533, 541; Attebury 1976, p. 37; Mercer 1927a, pp. 16–17; Jordan 1978, p. 43.

73. Strong 1914; Jordan 1978, p. 106.

74. Acrelius 1874, p. 46; Kalm 1972, pp. 84, 260; Day 1843, p. 294; Wacker 1968, pp. 77–78; Wacker and Trindell 1968, pp. 253–55,

260; Watson 1830, p. 471; Bealer and Ellis 1978, pp. 147–50; Holm 1834, p. 80; Nothnagle Log House; Lower Swedish Cabin.

75. Jordan 1985, pp. 17, 48, 50, 148; Wacker and Trindell 1968, pp. 254–55, 265; Bealer and Ellis 1978, pp. 151–56.

76. Roe 1988, pp. 4–10.

77. Lönnrot 1963, p. 169; Lloyd 1870, p. 361; Sirelius 1909, pp. 26–29; Sirelius 1911, p. 116.

78. Kalm 1972, p. 84; Erixon 1957, p. 71.

79. Hall and Moncure, unpublished report.

80. Sirelius 1909, pp. 28, 70.

81. Sirelius 1909, pp. 70–72.

82. Glassie 1968, p. 345.

83. Kalm 1937, vol. 2, p. 727; Jordan 1985, p. 126–28.

84. Williams 1843, p. 445; Jordan 1985, pp. 22–23.

85. Copley 1912, p. 641. See also Strong 1914.

86. Bealer and Ellis 1978, p. 19; Thomas 1974, p. 791; Jordan 1985, p. 60. For examples of ridgepole-purlin roofs in the West, see Florin 1970, pp. 339, 406, 448, 456, 471, 726, 820; Welsch 1980, pp. 316, 323; Bailey 1899, p. 833; Clemson 1974, pp. 16–19, 24, 32; Attebury 1976, pp. 39–43; Weis 1971, pp. 115, 124, 152, 160; and Hudson 1975, pp. 10–11.

87. Gritzner 1971, pp. 60–61; Jordan 1978, p. 85.

88. Meitzen 1895, vol. 2, p. 211; Heikel 1888, p. 241.

89. Seurasaaren ulkomuseo, exhibit 7; Sirelius 1907, p. 112.

90. Jordan 1985, pp. 96, 112.

91. Doddridge 1824, p. 136; Howe 1898–1902, vol. 1, p. 316; Hutslar 1986, p. 237–38, and fig. 122.

92. Williams 1843, p. 445; Strong 1914; Howe 1898–1902, vol. 1, p. 316.

93. Doddridge 1824, p. 135; Harpster 1938, p. 210; Woods 1904, pp. 167–68; Johnson 1978, p. 7; Harris 1805, p. 15; Srygley 1891, p. 133.

94. Harpster 1938, p. 211; Hutslar 1986, fig. 122; Howe 1898–1902, vol. 1, p. 316; Woods 1904, pp. 167–68; Doddridge 1824, p. 136; Harris 1805, p. 15; Williams 1843, p. 445.

95. Williams 1843, p. 445; "Virginian Canaan" 1853, p. 21.

96. Gillon 1971, p. 112; Buck and Buck 1939, pp. 312–20; Nichols 1976, p. 114; Jordan 1978, p. 90; Johnson 1978, pp. 7–8; Weslager 1954, p. 7; Aurner 1912, p. 9; Copley 1912, p. 641; Hutslar 1986, pp. 237–38; Morton 1911, p. 88.

97. Martin 1984, p. 18; Kozee 1973, pp. 84, 87; Harris 1805, p. 15.

98. Sirelius 1909, pp. 34–36, 45, 76–78, 81–84; Sirelius 1921, vol. 2, p. 202; Manninen 1934, p. 283; Valonen 1963, p. 45; Ailonen and Kinnunen 1980, p. 32.

99. Tihase 1974, p. 74; Manninen 1934, pp. 281–83; Sirelius 1909, pp. 25, 45; Vuorela 1964, pp. 38, 207, 218–19; Latvijas etnogrāfiskais brīvdabas muzejs, exhibit from Gulbene, in Vidzeme.

100. Lönnrot 1963, p. 172; Vuorela 1975, p. 412; Sirelius 1921, vol. 2, pp. 186–87, 202, 209–11.

101. Ek 1959–60, pp. 38–39; Erixon 1922, p. 273; Phleps 1942, p. 93.

102. Brodhead 1853–58, vol. 1, p. 150; *Pennsylvania Archives*, 2nd ser., vol. 5, p. 79.

103. Yeomans 1981, pp. 9–18; Robinson 1984, pp. 136, 139, 143.

104. Peck 1965, p. 144; Smithwick 1983, p. 4; Jordan 1978, p. 83.

105. Hunter 1925, p. 415; Patrick and Tomlan 1981, p. 17; Srygley 1891, p. 132; Pitman 1973, pp. 120–21; Jordan 1978, p. 83.

106. Sirelius 1911, pp. 63–66, 76–77; Vikinge skipene museum, displays.
107. Harris 1805, p. 15; Michaux 1805, p. 109; Smithwick 1983, p. 4; Patrick and Tomlan 1981, p. 17.
108. Harpster 1938, p. 195; Jordan 1978, p. 143; Srygley 1891, p. 136.
109. Strong 1914; Peck 1965, p. 144; Jordan 1978, p. 106; Srygley 1891, pp. 120–21.
110. National Museum of Finland, Archives, photo 1463.5; Falk 1921, pl. 1, following p. 272; Sirelius 1909, pp. 94–95; Sirelius 1911, pp. 49, 79–83, 86–87.
111. Lloyd 1870, p. 352; Kalm 1972, p. 260; Retzius 1885, p. 75; Sirelius 1909, p. 109.
112. Strong 1914; Peck 1965, pp. 144, 149; Harris 1805, p. 15; Srygley 1891, pp. 135–38; Hutslar 1986, fig. 122; Jordan 1978, pp. 95, 98.
113. Schiffer 1976, p. 245.
114. Robinson 1984, p. 141.
115. Sirelius 1911, pp. 51–54; Kalm 1972, p. 260.
116. Copley 1912, p. 641.
117. Harris 1805, p. 15.
118. See, for example, Harpster 1938, pp. 195–96; Draper 1842; Jordan 1978, pp. 105–7; and Cooper 1986, p. 227.
119. Pitman 1973, pp. 60, 66, 117; Wright 1950, p. 36; Wilson 1969, pp. 19–21; Patrick and Tomlan 1981, p. 17; Vaughan and Ferriday 1974, p. 82.
120. Soininen 1974, p. 456.
121. See, for example, Nordiska museet, arkiv, photo no. 177Iy; specimens at Turkansaaren ulkomuseo and Funäsdalen hembygdsgård; and Jordan 1985, pp. 45–46.
122. Kaups 1972, 1976, 1981, 1983; Karni and Levin 1972.
123. Retzius 1885.
124. Jordan 1985, pp. 50, 70, 148.
125. Day 1843, p. 296; Armstrong 1860, p. 90.
126. Danckaerts 1913, p. 98; Armstrong 1860, p. 90.
127. Becker 1984, pp. 32, 98, 101–2, 184–91, 256; Day 1843, p. 483; Weslager 1955, pp. 263–65.
128. Brodhead 1853–58, vol. 2, p. 69.
129. Kalm 1937, vol. 2, p. 728; Wacker 1968, p. 78.
130. *Archives of Maryland*, vol. 1, p. 224; Lawson 1967, pp. 223–24; *Colonial and State Records of North Carolina*, vol. 1, p. 300.
131. Byrd 1967, p. 94.
132. Belknap 1831, pp. 195–96; Hyde Log Cabin Museum. See also Dwight 1969, vol. 2, pp. 82, 84, 90, 94, 96, 204, 210, 300, 315, 321–22, 326, 335, 339; vol. 3, p. 125; vol. 4, pp. 35–36, 41, 55, 88.
133. Exceptions include the following fine studies: Wilson 1984; Davidson 1977; and Attebury 1976.

Chapter 7. Backwoods Folk Architecture

Epigraph: Lönnrot 1963, p. 66 (poem 11, lines 331–34).
  1. Newton 1974, p. 152.
  2. Literature specifically on the dogtrot plan includes Hulan 1975, 1977; Wright 1958; Murray 1982; Ferris 1986; Evans 1952; Price 1970; Gettys 1981; and Wilson 1971.
  3. Wacker and Trindell 1968, p. 259; Haines 1888, p. 16, Parker 1985,

p. 60; Gould 1975, p. 73; Evans 1952, pp. 1–2; Wright 1958, p. 109; Haycraft 1921, p. 26; Johnston and Waterman 1941, pp. 7, 16, 19; Randolph 1933, p. 48; Randolph and Clemens 1936, pp. 314–15; Woodbridge 1955a, pp. 80–81; Woodbridge 1955b, pp. 107–8; Garth 1947, p. 230.

4. Parker 1984, p. 60.

5. Hall 1930, vol. 3, p. 271.

6. Jordan and Kaups 1987; this article forms the basis of much of the present chapter.

7. Melville 1969, p. 329.

8. Glassie 1968a, pp. 88–89, 96–98; Kniffen 1965, p. 561.

9. Pillsbury 1983, p. 65; Wright 1950, p. 42; Evans 1969, p. 80; R. Pillsbury, letter to T.G.J., March 30, 1983; Wilson 1971, pp. 8–14.

10. Lounsbury 1977, p. 18; Glassie 1968a, pp. 89, 94–96; Wilson 1971, p. 13.

11. Montell and Morse 1976, pp. 20–21; Morrison 1952, pp. 169–70.

12. Evans 1969, p. 80.

13. Lounsbury 1977, p. 18; Evans 1969, p. 80; Wilson 1971, pp. 10–11.

14. Wright 1958, p. 115; Wilson 1971, pp. 10–12.

15. Penn 1912b, p. 270; Craigie and Hulbert 1940, vol. 2, p. 801; Mathews 1951, vol. 1, p. 512; Watson 1830, p. 388; Clark 1970, pp. 220, 228; Keen 1878a, p. 446.

16. Jordan 1985, p. 68.

17. Evans 1952, p. 2; Garth 1947, p. 230; Wacker and Trindell 1968, p. 259; Haines 1888, p. 16. Kniffen (1965) confused this issue by applying the term *saddlebag* only to the central chimney type, a usage that has since become standard in the literature.

18. Jordan 1985, pp. 109–12.

19. Wright 1958, p. 111.

20. Zelinsky 1973, p. 83; Jordan 1985, pp. 5, 154.

21. Wright 1956, p. 51; Hulan 1977, pp. 25–32; Jordan 1985, pp. 67–70, 146, 149; Wright 1958, pp. 109, 113–17; Kniffen and Glassie 1966, pp. 58–59, 63; Glassie 1972, p. 49; Zelinsky 1973, p. 20.

22. Wright 1950, p. 42; Ferris 1986.

23. Hutslar 1977, pp. 25–29; Hutslar 1986, p. 99; J. M. Denny, letter to T.G.J., October 30, 1985.

24. Hulan 1975, 1977.

25. Morton House Museum; Boulden-Stubbs house; Weslager 1955, pp. 259, 261; Weslager 1969, pp. 166–67.

26. Johnston 1906, pp. 396–98; Reynolds 1938, pp. 32–34; Rempel 1967, pp. 34, 69; Linley 1972, p. 23; Black 1976, pp. 5–6, 12–13; White 1898, vol. 1, p. 126; Connelley 1910, p. 26; Wacker and Trindell 1968, p. 259; Haines 1888, p. 16; Hulan 1975; Haycraft 1921, p. 26.

27. Reynolds 1938, pp. 31–34, 69, 244–45.

28. Williams 1968, vol. 1, pp. 23, 27.

29. Hood 1978, p. 206.

30. Kniffen 1965, p. 561; Weslager 1969, p. 72; Hutslar 1986, pp. ii, 254, 257.

31. Martin 1984, pp. 38, 109.

32. Flower 1882, p. 72. See also Baily 1969, p. 105.

33. Newton and Pulliam–Di Napoli 1977; Smithwick 1983, p. 169; Barrow 1849, p. 48.

34. Johnston 1957, pp. 121, 186; Stotz 1966, pp. 34–36, 42; Linley 1982, p. 310; Kozee 1973, p. 87; Newcomb 1950, pp. 50–51 and pl. 10;

Newcomb 1953, pp. 32, 35; Howe 1898–1902, vol. 1, p. 700; vol. 2, p. 327; Esarey 1918, vol. 1, pp. 477, 485; Flower 1882, pp. 128–29; Ball 1932, p. 15; Harrington 1935, pp. 43, 47; Hulan 1977, p. 27; Hutslar 1977, pp. 27–28; Smithwick 1983, pp. 40–41.

35. Hemmensdorff and Jonsson 1984, p. 12; Berg 1965, pp. 45–47; Berg 1967, pp. 70–72; Levander 1943–47, vol. 3, pp. 46, 56; Erixon 1947, pp. 13, 197–98, 212, 215; Wright 1958, p. 115; Meitzen 1895, vol. 3, p. 479; *Kulturhistorisk leksikon* 1956–75, vol. 5, cols. 56–60; vol. 17, cols. 712–17.

36. Berg 1967, pp. 70–72; Vreim 1947, p. 9. According to Smeds (1944), the *fäbod* system in western Finland dates from the sixteenth century, but it is uncertain whether the open-passage house was present then. Photographic evidence suggests not; see Ahlbäck 1983, pp. 368–70.

37. Kephart 1916, p. 76.

38. Kaups 1981, pp. 140, 143; Hämäläinen 1930, pp. 46, 51–58; Sirelius 1909, pp. 34–35; Sirelius 1911, p. 97; Heikel 1888, pp. 234, 292; Valonen 1963, p. 61; Kolehmainen and Laine 1979, pp. 124–25; Hämäläinen 1945, p. 20; Weslager 1969, p. 153; Soininen 1959, pp. 150–66; Soininen 1961; Talve 1979, pp. 33, 38; Vuorela 1971, pp. 306–8; Sirelius 1921, vol. 2, p. 208.

39. Thompson 1967, pp. 41–43; Vuorela 1964, p. 214; Ränk 1962, pp. 30–34; *Kulturhistorisk leksikon* 1956–75, vol. 13, cols. 120–21; Erixon 1947, pp. 291, 343.

40. Kaups 1981, p. 144; Heikel 1888, pp. 112–22, 231–33; Nilsson 1950; Tvengsberg 1961, pp. 121–46; Hämäläinen 1945; Dmitrieva 1982–83, pp. 29–54.

41. Kaups 1981, pp. 140, 143; Segerstedt MS, vol. 1, pt. 1, pp. 581–83; Heikel 1888, pp. 213, 232–33.

42. Schoultz 1951, pp. 44–45; Kaups 1981, pp. 140, 143; Hämäläinen 1945, p. 20; Axelson 1852, p. 110; Vuorela 1975, pp. 307–8; Sirelius 1911, p. 97.

43. Segerstedt MS, vol. 1, pt. 1, p. 582; Soininen 1961, p. 434; Montelius 1953, p. 50; Sirelius 1911, pp. 51, 92.

44. Heikel 1888, pp. 231, 233; Hutslar 1986, fig. 13; Nordiska museet, arkiv, photo no. 253Mm; National Museum of Finland, Archives, photo no. 3490.648.

45. Retzius 1885, pp. 62–79; Heikel 1888, p. 207; Sirelius 1909, pp. 24–25, 31–33, 90; Nordmann 1888, pp. 91–92; Levander 1943–47, vol. 2, p. 19; Lönborg 1902, p. 376; Hämäläinen 1945, p. 39.

46. Sirelius 1906, p. 90; Sirelius 1909 pp. 26–27, 58–59, 112–13.

47. Nordiska museet, arkiv, photos no. 28Bx, 70Fl, 303Be, 428Fd, 494Sai, EU50715; National Museum of Finland, Archives, photos no. 1575.30, 2195.9, 2884.521; Zornsamlingarna, museet, arkiv, Hedbodarna (Älvdalen) files; Meitzen 1895, vol. 2, p. 206; vol. 3, pp. 506–7; Hämäläinen 1945, p. 45.

48. Wilson 1984, pt. 1, pp. 12, 33–34; Jordan 1985, pp. 24–27.

49. Johnson 1911, vol. 2, p. 537; Weslager 1969, p. 164.

50. Thomas 1954, pp. 138–39; Hoover and Rodman 1980, p. 49; Hutslar 1986, p. 45, fig. 13; Eastman 1961, p. 17; Tuttle 1868, p. 411; Hoyt 1907, p. 144; Perrin 1966, p. 867; Guillet 1963a, illus. following p. 52. See also Howe 1898–1902, vol. 2, p. 77.

51. Madden 1974, p. 39; *Palimpsest*, 1960, cover illustration.

52. Adirondack Museum, cabin display; Randolph 1979, pp. 6, 8; Central New Brunswick Woodmen's Museum, cabin display; Fowler

1968, pp. 66–67; Mann, Skinulis, and Shanoff 1979, pp. 17, 19.

53. Parrington, Schenck, and Thibault 1984, p. 133; Miller, Lanier, and Rodenbough 1911–12, vol. 4, pp. 36–37; vol. 8, p. 23; Nelson 1982, p. 83; Rutsch and Peters 1977, pp. 32, 34.

54. Rehder, Morgan, and Medford 1979; Lyle 1970–74, p. 4; Stemmons 1972, p. viii; Jordan 1985, pp. 30–33, 38; Jordan 1978, pp. 139, 142, 161–63, 178–79; Hämäläinen 1945, pp. 33–36; Mariebergsskogen Open-Air Museum, exhibit from Vitsand, Värmland; Nordiska museet, arkiv, items no. 5 Yab, 5 Yai, 53 Hx; Roe 1988, p. 13.

55. Gailey 1984, pp. 37–39, 101, 108, 235; Evans 1969, p. 79; Jordan 1985, pp. 23–25.

56. Mercer 1975, pp. 24, 153, 156, 203; Sandon 1977, pp. 63–64; Gailey 1984, pp. 175, 186; Fox and Raglan 1954, p. 132; Jordan 1985, pp. 24, 29, 149.

57. Jordan 1985, pp. 24, 28, 149.

58. Evans 1969, p. 79.

Chapter 8. Hunting and Gathering

Epigraph: Lönnrot 1963, p. 88 (poem 15, lines 77–78).

1. Doolittle 1973, p. 35; Newton 1974, p. 152.

2. Evans 1966, p. 78; Muntz 1959, p. 36; Mahr 1954, p. 384; Brinton and Anthony 1888, p. 130.

3. Retzius 1885, pp. 49–55; Talve 1953, pp. 35–40; Gothe 1942, pp. 123–51; Gothe 1945, pp. 153–61; Levander 1943–47, vol. 1, pp. 5–51; Falk 1921, pp. 259–63; Nordmann 1888, pp. 64–69; Keyland 1954, pp. 29–42.

4. Bromander 1902, p. 287; Retzius 1885, p. 23.

5. Magnusson 1877, p. 135; Gothe 1945, p. 135; Johnson 1911, vol. 1, p. 239.

6. Brodhead 1853–58, vol. 2, p. 242.

7. Doddridge 1824, p. 123; Hinke and Kemper 1903–4, p. 123.

8. Howe 1898–1902, vol. 2, p. 65.

9. Smithwick 1983, p. 3; Peck 1965, pp. 122, 132–33; Harris 1805, p. 59; Johnson 1978, pp. 79–86; Sauer 1920, p. 151; Rice 1975, p. 43.

10. Michaux 1805, p. 263.

11. Thorpe 1858, pp. 620–21.

12. Johnson 1978, p. 79.

13. Flower 1882, p. 68; Smithwick 1983, p. 24; Hinke and Kemper 1903–4, p. 123.

14. Peck 1965, p. 145; Smithwick 1983, p. 50.

15. Evans 1965, p. 48; Brinton and Anthony 1888, p. 71.

16. Segerstedt MS, vol. 1, pt. 1, p. 33; Levander 1943–47, vol. 2, p. 260; Retzius 1885, p. 107; Kalm 1972, p. 260; Watson 1830, p. 471.

17. Armstrong 1860, p. 76; Campbell 1921, p. 29; Smithwick 1983, p. 8; Sauer 1920, p. 151.

18. Harpster 1938, p. 134.

19. Rice 1975, pp. 21–23.

20. Doddridge 1824, pp. 123–24.

21. Flanders 1985, p. 4.

22. Howe 1898–1902, vol. 2, p. 460.

23. Doddridge 1824, p. 123.

24. Hinke and Kemper 1903–4, p. 121; Michaux 1805, p. 85.

25. Kephart 1916, pp. 75–109.

26. Michaux 1805, p. 108; Doddridge 1824, p. 123.
27. Lönnrot 1963, pp. 232–35, 305–7; Retzius 1885, pp. 49–50; Larsson 1876; Segerstedt MS, vol. 2, pt. 1, fig. xviii; Talve 1953, p. 36; Falk 1921, p. 263.
28. Retzius 1885, p. 50; Talve 1953, p. 36; Falk 1921, p. 259.
29. Retzius 1885, pp. 50–55.
30. Acrelius 1874, p. 310; Kalm 1972, p. 66; Holm 1834, p. 90; Thomas 1912, p. 349; Leiby 1964, p. 99.
31. Taylor 1909, p. 248.
32. Rice 1975, pp. 20–28; Taylor 1909, p. 248.
33. Rice 1975, pp. 20–28.
34. Howe 1898–1902, vol. 1, p. 953.
35. Rice 1975, p. 21.
36. Evans 1966, p. 78; Kay 1979, pp. 414, 418.
37. Brodhead 1853–58, vol. 2, p. 88.
38. Williams 1936, pp. 26–31; Osburn 1963, p. 309.
39. Doddridge 1824, p. 124; Coffey 1984, p. 64; Hoover and Rodman 1980, p. 49; Leyburn 1962, pp. 258, 262; Elbert and Sculle 1982, p. 2; Rice 1975, p. 21.
40. Harpster 1933, pp. 223–24.
41. Doddridge 1824, p. 124.
42. Belknap 1812, pp. 60–61, 194.
43. Hoover and Rodman 1980, p. 49; Johnson 1978, p. 6.
44. Sirelius 1908, pp. 8, 12, 15–19, 28, 30–32; Sirelius 1909, pp. 17–19; Levander 1943–47, vol. 1, p. 218; Segerstedt MS, vol. 2, pt. 1, fig. xii-d; Hämäläinen 1945, pp. 25–27; Nordiska museet, arkiv, photos no. 303Bo, 495Bac; National Museum of Finland, Archives, photos no. 1202:8, 1463:112, 1482:80, 3184:1581, 3211:208; Zornsamlingarna, museet, archive, photo collection on Älvdalen, Rälldalen. See also displays at the following regional and local museums: Kuopion museo; Lycksele; Orsa; and Pielisen museo, outdoor exhibit no. 68.
45. Guillet 1963b, vol. 1, pp. 23, 50; Russell 1977, p. 339; Coffey 1984, pp. 61–63; Martin 1984, pp. 60–64; Bealer and Ellis 1978, p. 20; Howe 1898–1902, vol. 1, p. 680; Guillet 1963a, p. 157.
46. National Museum of Finland, Archives, photos no. 1427:14, 1482:34, 1574:5, 3184:297, 3184:1239, 3210:134; Nordiska museet, arkiv, photos no. 13Yi, 33Eg, 409In; Pielisen museo, outdoor exhibit no. 68.
47. Semple 1901, pp. 621–22.
48. Pohl and Hardin 1985–86, pp. 282–83.
49. Flower 1882, p. 72.
50. Michaux 1805, p. 263.
51. Johnson 1978, p. 75.
52. Moize 1985, pp. 820–21; Johnson 1978, pp. 75–76.
53. Ford 1915, p. 279.
54. Harpster 1938, p. 134; Johnson 1978, p. 76.
55. Thorpe 1858, p. 619.
56. Nordmann 1888, app. 4, pp. xv–xvii.
57. Talve 1953, pp. 36–37, 40; Värmlands museum, "Jakt och fiske" file, item no. 19165.
58. Levander 1943–47, vol. 1, p. 5; Glomdalsmuseet, exhibit on "flintelås."
59. See, for example, the exhibit of Finnish log buildings at Glomdals-

museet; and National Museum of Finland, Archives, photo no. 3211:131 from Karelia.

60. Talve 1953, pp. 36–37; Levander 1943–47, vol. 1, pp. 5–7; Björklund 1972, p. 57; Zornsamlingarna, museet, file on "Gammelgården föremålssamlingen," items no. 494, 495, 504, 511, 512; Norsk folkemuseum, archive, items no. L89.755, L89.756; Nordiska museet, arkiv, "etnologiska undersökningen" files, "Jakt," vol. 1 (1928–36), pp. 127, 755; National Museum of Finland, Archives, photo no. 2860:15. See also exhibits at the following museums: Glommersträsk hangengården; Ylä-savon kotiseutumuseo; Kuopion museo; Pielaveden; and Pielisen museo.

61. Itkonen 1948, vol. 2, p. 19; Nordiska museet, arkiv, photo no. 150Vb and "etnologiska undersökningen" files, "Jakt," vol. 1 (1928–36), pp. 87–127.

62. Armstrong 1860, pp. 50, 60; Johnson 1911, vol. 2, p. 537.

63. Thorpe 1858, pp. 614–15; Johnson 1978, pp. 80, 84; Driver 1969, p. 86; Talve 1953, pp. 37–38.

64. Segerstedt MS, vol. 2, pt. 1, fig. xviii; Talve 1953, pp. 37, 39, 40; Nordiska museet, arkiv, "etnologiska undersökningen" files, "Jakt," vol. 1 (1928–36), pp. 87–126.

65. Smith 1836, pp. 175, 186; Smithwick 1983, pp. 5, 174; Johnson 1978, pp. 86, 90.

66. Norsk folkemuseum, archive, item no. NF9811; Nordiska museet, arkiv, "etnologiska undersökningen" files, "Jakt" file, vol. 1, "hunden" folder; Nordmann 1888, app. 4, p. xvi.

67. Thorpe 1858, pp. 613–14; Muntz 1959, p. 36.

68. Michaux 1805, p. 263; Thorpe 1858, pp. 615–18.

69. Talve 1953, p. 38; Nordmann 1888, app. 4, p. xvii; Nordiska museet, arkiv, "etnologiska undersökningen" files, "Jakt," vol. 1, folder on "drev."

70. Driver 1969, p. 85.

71. Harris 1805, pp. 22–23; Taylor 1909, p. 249.

72. *Pennsylvania Archives*, 1st ser., vol. 1, p. 254; Lindeström 1925, pp. 213–14; Driver 1969, pp. 85–86.

73. Levander 1943–47, vol. 1, pp. 6–7; Talve 1953, pp. 38, 40; Nordiska museet, arkiv, "etnologiska undersökningen" files, "Jakt," vol. 1, item 8; Russell 1983, pp. 78, 85–86.

74. Thorpe 1858, p. 618; Rice 1975, p. 22; Doddridge 1824, p. 124.

75. Thorpe 1858, p. 619.

76. Smith 1836, p. 193.

77. Peck 1965, p. 128.

78. *Davy Crockett's Almanack* 1837, p. 18; Meine 1955, pp. 62, 132; Smith 1836, pp. 176, 190.

79. Johnson 1911, vol. 1, p. 148.

80. Axelson 1852, p. 97.

81. Kalm 1972, p. 150; Thomas 1912, p. 349.

82. Leiby 1964, p. 96; Watson 1830, p. 471.

83. Johnson 1978, p. 92.

84. Budd 1685, p. 5.

85. *Pennsylvania Archives*, 2nd ser., vol. 4, p. 558; Peck 1965, p. 132; Smithwick 1983, p. 3; Horsman 1970, pp. 116–17.

86. Green 1979, p. 84.

87. *Pennsylvania Archives*, 1st ser., vol. 2, p. 320; 2nd ser., vol. 4, p. 558; Harpster 1938, p. 133; Hutslar 1986, p. 51.

88. Sauer 1920, p. 151.
89. Kalm 1972, p. 250; Evans 1969, p. 81.
90. Kalm 1972, pp. 71–72, 102–5, 109–10, 175–79, 248–50, 303; Watson 1830, pp. 470–71; Brinton and Anthony 1888, p. 72.
91. Thomas 1912, p. 324.
92. Lönnrot 1963, pp. 52–53, 92–94, 136; Lloyd 1870, p. 365.

Chapter 9. Backwoods Frontier Expansion, 1725–1825

Epigraph: Lönnrot 1963, p. 210 (poem 29, line 193).
1. Glass 1986.
2. Leyburn 1962, pp. 195–96, 248–49.
3. Semple 1903, p. 58 and map following p. 54.
4. Ford 1915, p. 265; Evans 1969, pp. 70–71, 75.
5. Akenson 1984.
6. McDonald and McDonald 1980, p. 198; Purvis 1984, pp. 96–98; U.S. Bureau of the Census 1909, p. 116; American Council of Learned Societies 1932, p. 396.
7. Purvis 1982b, pp. 16, 22, 28.
8. McWhiney and McDonald 1983, pp. 94–95. On the exaggeration of Celtic influence, see Berthoff 1986.
9. Reed 1967, pp. 26, 44; Howe 1898–1902, vol. 1, p. 125; Braderman 1939, p. 454; Browning 1915, p. 483; Arthur 1914, p. 13; Purvis 1982a, pp. 258–59.
10. On generational surname shifts in America, see Armstrong 1860, pp. 80, 112; Dunlap 1954, p. 42; and *New Jersey Archives*, vol. 21, p. 42; vol. 30, p. 434.
11. For some genealogies of these and related families, see Williams 1916; Keen 1878a, 1879a, 1880, 1881, 1882, 1883b; Vacher 1947; Holstein 1892; Williams 1936; Rambo 1948; Rambo and Watson 1983; Dye and Dye 1983–85; Craig and Yocom 1983; McRaven 1937; Hulan 1980b; Rauanheimo 1938. A list of Finnish surnames common in Sweden can be found in Nordmann 1888, app. 1, p. i; and Gottlund 1931, p. 97. For early surname lists of New Sweden, see Acrelius 1874, pp. 190–93; Clay 1858, pp. 69–70; Ferris 1846, pp. 307–8; Johnson 1911, vol. 2, pp. 673–726; Federal Writers' Project 1938c, bull. 4, p. 4; Dunlap and Moyne 1952, p. 88; and Purvis 1982b, p. 30.
12. The Yokum problem is revealed in Hinke and Kemper 1903–4, pp. 119, 227, 237; Hinke and Kemper 1904–5, p. 58. On the Ericson problem, see *Archives of Maryland*, vol. 37, p. 199. See also Carlsson 1978; and Ryden 1930, 1931a, 1931b.
13. Springer and Springer 1952–53b, vol. 5, p. 275; Craig and Yocom 1983, pp. 254–56.
14. Kegley 1938, p. 145; Williams 1936; Hulan 1981 pp. 10–12; Hulan 1980b.
15. Collins 1874, vol. 2, p. 606; Kegley 1938, pp. 589, 615.
16. McRaven 1937, pp. 17–19.
17. Grimes 1967, p. 215; Vacher 1947, p. 25; John 1982–83, p. 433.
18. Rambo 1948, p. 2; Dunlap and Weslager 1967, p. 38.
19. Hulan 1980b.
20. *Pennsylvania Archives*, 1st ser., vol. 1, pp. 213–14; McKnight 1905, p. 588.
21. Nordmann 1888, p. 153.

22. Johnson 1911, vol. 2, p. 513; Vacher 1947; Nordmann 1888, pp. 35, 108; Acrelius 1874, p. 90.
23. U.S. Geological Survey, "Geographic Names Information System."
24. Ely 1887, p. 445.
25. U.S. Bureau of the Census 1908k, p. 24; Durham 1969, pp. 82–83.
26. Lönnrot 1963, p. 108.
27. Jordan 1985, p. 151.

Chapter 10. Conclusion

Epigraph: Lönnrot 1963, p. 17 (poem 3, lines 213–14).
1. Denevan 1983, p. 399.
2. Keen 1879b; Acrelius 1874, pp. 95–96.
3. Green 1979, p. 100.
4. *Pennsylvania Archives*, 2nd ser., vol. 5, p. 470.
5. Kirch 1980, p. 137.
6. Bowman 1931, p. 4.
7. Kirch 1980, p. 123.
8. Hess 1979, pp. 135–36; Butzer 1982, pp. 281, 285; Kirch 1980, p. 139; Weslager 1957, p. 2.
9. Lewis 1984, p. 16.
10. Diamond 1977, p. 259.
11. Green 1979, p 75.
12. Diamond 1977, p. 259; Kirch 1980, p. 130.
13. Kirch 1980, p. 123; Zelinsky 1973, p. 34.
14. Semple 1903, p. 74.

BIBLIOGRAPHY

Books, Articles, Theses, Dissertations, and Manuscripts

Aaltonen, V. T. 1952. "Soil Formation and Soil Types." *Fennia* 72:65–73.

Acrelius, Israel. 1874. *A History of New Sweden; or, The Settlements on the River Delaware.* Translated by William M. Reynolds. Philadelphia: Historical Society of Pennsylvania.

————. 1912. "From the 'Account of the Swedish Churches in New Sweden,' by Reverend Israel Acrelius, 1759." In *Narratives of Early Pennsylvania, West New Jersey, and Delaware, 1630–1707,* edited by Albert C. Myers, pp. 57–81. New York: Charles Scribner's Sons, 1912.

Adams, James N., and Keller, William E. 1969. *Illinois Place Names.* Illinois State Historical Society Occasional Publications, no. 54. Springfield: The Society.

Ahlbäck, Ragna. 1983. *Bonden i svenska Finland.* Helsinki: Skrifter utgivna av Svenska litteratursällskapet i Finland.

Ailonen, Riitta, and Kinnunen, Ritva. 1980. *Seurasaari Open-Air Museum Visitor's Guide.* Helsinki: Government Printing Office.

Akenson, Donald H. 1984. "Why the Accepted Estimates of the Ethnicity of the American People, 1790, Are Unacceptable." *William and Mary Quarterly,* 3rd ser. 41:102–19.

Åkerhielm, Gösta. 1907. "En antropologisk resa genom Värmlands finnskogar i mars 1907." *Ymer* 27:187–95.

American Council of Learned Societies. 1932. *Report of the Committee on Linguistic and National Stocks in the Population of the United States.* Washington, D.C.: Government Printing Office. Annual report of the American Historical Association, 1931, vol. 1, *Proceedings.*

Archives of Maryland. 1883–1964. 70 vols. Baltimore: Maryland Historical Society.

Ardoin, Robert B. L., ed. 1970–77. *Louisiana Census Records.* 3 vols. Baltimore: Genealogical Publishing Co., 1970, 1972. New Orleans: Polyanthos, 1977.

Arfwedson, Carolus David. 1909. *A Brief History of the Colony of New Sweden.* Translated by K. W. Granlund. Lancaster, Pa.: New Era Printing.

Armstrong, Edward, ed. 1860. "Record of Upland Court from the 14th of November, 1676, to the 14th of June, 1681." *Memoirs of the Historical Society of Pennsylvania* 7:11–203.

Armstrong, Zella. 1931. *The History of Hamilton County and Chattanooga, Tennessee.* Chattanooga: Lookout Publishing Co.

Arnstberg, Karl-Olov. 1976. *Datering av knuttimrade hus i Sverige.* Stockholm: Nordiska museet.

Arthur, Eric, and Witney, Dudley. 1972. *The Barn: A Vanishing Landmark in North America.* Toronto: M. F. Feheley Arts Co.

Arthur, John P. 1914. *Western North Carolina: A History.* Raleigh, N.C.: Edwards & Broughton.

Åstrom, Sven-Erik. 1978. *Natur och byte: Ekologiska synpunkter på Finlands ekonomiska historia.* Ekenäs, Finland: Söderström & C:o Förlags AB.

Attebury, Jennifer Eastman. 1976. "Log Construction in the Sawtooth Valley of Idaho." *Pioneer America* 8 (January): 36–46.

Auer, Väinö, and Jutikkala, Eino. 1941. *Finnlands Lebensraum: Das geographische und geschichtliche Finnland.* Berlin: Alfred Metzner Verlag.

Aurner, Charles R. 1912. *Leading Events in Johnson County, Iowa, History.* Cedar Rapids, Ia.: Western Historical Press.

Axelson, M[aximilian]. 1852. *Vandring i Wermlands Elfdal och finnskogar.* Stockholm: P. A. Huldberg.

Bailey, Dana R. 1899. *History of Minnehaha County, South Dakota.* Sioux Falls, S.D.: Broun & Saenger.

Baily, Francis. 1969. *Journal of a Tour in Unsettled Parts of North America in 1796 and 1797.* Edited by Jack D. L. Holmes. Carbondale and Edwardsville: Southern Illinois University Press.

Ball, William W. 1932. *The State That Forgot.* Indianapolis: Bobbs-Merrill.

Barrow, John. 1849. *Facts Relating to North-Eastern Texas, Condensed from Notes Made During a Tour through That Portion of the United States of America.* London: Simpkin, Marshall & Co.

Bealer, Alex W., and Ellis, John O. 1978. *The Log Cabin: Homes of the American Wilderness.* Barre, Mass.: Barre Publishing.

Becker, Gloria O. 1984. "Mill Creek Valley: Architecture, Industry, and Social Change in a Welsh Tract Community, 1682–1800." Ph.D. diss., University of Pennsylvania.

Belknap, Jeremy. 1812. *The History of New Hampshire.* Vol. 3. Dover: O. Crosby and J. Varney.

———. 1831. *The History of New-Hampshire.* Vol. 1. Dover: S. C. Stevens and Ela & Wadleigh.

Benson, Adolph B., and Hedin, Naboth. 1938. *Swedes in America, 1638–1938.* New Haven: Yale University Press.

Berg, Arne. 1965. "Byggjeskikken i Trysil." In *Trysilboka,* vol. 4, pt. 2. Elverum, Norway: Trysil Kommun.

———. 1967. *Tingbøkene og byggjeskikken i Glåmdalen.* Elverum, Norway: Skrifter frå Glomdalsmuseet.

Berthoff, Rowland. 1986. "Celtic Mist Over the South." *Journal of Southern History* 52:523–50.

Bielenstein, August. 1907. *Die Holzbauten und Holzgeräte der Letten. Ein Beitrag zur Ethnographie, Culturgeschichte und Archaeologie der Völker Russlands im Westgebiet.* Part 1. St. Petersburg: n.p.

Biggs, Nina M., and Mackoy, Mabel Lee. 1951. *History of Greenup County, Kentucky.* Louisville, Ky.: Franklin Press.

Bill, Ivan. 1982. "Om finnkolonisationen i Värmland." *Folkets Historia* 10 (January):18–23.

———. 1983. "Svedjefinnar koloniserade Delaware." *Folkets Historia* 11 (January):32–41.

Billington, Ray A. 1977. *America's Frontier Culture: Three Essays.* College Station: Texas A & M University Press.

Birch, Brian P. 1976. "Frontier Farm Settlement: A Pattern-Process Framework." *Geographic Dimensions of Rural Settlements*, pp. 33–40. National Geographical Society of India Publication no. 16. Varanasi, India: Banaras Hindu University.

Bjarnson, Donald E. 1976. "Swedish-Finnish Settlement in New Jersey in the Seventeenth Century." *Swedish Pioneer Historical Quarterly* 27:238–46.

Björklund, Stig. 1972. *Anders Zorn hembygdsvårdaren.* Malung, Sweden: Malungs Boktryckeri, för Zornmuseet Mora.

Black, Patti Carr. 1976. *Mississippi Piney Woods: A Photographic Study of Folk Architecture.* Jackson: Mississippi Department of Archives and History.

Boatright, Mody. 1941. "The Myth of Frontier Individualism." *Southwestern Social Science Quarterly* 22:12–32.

Boëthius, Gerda. 1927. *Studier i den nordiska timmerbyggnadskonsten från vikingatiden till 1800-talet.* Stockholm: Fritzes Hovbokhandel i Distribution.

Bollaert, William. 1956. *William Bollaert's Texas.* Edited by W. Eugene Hollon and Ruth L. Butler. Norman: University of Oklahoma Press.

Bowen, William A. 1978. *The Willamette Valley: Migration and Settlement on the Oregon Frontier.* Seattle: University of Washington Press.

Bowman, Isaiah. 1931. *The Pioneer Fringe.* New York: American Geographical Society.

Bowman, Mary K. 1965. *Reference Book of Wyoming County.* Parsons, W.Va.: McClain Printing Co.

Bowman, Virginia M. 1971. *Historic Williamson County: Old Homes and Sites.* Nashville, Tenn.: Blue & Gray Press.

Boyd, Julian P., ed. 1962–71. *The Susquehanna Papers.* 11 vols. Ithaca, N.Y.: Cornell University Press.

Bracey, Susan L. 1977. *Life by the Roaring Roanoke: A History of Mecklenburg County, Virginia.* Richmond, Va.: Whittet & Shepperson.

Braderman, Eugene M. 1939. "Early Kentucky: Its Virginia Heritage." *South Atlantic Quarterly* 38:449–61.

Bridenbaugh, Carl. 1976. "The Old and New Societies of the Delaware Valley in the Seventeenth Century." *Pennsylvania Magazine of History and Biography* 101:143–72.

Brinton, Daniel G., and Anthony, Albert S. 1888. *A Lenâpé-English Dictionary.* Philadelphia: Historical Society of Pennsylvania.

Broberg, Richard. 1953. "Värmlandsfinsk folktro." In *Värmland förr och nu* 51:67–99. Karlstad, Sweden.

———. 1967. "Invandringar från Finland till mellersta Skandinavien före 1700." *Svenska landsmål och folkliv*, no. 289, pp. 59–98.

———. 1973. "Språk-och kulturgränser i Värmland." *Svenska landsmål och svenskt folkliv* B.67:1–159.

———. 1981. "Äldre invandringar från Finland i historia och tradition." *Fataburen*, pp. 32–65.

Brodhead, John R., comp. 1853–58. *Documents Relative to the Colonial History of the State of New-York Procured in Holland, England, and France.* Vols. 1–5. Albany, N.Y.: Weed, Parsons & Co.

Bromander, C. V. 1901. "Höslåtter och löfskörd på Finnskogen." *Svenska turistföreningens årsskrift*, pp. 122–51.

———. 1902. "Svedjebruket på Finnskogen." *Svenska turistföreningens årsskrift*, pp. 259–96.

Brooks, Eugene C. 1916. *The Story of Corn and the Westward Migration*. Chicago: Rand McNally & Co.

Brown, Richard M. 1963. *The South Carolina Regulators*. Cambridge, Mass.: Belknap Press, Harvard University Press.

———. 1975. *Strain of Violence: Historical Studies of American Violence and Vigilantism*. New York: Oxford University Press.

Browne, W. A. 1929. "Some Frontier Conditions in the Hilly Portions of the Ozarks." *Journal of Geography* 28:181–88.

Browning, Charles H. 1915. "Pennsylvanians in Kentucky." *Pennsylvania Magazine of History and Biography* 39:483–84.

Brumbaugh, Thomas B.; Strayhorn, Martha I.; and Gore, Gary B. 1974. *Architecture of Middle Tennessee: The Historic American Buildings Survey*. Nashville, Tenn.: Vanderbilt University Press.

Buchanan, Ronald H. 1973. "Field Systems of Ireland." In *Studies of Field Systems in the British Isles*, edited by Alan R. H. Baker and Robin A. Butlin, pp. 580–618. Cambridge: Cambridge University Press.

Buck, Solon J., and Buck, Elizabeth H. 1939. *The Planting of Civilization in Western Pennsylvania*. Pittsburgh: University of Pittsburgh Press.

Budd, Thomas. 1685. *Good Order Established in Pennsilvania and New-Jersey in America, Being a true Account of the Country*. Philadelphia: William Bradford.

Buffington, Albert F. 1939. "Pennsylvania German: Its Relation to Other German Dialects." *American Speech* 14:276–86.

Butzer, Karl W. 1982. *Archaeology as Human Ecology*. Cambridge: Cambridge University Press.

Byrd, William. 1967. *William Byrd's Histories of the Dividing Line Betwixt Virginia and North Carolina*. Edited by William K. Boyd. New York: Dover Publications.

Campbell, Åke; Erixon, Sigurd; Lindqvist, Natan; and Sahlgren, Jöran. 1957. *Atlas över svensk folkkultur*, vol. 1, *Materiell och social kultur*. Uddevalla, Sweden: Bokförlaget Niloé.

Campbell, John C. 1921. *The Southern Highlander and His Homeland*. New York: Russell Sage Foundation.

Campbell, P[atrick]. 1937. *Travels in the Interior Inhabited Parts of North America in the Years 1791 and 1792*. Edted by H. H. Langton. Toronto: Champlain Society.

Candee, Richard M. 1976. "Wooden Buildings in Early Maine and New Hampshire: A Technological and Cultural History, 1600–1720." Ph.D. diss., University of Pennsylvania.

Carlisle, Ronald C. 1983. *Stonewall Jackson Lake, West Fork River, Lewis County, West Virginia: Architecture, History, Oral History, and Reconstructed Domains*. Pittsburgh: U.S. Army Corps of Engineers, Pittsburgh District.

Carlisle, Ronald C., and Ferenci, Andrea. 1978. *An Architectural Study of Some Log Structures in the Area of the Yatesville Lake Dam, Lawrence County, Kentucky*. Huntington, W.Va.: U.S. Army Corps of Engineers, Huntington District.

Carlsson, Alan. 1971. "New Sweden on the Delaware." *American Swedish Historical Foundation Yearbook*. pp. 1–22.

Carlsson, Sten. 1978. "John Hanson's Swedish Background." *Swedish Pioneer Historical Quarterly* 29:9–20.

Carter, Thomas. 1984. "North European Horizontal Log Construction in the Sanpete-Sevier Valleys." *Utah Historical Quarterly* 52:50–71.

Casagrande, Joseph B.; Thompson, Stephen I.; and Young, Philip D. 1964. "Colonization as a Research Frontier: The Ecuadorian Case." In *Process and Pattern in Culture: Essays in Honor of Julian H. Steward*, edited by Robert A. Manners, pp. 281–325. Chicago: Aldine.

Chapin, Lon F. 1931. *Early Days in Iowa*. Pasadena, Calif.: Southwest Publishing Co.

Chisholm, Michael. 1962. *Rural Settlement and Land Use*. London: Hutchinson.

Clark, Charles E. 1970. *The Eastern Frontier: The Settlement of Northern New England, 1610–1763*. New York: Alfred A. Knopf.

Clay, Jehu Curtis. 1858. *Annals of the Swedes on the Delaware*. Philadelphia: F. Foster.

Clement, John. 1893. "Swedish Settlers in Gloucester County, New Jersey, Previous to 1684." *Pennsylvania Magazine of History and Biography* 17:83–87.

Clemson, Donovan. 1974. *Living with Logs: British Columbia's Log Buildings and Rail Fences*. Saanichton, B.C.: Hancock House.

Clinton, Anita, and Lofton, Lynn. 1981. *Pioneer Places of Lawrence County, Mississippi*. N.p.: Lawrence County Historical Society.

Coffey, Brian. 1984. "From Shanty to House: Log Construction in Nineteenth-Century Ontario." *Material Culture* 16:61–75.

Coffey, Brian, and Noble, Allen G. 1986. "Residential Building Materials in New York State, 1855–1875." Paper read at the meetings of the Association of American Geographers, Minneapolis, May 7; copy in possession of T.G.J. (Abstract in *AAG '86, Twin Cities, Abstracts*, Washington, D.C.: Association of American Geographers, 1986, session 301.)

Collin, Nicholas. 1936. *The Journal and Biography of Nicholas Collin, 1746–1831*. Translated and edited by Amandus Johnson. Philadelphia: New Jersey Society of Pennsylvania.

Collins, Lewis. 1874. *History of Kentucky*. 2 vols. Covington, Ky.: Collins & Co.

Colonial and State Records of North Carolina. 1886–1914. 30 vols. Various editors. Raleigh and other places: Various publishers, including Hale, Daniels, Stewart, Nash, and Uzzell.

Colonial Records [of Pennsylvania]. 1852–53. 16 vols. Philadelphia: J. Severns & Co.; Harrisburg: T. Fenn & Co.

Connelley, William E. 1910. *The Founding of Harman's Station*. New York: Torch Press.

Conzen, Michael P. 1983. "Land and Society Through the Ages: A Cartographic Essay." In *The Western Experience*, vol. 2, *The Early Modern Period*, edited by Mortimer Chambers et al. 3rd ed. New York: Alfred A. Knopf.

Cooper, Patricia Irvin. 1986. "Toward a Revised Understanding of American Log Building." In *Perspectives in Vernacular Architecture*, vol. 2, edited by Camille Wells, pp. 227–28. Columbia: University of Missouri Press.

Copley, A. B. 1912. "Sturdy Pioneers of Van Buren and Cass." *Michigan Pioneer and Historical Collections* 38:637–45.

Cox, Thomas R.; Maxwell, Robert S.; Thomas, Phillip D.; and Malone, Joseph J. 1985. *This Well-Wooded Land: Americans and Their Forests from Colonial Times to the Present*. Lincoln: University of Nebraska Press.

Cox, William E. 1978. *Hensley Settlement: A Mountain Community.* N.p.: Eastern National Park & Monument Association.

Craig, Peter S., and Yocom, Henry W. 1983. "The Yocums of Aronameck in Philadelphia, 1648–1702." *National Genealogical Quarterly* 71 (December): 243–79.

Craigie, William A., and Hulbert, James R., eds. 1940. *A Dictionary of American English on Historical Principles.* 4 vols. Chicago: University of Chicago Press.

Crayon, Porte [David H. Strother, pseud.]. 1857. "A Winter in the South." Part 3. *Harper's New Monthly Magazine* 15 (November): 721–40.

———. 1858. "A Winter in the South." Part 4. *Harper's New Monthly Magazine* 16 (January): 167–83.

Creekmore, Pollyanna. 1980. *Early East Tennessee Taxpayers.* Easley, Tenn.: Southern Historical Press.

Crockett's Almanac, 1848. 1848. Boston: James Fisher.

Cronon, William. 1983. *Changes in the Land: Indians, Colonists, and the Ecology of New England.* New York: Hill & Wang.

Cummings, Abbott L. 1979. *The Framed Houses of Massachusets Bay, 1625–1725.* Cambridge, Mass.: Harvard University Press.

Danckaerts, Jasper. 1913. *Journal of Jasper Danckaerts, 1679–1680.* Edited by Bartlett B. James and J. Franklin Jameson. New York: Charles Scribner's Sons.

Dankers, Jasper, and Sluyter, Peter. 1867. *Journal of a Voyage to New York and a Tour in Several of the American Colonies in 1679–80.* Brooklyn, N.Y.: Long Island Historical Society.

Darby, H. Clifford. 1956. "The Clearing of the Woodland in Europe." In *Man's Role in Changing the Face of the Earth*, edited by William L. Thomas, Jr., pp. 183–216. Chicago: University of Chicago Press.

Davidson, David. 1977. "Log Building in the San Francisco Peaks Area of Northern Arizona." *Southwest Folklore* 1:1–28.

Davies, Margaret. 1973. "Field Systems of South Wales." In *Studies of Field Systems in the British Isles*, edited by Alan R. H. Baker and Robin A. Butlin, pp. 480–529. Cambridge: Cambridge University Press.

Davy Crockett's Almanack, 1837, of Wild Sports in the West, Life in the Backwoods, and Sketches of Texas. 1837. Nashville, Tenn.: By the heirs of Col. Crockett.

Day, Sherman. 1843. *Historical Collections of the State of Pennsylvania.* Philadelphia: George W. Gorton.

Denevan, William M. 1983. "Adaptation, Variation, and Cultural Geography." *Professional Geographer* 35:399–407.

De Valinger, Leon, Jr. 1954. *Reconstructed 1790 Census of Delaware.* Washington, D.C.: National Genealogical Society.

Diamond, Jared M. 1974. "Colonization of Exploded Volcanic Islands by Birds: The Supertramp Strategy." *Science* 184:803–6.

———. 1977. "Colonization Cycles in Man and Beast." *World Archaeology* 8:249–61.

Djurklou, G. 1873. "Från Vermlands Finnskogar." *Land och Folk*, pp. 241–68.

Dmitrieva, S. I. 1982–83. "Architectural and Decorative Features of the Traditional Dwelling of the Mezen' River Russians." *Soviet Anthropology and Archeology* 21 (Winter): 29–54.

Doddridge, Joseph. 1824. *Notes, on the Settlement and Indian Wars, of the Western Parts of Virginia and Pennsylvania.* Wellsburgh, Va.: The Gazette.

Dodge, Stanley D. 1942. "The Frontier of New England in the Seventeenth and Eighteenth Centuries and Its Significance in American History." *Papers of the Michigan Academy of Science, Arts, and Letters* 28:435–39.

Doolittle, Graydon. 1973. "Culture and Environment on the Cumberland Frontier." *Papers in Anthropology* (Department of Anthropology, University of Oklahoma) 14 (Spring):31–43.

Douglass, Truman O. 1922–23. "Platteville in Its First Quarter Century." *Wisconsin Magazine of History* 6:48–56.

Dovell, J. E. 1952. *Florida: Historic, Dramatic, Contemporary*, vol. 1. New York: Lewis Historical Publishing Co.

Draper, Philander. 1842. "Farming in Missouri in 1842." Manuscript provided by Division of Parks and Historic Preservation, Department of Natural Resources, State of Missouri, Jefferson City, Mo.; copy in possession of T.G.J.

Driver, Harold E. 1969. *Indians of North America*. 2nd ed. Chicago: University of Chicago Press.

Duncan, James S. 1980. "The Superorganic in American Cultural Geography." *Annals of the Association of American Geographers* 70:181–98.

Dunlap, A. R., ed. 1954. "Dutch and Swedish Land Records Relating to Delaware—Some New Documents and a Checklist." *Delaware History* 6, no. 1: 25–52.

Dunlap, A. R., and Moyne, E. J. 1952. "The Finnish Language on the Delaware." *American Speech* 27:81–90.

Dunlap, A. R., and Weslager, C. A. 1967. "More Missing Evidence: Two Depositions by Early Swedish Settlers." *Pennsylvania Magazine of History and Biography* 91:35–45.

Durham, W. H. 1976. "The Adaptive Significance of Cultural Behavior." *Human Ecology* 4:89–121.

Durham, Walter T. 1969. *The Great Leap Westward: A History of Sumner County, Tennessee, from Its Beginnings to 1805*. Gallatin, Tenn.: Sumner County Public Library Board.

Dwight, Timothy. 1969. *Travels in New England and New York*. Edited by Barbara M. Solomon and Patricia M. King. 4 vols. Cambridge, Mass.: Harvard University Press.

Dye, John, and Dye, Judy, eds. 1983–85. *Rambo References*. 5 vols. Spokane, Wash.: K.A.R.D. Files.

Eastman, Seth. 1961. *A Seth Eastman Sketchbook, 1848–1849*. Edited by Lois Burkhalter. Austin: University of Texas Press.

Edmundson, William. 1715. *A Journal of the Life, Travels, Sufferings, and Labour of Love in the Work of the Ministry*. London: J. Sowle.

Ehlers, Eckart. 1967. "Kuparivaara—Puolakkavaara—Jouttiaapa: Beispiele gegenwärtiger Agrarkolonisation in Nordfinnland." *Erdkunde* 21:212–26.

Ek, Sven B. 1959–60. "Nybilding och tradition: förändringar inom allmogens bostadsskick i norra Ångermanland." *Arkiv för norrländsk hembygdsforskning* 16:7–124. Härnösand, Sweden.

Eklund, Arne. 1953. "Litteratur om Värmlandsfinnarna." In *Värmland förr och nu* 51:145–241. Karlstad, Sweden.

Elbert, E. Duane, and Sculle, Keith A. 1982. "Log Buildings in Illinois: Their Interpretation and Preservation." *Illinois Preservation Series*, no. 3, pp. 1–8.

Ely, William. 1887. *The Big Sandy Valley*. Catlettsburg, Ky.: Central Methodist.

Epstein, D. M., and Valmari, A. 1984. "Reindeer Herding and Ecology in Finnish Lapland." *GeoJournal* 8:159–69.

Erixon, Sigurd. 1922. "Svensk byggnadskultur och dess geografi." *Ymer* 42:249–90.

————. 1933. "Hur Norge och Sverige mötas: studier rörande kulturgränser och kultursamband på skandinaviska halvön." *Instituttet for sammenlignende kulturforskning*, ser. A. no. 15 (Bidrag til bondesamfundets historie), pt. 2, pp. 183–299. Oslo: H. Aschehoug.

————. 1937. "The North-European Technique of Corner Timbering." *Folkliv*, no. 1, pp. 13–60 and plates.

————. 1947. *Svensk byggnads kultur: studier och skildringar belysande den svenska byggnadskulturens historia*. Stockholm: Aktiebolaget Bokverk.

————. 1955–56. "Är den nordamerikanska timringstekniken överförd från Sverige?" *Folkliv* 19:56–68.

————. 1957. "Schwedische Holzbautechnik in vergleichender Beleuchtung." *Liv och Folkkultur* 8:42–112.

————. 1961. "Swedish Villages without Systematic Regulation." *Geografiska Annaler* 43:57–74.

————, ed. 1962–63. *Sveriges bebyggelse. Statistisk-topografisk uppslagsbok: landsbygden, Värmlands län*. 3 vols. Uddevalla, Sweden: Olof Ericson, Bokförlaget Hermes.

Esarey, Logan. 1918. *A History of Indiana from Its Exploration to 1850*. Indianapolis: B. F. Bowen.

Evans, Elliot A. P. 1952. "The East Texas House." *Journal of the Society of Architectural Historians* 11 (December) 1–7.

Evans, E. Estyn. 1939. "Some Survivals of the Irish Open Field System." *Geography* 24:24–36.

————. 1965. "The Scotch-Irish in the New World: An Atlantic Heritage." *Royal Society of Antiquaries of Ireland* 35:39–49.

————. 1966. "Culture and Land Use in the Old West of North America." *Heidelberger Geographische Arbeiten*, no. 15, pp. 72–80.

————. 1967. *Mourne Country: Landscape and Life in South Down*. 2nd ed. Dundalk, Republic of Ireland: Dundalgan Press.

————. 1969. "The Scotch-Irish: Their Cultural Adaptation and Heritage in the American Old West." In *Essays in Scotch-Irish History*, edited by E. R. R. Green, pp. 69–86. London: Routledge & Kegan Paul.

Evjen, John O. 1916. *Scandinavian Immigrants in New York, 1630–1674*. Minneapolis: K. C. Holter Publishing Co.

Fairhurst, Horace. 1960. "Scottish Clachans." *Scottish Geographical Magazine* 76:67–76.

Falk, Erik. 1921. "Finnarna i Värmland intill 1600-talets slut." In *En bok om Värmland*, vol. 3, edited by H. H. Hildebrandsson and Sixten Samuelsson, pp. 229–84. Uppsala and Stockholm: Almqvist & Wiksells Boktryckeri.

Faris, Paul. 1983. *Ozark Log Cabin Folks the Way They Were*. Little Rock: Rose Publishing Co.

Federal Writers' Project of the Works Progress Administration (Illinois). 1937. *Galena Guide*. Galena, Ill.: City of Galena.

————. (New Jersey). 1938a. *The Records of the Swedish Lutheran Churches at Raccoon and Penns Neck, 1713–1786*. Elizabeth, N.J.: Colby & McGowan.

————. (New Jersey). 1938b. *The Swedes and Finns in New Jersey*. Bayonne, N.J.: Jersey Printing Co. (Probable author, Irene Fuhlbruegge.)

————. (New Jersey) 1938c. *The Swedes and Finns in New Jersey* (4 bulletins). N.p.: New Jersey State Board of Education. (Probable author, Irene Fuhlbruegge.)

Fernow, B., comp., ed., trans. 1877. *Documents Relating to the History of the Dutch and Swedish Settlements on the Delaware River, Translated and Compiled from Original Manuscripts in the Office of the Secretary of State, at Albany, and in the Royal Archives, at Stockholm* (vol. 12 of *Documents Relative to the Colonial History of the State of New York*). Albany, N.Y.: Argus Co.

Fernow, Erik. 1977. *Beskrivning över Värmland.* Edited by Arvid Ernvik. 2 vols. Karlstad, Sweden: NWT:s Förlag. (Originally published Göteborg, Sweden, 1773–79.)

Ferris, Benjamin. 1846. *History of the Original Settlements on the Delaware.* Wilmington, Del.: Wilson & Heald.

Ferris, William R., Jr. 1973. "Mississippi Folk Architecture: Two Examples." *Mississippi Folklore Register* 7:101–14.

———. 1986. "The Dogtrot: A Mythic Image in Southern Culture." *Southern Quarterly* 25 (Fall): 72–85.

Fiske, John. 1897. *Old Virginia and Her Neighbours.* 2 vols. Boston and New York: Houghton Mifflin Co.

Flanders, Robert. 1984. "Caledonia, an Ozarks Village: History, Geography, Architecture." Springfield, Mo.: Center for Ozarks Studies, Southwest Missouri State University, for the Missouri Department of Natural Resources.

———. 1985. "Alley, an Ozarks Mill Hamlet, 1890–1925: Society, Economy, Landscape." Springfield, Mo.: Center for Ozarks Study, Southwest Missouri State University, for the Ozark National Scenic Riverways, National Park Service.

———. 1986. "Caledonia: Ozark Legacy of the High Scotch-Irish." *Gateway Heritage* 6 (Spring):34–52.

Fletcher, Stevenson W. 1950. *Pennsylvania Agriculture and Country Life, 1640–1840.* Harrisburg: Pennsylvania Historical and Museum Commission.

Florin, Lambert. 1970. *Ghost Towns of the West.* N.p.: Promontory Press.

Flower, George. 1882. *History of the English Settlement in Edwards County, Illinois.* Chicago Historical Society Collection, vol. 1. Chicago: Fergus.

Ford, Henry J. 1915. *The Scotch-Irish in America.* Princeton: Princeton University Press.

Fort Necessity and Historic Shrines of the Redstone Country. 1932. Uniontown, Pa.: Fort Necessity Chapter, Pennsylvania Society of the Sons of the American Revolution.

Foster, George M. 1960. *Culture and Conquest: America's Spanish Heritage.* New York: Wenner-Gren Foundation for Anthropological Research.

Fothergill, Augusta B., and Naugle, John M. 1978. *Virginia Tax Payers, 1782–87, Other Than Those Published by the United States Census Bureau.* Baltimore: Genealogical Publishing Co.

Fowler, Albert. 1968. *Cranberry Lake from Wilderness to Adirondack Park.* Syracuse, N.Y.: Syracuse University Press and Adirondack Museum.

Fox, Cyril, and Raglan, Lord. 1954. *Monmouthshire Houses*, pt. 3. Cardiff: National Museum of Wales.

Freeman, Ira S. 1958. *A History of Montezuma County, Colorado.* Boulder, Colo.: Johnson.

Friis, Herman R. 1940. "A Series of Population Maps of the Colonies and the United States, 1625–1790." *Geographical Review* 30: 463–70.

Gailey, Alan. 1984. *Rural Houses of the North of Ireland.* Edinburgh: John Donald.

Garber, John P. 1934. *The Valley of the Delaware and Its Place in American History.* Philadelphia: John C. Winston.

Gard, Wayne. 1949. *Frontier Justice.* Norman: University of Oklahoma Press.

Garth, Thomas R., Jr. 1947. "Early Architecture in the Northwest." *Pacific Northwest Quarterly* 38:215–32.

Gates, Paul W. 1968. *History of Public Land Law Development.* Washington, D.C.: Government Printing Office.

Gehring, Charles T., ed. 1977. *New York Historical Manuscripts: Dutch, Delaware Papers.* Baltimore: Genealogical Publishing Co.

Geike, John C., ed. 1864. *George Stanley; or, Life in the Woods.* London: Routledge, Warne, & Routledge.

Geographical Society of Finland. 1925. *Atlas of Finland.* Helsinki: Kustannusosakeyhtiö Otava. (Trilingual: Finnish, Swedish, and English.)

Georgia Historical Society. 1969. *Index to United States Census of Georgia for 1820.* 2nd ed. Baltimore: Genealogical Publishing Co.

Gerlach, Russel L. 1976. *Immigrants in the Ozarks: A Study in Ethnic Geography.* Columbia: University of Missouri Press.

———. 1984. "The Ozark Scotch-Irish: The Subconscious Persistence of an Ethnic Culture." *Pioneer America Society Transactions* 7:47–57.

Gettys, Marshall. 1981. "The Dogtrot Log Cabin in Oklahoma." *Outlook in Historic Conservation,* January/February.

Gibbons, Edward J. 1968. "The Swedes' Tract in Upper Merion Township, Montgomery County, Pennsylvania: Land Transaction and Settlement, 1684–1710." *American Swedish Historical Foundation Yearbook,* pp. 1–10.

Gibson, James R. 1976. *Imperial Russia in Frontier America: The Changing Geography of Supply of Russian America, 1784–1867.* New York: Oxford University Press.

Gillis, Irene S., and Gillis, Norman E., eds. 1963. *Mississippi 1820 Census.* Baton Rouge, La.: By the Editors.

Gillis, Norman E. 1963. *Early Inhabitants of the Natchez District.* Baton Route, La.: N.p.

Gillon, Edmund, Jr. 1971. *Early Illustrations and Views of American Architecture.* New York: Dover Publications.

Glass, Joseph W. 1986. *The Pennsylvania Culture Region: A View from the Barn.* Ann Arbor, Mich.: UMI Research Press.

Glassie, Henry. 1963. "The Appalachian Log Cabin." *Mountain Life and Work* 39 (Winter): 5–14.

———. 1965. "The Old Barns of Appalachia." *Mountain Life and Work* 41 (Summer): 21–30.

———. 1968a. *Pattern in the Material Folk Culture of the Eastern United States.* Philadelphia: University of Pennsylvania Press.

———. 1968b. "The Types of the Southern Mountain Cabin." In *The Study of American Folklore: An Introduction,* edited by Jan H. Brunvand, pp. 338–70. New York: W. W. Norton & Co.

———. 1969a. "The Double-Crib Barn in South-Central Pennsylvania." Part 1. *Pioneer America* (January): 9–16.

———. 1969b. "The Double-Crib Barn in South-Central Pennsylvania." Part 2. *Pioneer America* 1 (July): 40–45.

————. 1970a. "The Double-Crib Barn in South-Central Pennsylvania." Part 3. *Pioneer America* 2 (January): 47–52.

————. 1970b. "The Double-Crib Barn in South-Central Pennsylvania." Part 4. *Pioneer America* 2 (July): 23–34.

————. 1972. "Eighteenth-Century Cultural Process in Delaware Valley Folk Building." *Winterthur Portfolio* 7:29–57.

Goddard, Ives. 1971. "The Ethnohistorical Implications of Early Delaware Linguistic Materials." *Man in the Northeast* 1:14–26.

Goins, Charles R., and Morris, John W. 1980. *Oklahoma Homes, Past and Present*, Norman: University of Oklahoma Press.

Gothe, Richard. 1942. *Hassela-finnarna*. Stockholm: Författarens Förlag.

————. 1945. *Medelpads finnmarker. Kulturhistoriska undersökningar rörande den finska kolonisationen inom mellersta Norrland under 15-, 16- och 1700-talen*. Stockholm: Författarens Förlag.

————. 1948. *Finnkolonisationen inom Ångermanland, södra Lappmarken och Jämtland*. Stockholm: Författarens Förlag.

————. 1950. "Orsafinnarna." In *Orsa. En sockenbeskrivning*, vol. 1, edited by Johannes Boëthius, pp. 481–542. Stockholm: Nordisk rotogravyr.

Gottlund, Carl A. 1931. *Dagbok öfver dess Resor på Finnskogarne i Dalarne, Helsingland, Vestmanland och Vermland år 1817*. Stockholm: Nordisk rotogravyr.

Gould, John. 1975. *Maine Lingo*. Camden, Me.: Down East Magazine.

Graves, Donald, and Colby, Michael. 1986. "An Overview of Flax and Linen Production in Pennsylvania." *Pennsylvania Folklife* 35 (Spring): 108–26.

Green, Stanton. 1979. "The Agricultural Colonization of Temperate Forest Habitats: An Ecological Model." In *The Frontier*, vol. 2, edited by William W. Savage, Jr., and Stephen I. Thompson, pp. 69–103. Norman: University of Oklahoma Press.

Green, Stanton W., and Perlman, Stephen M., eds. 1985. *The Archaeology of Frontiers and Boundaries*. Orlando, Fla.: Academic Press.

Gregorie, Anne K. 1954. *History of Sumter County, South Carolina*. Sumter, S.C.: Library Board of Sumter County.

Grimes, J. Bryan. 1967. *Abstracts of North Carolina Wills*. Baltimore: Genealogical Publishing Co.

Gritzner, Charles F. 1971. "Log Housing in New Mexico." *Pioneer America* 3 (July): 54–62.

Groefsema, Olive. 1949. *Elmore County: Its Historical Gleanings*. Caldwell, Idaho: Caxton Printers.

Grotenfelt, Gösta. 1899. *Det primitiva jordbrukets metoder i Finland under den historiska tiden*. Helsingfors, Finland: Simelii.

Guillet, Edwin C. 1963a. *Early Life in Upper Canada*. Toronto: University of Toronto Press.

————. 1963b. *The Pioneer Farmer and Backwoodsman*. 2 vols. Toronto: Ontario Publishing Co.

Gulley, J. L. M. 1959. "The Turnerian Frontier: A Study in the Migration of Ideas." *Tijdschrift voor economische en sociale geografie* 50:65–72, 81–91.

Gunter, Mrs. A. Y. n.d. "Recollection of an Early Cooke County Settler." Manuscript essay offered to the Historical Committee of the XLI Club of Gainesville, Tex.; copy in the Historical Collection, Museum, North Texas State University, Denton.

Gustafsson, Berndt. 1957. *Svensk kyrkogeografi, med samfundsbeskrivning*. Lund, Sweden: C. W. K. Gleerup.

Habicht, Tamara. 1977. *Rahvapärane arhitektuur.* Tallinn, Estonia, U.S.S.R.: Kirjastus "Kunst."

Haines, Alanson A. 1888. *Hardyston Memorial: A History of the Township and the North Presbyterian Church, Hardyston, Sussex County, New Jersey.* Newton: New Jersey Herald Print.

Hale, Richard W., Jr. 1957–60. "The French Side of the Log Cabin Myth." *Proceedings of the Massachusetts Historical Society,* 3rd ser., 72 (October 1957–December 1960): 118–25.

Hall, Basil. 1830. *Travels in North America in the Years 1827–1828.* 2nd ed. 3 vols. Edinburgh: Robert Cadell; London: Simkin & Marshall.

Hall, Clayton C., ed. 1910. *Narratives of Early Maryland.* New York: Charles Scribner's Sons.

Hall, John W. 1985. "Toward a Culture History of Whiskey." *North American Culture* 2, no. 1:49–54.

Hallowell, A. Irving. 1957a. "The Backwash of the Frontier: The Impact of the Indian on American Culture." In *The Frontier in Perspective,* edited by Walker D. Wyman and Clifton B. Kroeber, pp. 229–58. Madison: University of Wisconsin Press.

————. 1957b. "The Impact of the American Indian on American Culture." *American Anthropologist* 59:201–17.

Halsey, Francis W. 1901. *The Old New York Frontier.* New York: Charles Scribner's Sons.

————. 1902. *The Pioneers of Unadilla Village, 1784–1840.* Unadilla, N.Y.: St. Matthew's Church.

Hämäläinen, Albert. 1930. *Keski-Suomen kansanrakennukset.* Helsinki: Suomalaisen kirjallisuuden seuran toimituksia 186. Osa. Kansatieteellisiä kuvauksia II.

————. 1945. *Bostads- och byggnadsskick hos skogsfinnarna i Mellan-Skandinavien.* Stockholm: Nordiska museets handlingar, no. 23.

Hanna, Charles A. 1902. *The Scotch-Irish; or, The Scot in North Britain, North Ireland, and North America.* 2 vols. New York and London: G. P. Putnam's Sons.

Hanson, George A. 1876. *Old Kent: The Eastern Shore of Maryland.* Baltimore: John P. Des Forges.

Hardesty, Donald L. 1980–81. "Historic Sites Archaeology on the Western American Frontier: Theoretical Perspectives and Research Problems." *North American Archaeologist* 2:67–82.

————. 1986. "Rethinking Cultural Adaptation." *Professional Geographer* 38:11–18.

Harpster, John W., ed. 1938. *Pen Pictures of Early Western Pennsylvania.* Pittsburgh: University of Pittsburgh Press.

Harrington, Grant W. 1935. *Historic Spots, or Mile-Stones in the Progress of Wyandotte County, Kansas.* Merriam, Kans.: Mission Press.

Harris, R. Colebrook. 1966. *The Seigneurial System in Early Canada: A Geographical Study.* Madison: University of Wisconsin Press.

————. 1977. "The Simplification of Europe Overseas." *Annals of the Association of American Geographers* 67:469–83.

Harris, Thaddeus M. 1805. *The Journal of a Tour into the Territory Northwest of the Alleghany Mountains.* Boston: Manning & Loring.

Hart, John F. 1977. "Land Rotation in Appalachia." *Geographical Review* 67:148–66.

Hartz, Louis. 1964. *The Founding of New Societies: Studies in the History of the United States, Latin America, South Africa, Canada, and Australia.* New York: Harcourt, Brace & World.

Haycraft, Samuel. 1921. *A History of Elizabethtown, Kentucky and Its Surroundings*. Elizabethtown, Ky.: Woman's Club.

Hayes, Rutherford B. 1922. *Diary and Letters of Rutherford Birchard Hayes*, vol. 2. Edited by Charles R. Williams. Columbus: Ohio State Archaeological and Historical Society.

Heckscher, Eli F. 1935–49. *Sveriges ekonomiska historia från Gustav Vasa*. 2 vols., each with 2 parts. Stockholm: Albert Bonniers Förlag.

———. 1954. *An Economic History of Sweden*. Translated by Göran Ohlin. Cambridge, Mass.: Harvard University Press.

Heikel, Axel O. 1888. *Die Gebäude der Čeremissen, Mordwinen, Esten und Finnen*. Vol. 4 of *Suomalais-ugrilaisen seuran aikakauskirja*. Helsinki: Suomalaisen kirjallisuuden seura.

Heikkenen, Herman J., and Edwards, M. R. 1983. "The Key-Year Dendrochronology Technique and Its Application in Dating Historic Structures in Maryland." *Bulletin, Association for Preservation Technology*, 15, no. 3: 3–25.

Heinemann, Charles B., comp. 1965. *First Census of Kentucky, 1790*. Baltimore: Genealogical Publishing Co.

Heiss, Willard, comp. 1966. *1820 Federal Census for Indiana*. Indianapolis: Genealogical Section of the Indiana Historical Society.

Hemmensdorff, Ove, and Jonsson, Marie. 1984. *Fäbodar i Bergs kommun*. Östersund, Sweden: Jämtlands läns museum, kulturhistorisk utredning, no. 25.

Herman, Bernard. 1987. *Architecture and Rural Life in Central Delaware, 1700–1900*. Knoxville: University of Tennessee Press.

Hess, David W. 1979. "Pioneering as Ecological Process: A Model and Test Case of Frontier Adaptation." In *The Frontier*, vol. 2, edited by William W. Savage, Jr., and Stephen I. Thompson, pp. 123–51. Norman: University of Oklahoma Press.

Hewes, Leslie. 1982. "Early Fencing on the Western Margin of the Prairie." *Nebraska History* 63:300–348.

Hilliard, Sam B. 1969. "Pork in the Ante-Bellum South: The Geography of Self-Sufficiency." *Annals of the Association of American Geographers* 59:461–80.

———. 1972. *Hog Meat and Hoe Cake: Food Supply in the Old South, 1840–1860*. Carbondale: Southern Illinois University Press.

Hinke, William J., and Kemper, Charles E. 1903–4. "Moravian Diaries of Travels through Virginia." Part 1. *Virginia Magazine of History and Biography* 11:113–31, 225–42, 370–93.

———. 1904–5. "Moravian Diaries of Travels through Virginia." Part 2. *Virginia Magazine of History and Biography* 12:55–61, 134–53, 271–81.

Historic and Architectural Resources of the Tar-Neuse River Basin. 1977. Appendices. Raleigh: North Carolina Department of Cultural Resources, Division of Archives and History.

Hoffman, Charles F. 1835. *A Winter in the West*. 2 vols. New York: Harper & Brothers.

Holm, Thomas Campanius. 1702. *Kort beskrifning om provincien Nya Sverige uti America, som nu förtjden af the Engelske kallas Pensylvania*. Stockholm: J. H. Werner.

———. 1834. "A Short Description of the Province of New Sweden, now called, by the English, Pennsylvania, in America," translated by Peter S. du Ponceau. *Memoirs of the Historical Society of Pennsylvania* 3:1–166.

Holme, Thomas. 1876. "A Mapp of the Improved Part of Pensilvania in America, Divided into Countyes, Townships and Lotts [1687]." Philadelphia: Samuel L. Smedley, Chief Engineer and Surveyor of the City of Philadelphia.

Holmes, H. B., Jr. 1962. *Index of the Surface Waters of Virginia.* Virginia Place Name Society, Occasional Paper no. 3. Charlottesville: University of Virginia.

Holstein, Anna M. 1892. *Swedish Holsteins in America from 1644 to 1892.* Norristown, Pa.: M. R. Wills.

A Home in the Wilderness [Currier & Ives print]. 1960. *Palimpsest* 41, no. 11 (November): cover.

[Homman, Olle]. 1964. "Knuttyper i Dalarna, 1100–1900." *Dalarnas hembygdsbok.* pp. 45–52.

Hood, Davyd F. 1978. "The Architecture of the New River Valley." In *Carolina Dwelling: Towards Preservation of Place, in Celebration of the North Carolina Vernacular Landscape,* edited by Doug Swaim, pp. 202–15. Raleigh: School of Design, North Carolina State University.

———. 1983. *The Architcture of Rowan County.* Salisbury, N.C.: Rowan County Historic Properties Commission.

Hoover, Dwight W., and Rodman, Jane. 1980. *A Pictorial History of Indiana.* Bloomington: Indiana University Press.

Horner, Thomas M. 1971. "Sauna Baths Along the Delaware, 1638–1682." *American Swedish Historical Foundation Yearbook,* pp. 23–28.

Horsman, Reginald. 1970. *The Frontier in the Formative Years, 1783–1815.* New York: Holt, Rinehart & Winston.

Horton, Loren N. 1974. "Early Architecture in Dubuque." *Palimpsest* 55:130–51.

Howe, Henry. 1898–1902. *Historical Collections of Ohio.* 2 vols. Norwalk, Ohio: Laning Printing.

Hoyt, Mary M. L. 1907. "Life of Leonard Slater." *Michigan Pioneer and Historical Society, Historical Collections* 35:142–55.

Hudson, G. E. 1951. "Copedology for the Ornithologist." *Ecology* 32:571–76.

Hudson, John C. 1975. "Frontier Housing in North Dakota." *North Dakota History* 42 (Fall): 4–15.

———. 1977. "Theory and Methodology in Comparative Frontier Studies." In *The Frontier: Comparative Studies,* edited by David H. Miller and Jerome O. Steffen, pp. 11–31. Norman: University of Oklahoma Press.

———. 1984. "Cultural Geography and the Upper Great Lakes Region." *Journal of Cultural Geography* 5, no. 1:19–32.

Hughes-Jones, Alicia, and Gettys, Marshall. 1981. "Single Pen Log Cabins in Oklahoma." *Outlook in Historic Conservation,* May–June.

Hulan, Richard H. 1975. "Middle Tennessee and the Dogtrot House." *Pioneer America* 7, no. 2 (July): 37–46.

———. 1977. "The Dogtrot House and Its Pennsylvania Associations." *Pennsylvania Folklife* 26 (Summer): 25–32.

———. 1980a. "The Delaware Valley Double-House and Its European Origin." Unpublished manuscript; copy in possession of T.G.J.

———. 1980b. "Whatever Happened to Baby Swain? Diffusion of New Sweden's Folk Culture to the Interior." Paper read at the annual meeting of the American Folklore Society, Pittsburgh, Pa., October; copy in possession of T.G.J.

———. 1981. "The Swedes in the Shenandoah Valley." Paper read before Virginia Folklore Society, November; copy in possession of T.G.J.

———. 1984. *From Northern Shore: The Swedish and Finnish Presence in Colonial Maryland.* Rockville, Md.: Daystarr Press. (Brochure accompanying museum exhibit.)

———. 1986. "The Batsto Boat: Evidence of Delaware Valley Swedish Technology?" In *The Challenge of Folk Materials for New Jersey's Museums*, edited by Cynthia Koch and Eliot Werner, pp. 63–69. New Brunswick: Museums Council of New Jersey.

Humphrey, H. N. 1916. "Cost of Fencing Farms in the North Central States." *United States Department of Agriculture Bulletin No. 321.* Washington, D.C.: Government Printing Office. 32 pp.

Hunter, J. Marvin. 1925. *The Trail Drivers of Texas.* Nashville, Tenn.: Cokesbury Press.

Huovinen, Sulo. 1986. *Värmlandsfinnar: om Finnskogens historia och kultur.* Stockholm: Kulturfonden för Sverige och Finland.

Hutslar, Donald A. 1977. *The Log Architecture of Ohio.* Columbus: Ohio Historical Society.

———. 1986. *The Architecture of Migration: Log Construction in the Ohio Country, 1750–1850.* Athens: Ohio University Press.

Ilmonen, S. 1916. *Amerikan ensimäiset soumalaiset eli Delawaren siirtokunnan historia.* Hancock, Mich.: Suomalais-Luteerilaisen Kustannusliikkeen Kirjapaino.

Index to the Headright and Bounty Grants of Georgia, 1756–1909. 1970. Vidalia, Ga.: Georgia Genealogical Reprints.

Index to the Wills of Charleston County, South Carolina, 1671–1868. 1950. Charleston, S.C.: Charleston Free Library.

Itkonen, T. I. 1947. "Lapparnas förekomst i Finland." *Ymer* 67:43–57.

———. 1948. *Suomen lappalaiset vuoteen 1945.* 2 vols. Porvoo and Helsinki: Werner Söderström.

Jackson, Ronald V., ed. 1981a. *Alabama 1820 Census Index.* Bountiful, Utah: Accelerated Indexing Systems.

———, ed. 1981b. *Michigan 1820 Index Census.* Bountiful, Utah: Accelerated Indexing Systems.

———, ed. 1981c. *Virginia 1820 Census Index.* Salt Lake City, Utah: Accelerated Indexing Systems.

Jackson, Ronald V., and Schaefermeyer, David, eds. 1976. *South Carolina 1820 Census Index.* Bountiful, Utah: Accelerated Indexing Systems.

Jackson, Ronald V., and Teeples, Gary R., eds. 1974. *Tennessee 1820 Census.* Bountiful, Utah: Accelerated Indexing Systems.

———, eds. 1976. *Kentucky 1820 Census Index.* Bountiful, Utah: Accelerated Indexing Systems, 1976.

Jackson, Ronald V.; Teeples, Gary R.; and Schaefermeyer, David, eds. 1974. *Delaware 1820 Census Index.* Bountiful, Utah: Accelerated Indexing Systems.

———, eds. 1976a. *Georgia 1820 Census Index.* Bountiful, Utah: Accelerated Indexing Systems.

———, eds. 1976b. *Louisiana 1820 Census Index.* Bountiful, Utah: Accelerated Indexing Systems.

———, eds. 1976c. *Maine 1820 Census Index.* Bountiful, Utah: Accelerated Indexing Systems.

———, eds. 1976d. *Massachusetts 1820 Census Index.* Bountiful, Utah: Accelerated Indexing Systems.

———, eds. 1976e. *New Hampshire 1820 Census Index.* Bountiful, Utah: Accelerated Indexing Systems.

————, eds. 1976f. *North Carolina 1820 Census Index*. Bountiful, Utah: Accelerated Indexing Systems.

————, eds. 1976g. *Rhode Island 1820 Census Index*. Bountiful, Utah: Accelerated Indexing Systems.

————, eds. 1976h. *Vermont 1820 Census Index*. Bountiful, Utah: Accelerated Indexing Systems.

————, eds. 1977a. *Connecticut 1820 Census Index*. Bountiful, Utah: Accelerated Indexing Systems.

————, eds. 1977b. *Maryland 1820 Census Index*. Bountiful, Utah: Accelerated Indexing Sytems.

————, eds. 1977c. *New York 1820 Census Index*. Bountiful, Utah: Accelerated Indexing Sytems.

————, eds. 1977d. *Pennsylvania 1820 Census Index*. Bountiful, Utah: Accelerated Indexing Systems.

Jacobs, Wilbur R. 1973. "The Indian and the Frontier in American History—A Need for Revision." *Western Historical Quarterly* 4:43–56.

Jacobsen, Kari S. 1985. "Bebyggelsen på Finnskogen—hva med den?" *Årbok, Foreningen til norske fortidsminnesmerkers bevaring*, no. 139, pp. 91–114.

James, William. 1916. *Talks to Teachers on Psychology: And to Students on Some of Life's Ideals*. New York: Henry Holt.

Jeane, D. Gregory, and Purcell, Douglas C., eds. 1978. *The Architectural Legacy of the Lower Chattahoochee Valley in Alabama and Georgia*. University: University of Alabama Press.

Jennewein, J. Leonard, and Boorman, Jane, eds. 1961. *Dakota Panorama*. Sioux Falls, S.Dak.: Midwest-Beach.

Jennings, Francis. 1984. *The Ambiguous Iroquois Empire*. New York: W. W. Norton & Co.

Jessee, Glenn J. 1983. "Culture Contact and Acculturation in New Sweden, 1638–1655." M.A. thesis, College of William and Mary.

Jillson, Willard R. 1925. *The Kentucky Land Grants: A Systematic Index to All of the Land Grants Recorded in the State Land Office at Frankfort, Kentucky*. Louisville, Ky.: Standard Printing Co.

————. 1926. *Old Kentucky Entries and Deeds*. Louisville, Ky.: Standard Printing Co.

John, Elizabeth A. H. 1982–83. "Portrait of a Wichita Village, 1808." *Chronicles of Oklahoma* 60:412–37.

Johnson, Amandus. 1911. *The Swedish Settlements on the Delaware, 1638–1664*. 2 vols. New York: D. Appleton for the University of Pennsylvania.

————. 1955. "Sweden Gave America the Rail Fence." *American Swedish Monthly* 49 (June): 6–7, 29.

Johnson, Howard, ed. 1978. *A Home in the Woods: Pioneer Life in Indiana. Oliver Johnson's Reminiscences of Early Marion County*. Bloomington: Indiana University Press.

Johnson, L. F. 1912. *History of Franklin County, Kentucky*. Frankfort, Ky.: Roberts Printing.

Johnson, William. 1921–53. *The Papers of Sir William Johnson*. 14 vols. Edited by James Sullivan et al. Albany: University of the State of New York.

Johnston, David E. 1906. *History of Middle New River Settlements and Contiguous Territory*. Huntington, W.V.: Standard Printing & Publishing.

Johnston, Frances B. 1957. *The Early Architecture of Georgia*. Chapel Hill: University of North Carolina Press.

Johnston, Frances B., and Waterman, Thomas T. 1941. *The Early Architecture of North Carolina: A Pictorial Survey*. Chapel Hill: University of North Carolina Press.

Jokipii, Mauno. 1961. "Satakunnan asuinrakennuksista ennen isoavihaa." *Satakunta* 17:34–64.

Jones, Glanville R. J. 1973. "Field Systems of North Wales." In *Studies of Field Systems in the British Isles*, edited by Alan R. H. Baker and Robin A. Butlin, pp. 430–79. Cambridge: Cambridge University Press.

Jones, John. 1912. "Letter of John Jones, 1725." In *Narratives of Early Pennsylvania, West New Jersey and Delaware, 1630–1707*, edited by Albert C. Myers, pp. 449–59. New York: Charles Scribner's Sons.

Jones, Louis C., ed. 1965. *Growing Up in the Cooper Country: Boyhood Recollections of the New York Frontier*. Syracuse, N.Y.: Syracuse University Press.

Jordan, Terry G. 1976. "Abandonment of Farm-Village Tradition in New-Land Settlement: The Example of Anglo-America." In *Geographic Dimensions of Rural Settlements*, pp. 84–88. National Geographical Society of India, Research Publication Series, no. 16.

———. 1978. *Texas Log Buildings: A Folk Architecture*. Austin: University of Texas Press.

———. 1980. "Alpine, Alemannic, and American Log Architecture." *Annals of the Association of American Geographers* 70:154–80.

———. 1981. *Trails to Texas: Southern Roots of Western Cattle Ranching*. Lincoln: University of Nebraska Press.

———. 1982. *Texas Graveyards: A Cultural Legacy*. Austin: University of Texas Press.

———. 1983. "A Reappraisal of Fenno-Scandian Antecedents for Midland American Log Construction." *Geographical Review* 73:58–94.

———. 1983–84. "Moravian, Schwenkfelder, and American Log Construction." *Pennsylvania Folklife* 33:98–124.

———. 1985. *American Log Buildings: An Old World Heritage*. Chapel Hill: University of North Carolina Press.

———. 1986. "Evolution of American Backwoods Pioneer Culture: The Role of the Delaware Finns." In *Mississippi's Piney Woods: A Human Perspective*, edited by Noel Polk, pp. 25–39. Jackson: University Press of Mississippi.

———. 1988. *The European Culture Area: A Systematic Geography*. 2nd ed. New York: Harper & Row.

Jordan, Terry G., and Kaups, Matti. 1987. "Folk Architecture in Cultural and Ecological Context." *Geographical Review* 77:52–75.

Jordan, Terry G.; Kaups, Matti; and Lieffort, Richard M. 1986–87a. "Diamond Notching in America and Europe." *Pennsylvania Folklife* 36:70–78.

———. 1986–87b. "New Evidence on the European Origin of Pennsylvanian V Notching." *Pennsylvania Folklife* 36:20–31.

Jordan, Terry G., and Rowntree, Lester. 1986. *The Human Mosaic: A Thematic Introduction to Cultural Geography*. 4th ed. New York: Harper & Row.

Jutikkala, Eino. 1963. *Bonden i Finland genom tiderna*. Stockholm: LTs Förlag.

Jutikkala, Eino; Kaukiainen, Yrjö; and Åström, Sven-Erik, eds. 1980. *Suomen taloushistoria*, vol. 1. Helsinki: Kustannusosakeyhtiö Tammi.

Jutikkala, Eino, and Pirinen, Kauko. 1974. *A History of Finland*. Translated by Paul Sjöblom. Rev. ed. New York: Praeger Publishers.

Kalm, Pehr. 1929. *Pehr Kalms resa till Norra Amerika.* Helsinki: Skrifter utgivna av Svenska litteratursällskapet i Finland.

———. 1937. *Peter Kalm's Travels in North America: The English Version of 1770.* Edited by Adolph B. Benson. 2 vols. New York: Wilson-Erickson.

———. 1972. *Travels into North America.* Translated by John R. Forster. Barre, Mass.: Imprint Society.

Kaplan, Peter R. 1981. *The Historic Architecture of Cabarrus County, North Carolina.* Concord, N.C.: Historic Cabarrus, Inc.; Concord and Raleigh: North Carolina Division of Archives and History.

Karni, Michael, and Levin, Robert. 1972. "Northwoods Vernacular Architecture: Finnish Log Building in Minnesota." *Northwest Architect* 36 (May–June): 92–99.

Kauffman, Henry J. 1975. *The American Farmhouse.* New York: Hawthorn Books.

Kaups, Matti. 1972. "A Finnish *Riihi* in Minnesota." *Journal of the Minnesota Academy of Science* 38:66–71.

———. 1976. "A Finnish Savusauna in Minnesota." *Minnesota History* 45:11–20.

———. 1981. "Log Architecture in America: European Antecedents in a Finnish Context." *Journal of Cultural Geography* 2, no. 1:131–53.

———. 1983. "Finnish Log Houses in the Upper Middle West, 1890–1920." *Journal of Cultural Geography* 3, no. 2:2–26.

Kay, Jeanne. 1979. "Wisconsin Indian Hunting Patterns, 1634–1836." *Annals of the Association of American Geographers* 69:402–18.

Keen, Gregory B. 1878a. "The Descendants of Jöran Kyn, the Founder of Upland." Part 1. *Pennsylvania Magazine of History and Biography* 2:325–35, 443–56.

———, ed. and trans. 1878b. "Early Swedish Records—Extracts from Parish Records of Gloria Dei Church, Philadelphia." *Pennsylvania Magazine of History and Biography* 2:224–28.

———. 1879a. "The Descendants of Jöran Kyn, the Founder of Upland." Part 2. *Pennsylvania Magazine of History and Biography* 3:88–95, 206–33, 331–41, 447–57.

———, ed. 1879b. "Taxables Living Within the Jurisdiction of New Castle Court in November, 1677." *Pennsylvania Magazine of History and Biography* 3:352–54.

———. 1879c. "The Third Swedish Expedition to New Sweden." *Pennsylvania Magazine of History and Biography* 3:462–64.

———. 1880. "The Descendants of Jöran Kyn, the Founder of Upland." Part 3. *Pennsylvania Magazine of History and Biography* 4:99–112, 234–45, 343–60, 484–500.

———. 1881. "The Descendants of Jöran Kyn, the Founder of Upland." Part 4. *Pennsylvania Magazine of History and Biography* 5:85–101, 217–22, 334–42, 451–61, 480.

———. 1882. "The Descendants of Jöran Kyn, the Founder of Upland." Part 5. *Pennsylvania Magazine of History and Biography* 6:106–10, 207–16, 329–41, 453–57.

———, ed. and trans. 1883a. "An Account of the Seditious False Königsmark in New Sweden." *Pennsylvania Magazine of History and Biography* 7:219–20.

———. 1883b. "The Descendants of Jöran Kyn, the Founder of Upland." Part 6. *Pennsylvania Magazine of History and Biography* 7:94–100, 200–205, 299–308, 464–74.

———, ed. 1883c. "Returns of Inhabitants and Lands Owned and Improved in Portions of Philadelphia County in 1684." *Pennsylvania Magazine of History and Biography* 7:106–7.

Kegley, F. B. 1938. *Kegley's Virginia Frontier.* Roanoke: Southwest Virgina Historical Society.

Keith, Charles P. 1969. *Chronicles of Pennsylvania from the English Revolution to the Peace of Aix-la-Chapelle.* 3 vols. Port Washington, N.Y.: Ira J. Friedman.

Keller, Albert G. 1947. *Societal Evolution.* New Haven: Yale University Press.

Kelly, J. Frederick. 1940. "A Seventeenth-Century Connecticut Log House." *Old-Time New England* 31 (October): 28–40.

Kennedy, Michael S., ed. 1964. *Cowboys and Cattlemen: A Roundup from Montana.* New York: Hastings House.

Kenny, James. 1913. "Journal of James Kenny, 1761–1763." *Pennsylvania Magazine of History and Biography* 37:1–47, 152–201.

Kentucky Heritage Commission and Boone County Fiscal Court. 1979. *Survey of Historic Sites in Kentucky: Boone County.* Newport, Ky.: Otto Printing.

Kephart, Horace. 1916. *Our Southern Highlanders.* New York: Outing Publishing Co.

Keränen, Jorma. 1984. *Kainuun asuttaminen.* Jyväskylä: Studia historica Jyväskyläensia, no. 28.

Kerkhoff, Jennie Ann. 1962. *Old Homes of Page County, Virginia.* Luray, Va.: Lauck & Co.

Kerkkonen, Martti. 1938. "Delawaren siirtokunta ja Pietari Kalm." *Historiallinen aikakauskirja* 36:96–121.

———. 1969–70. "New Sweden and Finland." *American Swedish Historical Foundation Yearbook,* pp. 38–41.

Keyland, Nils. 1954. *Folkliv i Värmlands finnmarker: Efterlämnade uppsatser och bilder.* Stockholm: Nordiska museets handlingar, no. 46.

Kimball, Fiske. 1922. *Domestic Architecture of the American Colonies.* New York: Charles Scribner's Sons.

Kimball, Gorham G. 1954. "Trailing Sheep from California to Idaho in 1865: The Journal of Gorham Gates Kimball," edited by Edward N. Wentworth. *Agricultural History* 28:49–83.

Kirch, Patrick. 1980. "The Archaeological Study of Adaptation: Theoretical and Methodological Issues." In *Advances in Archaeological Method and Theory,* vol. 3, edited by Michael B. Schiffer, pp. 101–56. New York: Academic Press.

Klepp, Susan. 1982. "Five Early Pennsylvania Censuses." *Pennsylvania Magazine of History and Biography* 106:483–514.

Kniffen, Fred B. 1936. "Louisiana House Types." *Annals of the Association of American Geographers* 26:179–93.

———. 1965. "Folk Housing: Key to Diffusion." *Annals of the Association of American Geographers* 55:549–77.

———. 1969. "On Corner Timbering." *Pioneer America* 1 (January): 1–8.

Kniffen, Fred B., and Glassie, Henry. 1966. "Building in Wood in the Eastern United States: A Time-Place Perspective." *Geographical Review* 56:40–66.

Koivukangas, Olavi, and Toivonen, Simo. 1978. *Suomen siirtolaisuuden ja maassamuuton bibliografia.* Turku/Åbo, Finland: Siirtolaisuusinstituutti.

Kolehmainen, Alfred, and Laine, Veijo A. 1979. *Suomalainen talonpoikaistalo.* Helsinki: Kustannusosakeyhtiö Otava.

Konrad, Victor. 1986. "Soil Analysis and Archaeology in the Northeastern Woodlands." Paper read at the meetings of the Association of American Geographers, Minneapolis, May 6. (Abstract in *AAG '86, Twin Cities, Abstracts,* Washington, D.C.: Association of American Geographers, 1986, session 153.)

Korhonen, Teppo. 1985. "Kansankulttuurin juuret." In *Suomen historia,* vol. 2, edited by Yrjö Blomstedt, pp. 349–414. Helsinki: Weilin and Göös.

Kortesalmi, J. Juhani. 1969. "Suomalaisten huuhtaviljely." *Oulun historiaseuran julkaisuja, Scripta Historica* 2:278–362.

Koskela, Alice. 1985. "Finnish Log Homestead Buildings in Long Valley." In *Idaho Folklife: Homesteads to Headstones,* edited by Louie W. Attebery, pp. 29–36. Salt Lake City: University of Utah Press; Boise: Idaho State Historical Society.

Kozee, William C. 1973. *Pioneer Families of Eastern and Southeastern Kentucky.* Baltimore: Genealogical Publishing Co.

Kuethe, J. Louis. 1936. "A List of Maryland Mills, Taverns, Forges, and Furnaces of 1795." *Maryland Historical Magazine* 31:155–69.

Kujala, Viljo. 1952. "Vegetation." *Fennia* 72:209–34.

Kulturhistorisk leksikon for nordisk middelalder. 1956–77. Vols. 1–21. København, Denmark: Rosenkilde og Bagger.

Laer, A. J. F. van. 1920–23. *Minutes of the Court of Fort Orange and Beverwyck.* 2 vols. Albany: University of the State of New York.

Lagus, F. H. B. 1893. *Kertomus asuinrakennuksista Sumiaisissa.* Helsinki: Suomalaisen kirjallisuuden seuran toimituksia, 81 osa, Kansatieteellisiä kertomuksia, 1.

Lancaster, Clay. 1961. *Ante Bellum Houses of the Bluegrass: The Development of Residential Architecture in Fayette County, Kentucky.* Lexington: University of Kentucky Press.

Langsam, Walter E., and Johnson, William G. 1985. *Historic Architecture of Bourbon County, Kentucky.* Georgetown, Ky.: Historic Paris-Bourbon County, Inc., and Kentucky Heritage Council.

Larson, Eather E. 1963. *Swedish Commentators on America, 1638–1865: An Annotated List of Selected Manuscript and Printed Materials.* New York: New York Public Library and Chicago: Swedish Pioneer Historical Society.

Larsson, C. 1876. *Björnjagten i Vermlands finbygd.* Published print. Copy available in Värmlands Museum, Karlstad.

Laukkanen, Kari. 1982. "Metsäsuomalaisten sananlaskut." In *Ulkosuomalaisia,* pp. 207–38. Kalevalaseuran vuosikirja, no. 62. Helsinki: Suomalaisen kirjallisuuden seura.

Lawson, John. 1967. *A New Voyage to Carolina.* Edited by Hugh T. Lefler. Chapel Hill: University of North Carolina Press.

Lefferts, H. L. 1977. "Frontier Demography: An Introduction." In *The Frontier: Comparative Studies,* edited by David H. Miller and Jerome O. Steffen, pp. 33–55. Norman: University of Oklahoma Press.

Leiby, Adrian C. 1964. *The Early Dutch and Swedish Settlers of New Jersey.* Princeton: D. van Nostrand Co.

Lemon, James T. 1966. "The Agricultural Practices of National Groups in Eighteenth-Century Southeastern Pennsylvania." *Geographical Review* 56:467–96.

———. 1972. *The Best Poor Man's Country: A Geographical Study of Early Southeastern Pennsylvania.* Baltimore: Johns Hopkins Press, 1972.

Levander, Lars. 1943–47. *Övre Dalarnes bondekultur under 1800-talets förra hälft.* Skrifter utgivna av kungl. Gustav Adolfs akademien för folklivsforskning, no. 11, pts. 1–3. 3 vols. Stockholm: Jonson & Winter, 1943, 1944; Lund: Carl Bloms Boktryckeri, 1947.

Levick, James J. 1893. "The Early Welsh Quakers and Their Emigration to Pennsylvania." *Pennsylvania Magazine of History and Biography* 17:385–413.

Lewis, Kenneth E. 1984. *The American Frontier: An Archaeological Study of Settlement Pattern and Process.* Orlando, Fla.: Academic Press.

——. 1987. "The Agricultural Colonization of Southern Michigan: A Perspective for Archaeological Research." Paper presented at the Second Conference on Historic Archaeology in Illinois, Normal, Ill., August 7.

Leyburn, James G. 1935. *Frontier Folkways.* New Haven: Yale University Press.

——. 1962. *The Scotch-Irish: A Social History.* Chapel Hill: University of North Carolina Press.

Linderholm, Helmer. 1974. *Sveriges finnmarker.* Stockholm: Tidens förlag.

——. 1976. *Nya Sveriges historia: vårt stora Indianäventyr.* Stockholm: Tidens förlag.

Lindeström, Peter. 1925. *Geographia Americae, with an Account of the Delaware Indians.* Translated and edited by Amandus Johnson. Philadelphia: Swedish Colonial Society.

Lindgren, Gunnar. 1939. *Falbygden och dess närmaste omgivning vid 1600-talets mitt: en kulturgeografisk studie.* Geographica: skrifter från Upsala Universitets Geografiska Institution, no. 6. Uppsala, Sweden: Appelbergs boktryckeriaktiebolag.

Linley, John. 1972. *Architecture of Middle Georgia: The Oconee Area.* Athens: University of Georgia Press.

——. 1982. *The Georgia Catalogue, Historic American Buildings Survey: A Guide to the Architecture of the State.* Athens: University of Georgia Press.

Little-Stokes, Ruth, ed. 1979. *An Inventory of Historic Architecture, Caswell County, North Carolina.* Raleigh: Division of Archives and History, North Carolina Department of Cultural Resources and Caswell County Historical Association.

Lloyd, L. 1870. *Peasant Life in Sweden.* London: Tinsley Brothers.

Lockridge, Kenneth A. 1970. *A New England Town, the First Hundred Years: Dedham, Massachusetts, 1636–1736.* New York: W. W. Norton & Co.

Lönborg, Sven. 1901. "Till finnskogen." *Svenska Turistföreningens Årsskrift,* pp. 227–43.

——. 1902. "Finnmarkerna i mellersta Skandinavien." *Ymer* 22:65–90, 361–408, 465–504.

Long, Amos, Jr. 1961. "Fences in Rural Pennsylvania." *Pennsylvania Folklife* 12 (Summer): 30–35.

Longyear, Harriet M. 1915. "The Settlement of Clinton County." *Michigan Historical Collections* 39:360–64.

Lönnrot, Elias. 1963. *The Kalevala, or Poems of the Kaleva District.* Translated by Francis P. Magoun, Jr. Cambridge, Mass.: Harvard University Press.

Lossing, Benson J. 1859. "Daniel Boone." *Harper's New Monthly Magazine* 19 (October): 577–601.

Louhi, E. A. 1925. *The Delaware Finns; or, The First Permanent Settle-*

ments in Pennsylvania, Delaware, West New Jersey, and Eastern Part of Maryland. New York: Humanity Press, 1925.

Lounsbury, Carl. 1977. "The Development of Domestic Architecture in the Albemarle Region." *North Carolina Historical Review* 54:17–48.

———. 1980. *Alamance County Architectural Heritage.* N.p.: Alamance County Historical Properties Commission.

Lundén, Thomas. 1981. "Proximity, Equality, and Difference: The Evolution of the Norwegian-Swedish Boundary Landscape." *Regio Basiliensis* 22:128–39.

Lyle, Royster, Jr. 1970–74. "Log Buildings in Rockbridge County." *Proceedings of the Rockbridge Historical Society* 8:3–12.

———. 1972. "Log Buildings in the Valley of Virginia." *Roanoke Valley Historical Society Journal* 8, no. 1:24–31.

Madden, Betty I. 1974. *Art, Crafts, and Architecture in Early Illinois.* Urbana: University of Illinois Press.

Magnusson, Jan. 1877. "Fryksdals härad och Finnskogar i äldre tider." *Land och Folk*, no. 3, pp. 129–56.

Mahr, August C. 1954. "Aboriginal Culture Traits as Reflected in Eighteenth-Century Delaware Indian Tree Names." *Ohio Journal of Science* 54, no. 6:380–87.

———. 1955. "Eighteenth Century Terminology of Delaware Indian Cultivation and Use of Maize: A Semantic Analysis." *Ethnohistory* 2:209–40.

Mann, Dale; Skinulis, Richard; and Shanoff, Nancy. 1979. *The Complete Log House Book: A Canadian Guide to Building with Log.* Toronto: McGraw-Hill Ryerson.

Manninen, I. 1934. "Rakennukset." In *Suomen suku*, vol. 3, edited by A. Kannisto et al., pp. 242–96. Helsinki: Kustannusosakeyhtiö Otava.

Margolis, Maxine. 1977. "Historical Perspectives on Frontier Agriculture as an Adaptive Strategy." *American Ethnologist* 4:42–64.

Marshall, Howard W. 1981. *Folk Architecture in Little Dixie: A Regional Culture in Missouri.* Columbia: University of Missouri Press.

Martin, Charles E. 1984. *Hollybush: Folk Building and Social Change in an Appalachian Community.* Knoxville: University of Tennessee Press.

Martin, Sheila. 1969–70. "Margaret Mattson, Accused Witch." *American Swedish Historical Foundation Yearbook*, pp. 15–20.

Mathews, Mitford M., ed. 1951. *A Dictionary of Americanisms on Historical Principles.* 2 vols. Chicago: University of Chicago Press.

Matson, Ole. 1902–8. "Fra Solørs Finnskog." *Norvegia: Tidsskrift for det norske folks maal og minder* 2:22–38, 98–120, 190–224, 256–80.

McDonald, Forrest, and McDonald, Ellen Shapiro. 1980. "The Ethnic Origins of the American People, 1790." *William and Mary Quarterly*, 3rd ser., 37 (April): 179–99.

McDonald, Forrest, and McWhiney, Grady. 1980a. "The Celtic South." *History Today* 30:11–15.

———. 1980b. "The South from Self-Sufficiency to Peonage: An Interpretation." *American Historical Review* 85:1095–118.

McDowell, Bart, and Abell, Sam. 1986. "C. M. Russell, Cowboy Artist." *National Geographic* 169 (January): 60–95.

McKnight, William J. 1905. *A Pioneer Outline History of Northwestern Pennsylvania.* Philadelphia: J. B. Lippincott.

McManis, Douglas R. 1975. *Colonial New England: A Historical Geography.* New York: Oxford University Press.

McRaven, William H. 1937. *Life and Times of Edward Swanson.* Nashville and Kingsport, Tenn.: Kingsport Press.

McWhiney, Grady, and McDonald, Forrest. 1983. "Celtic Names in the Antebellum Southern United States." *Names* 31:89–102.

Mead, W. R. 1959. "Frontier Themes in Finland." *Geography* 44:145–56.

Meine, F. J. 1955. *The Crockett Almanacks, 1835–1838.* Chicago: Caxton Club.

Meinig, Donald W. 1957–58. "The American Colonial Era: A Geographic Commentary." *Proceedings of the Royal Geographical Society, South Australian Branch Session,* pp. 1–22.

———. 1965. "The Mormon Culture Region: Strategies and Patterns in the Geography of the American West, 1847–1964." *Annals of the Association of American Geographers* 55:191–220.

———. 1969. *Imperial Texas: An Interpretive Essay in Cultural Geography.* Austin: University of Texas Press.

———. 1972. "American Wests: Preface to a Geographical Interpretation." *Annals of the Association of American Geographers* 62:159–84.

———. 1976. "Spatial Models of a Sequence of Transatlantic Interactions." *Twenty-third International Geographical Congress: Historical Geography, Section 9,* pp. 30–35. Moscow: I.G.C.

———. 1986. *The Shaping of America: A Geographical Perspective on Five Hundred Years of History,* vol. 1. New Haven: Yale University Press.

Meitzen, August. 1895. *Siedelung und Agrarwesen der Westgermanen und Ostgermanen, der Kelten, Römer, Finnen und Slawen.* 3 vols. and atlas. Berlin: Wilhelm Hertz.

Melville, Herman. 1969. *Great Short Works of Herman Melville.* Edited by Warner Berthoff. New York: Harper & Row.

Mercer, Eric. 1975. *English Vernacular Houses: A Study of Traditional Farmhouses and Cottages.* London: Her Majesty's Stationery Office.

Mercer, Henry C. 1927a. "The Origin of Log Houses in the United States." Part 1. *Old-Time New England* 18 (July): 2–20.

———. 1927b. "The Origin of Log Houses in the United States." Part 2. *Old-Time New England* 18 (October): 51–63.

Meredith, Mamie. 1951. "The Nomenclature of American Pioneer Fences." *Southern Folklore Quarterly* 15:109–51.

Merrill, Boynton, Jr. 1985. *Old Henderson Homes and Buildings.* Henderson, Ky.: Historic Henderson Publishing Council.

Michael, Ronald L., and Carlisle, Ronald C. 1976. "A Log Settler's Fort/Home." *Pennsylvania Folklife* 25 (Spring): 39–46.

———. 1979. *Historical and Architectural Study of Buildings and Artifacts Associated with the Bulltown Historic Area, Burnsville Lake Project, Braxton County, West Virginia.* Huntington, W.Va.: U.S. Army Corps of Engineers.

Michaux, F. A. 1805. *Travels to the West of the Alleghany Mountains, in the States of Ohio, Kentucky, and Tennessea.* London: B. Crosby & Co.

Mikesell, Marvin W. 1960. "Comparative Studies in Frontier History." *Annals of the Association of American Geographers* 50:62–74.

Miller, David H., and Savage, William W., Jr. 1977. "Ethnic Stereotypes and the Frontier: A Comparative Study of Roman and American Experience." In *The Frontier: Comparative Studies,* edited by David H. Miller and Jerome O. Steffen, pp. 109–37. Norman: University of Oklahoma Press.

Miller, Donald C. 1977. *Ghost Towns of Washington and Oregon.* Boulder, Colo.: Pruett Publishing Co.

Miller, Francis T.; Lanier, Robert S.; and Rodenbough, Theo. F. 1911–12. *The Photographic History of the Civil War.* 10 vols. New York: Review of Reviews.

Mitchell, Robert D. 1966. "The Presbyterian Church as an Indicator of Westward Expansion in Eighteenth Century America." *Professional Geographer* 18:293–99.

———. 1977. *Commercialism and Frontier: Perspectives on the Early Shenandoah Valley.* Charlottesville: University Press of Virginia.

———. 1978. "The Formation of Early American Cultural Regions: An Interpretation." In *European Settlement and Development in North America: Essays on Geographical Change in Honour and Memory of Andrew Hill Clark,* edited by James R. Gibson, pp. 66–90. Toronto: University of Toronto Press.

Moffett, Marian, and Wodehouse, Lawrence. 1984. *The Cantilever Barn in East Tennessee.* Knoxville: University of Tennessee School of Architecture.

Moize, Elizabeth A. 1985. "Daniel Boone: First Hero of the Frontier." *National Geographic* 168 (December): 812–41.

Montelius, Sigvard. 1953. "The Burning of Forest Land for the Cultivation of Crops: 'Svedjebruk' in Central Sweden." *Geografiska Annaler* 35:41–54.

———. 1960. "Finn Settlement in Central Sweden." *Geografiska Annaler* 42:285–93.

Montell, W. Lynwood. 1986. *Killings: Folk Justice in the Upper South.* Lexington: University Press of Kentucky.

Montell, W. Lynwood, and Morse, Michael. 1976. *Kentucky Folk Architecture.* Lexington: University Press of Kentucky.

Mood, Fulmer. 1952. "Studies in the History of American Settled Areas and Frontier Lines." *Agricultural History* 26:16–34.

Morrison, Hugh. 1952. *Early American Architecture: From the First Colonial Settlements to the National Period.* New York: Oxford University Press.

Morton, Oren F. 1911. *A History of Highland County, Virginia.* Monterey, Va.: By the author.

Mulkearn, Lois, and Pugh, Edwin. 1954. *A Traveller's Guide to Historic Western Pennsylvania.* Pittsburgh: University of Pittsburgh Press.

Muntz, Alfred P. 1959. "The Changing Geography of the New Jersey Woodlands, 1600–1900." Ph.D. diss., University of Wisconsin.

Murray, Ruth C. 1982. "The Absalom Autrey Log House, Lincoln Parish, Louisiana." *Pioneer America* 14:137–40.

Myers, Albert C., ed. 1912. *Narratives of Early Pennsylvania, West New Jersey, and Delaware, 1630–1707.* New York: Charles Scribner's Sons.

Myrdal, Janken. 1979. "Hägnadernas historia." *Bygd och natur,* pp. 97–110.

Nelson, Dean E. 1982. "Right Nice Little Houses: Impermanent Camp Architecture of the American Civil War." In *Perspectives in Vernacular Architecture,* edited by Camille Wells, pp. 79–93. Annapolis, Md.: Vernacular Architecture Forum.

Nelson, Helge. 1943. *The Swedes and the Swedish Settlements in North America.* Lund, Sweden: C. W. K. Gleerup.

Newcomb, Rexford. 1950. *Architecture of the Old Northwest Territory.* Chicago: University of Chicago Press.

———. 1953. *Architecture in Old Kentucky.* Urbana: University of Illinois Press.

New Jersey Archives (Documents Relating to the Colonial History of the State of New Jersey). 1880–1924. 1st ser. 33 vols. Various places, publishers, and editors.

Newton, Milton B., Jr. 1974. "Cultural Preadaptation and the Upland South." *Geoscience and Man* 5:143–54.

Newton, Milton B., Jr., and Pulliam–Di Napoli, Linda. 1977. "Log Houses as Public Occasions: A Historical Theory." *Annals of the Association of American Geographers* 67:360–83.

Nichols, Frederick D. 1976. *The Architecture of Georgia.* Savannah, Ga.: Beehive Press.

Nickels, Sylvie; Kallas, Hillar; and Friedman, Phillipa. 1973. *Finland: An Introduction.* New York and Washington: Praeger.

Nickul, Karl. 1977. *The Lappish Nation: Citizens of Four Countries.* Bloomington: Indiana University Research Center for Language and Semiotic Studies.

Nilsson, Yngve. 1938. "Norra Värmland vid tiden för den finska kolonisationen." *Svensk Geografisk Årsbok,* no. 14, pp. 7–28.

———. 1950. *Bygd och näringsliv i norra Värmland: en kulturgeografisk studie.* Meddelanden från Lunds Universitets Geografiska Institution, Avhandlingar, no. 18. Lund, Sweden: C. W. K. Gleerup.

Noble, Allen G. 1984. *Wood, Brick, and Stone: The North American Settlement Landscape.* 2 vols. Amherst: University of Massachusetts Press.

Nordmann, Petrus. 1888. *Finnarna i mellersta Sverige.* Helsinki: Tidnings- & Tryckeri-Aktiebolagets Tryckeri.

Nordström, Fritz. 1986. "Olof Stille of New Sweden." *Swedish American Genealogist,* 6:97–106.

Norris, Darrell A. 1982. "Ontario Fences and the American Scene." *American Review of Canadian Studies* 12 (Summer): 37–50.

Norton, James S., ed. 1973. *New Jersey in 1793: An Abstract and Index of the 1793 Militia Census of the State of New Jersey.* Salt Lake City: N.p.

Norton, Margaret C., ed. 1934. *Illinois Census Returns 1820.* Collections of the Illinois State Historical Library, vol. 26. Springfield: Trustees of the Illinois State Historical Library.

Nowlin, William. 1883. "The Bark-Covered House; or, Pioneer Life in Michigan." *Report of the Pioneer Society of the State of Michigan* 4:480–541.

Odhner, C. T. 1879. "The Founding of New Sweden, 1637–1642." *Pennsylvania Magazine of History and Biography* 3:269–84, 395–411.

Ohio Library Foundation. 1964. *1820 Federal Population Census, Ohio: Index.* Columbus: Ohio Library Foundation.

Olovsson, Olov. 1979. *Finska släktnamn i mellersta Sverige och Norge.* Torsby, Sweden: ABE-Tryck.

Osburn, Mary M., ed. "The Atascosita Census of 1826." *Texana* 1 (1963): 299–321.

Østberg, Kristian. 1931. "Finnskogene i Norge." Part 1. *Norsk geografisk tidsskrift* 3:438–88.

———. 1932. "Finnskogene i Norge." Part 2. *Norsk geografisk tidsskrift* 4:121–63, 213–54.

———. 1935. "Trekk av finnskogenes kulturhistorie." *Norsk geografisk tidsskrift* 5:272–93.

Oszuscik, Philippe. 1986. "The Carolina Heritage in Mobile and Southwest Alabama." *Pioneer America Society Transactions* 9:63–70.

Otto, John S. 1983. "Southern 'Plain Folk' Agriculture: A Reconsideration." *Plantation Society in the Americas* 2 (April):29–36.

Otto, John S., and Anderson, Nain E. 1982. "The Diffusion of Upland South Folk Culture, 1790–1840." *Southeastern Geographer* 22 (November): 89–98.

Otto, John S., and Burns, Augustus M., III. 1981. "Traditional Agricultural Practices in the Arkansas Highlands." *Journal of American Folklore* 94:166–87.

Palimpsest. 1960. Vol. 41 (November): cover illustration.

Palmqvist, Albert. 1953. "När kom finnarna till Värmland." In *Värmland förr och nu* 51:21–34. Karlstad, Sweden.

Papenfuse, Edward C., and Coale, Joseph M., III. 1982. *The Hammond-Harwood House Atlas of Historical Maps of Maryland, 1608–1908.* Baltimore: Johns Hopkins University Press.

Parker, W. B. 1984. *Notes Taken during the Expedition Commanded by Capt. R. B. Marcy, U.S.A., through Unexplored Texas.* Austin: Texas State Historical Association.

Parrington, Michael; Schenck, Helen; and Thibault, Jacqueline. 1984. "The Material World of the Revolutionary War Soldier at Valley Forge." In *The Scope of Historical Archaeology: Essays in Honor of John L. Cotter,* edited by David G. Orr and Daniel G. Crozier, pp. 125–61. Philadelphia: Occasional Publication of the Department of Anthropology, University of Pennsylvania.

Paschall, Thomas. 1912. "Letter of Thomas Paschall, 1683." In *Narratives of Early Pennsylvania, West New Jersey, and Delaware, 1630–1707,* edited by Albert C. Myers, pp. 245–54. New York: Charles Scribner's Sons.

Pastorius, Francis Daniel. 1912. "Circumstantial Geographical Description of Pennsylvania, by Francis Daniel Pastorius, 1700." In *Narratives of Early Pennsylvania, West New Jersey, and Delaware, 1630–1707,* edited by Albert C. Myers, pp. 353–448. New York: Charles Scribner's Sons.

Patrick, James, and Tomlan, Michael A. 1981. *Architecture in Tennessee, 1768–1897.* Knoxville: University of Tennessee Press.

Paulaharju, Samuli. 1906. *Kansatieteellinen kuvaus asuinrakennuksista Uudellakirkolla Viipurin läänissä.* Helsinki: Suomalaisen kirjallisuuden seuran toimituksia, 81 osa. Kansatieteellisiä kertomuksia, 6.

Paulsen, Frederik. 1972. "Das neue Rom: Der Anteil der Friesen an der Entstehung New Yorks." *Nordfriesland: Kultur-Politik-Wirtschaft,* pp. 265–76.

Paynter, Robert. 1982. *Models of Spatial Inequality: Settlement Patterns in Historical Archeology.* New York: Academic Press.

Peck, John M. 1965. *Forty Years of Pioneer Life: Memoir of John Mason Peck.* Edited by Rufus Babcock. Carbondale and Edwardsville: Southern Illinois University Press.

Peet, Richard. 1969. "The Spatial Expansion of Commercial Agriculture in the Nineteenth Century: A von Thünen Explanation." *Economic Geography* 45:283–301.

———. 1970–71. "Von Thünen Theory and the Dynamics of Agricultural Expansion." *Explorations in Economic History* 8:181–201.

Penn, William. 1912a. "Letter from William Penn to the Committee of the Free Society of Traders, 1683." In *Narratives of Early Pennsylva-*

nia, *West New Jersey, and Delaware, 1630–1707,* edited by Albert C. Myers, pp. 217–44. New York: Charles Scribner's Sons.

————. 1912b. "A Further Account of the Province of Pennsylvania, by William Penn, 1685." In *Narratives of Early Pennsylvania, West New Jersey, and Delaware, 1630–1707,* edited by Albert C. Myers, pp. 255–78. New York: Charles Scribner's Sons.

Pennsylvania Archives. 1852–1934. Ser. 1–9. 119 vols. Philadelphia and Harrisburg: Joseph Severns, Lane S. Hart, State Library, and others.

Perrin, Richard W. E. 1966. "Log Houses in Wisconsin." *Antiques* 89 (June): 867–71.

Peters, Bernard D. 1973. "Changing Ideas about the Use of Vegetation as an Indicator of Soil Quality: Example of New York and Michigan." *Journal of Geography* 72:18–28.

Petersen, William J. 1960. "The Pioneer Log Cabin." *Palimpsest* 41 (November): 485–516.

Phleps, Hermann. 1942. *Holzbaukunst: Der Blockbau.* Karlsruhe, Germany: Fachblattverlag Dr. Albert Bruder.

Pierson, George W. 1940. "The Frontier and Frontiersmen of Turner's Essays." *Pennsylvania Magazine of History and Biography* 64:449–78.

Pillsbury, Richard. 1977. "Patterns in the Folk and Vernacular House Forms of the Pennsylvania Culture Region." *Pioneer America* 9:12–31.

————. 1983. "The Europeanization of the Cherokee Settlement Landscape Prior to Removal: A Georgia Case Study." *Geoscience and Man* 23:59–69.

Pitman, Leon S. 1973. "A Survey of Nineteenth-Century Folk Housing in the Mormon Culture Region." Ph.D. diss., Louisiana State University.

Platt, Kenneth B. 1978. *Salmon River Saga.* Fairfield, Wash.: Ye Galleon Press.

Pocius, Gerald L. 1977. "Walls and Fences in Susquehanna County, Pennsylvania." *Pennsylvania Folklife* 26 (Spring): 9–20.

Pohl, James W., and Hardin, Stephen L. 1985–86. "The Military History of the Texas Revolution: An Overview." *Southwestern Historical Quarterly* 89:209–308.

Potter, Dorothy W., ed. and comp. 1974. *Index to 1820 North Carolina Census, Supplemented from Tax Lists and Other Sources.* N.p.: By the author.

Potter, Theodore E. 1907. "A Boy's Story of Pioneer Life in Michigan." *Michigan Pioneer and Historical Society, Historical Collections* 35:393–99.

Price, Beulah M. D'Olive. 1970. "The Dog-Trot Log Cabin: A Development in American Folk Architecture." *Mississippi Folklore Register* 4, no. 3: 84–89.

Price, Cynthia R., and Price, James E. 1981. "Investigation of Settlement and Subsistence Systems in the Ozark Border Region of Southeast Missouri during the First Half of the Nineteenth Century: The Widow Harris Cabin Project." *Ethnohistory* 28 (Summer): 237–58.

Price, Edward T. 1951. "The Melungeons: A Mixed-Blood Strain of the Southern Appalachians." *Geographical Review* 41:256–71.

Price, H. Wayne. 1980. "The Double-Crib Log Barns of Calhoun County." *Journal of the Illinois State Historical Society* 73 (Summer): 140–60.

Prigogine, Ilya; Nicolis, Gregoire; and Babloyantz, Agnes. 1972a. "Thermodynamics of Evolution." Part 1. *Physics Today* 25 (November): 23–28.

———. 1972b. "Thermodynamics of Evolution." Part 2. *Physics Today* 25 (December): 35–41.

Primack, Martin L. 1962. "Land Clearing under Nineteenth-Century Techniques: Some Preliminary Calculations." *Journal of Economic History* 22:484–97.

Printz, Johan. 1912a. "Report of Governor Johan Printz, 1644." In *Narratives of Early Pennsylvania, West New Jersey, and Delaware, 1630–1707*, edited by Albert C. Myers, pp. 91–116. New York: Charles Scribner's Sons.

———. 1912b. "Report of Governor John Printz, 1647." In *Narratives of Early Pennsylvania, West New Jersey, and Delaware, 1630–1707*, edited by Albert C. Myers, pp. 117–29. New York: Charles Scribner's Sons.

Proudfoot, V. B. 1959. "Clachans in Ireland." *Gwerin* 2:110–22.

Purvis, Thomas L. 1982a. "The Ethnic Descent of Kentucky's Early Population: A Statistical Investigation of European and American Sources of Emigration, 1790–1820." *Register of the Kentucky Historical Society* 80 (July): 253–66.

———. 1982b. "The European Origins of New Jersey's Eighteenth-Century Population." *New Jersey History* 100:15–31.

———. 1984. "The European Ancestry of the United States Population, 1790." *William and Mary Quarterly*, 3rd ser., 41:85–101.

Rambo, Ormond Jr. 1948. "The First Pioneers: The Rambo Family." *American Swedish Historical Foundation Yearbook*, pp. 1–19.

Rambo, Simmeon B., and Watson, Sara Rambo. 1983. *The Rambo Heritage*. Easley, S.C.: Southern Historical Press.

Randolph, Vance. 1933. "A Fourth Ozark Word-List." *American Speech* 8:47–53.

Randolph, Vance, and Clemens, Nancy. 1936. "A Fifth Ozark Word List." *American Speech* 11:314–18.

Randolph, Wayne. 1979. "Wilderness Architecture: A Trapper's Cabin Survey." *Fourteenth Annual Traditional Craft Days: Studies in Traditional American Crafts*, pp. 6–8. Oneida, N.Y.: Madison County Historical Society.

Ränk, Gustav. 1962. *Die Bauernhausformen im baltischen Raum*. Würzburg, West Germany: Holzner-Verlag.

Rauanheimo, Akseli. 1921. "Rautalammin lahja Amerikalle." *Kansanvalistus–seuran kalenteri*, pp. 29–40.

Rauanheimo, Yrjö. 1938. "Delawaren suomalaiset." *Genos*, pp. 37–39.

Raup, H. F. 1947. "The Fence in the Cultural Landscape." *Western Folklore* 6:1–12.

Ravenswaay, Charles van. 1977. *The Arts and Architecture of German Settlements in Missouri*. Columbia: University of Missouri Press.

Rawle, William B. 1884. "The First Tax List for Philadelphia County, A.D. 1693." *Pennsylvania Magazine of History and Biography* 8:82–105.

Raymond, Eleanor. 1931. *Early Domestic Architecture of Pennsylvania*. New York: William Helburn.

Reed, Louis. 1967. *Warning in Appalachia: A Study of Wirt County, West Virginia*. Morgantown: West Virginia University Library.

Rehder, John B.; Morgan, John; and Medford, Joy L. 1979. "The Decline of Smokehouses in Grainger County, Tennessee." *West Georgia College Studies in the Social Sciences* 18 (June): 75–83.

Remington, Frederic. 1961. *Pony Tracks*. Norman: University of Oklahoma Press.

Rempel, John I. 1960. "The History and Development of Early Forms of

Building Construction in Ontario." Part 1. *Ontario History* 52:235–44.

———. 1961. "The History and Development of Early Forms of Building Construction in Ontario." Part 2. *Ontario History* 53:1–35.

———. 1967. *Building With Wood and Other Aspects of Nineteenth-Century Building in Ontario.* Toronto: University of Toronto Press.

Rennick, Robert M. 1984. *Kentucky Place Names.* Lexington: University Press of Kentucky.

Renqvist, Henrik. 1952. "The Inland Waters." *Fennia* 72:161–201.

Reponen, Astrid. 1934. "Vermlannin suomalaisalueen tuvista, saunoista ja riihistä." *Suomen museo* 41:55–77.

Retzius, Gustaf. 1885. *Finnland: Schilderungen aus seiner Natur, seiner alten Kultur und seinem heutigen Volksleben.* Translated by C. Appel. Berlin: Georg Reimer.

Reynolds, John E. 1938. *In French Creek Valley.* Meadville, Pa.: Crawford County Historical Society.

Rhoades, Robert E., and Thompson, Stephen I. 1975. "Adaptive Strategies in Alpine Environments: Beyond Ecological Particularism." *American Ethnologist* 2:535–51.

Rice, Otis K. 1975. *Frontier Kentucky.* Lexington: University Press of Kentucky.

Ridge, Martin. 1964. "Why They Went West." *American West* 1 (Summer): 40–57.

Riedl, Norbert F.; Ball, Donald B.; and Cavender, Anthony P. 1976. *A Survey of Traditional Architecture and Related Material Folk Culture Patterns in the Normandy Reservoir, Coffee County, Tennessee.* Department of Anthropology Report of Investigations, no. 17. Knoxville: University of Tennessee and Tennessee Valley Authority.

Rikkinen, Kalevi. 1977. *Suomen asutusmaantiede.* Helsinki: Kustannusosakeyhtiö Otava.

Rising, Johan. 1912a. "Report of Governor Johan Rising, 1654." In *Narratives of Early Pennsylvania, West New Jersey, and Delaware, 1630–1707,* edited by Albert C. Myers, pp. 131–51. New York: Charles Scribner's Sons.

———. 1912b. "Report of Governor Johan Rising, 1655." In *Narratives of Early Pennsylvania, West New Jersey, and Delaware, 1630–1707,* edited by Albert C. Myers, pp. 153–65. New York: Charles Scribner's Sons.

Roberts, Warren E. 1976a. "Field Work in Du Bois County, Indiana." *Echoes of History* 6 (January): 12–14.

———. 1976b. "Some Comments on Log Construction in Scandinavia and the United States." *Folklore Today: A Festschrift for Richard M. Dorson,* edited by Linda Dégh, Henry Glassie, and Felix J. Oinas, pp. 437–50. Bloomington: Indiana University Research Center for Language and Semiotic Studies.

———. 1985. *Log Buildings of Southern Indiana.* Bloomington: Ind.: Trickster Press.

Robinson, Philip S. 1984. *The Plantation of Ulster: British Settlement in an Irish Landscape, 1600–1670.* New York: St. Martin's Press.

Roe, Keith E. 1988. *Corncribs in History, Folklife, and Architecture.* Ames: Iowa State University Press.

Rohe, Randall. 1985. "Settlement Patterns of Logging Camps in the Great Lakes Region." *Journal of Cultural Geography* 6 (Fall/Winter): 79–108.

Romig, Walter. N.d. *Michigan Place Names.* Grosse Pointe, Mich.: By the author.

Rothert, Otto A. 1913. *A History of Muhlenberg County.* Louisville, Ky.: John P. Morton.

Russell, Carl P. 1977. *Firearms, Traps, and Tools of the Mountain Men.* Albuquerque: University of New Mexico Press.

Russell, Emily W. B. 1983. "Indian-Set Fires in the Forests of the Northeastern United States." *Ecology* 64:78–88.

Russell, George E. 1978. "The Swedish Settlement in Maryland, 1654." *American Genealogist* 54 (October): 203–10.

Russell, Jervis, ed. 1971. *Jimmy Come Lately: History of Clallam County.* Port Angeles, Wash.: Clallam County Historical Society.

Rutsch, Edward S., and Peters, Kim M. 1977. "Forty Years of Archaeological Research at Morristown National Historical Park, Morristown, New Jersey." *Historical Archaeology* 11:15–38.

Rydberg, Alexander. 1929. "Finnarna i Värmland." *Historisk Tidskrift* 41:418–24.

Ryden, George H. 1930. "The Hanson Family of Maryland." Part 1. *Swedish-American Historical Bulletin* 3 (June): 53–59. 4

———. 1931a. "The Hanson Family of Maryland." Part 2. *Swedish-American Historical Bulletin* 4 (February): 55–68.

———. 1931b. "The Hanson Family of Maryland." Part 3. *Swedish-American Historical Bulletin* 4 (June): 35–44.

Sahlins, Marshall D., and Service, Elman R., eds. 1960. *Evolution and Culture.* Ann Arbor: University of Michigan Press.

Salley, A. S., Jr. 1898. *History of Orangeburg County.* Orangeburg, S.C.: R. Lewis Berry.

Sandel, Andreas. 1906. "Extracts from the Journal of Rev. Andreas Sandel, Pastor of Gloria Dei Swedish Lutheran Church, Philadelphia, 1702–1719." *Pennsylvania Magazine of History and Biography* 30:287–99, 445–52.

Sandon, Eric. 1977. *Suffolk Houses: A Study of Domestic Architecture.* Woodbridge, Suffolk, England: Baron.

Sandvig, Anders. 1947. *Vår gamle bondebebyggelse.* Lillehammer, Norway: Maihaugen.

Sauer, Carl O. 1920. *The Geography of the Ozark Highland of Missouri.* Geographic Society of Chicago, Bulletin no. 7. Chicago: University of Chicago Press.

———. 1930. "Historical Geography and the Western Frontier." In *The Trans-Mississippi West*, edited by James F. Willard and Colin B. Goodykoontz, pp. 267–89. Boulder: University of Colorado.

———. 1941. "Foreword to Historical Geography." *Annals of the Association of American Geographers* 31:1–24.

Schafer, Joseph. 1936–37. "High Society in Pioneer Wisconsin." *Wisconsin Magazine of History* 20:447–61.

Schiffer, Margaret B. 1976. *Survey of Chester County, Pennsylvania, Architecture: Seventeenth, Eighteenth and Nineteenth Centuries.* Exton, Pa.: Schiffer Publishing.

Schoultz, Gösta von. 1951. *Dalslandsgårdar.* Stockholm: Tryckeri A.-B. Thule.

———. 1979. "Construction Techniques and Interior Layouts of Swedish Folk Houses," translated by Gary Stanton. *Folklore Forum* 12, nos. 2–3: 237–59.

Schroeder, Walter A. 1983. "Types of Settlement Patterns in the Ste. Genevieve District, 1750–1806." In *Cultural Geography of Missouri*, edited by Michael O. Roark, pp. 1–10. Cape Girardeau: Department of Earth Science, Southeast Missouri State University.

————. 1986. "Local Population Movement on the Eastern Ozarks Frontier, 1770–1820." Paper read at the meetings of the Association of American Geographers, Minneapolis, May 6. (Abstract in *AAG '86, Twin Cities, Abstracts*, Washington, D.C.: Association of American Geographers, 1986, session 182.)

Schultz, LeRoy G. 1983. "Log Barns of West Virginia." *Goldenseal*, Spring, pp. 40–45.

Schwartz, Sally. 1982. "Society and Culture in the Seventeenth-Century Delaware Valley." *Delaware History* 20 (Fall/Winter): 98–122.

Scisco, Louis D. 1930. "Baltimore County Records of 1668 and 1669." *Maryland Historical Magazine* 25:255–62.

————. 1933. "Baltimore County Land Records of 1673." *Maryland Historical Magazine* 28:345–50.

Schofield, Edna. 1936. "The Evolution and Development of Tennessee Houses." *Journal of the Tennessee Academy of Science* 11 (October): 229–40.

————. 1938. "The Origin of Settlement Patterns in Rural New England." *Geographical Review* 28:652–63.

Segerstedt, Albrekt J. N.d. "Finnbefolkningen i mellersta Sverige och sydöstra Norge." Manuscript. 5 vols. Kungliga Vitterhetsakademiens bibliotek, Stockholm, Sweden.

Séguin, Robert-Lionel. 1963. *Les granges du Québec du XVIIe au XIXe siècle*. Ottawa: Musée National du Canada.

Semple, Ellen C. 1901. "The Anglo-Saxons of the Kentucky Mountains." *Geographical Journal* 17:588–623.

————. 1903. *American History and Its Geographic Conditions*. Boston and New York: Houghton Mifflin Co.

Sherman, James E., and Sherman, Barbara H. 1969. *Ghost Towns of Arizona*. Norman: University of Oklahoma Press.

Shortridge, James R. 1980. "The Expansion of the Settlement Frontier in Missouri." *Missouri Historical Review* 75:64–90.

Shurtleff, Harold R. 1939. *The Log Cabin Myth: A Study of the Early Dwellings of the English Colonists in North America*. Cambridge: Harvard University Press.

Sipe, C. Hale. 1931. *The Indian Wars of Pennsylvania*. Harrisburg, Pa.: Telegraph Press.

Sirelius, U. T. 1906. "Über die primitiven Wohnungen der finnischen und ob-ugrischen Völker." Part 1. *Finnisch-ugrische Forschungen: Zeitschrift für finnisch-ugrische Sprach- und Volkskunde* 6:74–104, 121–54.

————. 1907. "Über die primitiven Wohnungen der finnischen und ob-ugrischen Völker." Part 2. *Finnisch-ugrische Forschungen: Zeitschrift für finnisch-ugrische Sprach- und Volkskunde* 7:55–128.

————. 1908. "Über die primitiven Wohnungen der finnischen und ob-ugrischen Völker." Part 3. *Finnisch-ugrische Forschungen: Zeitschrift für finnisch-ugrische Sprach- und Volkskunde* 8:8–59.

————. 1909. "Über die primitiven Wohnungen der finnischen und ob-ugrischen Völker." Part 4. *Finnisch-ugrische Forschungen: Zeitschrift für finnisch-ugrische Sprach- und Volkskunde* 9:17–113.

————. 1911. "Über die primitiven Wohnungen der finnischen und ob-ugrischen Völker." Part 5. *Finnisch-ugrische Forschungen: Zeitschrift für finnisch-ugrische Sprach- und Volkskunde* 11:23–122.

————. 1921. *Suomen kansanomaista kulttuuria*. 2 vols. Helsinki: Kustannusosakeyhtiö Otava.

———. 1923. "Väster och öster i Finlands materiella kultur." *Rig* 6:97–110.

Skottsberg, Carl. 1960. *Pehr Kalms brev till friherre Sten Carl Bielke.* Åbo, Finland: Skrifter utgivna av Svenska Litteratursällskapet i Finland, no. 382.

Sloane, Eric. 1955. *Our Vanishing Landscape.* New York: Funk & Wagnalls.

Smeds, Helmer. 1944. "Fäbodbebyggelsen i Finland: En historisk-geografisk översikt." *Geographica* 15:192–232.

Smith, Joseph. 1854. *Old Redstone; or, Historical Sketches of Western Presbyterianism, Its Early Ministers, Its Perilous Times, and Its First Records.* Philadelphia: Lippincott, Grambo & Co.

Smith, Philip H. 1877. *General History of Dutchess County.* Amenia, N.Y.: De Lacey & Walsh.

[Smith, Richard P.] 1836. *Col. Crockett's Exploits and Adventures.* Philadelphia: T. K. & P. G. Collins.

Smith, Samuel D. 1980. *Historical Background and Archaeological Testing of the Davy Crockett Birthplace State Historic Area, Greene County, Tennessee.* Nashville: Division of Archaeology, Tennessee Department of Conservation, Research Series, no. 6.

Smithwick, Noah. 1983. *The Evolution of a State; or, Recollections of Old Texas Days.* Rev. ed. Austin: University of Texas Press.

Snoddy, Daniel. N.d. "Daniel Snoddy Papers." Joint manuscripts, University of Missouri at Columbia. Copy provided by Division of Parks and Historic Preservation, Department of Natural Resources, State of Missouri, Jefferson City, Mo.

Soininen, Arvo M. 1959. "Burn-beating as the Technical Basis of Colonisation in Finland in the Sixteenth and Seventeenth Centuries." *Scandinavian Economic History Review,* no. 7, pp. 150–66.

———. 1961. *Pohjois-savon asuttaminen keski—ja uuden ajan vaihteessa.* Helsinki: Historiallisia tutkimuksia, julkaissut Suomen historiallinen seura 53.

———. 1974. *Vanha maataloutemme: maatalous ja maatalousväestö soumessa perinnäisen maatalouden loppukaudella 1720-luvulta 1870-luvulle.* Helsinki: Historiallisia tutkimuksia, julkaissut Suomen historiallinen seura 96.

Sømme, Axel. 1960. *A Geography of Norden.* Oslo: J. W. Cappelens Forlag.

Soper, Sarah E. 1900. "Reminiscence of Pioneer Life in Oakland County." *Michigan Pioneer and Historical Society, Historical Collections* 28:399–408.

Spenser, Edmund. 1970. *A View of the Present State of Ireland.* Edited by W. L. Renwick. Oxford: Clarendon Press. (Originally published 1598).

Sprinchorn, Carl K. S. 1883. "The History of the Colony of New Sweden." Part 1. Translated by Gregory B. Keen. *Pennsylvania Magazine of History and Biography* 7:395–419.

———. 1884. "The History of the Colony of New Sweden." Part 2. Translated by Gregory B. Keen. *Pennsylvania Magazine of History and Biography* 8:17–44, 129–59, 241–54.

Springer, Courtland B., and Springer, Ruth L. 1952–53a. "Burial Records, 1713–65, Holy Trinity (Old Swedes) Church." *Delaware History* 5:178–205.

———, eds. 1952–53b. "Communicant Records, 1713–56, Holy Trinity (Old Swedes) Church." Part 1. *Delaware History* 5:270–91.

———, eds. 1954–55. "Communicant Records, 1713–56, Holy Trinity

(Old Swedes) Church." Part 2. *Delaware History* 6:53–67, 140–58, 233–51, 307–32.

Srygley, F. D. 1891. *Seventy Years in Dixie: Recollections and Sayings of T. W. Caskey and Others*. Nashville, Tenn.: Gospel Advocate Co.

Stårck, Erik. 1909. "Till Johola. Skogsäfventyr från sommaren 1908." *Svenska turistföreningens årsskrift*, pp. 165–85.

Stansfield, Charles A., Jr. 1983. *New Jersey: A Geography*. Boulder, Colo.: Westview Press.

Steiner, Bernard C. 1913. "Kent County and Kent Island, 1656–1662." *Maryland Historical Magazine* 8:1–33.

Stemmons, John D., ed. 1972. *Pennsylvania in 1800: A Computerized Index to the 1800 Federal Population Schedules of the State of Pennsylvania*. Salt Lake City: By the author.

Stewart, Aura P. 1883. "St. Clair County." *Report of the Pioneer Society of the State of Michigan* 4:324–55.

Stewart-Abernathy, Leslie C. 1985. *Independent but Not Isolated: The Archeology of a Late Nineteenth Century Ozark Farmstead*. Pine Bluff: Arkansas Archeology Survey.

Stilgoe, John R. 1982. *Common Landscape of America, 1580 to 1845*. New Haven: Yale University Press.

Stone, Kirk H. 1973. *Northern Finland's Post-War Colonizing and Emigration: A Geographical Analysis of Rural Demographic Counter-Currents*. The Hague: Martinus Nijhoff.

Stoner, Paula. 1977. "Early Folk Architecture of Washington County." *Maryland Historical Magazine* 72:512–22.

Storrie, Margaret C. 1962. "The Scotch Whiskey Industry." *Institute of British Geographers, Transactions and Papers*, no. 31, pp. 97–114.

Stotz, Charles M. 1966. *The Architectural Heritage of Early Western Pennsylvania: A Record of Building before 1860*. Pittsburgh: University of Pittsburgh Press.

Strang, Everett N. 1970. "The Strang Family of Southern Jersey." *Genealogical Magazine of New Jersey* 45 (September): 111–19.

Strong, W. R. 1914. "Reminiscences." *Gainesville (Texas) Register*, June 16.

Stryker-Rodda, Kenn, ed. 1972. *Revolutionary Census of New Jersey: An Index, Based on Ratables, of the Inhabitants of New Jersey during the Period of the American Revolution*. Cottonport, La.: Polyanthos.

Sturgis, Samuel B. 1962. "Where Pennsylvania History Began." *American Swedish Historical Museum Yearbook*, pp. 25–38.

Substitutes for Georgia's Lost 1790 Census. 1975. Albany, Ga.: Delwyn Associates.

Summers, Lewis P. 1966. *History of Southwest Virginia, 1746–1786*. Baltimore: Genealogical Publishing Co.

"Suomalais-ugrilaisten kansojen asumus-alat [1885]." 1886. *Suomalais-ugrilaisen seuran aikakauskirja* 1: map following p. 135.

Suomen asutus 1560-luvulla: Kartasto. 1973. Forssa, Finland: Suomen historiallinen seura, käsikirjoja 7.

Suomen maantieteellinen seura. 1960. *Suomen kartasto*. Helsinki: Kustannusosakeyhtiö Otava.

"Surry County, North Carolina." 1862. *Harper's New Monthly Magazine* 25 (July): 178–85.

Sutherland, Stella H. 1936. *Population Distribution in Colonial America*. New York: Columbia University Press.

Svensk Ortförteckning 1960. 1960. Örebro, Sweden: Kungl. Generalpoststyrelsen, Kungl. Telestyrelsen & Kungl. Järnvägsstyrelsen. 882 pp.

Swaim, Doug, ed. 1978. *Carolina Dwelling: Towards Preservation of Place, in Celebration of the North Carolina Vernacular Landscape.* Raleigh: School of Design, North Carolina State University.

————. 1981. *Cabins and Castles: The History and Architecture of Buncombe County, North Carolina.* Raleigh: North Carolina Department of Cultural Resources.

Swank, Scott T. 1983. "The Architectural Landscape." In *Arts of the Pennsylvania Germans,* edited by Scott T. Swank, et al., pp. 20–34. New York: W. W. Norton & Co., for the Winterthur Museum.

Swanson, Roy W. 1930. "The Swedes and the New History." *Swedish-American Historical Bulletin* 3 (September): 7–21.

Swanton, John R. 1946. *The Indians of the Southeastern United States.* Bureau of American Ethnology, Bulletin no. 137. Washington, D.C.: Government Printing Office.

Sweden: Official Standard Names Approved by the United States Board on Geographic Names. 1963. Washington, D.C.: Office of Geography, Department of the Interior.

Swem, Earl G. 1934–36. *Virginia Historical Index.* 2 vols. Roanoke, Va.: Stone Co.

Swoboda, Otto. 1975–78. *Alte Holzbaukunst in Österreich.* 2 vols. Salzburg: Otto Müller.

Talve, Ilmar. 1953. "Drag ur finnbygdens näringsliv." In *Värmland förr och nu* 51:35–66. Karlstad, Sweden.

————. 1973–74. "Kulturgrenzen und Kulturgebiete Finnlands." *Ethnologia Europaea* 7, no. 1: 55–103.

————. 1979. *Suomen kansankulttuuri.* Helsinki: Suomalaisen kirjallisuuden seuran toimituksia 355.

————. 1982. "Metsäsuomalaiset ja Suomen kansankulttuuri." In *Ulkosuomalaisia,* pp. 175–89. Kalevalaseuran vuosikirja, no. 62. Helsinki: Suomalaisen kirjallisuuden seura.

Taylor, George R., ed. 1972. *The Turner Thesis Concerning the Role of the Frontier in American History.* 3rd ed. Lexington, Mass.: D. C. Heath & Co.

Taylor, Gwynne Stephens. 1981. *From Frontier to Factory: An Architectural History of Forsyth County.* Winston-Salem, N.C.: North Carolina Department of Cultural Resources, Division of Archives and History, with Winston-Salem/Forsyth County Historic Properties Commission and City-County Planning Board of Forsyth County and Winston-Salem.

Taylor, Oliver. 1909. *Historic Sullivan: A History of Sullivan County, Tennessee, with brief Biographies of the Makers of History.* Bristol, Tenn.: King Printing.

Tebbetts, Diane. 1978. "Traditional Houses of Independence County, Arkansas." *Pioneer America* 10 (July): 36–55.

Terrell, Isaac L. 1970. *Old Houses in Rockingham County.* Verona, Va.: McClure Press.

Thomas, Benjamin P. 1954. *Lincoln's New Salem.* New York: Alfred A. Knopf.

Thomas, Gabriel. 1912. "An Historical and Geographical Account of Pensilvania and of West-New-Jersey, by Gabriel Thomas, 1698." In *Narratives of Early Pennsylvania, West New Jersey, and Delaware, 1630–1707,* edited by Albert C. Myers, pp. 307–52. New York: Charles Scribner's Sons.

Thomas, James C. 1974. "The Log Houses of Kentucky." *Antiques* 105:791–98.

Thomas, N. M. 1900. "Reminiscences." *Michigan Pioneer and Historical Society, Historical Collections* 28:533–36.

Thompson, Frances. 1977. *Mountain Relics.* South Brunswick and New York: A. S. Barnes.

Thompson, M. W. 1967. *Novgorod the Great.* New York and Washington, D.C.: Frederick A. Praeger.

Thompson, Stephen I. 1972–73. "Pioneer Colonization: A Cross-Cultural View." *Current Topics in Anthropology* 6, no. 33. (Addison-Wesley Modules in Anthropology.)

Thorpe, T. B. 1858. "The American Deer: Its Habits and Associations." *Harper's New Monthly Magazine* 17 (October): 606–21.

Thünen, Johann Heinrich von. 1966. *Von Thünen's Isolated State.* Translated by Carla M. Wartenberg. Oxford: Pergamon Press.

Tihase, K. 1974. *Eesti talurahvaarhitektuur.* Tallinn, Estonia, U.S.S.R.: Kirjastus "Kunst."

Torma, Carolyn, and Wells, Camille. [1986.] *Architectural and Historical Sites of Pulaski County.* N.p.: Kentucky Heritage Council and Pulaski Heritage, Inc.

Trewartha, Glenn T. 1946. "Types of Rural Settlement in Colonial America." *Geographical Review* 36:568–96.

Trigger, Bruce G. 1978. *Northeast.* Vol. 15 in the series *Handbook of North American Indians.* Washington, D.C.: Smithsonian Institution.

Turner, Frederick J. 1921. *The Frontier in American History.* New York: Henry Holt & Co.

Turner, Frederick J. 1962. *The Frontier in American History.* Introduction by Ray A. Billington. New York: Holt, Rinehart & Winston.

Turner, Orsamus. 1849. *Pioneer History of the Holland Purchase.* Buffalo, N.Y.: Jewett, Thomas.

Tuttle, J. M. 1868. "The Minnesota Pineries." *Harper's New Monthly Magazine* 36 (March): 409–23.

Tvengsberg, Per Martin. 1961. "Finsk byggeskikk i Grue: mer om røykstua i Tvengsberget." *Foreningen til norske fortidsminnesmerkers bevaring, årbok,* pp. 121–46.

———. 1982. "Gruen suomalaismetsän kaskiviljelystä." In *Ulkosuomalaisia,* pp. 190–206. Kalevalaseuran vuosikirja, no. 62. Helsinki: Suomalaisen kirjallisuuden seura.

Uhlig, Harald. 1961. "Old Hamlets with Infield and Outfield Systems in Western and Central Europe." *Geografiska Annaler* 43:285–312.

Umatilla County: A Backward Glance. 1981. [Oregon]: Umatilla County Historical Society.

U.S. Bureau of the Census. 1908a. *Heads of Families at the First Census of the United States Taken in the Year 1790: Connecticut.* Washington, D.C.: Government Printing Office.

———. 1908b. *Heads of Families at the First Census of the United States Taken in the Year 1790: Maine.* Washington, D.C.: Government Printing Office.

———. 1908c. *Heads of Families at the First Census of the United States Taken in the Year 1790: Maryland.* Washington, D.C.: Government Printing Office.

——— 1908d. *Heads of Families at the First Census of the United States Taken in the Year 1790: Massachusetts.* Washington, D.C.: Government Printing Office.

———. 1908e. *Heads of Families at the First Census of the United States*

Taken in the Year 1790: New Hampshire. Washington, D.C.: Government Printing Office.

————. 1908f. *Heads of Families at the First Census of the United States Taken in the Year 1790: New York.* Washington, D.C.: Government Printing Office.

————. 1908g. *Heads of Families at the First Census of the United States Taken in the Year 1790: North Carolina.* Washington, D.C.: Government Printing Office.

————. 1908h. *Heads of Families at the First Census of the United States Taken in the Year 1790: Pennsylvania.* Washington, D.C.: Government Printing Office.

————. 1908i. *Heads of Families at the First Census of the United States Taken in the Year 1790, Records of State Enumerations: 1782 to 1785, Virginia.* Washington, D.C.: Government Printing Office.

————. 1908j. *Heads of Families at the First Census of the United States Taken in the Year 1790: Rhode Island.* Washington, D.C.: Government Printing Office.

————. 1908k. *Heads of Families at the First Census of the United States Taken in the Year 1790: South Carolina.* Washington, D.C.: Government Printing Office.

————. 1908l. *Heads of Families at the First Census of the United States Taken in the Year 1790: Vermont.* Washington, D.C.: Government Printing Office.

————. 1909. *A Century of Population Growth from the First Census of the United States to the Twelfth.* Washington, D.C.: Government Printing Office.

————. 1983a. *Ancestry of the Population by State: 1980.* Supplementary Report PC80-S1-10. Washington, D.C.: Bureau of the Census.

————. 1983b. *1980 Census of Population.* Vol. 1, *Characteristics of the Population,* chap. C, "General Social and Economic Characteristics," pts. 1–51. Washington, D.C.: Bureau of the Census.

————. 1983c. "Microdata Sample A [Census of Population and Housing, 1980]." Unpublished computer tape, Bureau of the Census, Washington, D.C.

————. 1983d. "Technical Documentation [Census of Population and Housing, 1980]." Summary Tape File 4. Unpublished computer tape, Bureau of the Census, Washington, D.C.

U.S. Department of Agriculture. 1872. "Statistics of Fences in the United States." *Report of the Commissioner of Agriculture for the Year 1871,* pp. 497–512. Washington, D.C.: Government Printing Office.

U.S. Geological Survey, National Mapping Division, Office of Geographic and Cartographic Research, Branch of Geographic Names. "Geographic Names Information System." Reston, Va.: U.S. Geological Survey National Center. (Alphabetical indices of place names appearing on U.S.G.S. topographic sheets, available on microcards or computer print-outs, by state units.)

"The Upper Mississippi." 1858. *Harper's New Monthly Magazine* 16 (March): 433–54.

Upton, Dell. 1982. "Vernacular Domestic Architecture in Eighteenth-Century Virginia." *Winterthur Portfolio* 17:95–119.

Vacher, Edna Robertson. 1947. "A Genealogy of the Bankston (Benkestok) Family." Unpublished manuscript. Archives of the Center for Regional Studies, Southeastern Louisiana University, Hammond, La.

Valentine, Edward P. [1929.] *Edward Pleasants Valentine Papers.* 4 vols. Richmond, Va.: Valentine Museum.

Valonen, Niilo. 1958–59. "Rakennuksia tutkitaan." *Osma,* pp. 19–30.

———. 1963. *Zur Geschichte der finnischen Wohnstuben.* Helsinki: Suomalais-ugrilaisen seuran toimituksia, no. 133.

———. 1971. "Suomenselkä perinnealueena." *Ethnologia Fennica* 1, nos. 1–2: 14–40.

———. 1977. "En gård från järnåldern och dess traditioner: Gulldynt i Vörå, Österbotten." *Ethnologia Fennica* 7, nos. 1–2: 5–41.

"Värmland." 1955. *Svensk uppslagsbok* 31:1133–57. Malmö, Sweden: Förlagshuset Norden.

Vaughan, Alden T. 1965. *New England Frontier: Puritans and Indians, 1620–1675.* Boston and Toronto: Little, Brown & Co.

Vaughan, Thomas, and Ferriday, Virginia G., eds. 1974. *Space, Style, Structure: Building in Northwest America.* Portland: Oregon Historical Society.

Via, Vera T. 1962. "The Old Rail Fence." *Virginia Cavalcade* 12 (Summer): 33–40.

Vilkuna, Kustaa. 1948. "Pykäliköt ja suurkasket." *Kotiseutu,* pp. 99–105.

———. 1953. "Varpå beror den finske svedjebondens kolonisationsförmåga." In *Värmland förr och nu* 51:9–20. Karlstad, Sweden.

———. 1960. "Savolaiset erämaiden valloittajina." *Kotiseutu,* pp. 47–53.

"The Virginian Canaan." 1853. *Harper's New Monthly Magazine* 8 (December): 18–36.

Visted, Kristofer, and Stigum, Hilmar. 1951. *Vår gamle bondekultur,* vol. 1. Oslo: J. W. Cappelen.

Vlach, John M. 1972a. "The 'Canada Homestead': A Saddlebag Log House in Monroe County, Indiana." *Pioneer America* 4, no.2 (July): 8–17.

———. 1972b. "Form and House Types in American Folk Architecture." In *Introduction to Folklore,* edited by Robert J. Adams, pp. 116–54. Columbus, Ohio: Collegiate Publishing Co.

———. 1976. "The Shotgun House: An African Legacy." *Pioneer America* 8:47–70.

———. 1978. *The Afro-American Tradition in Decorative Arts.* Cleveland: Cleveland Museum of Art.

Vreim, Halvor. 1947. *Norsk trearkitektur.* Oslo: Gylendal Norsk forlag.

———. 1952. "Norsk byggekunst i middelalderen." *Nordisk Kultur* 17:348–70.

———. 1966. *Laftehus: Tømring og torvtekking.* 5th ed. Oslo: Noregs boklag.

Vuorela, Toivo. 1964. *The Finno-Ugric Peoples.* Bloomington: Indiana University Press.

———. 1975. *Suomalainen kansankulttuuri.* Porvoo and Helsinki: Werner Söderström osakeyhtiö.

———, ed. 1976. *Suomen kansankulttuurin kartasto,* vol. 1. Helsinki: Suomalaisen kirjallisuuden seura.

Wacker, Peter O. 1968. *The Musconetcong Valley of New Jersey: A Historical Geography.* New Brunswick, New Jersey: Rutgers University Press.

———. 1974. "Traditional House and Barn Types in New Jersey: Keys to Acculturation, Past Cultureographic Regions, and Settlement History." *Geoscience and Man* 5 (1974): 163–176.

———. 1975a. *The Cultural Geography of Eighteenth Century New Jersey.* New Jersey's Revolutionary Experience, no. 4. Trenton: New Jersey Historical Commission. 24 pp.

———. 1975b. *Land and People: A Cultural Geography of Preindustrial*

New Jersey: Origins and Settlement Patterns. New Brunswick, N.J.: Rutgers University Press.

——. 1979. "Relations between Cultural Origins, Relative Wealth, and the Size, Form, and Materials of Construction of Rural Dwellings in New Jersey during the Eighteenth Century." In *Géographie historique du Village et de la Maison Rurale,* pp. 201–30. Paris: Centre National de la Recherche Scientifique.

Wacker, Peter O., and Trindell, Roger T. 1968. "The Log House in New Jersey: Origins and Diffusion." *Keystone Folklore Quarterly* 13:248–68.

Wallin, Väinö. 1892–93. *Liiviläisten rakennukset.* Vähäisiä kirjelmiä 18. Helsinki: Suomalaisen kirjallisuuden seura, julkaissut.

Ward, Albert E., ed. 1983. *Forgotten Places and Things.* Albuquerque: Center for Anthropological Studies.

Ward, Christopher. 1930. *The Dutch and Swedes on the Delaware, 1609–64.* Philadelphia: University of Pennsylvania Press.

——. 1938. *New Sweden on the Delaware.* Philadelphia: University of Pennsylvania Press.

Waterman, Thomas Tileston. 1950. *The Dwellings of Colonial America.* Chapel Hill: University of North Carolina Press.

Watson, John F. 1830. *Annals of Philadelphia, Being a Collection of Memoirs, Anecdotes, & Incidents of the City and Its Inhabitants.* Philadephia: E. L. Carey & A. Hart; New York: G. & C. & H. Carvill.

Wayland, John W. 1930. *Virginia Valley Records.* Strasburg, Va.: Shenandoah Publishing House.

Webb, Walter P. 1931. *The Great Plains.* Boston: Ginn & Co.

——. 1951. *The Great Frontier.* Austin: University of Texas Press.

Weis, Norman D. 1971. *Ghost Towns of the Northwest.* Caldwell, Idaho: Caxton Printers.

Wells, Robin. 1973. "Frontier Systems as a Sociocultural Type." *Papers in Anthropology* 14, no. 1: 6–15.

Welsch, Roger L. 1980. "Nebraska Log Construction: Momentum in Tradition." *Nebraska History* 61:310–35.

Wertenbaker, Thomas J. 1938. *The Founding of American Civilization: The Middle Colonies.* New York and London: Charles Scribner's Sons.

Weslager, C. A. 1952. "Log Structures in New Sweden during the Seventeenth Century." *Delaware History* 5:77–95.

——. 1954. "Log Houses in Virginia during the Seventeenth Century." *Quarterly Bulletin, Archaeological Society of Virginia* 9, no. 2: 2–8.

——. 1955. "Log Houses in Pennsylvania during the Seventeenth Century." *Pennsylvania History* 22 (July): 256–66.

——. 1957. "The Swede Meets the Red Man." *Bulletin of the Archaeological Society of Delaware* 8, no. 1: 1–12.

——. 1967. *The English on the Delaware, 1610–1682.* New Brunswick, N.J.: Rutgers University Press.

——. 1969. *The Log Cabin in America from Pioneer Days to the Present.* New Brunswick, N.J.: Rutgers University Press.

——. 1982. "The City of Amsterdam's Colony on the Delaware, 1656–1664, with Unpublished Dutch Notarial Abstracts." *Delaware History* 20:1–26, 73–97.

——. ca. 1987. *The Swedes and Dutch at New Castle.* New York: Bart.

——. 1988. *New Sweden on the Delaware, 1638–1655.* Wilmington, Del.: Middle Atlantic Press.

Westman, Erik G., ed. 1931. *The Swedish Element in America.* 3 vols. Chicago: Swedish-American Biographical Society.

"What Did Early Settlers Grow on Their Farms?" 1984. *Daily Gleaner* (Fredericton, N.B., Canada), August 8, p. 10.

White, Truman C. 1898. *Our Country and Its People: A Descriptive Work on Erie County, New York*, vol. 1. Boston: Boston History Co.

Whittington, G. 1973. "Field Systems of Scotland." In *Studies of Field Systems in the British Isles*, edited by Alan R. H. Baker and Robin A. Butlin, pp. 530–79. Cambridge: University Press.

Whitwell, W. L., and Winborne, Lee W. 1982. *The Architectural Heritage of the Roanoke Valley*. Charlottesville: University Press of Virginia.

Wiklund, K. B. 1902. "Finska språkets nuvarande utbredning i Värmland och Grue finnskog." *Ymer* 22:15–18, plus map at end.

Wilhelm, Eugene J., Jr. 1965. "The Cultural Heritage of the Blue Ridge." *Mountain Life and Work* 40 (Summer): 16–20.

———. 1978. "Folk Settlements in the Blue Ridge Mountains." *Appalachian Journal* 5, no. 2 (Winter): 204–45.

Wilkie, D. 1834. *Sketches of a Summer Trip to New York and the Canadas*. Edinburgh: Ballantyne & Co.

Williams, John S. 1843. "Our Cabin; or, Life in the Woods." *American Pioneer* 2, no. 10 (October): 434–59.

Williams, Michael. 1982. "Clearing the United States Forests: Pivotal Years, 1810–1860." *Journal of Historical Geography* 8:12–28.

Williams, Michael A., and Dockery, Carl. 1984. *Marble and Log: The History and Architecture of Cherokee County, North Carolina*. Murphy, N.C.: Cherokee County Historical Museum; Raleigh: North Carolina Department of Cultural Resources, Division of Archives and History.

Williams, Samuel C. 1930. *Beginnings of West Tennessee*. Johnson City, Tenn.: Watauga Press.

———. 1936. "Stephen Holston and Holston River." *East Tennessee Historical Society's Publications* 8:26–34.

Williams, Thomas J. C. 1968. *A History of Washington County, Maryland*. 2 vols. Baltimore: Regional Publishing Co.

Williams, Thomas J. C. and McKinsey, Folger. 1967. *History of Frederick County, Maryland*. 2 vols. Baltimore: Genealogical Publishing Co.

Williams, W. A. 1916. *Early American Families: The Williams, Moore, McKitrick, Fonda, Van Alen, Lanning, King, Justice, Cunningham, Longacre, Swanson and Cox Families*. Philadelphia: By the author.

Wilson, Eugene M. 1969. "Folk Houses of Northern Alabama." Ph.D. diss., Louisiana State University.

———. 1970. "The Single Pen Log House in the South." *Pioneer America* 2 (January): 21–28.

———. 1971. "Some Similarities between American and European Folk Houses." *Pioneer America* 3 (July): 8–14.

Wilson, Mary. 1984. *Log Cabin Studies*, pt. 1, "The Rocky Mountain Cabin." Ogden, Utah: U.S. Department of Agriculture, Forest Service.

Winberry, John J. 1974. "The Log House in Mexico." *Annals of the Association of American Geographers* 64:54–69.

Withers, Robert S. 1950. "The Stake and Rider Fence." *Missouri Historical Review* 44:225–31.

Wood, Joseph S. 1982. "Village and Community in Early Colonial New England." *Journal of Historical Geography* 8:333–46.

Woodbridge, Hensley C. 1955a. "A Note on Dogtrots." *Kentucky Folklore Record*, pp. 80–81.

———. 1955b. "More on *Dogtrot*." *Kentucky Folklore Record*, pp. 107–8.

Woods, William. 1904. *Two Years Residence in the Settlement on the English Prairie.* Edited by Reuben G. Thwaites. Cleveland: A. H. Clark.

Wright, Martin. 1950. "The Log Cabin in the South." M.A. thesis, Louisiana State University.

———. 1956. "Log Culture in Hill Louisiana." Ph.D. diss., Louisiana State University.

———. 1958. "The Antecedents of the Double-Pen House Type." *Annals of the Association of American Geographers* 48:109–17.

Wuorinen, John H. 1938. *The Finns on the Delaware, 1638–1655: An Essay in American Colonial History.* New York: Columbia University Press.

Wyman, Walker D., and Kroeber, Clifton B., eds. 1957. *The Frontier in Perspective.* Madison: University of Wisconsin Press.

Wynn, Graeme. 1983. "Settler Societies in Geographical Focus." *Historical Studies* 20:353–66.

Yeager, Lyn Allison. 1977. *Log Structures in Warren County, Kentucky.* Bowling Green, Ky.: Citizens National Bank.

Yeomans, D. T. 1981. "A Preliminary Study of English Roofs in Colonial America." *Journal, Association of Preservation Technology* 13, no. 4: 9–18.

Zelinsky, Wilbur. 1953. "The Log House in Georgia." *Geographical Review* 43:173–93.

———. 1959. "Walls and Fences." *Landscape* 8 (Spring): 14–20.

———. 1973. *The Cultural Geography of the United States.* Englewood Cliffs, N.J.: Prentice-Hall.

Interviews, Letters, and Reports

Ailonen, Riitta, Curator. Museovirasto, Finland, National Board of Antiquities and Historical Monuments. Interview, Helsinki, January 8, 1981.

Brown, Don. Arkansas Historic Preservation Program, Little Rock. Letter to T.G.J. dated July 17, 1985.

Carter, Tom. Architectural Historian, State of Utah, Department of Community and Economic Development, Division of State History (Utah State Historical Society), Salt Lake City. Letter to T.G.J. dated October 12, 1984.

Cooper, Patricia Irvin. Athens, Georgia. Letter to T.G.J. dated June 29, 1987.

Daly, Charlotte S. Department of Art, Florida State University, Tallahassee. Letter to T.G.J. dated June 4, 1985.

Denny, James M. Chief, Survey and Registration, Division of Parks and Historic Preservation, Department of Natural Resources, State of Missouri, Jefferson City. Letters to T.G.J. dated October 30 and December 20, 1985.

Hall, Stephen A., and Moncure, Hank. University of Texas at Austin. Report of microscopic analysis of a chinking sample collected June 30, 1985, from a derelict semidugout log shanty 6 kilometers south of Saarijärvi on Highway 78 in northern Finland, between Rovaniemi and Ranua in Peräpohjola (Hinter-Bothnia) traditional province, February 7, 1986.

Holdsworth, Deryck. Department of Geography, University of Toronto, Canada. Letter to T.G.J. dated July 14, 1986.

Hulan, Richard. Arlington, Virginia. Letter to T.G.J. dated April 20, 1983.

Jauhiainen, Erkki. Department of Geography, University of Joensuu, Finland. Interview, Helsinki, June 20, 1985.

Koehler, Ove. Curator, Sågudden Museum, Arvika, Värmland, Sweden. Interview, May 23, 1985.

Moore, J. Roderick. Blue Ridge Institute, Ferrum College, Ferrum, Virginia. Letter to T.G.J. dated June 15, 1984.

Myrdal, Janken. Nordiska museet, Stockholm, Sweden. Interview, May 29, 1985.

Pillsbury, Richard. Department of Geography, Georgia State University, Atlanta. Letter to T.G.J. dated March 30, 1983.

Roede, Lars. Architect and Chief Curator, Norsk Folkemuseum, Bygdøy, Oslo, Norway. Interview, July 12, 1985.

Skre, Ivar. Director, Glomdalsmuseet, Elverum, Hedmark, Norway. Interview, May 18, 1985.

Tvengsberg, Per Martin, descendant of Finnskog settlers. Fylkeskonservator, Hedmark fylke, Østre Diesen, Hamar, Norway. Interviews, May 18, 24–25, 1985.

Wilson, Eugene M. Professor of Geography, University of South Alabama, Mobile. Letter to T.G.J. dated June 5, 1984.

Museums, Archives, Exhibits, and Symposia

Abborrtjärnsberg friluftsgård, near Röjdåfors, Värmland, Sweden. Visited May 20, 1985.

Adirondack Museum, Blue Mountain Lake, New York. Visited August 13, 1984.

Arkansas Historic Preservation Program, 225 East Markham, Little Rock. Files.

Arvidsjaur Lappstaden, Arvidsjaur, Lappland, Sweden. Visited July 6, 1985.

Black Creek Pioneer Village, Toronto, Ontario, Canada. Visited August 1, 1984.

Boulden-Stubbs house, 843 Elk Forest Road, Elkton, Maryland. Visited March 2, 1988.

Brunskog hembygdsgård, Brunskog, Värmland, Sweden. Visited May 23, 1985.

Calgary Heritage Park, Calgary, Alberta. Visited July 10, 1987.

Central New Brunswick Woodmen's Museum, Boiestown, New Brunswick, Canada. Visited August 8, 1984.

Cody Old Town Open-Air Museum, Cody, Wyoming. Visited July 4, 1987.

Cumberland County Historical Society Museum, Greenwich, New Jersey, log "Swedish" Granary on the grounds. Visited March 1, 1988.

Dalby hembygdsgård, Ransby, near Dalby, Värmland, Sweden. Visited May 21, 1985.

Darby Pioneer Heritage Museum, Darby, Montana. Visited July 7, 1987.

"Delaware 350: The Beginning of Finnish Migration to the New World." Exhibit prepared by the Institute of Migration, Turku, Finland, and displayed during March 1988 at the University of Delaware, Newark.

Enonkosken kotiseutumuseo, Enonkoski, Savo, Finland. Visited June 15, 1985.

Eskilstuna Open-Air Museum, Eskilstuna, Södermanland, Sweden. Visited June 8, 1981.

Fågelsjö gammelgården, Fågelsjö, Orsa Finnmark, Dalarna, Sweden. Visited June 6, 1985.

Fagersta hembygdsgård, Fagersta, Västmanland, Sweden. Visited May 26, 1985.

Filipstad hembygdsgård, Filipstad, Värmland, Sweden. Visited May 25, 1985.

Finnetunet (Finnish Museum), Svullrya, Grue Finnskog, Hedmark, Norway. Visited May 18 and 24, 1985.

Fort Missoula Museum, Missoula, Montana. Visited July 8, 1987.

Fort Steele Heritage Park, Fort Steele, British Columbia. Visited July 15, 1987.

Funäsdalen hembygdsgård, Funäsdalen, Härjedalen, Sweden. Visited July 8, 1985.

Genesee Country Village and Museum, Mumford, New York. Visited August 14, 1984.

Glomdalsmuseet, Elverum, Hedmark, Norway. Visited May 18, 1985.

Glommersträsk hangengården, Glommersträsk, Lappland, Sweden. Visited July 6, 1985.

Gräsmark hembygdsgården, Uddheden, Värmland, Sweden. Visited May 19, 1985.

Gunnarskog hembygdsgård, Gunnarskog, Värmland, Sweden. Visited May 23, 1985.

Hällefors hembygdsgård, Hällefors, Västmanland, Sweden. Visited May 25, 1985.

Hallingdal folkemuseum, Nesbyen, Buskerud, Norway. Visited June 24, 1981.

Hankasalmen kotiseutumuseo, Hankasalmi, Keski-Suomi, Finland. Visited June 11, 1985.

Hede hembygdsgård, Hede, Härjedalen, Sweden. Visited July 8, 1985.

Hedmarksmuseet og Domkirkeodden, Hamar, Hedmark, Norway. Visited May 18, 1985.

Hol Bygdemuseum, Hol, Hallingdal, Buskerud, Norway. Visited June 24, 1981.

Hyde Log Cabin Museum, Grand Isle, Vermont. Visited August 12, 1984.

Idaho Historical Museum, Pioneer Village, Julia Davis Park, Boise. Visited July 17, 1987.

Jämtlands läns museum, Östersund, Jämtland, Sweden. Visited July 8, 1985.

Jamtli Open-Air Museum, Östersund, Jämtland, Sweden. Visited July 7, 1985.

Johola friluftsgård, near Rödjåfors, Värmland, Sweden. Visited May 24, 1985.

Jokkmokk hembygdsgård, Jokkmokk, Lappland, Sweden. Visited July 5, 1985.

Jokkmokks museum, Jokkmokk, Lappland, Sweden. Visited July 5–6, 1985.

Jönköpings läns museum, Jönköping, Småland, Sweden. Visited June 6–7, 1981.

Juhani Ahon museo, near Iisalmi, Savo, Finland. Visited June 10, 1985.

Julita gård, Julita, Södermanland, Sweden. Visited June 8, 1981.

Kankaanpään talomuseo, near Laukaa, Keski-Suomi, Finland. Visited June 11, 1985.

Karjalainen kotitalo-ulkomuseo, Imatra-Pässiniemi, Savo, Finland. Visited June 27, 1985.

Kemin museo, Kemi, Peräpohjola, Finland. Visited June 9, 1985.

Kesälahden museo, Kesälahti, Karelia, Finland. Visited June 28, 1985.

Kings Landing Historical Settlement, near Fredericton, New Brunswick, Canada. Visited August 8, 1984.

Kollsberg hembygdsgård, Torsby, Värmland, Sweden. Visited May 21, 1985.

Konneveden kotiseutumuseo, Konnevesi, Keski-Suomi, Finland. Visited June 11, 1985.

Kuopion museo, Kuopio, Savo, Finland. Visited June 12, 1985.

Kvarntorps Finngård, near Lekvattnet, Värmland, Sweden. Visited May 19, 1985.

Latvian Soviet Socialist Republic Historical Museum, Rigas Pils, Riga, Latvia, U.S.S.R. Visited June 23, 1985.

Latvijas etnogrāfiskais brīvdabas muzejs, Riga-Berģi, Latvian Soviet Socialist Republic, U.S.S.R. Visited June 24, 1985.

Laukaan kotiseutumuseo, Laukaa, Keski-Suomi, Finland. Visited June 11, 1985.

Lekvattnet Barmen Rynna hembygdsgård, Lekvattnet, Värmland, Sweden. Visited May 19, 1985.

Lepikon torppa, Pielavesi, Savo, Finland. Visited June 13, 1985.

Library of Congress, Historic American Buildings Survey (H.A.B.S.), Washington, D.C. Files.

Lower Swedish Cabin, Creek Road, Clifton Heights, Pennsylvania. Visited July 28, 1980, and March 6, 1988. Dendrochronological report on the house by Landmark Preservation, Ltd., Westchester, Pennsylvania.

Luleå friluftsmuseet, Gammelstad, near Luleå, Norrbotten, Sweden. Visited June 9, 1985.

Lycksele hembygdsgård, Lycksele, Lappland, Sweden. Visited July 6, 1985.

MacLachlan Woodworking Museum, Grass Creek Park, Township of Pittsburgh, Frontenac County, Ontario, Canada. Visited August 2, 1984.

Mariebergsskogen Open-Air Museum, Karlstad, Värmland, Sweden. Visited May 22, 1985.

Mattila friluftsgård, near Rödjåfors, Värmland, Sweden. Visited May 24, 1985.

Missouri, Department of Natural Resources, Division of Parks and Historic Preservation, Survey and Registration (James M. Denny, Chief), P.O. Box 176, Jefferson City. Files.

———, State Historical Society, Columbia. Photograph collection.

Morton House Museum, Prospect Park, Pa. Visited July 28, 1980.

Museum of Soviet Ethnography, Leningrad, U.S.S.R. Visited January 6, 1981.

National Museum of Finland (Kansallismuseo), Archives (Kansatieteen toimisto), Nervanderinkatu 13, Helsinki, Finland. Visited June 17–24, 1985.

"New Sweden in America." Symposium held on the 350th anniversary of the founding of New Sweden, University of Delaware, Newark, March 3–5, 1988.

Nordiska museet, arkiv, Djurgården, Stockholm, Sweden. Used June 10, 1981, May 28–June 3, 1985, and April 7–June 20, 1986.

Nordmark hembygdsgård, Nordmark, Värmland, Sweden. Visited May 25, 1985.

Norsk folkemuseum, Oslo-Bygdøy, Norway. Visited June 28, 1981; May 16, 1985; and July 12, 1985.

C. A. Nothnagle Log House, home of Harry and Doris Rink, 406 Swedesboro Road, Gibbstown, New Jersey. Visited March 1, 1988.

Nyskoga hembygdsgård, Nyskoga, Värmland, Sweden. Visited May 21, 1985.

Ockelbo hembygdsgård, Ockelbo, Gästrikland, Sweden. Visited June 5, 1985.

Oregon Historical Society, Photograph Collection, Portland. Visited April 24, 1987.

Orsa hembygdsgård, Orsa, Dalarna, Sweden. Visited June 5, 1985.

Ortodoksinen kirkkomuseo, Kuopio, Savo, Finland. Visited June 12, 1985.

Östmark hembygdsgård, Östmark, Värmland, Sweden. Visited May 20, 1985.

Pennsylvania Historical and Museum Commission, Harrisburg. Files.

Peuran museo, Rautalampi, Keski-Suomi, Finland. Visited June 11, 1985.

Pielaveden kotiseutumuseo, Pielavesi, Savo, Finland. Visited June 13, 1985.

Pielisen museo, Lieksa, Karelia, Finland. Visited June 29, 1985.

Pienmäen talomuseo, Pienmäki, near Niemisjärvi, Keski-Suomi, Finland. Visited June 11, 1985.

Point Pelee National Park, De Laurier house exhibit, near Leamington, Ontario, Canada. Visited October 18, 1987.

Purala Finngård, near Rödjåfors, Värmland, Sweden. Visited May 25, 1985.

Putkinotko farmstead museum, near Savonlinna, Savo, Finland. Visited June 15, 1985.

Pyhäntä ulkomuseo, near Pyhäntä, Pohjanmaa, Finland. Visited June 10, 1985.

Ranching Heritage Center Museum, Texas Tech University, Lubbock. Visited September 21, 1984.

Ransäter hembygdsgård, Ransäter, Värmland, Sweden. Visited June 14, 1981.

Rantasalmen kotiseutumuseo, Rantasalmi, Savo, Finland. Visited June 14, 1985.

Rikenberg friluftsgård, near Bjurberget, Värmland, Sweden. Visited May 21, 1985.

Riksarkivet, Sverige, collection labelled "Kolonier, Nya Sverige," part of the Handel och Sjöfart Samlingen, Stockholm, Sweden. Visited September 11–12, 1984, and May 28–29, 1985.

Ritaberg (Ritamäki) Finngård friluftsgård, near Lekvattnet, Värmland, Sweden. Visited May 19 and 23, 1985.

Riuttalan talonpoikaismuseo, Riuttala, near Karttula, Savo, Finland. Visited June 13, 1985.

Saamelaismuseo, Inari, Lapland, Finland. Visited July 2, 1985.

Sågudden hembygdsmuseum, Arvika, Värmland, Sweden. Visited May 23, 1985.

Sandvig Maihaugen, Lillehammer, Oppland, Norway. Visited June 15, 1981.

Säter Hembygdsmuseum Åsgårdarna, Säter, Dalarna, Sweden. Visited June 12, 1981.

Seurasaaren ulkomuseo (Seurasaari Open-Air Museum, Seurasaari Island), Helsinki, Finland. Visited January 8, 1981, and June 19 and 21, 1985.

Skansen, on Djurgården Island, Stockholm, Sweden. Visited June 9, 1981, and May 26 and June 1, 1985.

Skråckarberget hembysgården tomta, near Södra Finnskoga, Värmland, Sweden. Visited May 21, 1985.

Södra Råda Ödekyrka, near Knekterud, Värmland, Sweden. Visited June 7, 1981.

Strömsund hembygdsgård, Strömsund, Jämtland, Sweden. Visited July 7, 1985.

Torp hembygdsgård, Torp, Medelpad, Sweden. Visited June 7, 1985.

Tröndelag folkemuseum, Sverresborg, Trondheim, Sör-Tröndelag, Norway. Visited June 17, 1981.

Turkansaaren ulkomuseo, near Oulu, Pohjanmaa, Finland. Visited June 10, 1985.

Upper Canada Village, Morrisburg, Ontario. Visited August 2, 1984.

Valdres folkemuseum, Fagernes, Oppland, Norway. Visited July 10, 1985.

Vallby Open-Air Museum, Västerås, Västmanland, Sweden. Visited May 26, 1985.

Värmlands museum, Karlstad, Värmland, Sweden. Visited May 22, 1985.

Vemdalen hembygdsgård, Vemdalen, Härjedalen, Sweden. Visited July 8, 1985.

Vesannon torpparimuseo, Vesanto, Keski Suomi, Finland. Visited June 13, 1985.

Viby By Farmstead Museum, near Sigtuna, Uppland, Sweden. Visited June 11, 1981.

Vikinge skipene museum, Oslo-Bygdøy, Norway. Visited June 28, 1981, and July 13, 1985.

Wadköping Open-Air Museum, Örebro, Närke, Sweden. Visited June 7–8, 1981.

Ylä-savon kotiseutumuseo, Iisalmi, Savo, Finland. Visited June 10, 1985.

Zornsamlingarna, incuding Zornmuseet and Zorns gammelgård, Mora, Dalarna, Sweden. Visited June 13, 1981, and June 6, 1985.

INDEX

333

Terry G. Jordan is Walter Prescott Webb Professor of History and Ideas, Department of Geography, University of Texas, Austin. He has published extensively on American folk cultures and their Old World backgrounds. Matti Kaups is professor of geography and ethnohistory, University of Minnesota, Duluth, and professor of Scandinavian Studies, University of Minnesota, Minneapolis. He has published numerous articles on Finns in America.

The American Backwoods Frontier

Designed by Chris L. Smith
Composed by Graphic Composition, Inc.,
    in Trump with display lines in Neuland
Printed by the Maple Press Company
    on 60-lb. Glatfelter Offset